Axiomatic theory of bargaining with a variable number of agents

Axiomatic theory of bargaining with a variable number of agents

WILLIAM THOMSON
University of Rochester
and
TERJE LENSBERG
Norwegian School of Economics and Business Administration
Bergen, Norway

The right of the University of Cambridge to print and sell all manner of books was granted by Henry VIII in 1534. The University has printed and published continuously since 1584.

CAMBRIDGE UNIVERSITY PRESS
Cambridge
New York New Rochelle Melbourne Sydney

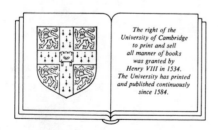

Published by the Press Syndicate of the University of Cambridge
The Pitt Building, Trumpington Street, Cambridge CB2 1RP
32 East 57th Street, New York, NY 10022, USA
10 Stamford Road, Oakleigh, Melbourne 3166, Australia

First published 1989

Printed in the United States of America

Library of Congress Cataloging-in-Publication Data

Thomson, William, 1949–

Axiomatic theory of bargaining with a variable number
of agents.

Bibliography: p.
Includes index.
1. Negotiation in business - Mathematical models.
2. Negotiation - Mathematical models. I. Lensberg,
Terje. II. Title.
HD58.6.T48 1988 658 88-9522
ISBN 0 521 34383 6

British Library Cataloguing in Publication Data

Thomson, William

Axiomatic theory of bargaining with a
variable number of agents

1. Economics. Game theory
I. Title II. Lensberg, Terje
330′.01′5193

ISBN 0 521 34383 6

To our parents

Contents

Acknowledgments

Many institutions and individuals have helped us in the preparation of this work. We would like to thank the Massachusetts Institute of Technology and Harvard University, where our collaboration started and where the first chapters of our manuscript were written; the Center for Applied Research at the Norwegian School of Economics and Business Administration and the University of Rochester, our home institutions, for their supportive intellectual climates; the National Science Foundation for its financial support; a number of seminar audiences across the United States and Europe, and several generations of students, for their questions and comments; and Rose Burgholzer for her expert typing of the successive drafts of the manuscript. Last, but not least, we thank our wives for their continued encouragement and patience over the course of this long project. This book would not exist without them.

Symbols and notation

$\mathbb{N}$	positive integers
$\mathbb{R}$	real numbers
$\mathbb{R}_+$	nonnegative real numbers
$\mathbb{R}_{++}$	positive real numbers
$\mathbb{R}^n_+$	n-fold Cartesian product of $\mathbb{R}_+$
I	set of agents
$i, j, \ldots$	generic elements of I
$\mathcal{P}$	set of finite subsets of I
$P, Q, \ldots$	generic elements of $\mathcal{P}$
$\|P\|$	cardinality of P
$\mathbb{R}^P_+$	Cartesian product of $\|P\|$ copies of $\mathbb{R}_+$, indexed by the elements of P
$x, y, \ldots$	generic elements of $\mathbb{R}^P_+, \mathbb{R}^Q_+, \ldots$
Σ^P	the class of convex, compact, comprehensive subsets of $\mathbb{R}_+$ containing at least one vector with all positive coordinates
$\tilde{\Sigma}^P$	subclass of Σ^P of strictly comprehensive problems
Σ^P_{dif}	subclass of Σ^P of problems with a differentiable undominated boundary
Σ^P_Δ	subclass of Σ^P of "triangular" problems

$\Sigma \equiv \bigcup \Sigma^P$

$\tilde{\Sigma} \equiv \bigcup \tilde{\Sigma}^P$

$\Sigma_{\text{dif}} \equiv \bigcup \Sigma^P_{\text{dif}}$

$\Sigma_\Delta \equiv \bigcup \Sigma^P_\Delta$

Given $S^1, \ldots, S^k \subset \mathbb{R}^P_+$,
- $\text{co}\{S^1, \ldots, S^k\}$ is the convex hull of $S^1, \ldots, S^k$;
- $\text{cch}\{S^1, \ldots, S^k\}$ is the convex and comprehensive hull of $S^1, \ldots, S^k$.

Given $P, Q \in \mathcal{P}$ with $P \subset Q$, $y \in \mathbb{R}^Q$, $T \subset \mathbb{R}^Q$,
- $Q \backslash P$ is the set of elements of Q that do not belong to P;
- y_P is the projection of y onto $\mathbb{R}^P$;
- T_P is the projection of T onto $\mathbb{R}^P$;
- $t^y_P(T)$ is the set of points $x \in \mathbb{R}^P$ such that $(x, y_{Q\backslash P}) \in T$.

Given $x \in \mathbb{R}^P$,

$\sum_P x_i$ is the sum of x_i for i ranging in P;

$\prod_P x_i$ is the product of x_i for i ranging in P.

Given $x, y \in \mathbb{R}^P$,

$x \geqq y$ means $x_i \geqq y_i$ for all $i \in P$;

$x \geq y$ means $x \geqq y$ but $x \neq y$;

$x > y$ means $x_i > y_i$ for all $i \in P$.

N Nash solution
K Kalai–Smorodinsky solution
E Egalitarian solution
L Leximin solution
U Utilitarian solution

Axioms

	Abbreviations	
	Fixed number of agents	Variable number of agents
Anonymity	*an*	*AN*
Bilateral Stability	–	*B.STAB*
Conflictual Juxtaposition	–	*C.J*
Conflictual Replication	–	*C.R*
Continuity	*cont*	*CONT*
Homogeneity	*hom*	*HOM*
Independence of Irrelevant Alternatives	*i.i.a*	*I.I.A*
Individual Monotonicity	*i.mon*	*I.MON*
Individual Optimality	–	*I.O*
Individual Rationality	*i.r*	*I.R*
Multilateral Stability	–	*M.STAB*
Nonconflictual Juxtaposition	–	*N.C.J*
Nonconflictual Replication	–	*N.C.R*
Pareto-Optimality	*p.o*	*P.O*
Population Monotonicity	–	*MON*
Scale Invariance	*s.inv*	*S.INV*
Strong Individual Rationality	*st.i.r*	*ST.I.R*
Symmetry	*sy*	*SY*
Weak Continuity	–	*W.CONT*
Weak Nonconflictual Juxtaposition	–	*W.N.C.J*
Weak Pareto-Optimality	*w.p.o*	*W.P.O*
Weak Stability	–	*W.STAB*

CHAPTER 1

Preliminaries

1.1 Introduction

We imagine a group of individuals to whom is available a certain set of choices over which their preferences differ. These choices may concern general features of society such as laws and institutions or concrete details of their daily lives such as who should perform a certain task on a given day or how much of a particular good each individual should receive. The problem they face is to make a choice that would provide an equitable compromise. The aim of the present study is to contribute to the understanding of how such a choice could, or should, be made.

The first step of any such study consists in precisely specifying the *class of choice problems* that the group may encounter; the analysis is confined to that class. The search is then for desirable *solutions,* a solution being a method of associating with each problem in the class an outcome feasible for that problem and interpreted as the "best" alternative.

Several important classes of problems have been extensively studied in the literature. In the Arrow (1951) tradition, an *abstract set of feasible alternatives,* on which the agents' preferences are defined, is given. In the most general formulation, these preferences are assumed to have only ordinal significance, and no structural assumptions are made on the feasible set.

At another extreme is the important class of *economic problems of fair division.* The issue there is to distribute a list of items among several claimants, a classical example being the division of an inheritance among several heirs. In economics textbooks, the standard problem is that of dividing a fixed bundle of infinitely divisible goods. Then the feasible set has a very special structure, and certain assumptions can be made about preferences that would not be meaningful in the Arrow framework.

In yet another formulation, which will be the one adopted here, the set of feasible alternatives is not given in all of its physical details but only as a *subset* of a Euclidean space interpreted as the *utility space;* agents are equipped with real-valued utility functions, defined up to transformations in a certain class. The extent to which the utility functions have cardinal significance, which determines how broad this class of transformations is, is specified as part of the description of the situation under study. A choice problem is a family of subsets of the utility space that are all equivalent under the class of transformations. Usually, the problem is given by one representative member of the family.

Once a class of problems has been specified, the search can begin for solutions. Two main approaches are available. The first one consists in producing solutions directly and in studying how well they perform. This is done mainly by analyzing examples. Particular problems about which one has some intuitive idea of how they should be solved are identified, and it is determined whether the solutions under consideration behave in conformity with this intuition.

The second approach is the axiomatic approach. It consists in formulating desiderata, or *axioms,* on how choice problems should be solved and in checking whether the axioms are compatible, that is, whether there exist solutions satisfying them all. The primary conceptual task within this approach is the formulation of the axioms. The axioms may, of course, be incompatible. It is indeed not rare that one would like to impose more axioms than are jointly compatible. It may also happen that a solution satisfying a list of axioms that all seem appealing on the basis of a one-by-one examination is found to behave unsatisfactorily in some particular situation. Then, the natural way to proceed is formally to identify the class of situations so exemplified and to formulate an additional axiom specifying how the solution should behave on that class and finally to determine the greatest subset of axioms of the original list that are compatible with the new axiom. Of course, compatibility may hold for several distinct such subsets. A systematic investigation of the maximal compatibilities clarifies the "cost" of each axiom and the "trade-offs" between axioms. It is ultimately on the basis of such information and of one's intuitive feeling concerning the various axioms that progress can be made in solving the problem of social choice.

The approach followed here is the axiomatic approach. Our purpose is to formulate what we hope will appear to the reader as appealing axioms and to exhibit various compatibilities between these axioms; it is not to make a final recommendation.

As mentioned earlier, our treatment is fairly abstract in that it involves no detailed description of the characteristics of the actual physical choices that are available; we only use the utilities attached by the individuals to these choices. Ours is therefore what Sen (1979) has called a "welfarist" theory. In a series of papers, Roemer has formulated a number of criticisms of this approach. An overview of these criticisms can be found in Roemer (1986).

Of particular importance is the fact that the utility functions have cardinal significance instead of being arbitrary numerical representations of the agents' ordinal preferences.

They can be given two possible interpretations. Either they are utility functions of the von Neumann–Morgenstern type (1944), representing agents' attitude toward risk, or, as in the classical theory, they measure intensities of preferences.

The choice problems under study are all the subsets of the utility space satisfying a list of elementary properties specified in the next section; and a solution is a function defined on that family of subsets that associates with each member of the family one of its points, interpreted as the optimal choice. This formulation is essentially that introduced by Nash (1950) in his fundamental paper on the "bargaining problem." The bargaining interpretation is, however, not the only admissible one. Since, in fact, an important aspect of the work presented here concerns normative issues of social choice, as opposed to the positive questions addressed in bargaining theory, the general term *problem* will often be used instead of the phrase *bargaining problem*.

The appeal of Nash's formulation is due to its generality and its potential applicability to a large class of specific situations. However, it should be noted that additional information on the structure of the underlying set of physical choices sometimes can enter in a useful way in the construction of solutions and in the formulation of axioms. For instance, as alluded to earlier, if the choice problems consist of distributing a fixed bundle of goods, the feasible alternatives constitute a convex compact subset of a Euclidean space. Preferences can then be required to have special properties (such as convexity and monotonicity) that would not be meaningful otherwise, and solutions (such as the Walrasian solution) that would otherwise not be well defined become available. Such economic problems are important in motivating our work, and our results are often illustrated with the help of economic problems. For that reason, these problems are formally defined in Section 1.3. However, our attention is always limited in the proofs to the abstract framework outlined in the preceding.

Several solutions to the bargaining problem have been proposed in the literature and have been given axiomatic characterizations, and these solutions turn out to be central to our analysis. In addition, new families of solutions are introduced. The well-known solutions are axiomatized in novel ways, and analogous rationalizations are provided for the new solutions.

The novelty of our approach is its essential focus on situations in which the number of agents involved is variable, in contrast with virtually all of the existing literature where the number of agents is assumed to be fixed.

The rest of this introductory chapter is organized as follows. Section 1.2 contains descriptions of the domain of problems with which the classical theory of bargaining has been concerned and of the domain considered here; several changes have indeed been introduced, motivated in large part by our desire to lighten the notation. The concept of a solution is formally introduced and illustrated by a description of Nash's well-known solution. Section 1.3 is devoted to a presentation of the class of economic problems. Section 1.4 motivates the study of social choice with a variable number of agents and introduces the additional concepts and notation that will be needed to deal with this more general situation. Section 1.5 contains an overview of the organization of the book and a short summary of its main conclusions.

1.2 Domains and solutions

The theory developed here has its origin in a fundamental paper by Nash (1950), where the following concepts are proposed. A *two-person bargaining problem* is a pair (S, d) where S, the *feasible set,* is a subset of the two-dimensional Euclidean space, and d, the *status quo* or *disagreement point,* is a point of S. The intended interpretation of (S, d) is as follows: Each point of S gives the utility levels, measured in von Neumann–Morgenstern scales, attained by the two agents through the choice of some joint action. If they agree on a particular point of S, then that is what they get; if they fail to reach an agreement, they get d.

It is assumed that S is *compact* and *convex* and that *there is a point x of S strictly dominating d.* As stated, S is compact: It is closed (contains its boundary) and bounded (it is contained in some sphere of finite radius). Closedness is assumed for mathematical convenience. Compactness of S is satisfied in most situations of interest, in particular, if S is generated through convexification from a finite set of basic alternatives, a not uncommon situation. More generally, compactness of S will hold if S is the image in utility space of some compact set of basic alternatives under a vector of continuous utility functions. Even if the set of basic alternatives is not bounded, its image in utility space will be bounded if the utility functions are bounded, a property that has been argued as necessary to avoid the St. Petersburg paradox (see, in particular, Aumann, 1977). Convexity of S (if two points are in S, then the segment connecting them is contained in S) results from allowing randomization among alternatives if the utility functions are of the von Neumann–Morgenstern type.

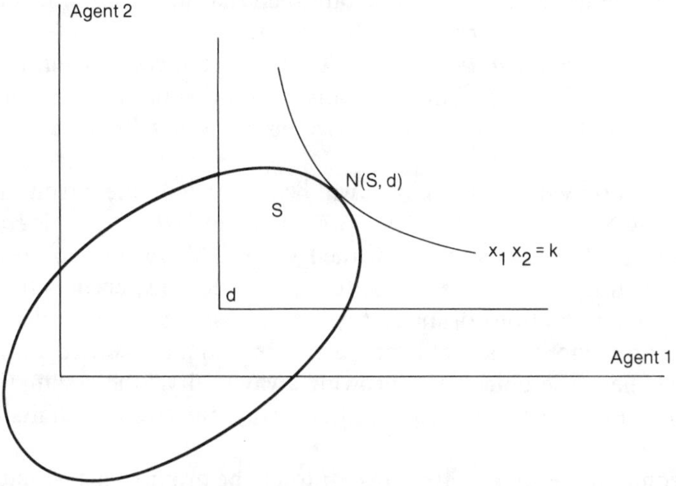

Figure 1.1. The Nash solution to the two-person bargaining problem.

The assumption that S contains at least one point strictly dominating d is made to ensure that both agents are nontrivially involved; both should have something to gain.

The class of such problems is denoted $\bar{\Sigma}^2$. A *solution* is a function F from $\bar{\Sigma}^2$ to $\mathbb{R}^2$ that associates with every bargaining problem $(S, d) \in \bar{\Sigma}^2$ a point of S, denoted $F(S, d)$, where $F(S, d)$ is interpreted as the compromise reached by the agents when they face the bargaining problem (S, d).

Nash proposed the following solution, which will be denoted N: Given $(S, d) \in \bar{\Sigma}^2$, $N(S, d)$ is the maximizer of the product $(x_1 - d_1)(x_2 - d_2)$ over the points x of S dominating d.

Nash's domain and his solution can directly be extended to the n-person case. (The n-person Nash solution associates with every $(S, d) \in \bar{\Sigma}^n$ the unique maximizer of the product $\prod (x_i - d_i)$ over the points x of S dominating d.)

The Nash solution has a simple geometric interpretation, represented in Figure 1.1. First, straight lines parallel to the axes are drawn through d. Then the highest rectangular hyperbola touching S, with these lines as asymptotes, is found. The point of contact of this hyperbola with S is the *Nash solution outcome of* (S, d).

Nash provided two rationalizations for his solution. One of them is based on noncooperative considerations, which we will not discuss here. The other is based on an axiomatic argument, after which all of our own studies will be patterned: Nash proposed a list of properties that he thought any solution should satisfy, and he established that his solution was the only one to satisfy these properties. In what follows we will refer to as an *axiomatic characterization of a solution* any such theorem identifying a particular solution as the only one satisfying a certain list of axioms. (The axioms used by Nash to characterize his solution will be described in Chapter 2.)

The domain on which our analysis will be conducted differs from that considered by Nash in three respects. First, we assume that (S, d) is *comprehensive:*[1] If $d \leqq y \leqq x$ and $x \in S$, then $y \in S$. This restriction on the domain, which is of no consequence for some solutions, ensures that a number of other solutions of interest will always select undominated alternatives, an obviously desirable property. Since in most concrete situations agents have the option of "throwing away utility," the assumption is a small price to pay to widen in significant ways the class of admissible solutions.

The second difference is that we take d to be the origin. This permits a major notational simplification; d is omitted altogether. This specification can be justified by assuming that the theory is independent of the choice of a zero for the utility functions used in the construction of the feasible set. Since all existing solutions are indeed invariant under translations of the origin and since our own formulation will also assume this invariance, it is convenient to take as admissible only problems that have already been subjected to a translation bringing their disagreement point to the origin. Consequently, $d = 0$ always, and a typical problem is simply denoted S instead of $(S, 0)$.

Finally, all problems are taken to be subsets of $\mathbb{R}^n_+$ (instead of $\mathbb{R}^n$). This means that all alternatives that would give any agent less than what he gets at the disagreement point $d = 0$ are disregarded; this assumption can be easily justified in situations where agents are *entitled* to 0 so that alternatives that do not meet this constraint can be judged irrelevant to the determination of the final compromise. It is, however, a little stronger than needed to guarantee the satisfaction of the constraint. Indeed, solutions exist that always select outcomes dominating d, although they do not depend only on the part of S that dominates d.

This discussion is summarized in the following definition.

Definition 1.1. *Σ^n is the family of n-person* ***problems*** *S such that*

(a) *S is a convex, compact subset of $\mathbb{R}^n_+$ containing at least one strictly positive vector.*

(b) *For all $x, y \in \mathbb{R}^n_+$, if $x \in S$ and $x \geqq y$, then $y \in S$.*

[1] Vector inequalities. Given two vectors $x, y \in \mathbb{R}^n$, $x \geqq y$ means $x - y \in \mathbb{R}^n_+$; $x \geq y$ means $x \geqq y$ and $x \neq y$; $x > y$ means $x - y \in \mathbb{R}^n_{++}$.

Convexity and compactness of S have already been discussed. The requirement that S contains a strictly positive vector is the form taken by our earlier requirement that S contains a point strictly dominating the disagreement point since the disagreement point is now the origin. Condition (b) is the form taken in the present context by our earlier assumption of comprehensiveness. It holds automatically if utility is freely disposable in the relevant region.

The subclass $\tilde{\Sigma}^n$ defined next will also be considered.

Definition 1.2. *$\tilde{\Sigma}^n$ is the subclass of Σ^n of problems S such that*

(c) *for all $x, y \in S$, if $y \geq x$, then there exists $z \in S$ with $z > x$.*

Condition (c), which we call *strict comprehensiveness,* says that the undominated boundary of S contains no segment parallel to a coordinate subspace. This property has important implications. In particular, there are a number of axioms that some solutions satisfy on $\tilde{\Sigma}^n$ but not on Σ^n. Since any element of Σ^n can be approximated by a sequence of elements of $\tilde{\Sigma}^n$, the subdomain $\tilde{\Sigma}^n$ will turn out to be quite useful in proofs. Of course, strict comprehensiveness also has conceptual significance since it guarantees that "utility transfers" are always possible along the north–east boundary of the problem. (It has also played a crucial role in several recent contributions to the theory of games in conditional function form.)

1.3 Economic problems

This section contains a brief description of an important class of choice problems that will often be used in the following pages for illustration and motivation. This is the class of traditional economic division problems, consisting in the allocation of a bundle of goods among a group of consumers. Such problems can be specified in several alternative ways. We have chosen the following formulation.

An *n-person economic division problem* is a list (l, Ω, u) where $l \in \mathbb{N}$ is the *number of goods,* $\Omega \in \mathbb{R}^l_+$ is the *vector of goods* to be distributed, and $u = (u_1, \ldots, u_n)$ is a vector of n real-valued *utility functions* defined on $\mathbb{R}^l_+$. The goods are infinitely divisible so that a *feasible allocation* is a vector $z = (z_1, \ldots, z_n) \in \mathbb{R}^{ln}_+$ satisfying the feasibility constraint $\sum z_i = \Omega$. The vector z_i is interpreted as agent i's *consumption*. If the goods are freely disposable, the feasibility constraint is written as $\sum z_i \leqq \Omega$. For each i, u_i is continuous, nondecreasing, and quasi-concave and satisfies $u_i(\Omega) > u_i(0)$ and the normalization condition $u_i(0) = 0$. It is well known that if the utility functions are in fact concave and the feasibility constraint is written as an inequality, then the image in the utility space of the set of feasible allocations is an element of Σ^n (given in Definition 1.1). If each u_i is strictly increasing, an element of $\tilde{\Sigma}^n$ results. Conditions under which, conversely, an element of Σ^n (or $\tilde{\Sigma}^n$) can be obtained as the image in the utility space of the set of feasible allocations of some n-person economy (l, Ω, u) satisfying the assumptions listed in the preceding have been analyzed by Billera and Bixby (1973) and others.

Choice problems of that nature have been extensively studied, in particular in the two-person case and often without the assumption that commodities are infinitely divisible. One of the oldest and best-known solutions is the "divide-and-choose" method, but there are others. We need not go into the details here, however, since we are not directly concerned with this problem per se.

1.4 Social choice with a variable population

In the traditional formulation of the bargaining problem, as presented in Section 1.2, the number of agents is assumed to be some fixed, although usually arbitrary, number. The contribution of this book is its focus on situations in which the number of agents may vary. This possibility has been recognized and exploited in other branches of economic theory and political science, such as the theory of the core (see Debreu and Scarf, 1963), the theory of indices of inequality (see Blackorby and Donaldson, 1982), and the theory of fair apportionment (see Balinski and Young, 1982). To our knowledge, Harsanyi (1959) and Kalai (1977a) are the only writers who considered it in bargaining theory. However, their investigations (which are presented in Chapters 7 and 12, respectively) remain limited. Here, we will engage in a systematic analysis of the bargaining problem in situations where the number of agents is variable.

These variations can be understood in two ways. First, they may be hypothetical. Thought experiments concerning situations that may not be encountered in actual fact may yield useful insights into the respective merits of solutions. Or, actual changes in the population may take place: Families become larger or smaller as new children are born, older children leave the home, or elderly members die; cities enlarge at the expense of the countryside as industries develop; nations lose population as a result of wars or emigration. In each of these cases, one may want to know how social decisions could, or should, be affected by variations in the actual number of agents.

The variations in the number of agents may be imposed on the agents from the outside, or the agents themselves may have control over them. The original agents may have veto power over the arrival of the newcomers, which they will be more likely to exercise if they stand to lose much.

Conversely, the original agents may have a right, and the possibility, to bring in additional agents and should be expected to do so if it is to their benefit. A situation of particular interest is when subgroups of agents have similar preferences. Then, a given agent may find that by bringing in agents with tastes similar to hers, she strengthens her position. The opposite is possible too. A group of agents with similar interests may want to be represented by only one of them and drop out of sight while the problem is being resolved.

To allow for this kind of analysis, a more general concept of solutions is needed, which it is the purpose of the next few paragraphs to develop.

There is a universe I of "potential agents." Alternatively, I can be thought of as being a set of "positions" to which individuals would be assigned. The running index of an agent in I is i. Usually, I will be taken to be the positive integers and sometimes some finite subset of the positive integers.

The class of (finite) subsets of I is designated $\mathcal{P}$, with generic elements $P, Q, \ldots,$. Choice problems may involve any such subset of I. The cardinality of $P \in \mathcal{P}$ is denoted $|P|$. Given $P \in \mathcal{P}$, $\mathbb{R}^P_+$ designates the Cartesian product of $|P|$ copies of $\mathbb{R}_+$ indexed by the members of P, and Σ^P is the class of subsets of $\mathbb{R}^P_+$ with properties (a) and (b) required in Definition 1.1 of the elements of Σ^n. Each element of Σ^P is to be interpreted as a problem that the group P may conceivably face. Finally, $\Sigma \equiv \bigcup_{P \in \mathcal{P}} \Sigma^P$ is the class of all possible problems that some admissible group may face.

A *solution* is a function F that associates with each $S \in \Sigma$ a unique point of S, denoted $F(S)$, and called the *solution outcome of* S. A solution provides a compromise for any conceivable problem faced by any admissible group of agents. Given $P \in \mathcal{P}$, the restriction of the solution to Σ^P is called the *component of the solution relative to* P.

Solutions initially defined for the case of a fixed number of agents usually can trivially be extended to deal with arbitrary numbers of agents. For instance, the *Nash solution* N is the solution that coincides with the $|P|$-person Nash solution (Section 1.2) for each $P \in \mathcal{P}$.

This book is devoted to an axiomatic study of solutions as just defined. It is organized in a series of chapters, many of which center on only one solution. Each of the best-known solutions is studied in one or more chapters.

The proofs of the theorems, which are sometimes involved, are all essentially geometric. To make them easier to read, we have included a large number of figures. We have sometimes offered two proofs of the same result; a basic understanding can be obtained by reading one proof pertaining to a simple case, whereas the general case is treated in the other proof. In order to allow the chapters to be read independently, we have occasionally restated a definition introduced in an early chapter.

1.5 Summary of results

This chapter concludes with an overview of this book. Chapter 2 is devoted to a summary of the current status of the axiomatic theory of bargaining when the number of agents is fixed. More comprehensive treatments can be found in Roth (1979c) and Thomson (1987b). The rest of the book is essentially organized around four main issues: monotonicity, guarantees and opportunities, stability, and replication.

The property of *monotonicity,* which should here be understood as monotonicity in response to variations in the number of agents, is satisfied by a solution when the solution forces every one of the agents originally present to help out in supporting newcomers if the arrival of the newcomers is not accompanied by an expansion of opportunities. This property expresses a form of solidarity among agents. We use it to develop axiomatic characterizations of the Kalai–Smorodinsky solution (Chapter 3) and of the Egalitarian solution (Chapter 4). We also introduce and analyze two families of solutions generalizing the Egalitarian solution but still satisfying the property (Chapter 5).

When a solution does not satisfy monotonicity, it sometimes gives one, or perhaps several, of the agents initially present the opportunity to benefit from the arrival of the newcomers. We propose next a quantitative measure of the extent to which this undesirable phenomenon is permitted by solutions, and we use this measure to rank them. Similarly, we examine and quantify the extent of the losses that are imposed on the agents initially present in order to accommodate the newcomers. Solutions that limit opportunities for gains and offer good protections from large drops in utility are of course preferable. We show that when either *opportunities* for gains or *guarantees* are considered, the Kalai–Smorodinsky solution is best among a large class of solutions. However, when it is the opportunities for gains or the guarantees offered to the initial *group* seen as a whole that are considered, it is the Nash solution that comes out best (Chaper 6).

The third theme is that of *stability.* A solution is stable if what it recommends for each group is consistent with what it recommends for each subgroup (individual by individual) subject to the constraint that each of the agents in the complementary subgroup receives what was originally proposed he should receive. We give axiomatic characterizations involving this axiom for the Nash solution (Chapter 7), a new family of multivalued solutions related to the Nash solution (Chapter 8), and the Leximin solution (Chapter 9).

Next, we combine the themes of monotonicity and stability in a characterization of the Egalitarian solution (Chapter 10).

Generalizations of the results on stability are then developed (Chapter 11), yielding a characterization of a whole family of new solutions referred to as additive Bergson–Samuelson solutions.

Chapter 12 is devoted to a study of solutions in situations in which the preferences of the new agents bear some simple relation to those of the agents originally present, such as when they precisely replicate them. We propose several notions of *invariance of solutions under* (various kinds of) *juxtapositions and replications* of problems, and we investigate whether the well-known solutions satisfy these invariance properties. There, the answers are mostly positive.

A bibliography concludes.

1.6 Other notational conventions

Given $P, Q \in \mathcal{P}$ with $P \subset Q$, $Q \backslash P$ designates the set consisting of the elements of Q that do not belong to P. If $P = \{i\}$, where i is an element of I, we write $P \backslash i$ instead of $P \backslash \{i\}$.

Given $P \in \mathcal{P}$, e_P designates the vector of $\mathbb{R}^P$ that has all of its coordinates equal to 1. If $P = \{i\}$, we write e_i instead of $e_{\{i\}}$; this is the unit vector corresponding to agent i. Given $P, Q \in \mathcal{P}$ with $P \subset Q$ and $y \in \mathbb{R}^Q_+$, y_P designates the projection of y on $\mathbb{R}^P_+$. Similarly, if $T \subset \mathbb{R}^Q_+$, T_P designates the projection of T on $\mathbb{R}^P_+$.

Given $S^1, \ldots, S^k \subset \mathbb{R}^P_+$, $\text{co}\{S^1, \ldots, S^k\}$ is the convex hull of $S^1, \ldots, S^k$ (the intersection of all the convex sets containing $S^1, \ldots, S^k$); $\text{cch}\{S^1, \ldots, S^k\}$ is the convex and comprehensive hull of $S^1, \ldots, S^k$ (the intersection of all the convex and comprehensive sets containing $S^1, \ldots, S^k$). Given $A \subset \mathbb{R}^P_+$, rel. int. A is the relative interior of A.

In the course of this book, we will often have to enlarge the dimensionality of the space in which we work. To simplify the notation, we will designate by the same letter a set initially given in the space of lower dimensionality and that same set embedded in the space of higher dimensionality. We believe that no ambiguity will result from this abuse of notation. In the few places where we feared that confusion might arise, we have adopted more explicit notation.

CHAPTER 2

Axiomatic theory of bargaining with a fixed number of agents

2.1 Introduction

In this chapter we survey the axiomatic theory of bargaining for a fixed number of agents. Although Nash's paper has enjoyed great popularity since its publication, and the Nash solution has been used in numerous studies of actual conflict situations, the central role played by this solution was very seriously challenged in the mid-1970s by the introduction and the characterization of other solutions, notably the Kalai–Smorodinsky and Egalitarian solutions. Largely spurred by these developments, an explosion of contributions to the theory has occurred since. Here, we will describe the main aspects of the theory, with particular emphasis on results concerning the solutions that will be at the center of our own theory.

2.2 The main solutions

Although alternatives to the Nash solution were proposed soon after the publication of Nash's paper, it is fair to say that until the mid-1970s, the Nash solution was often seen by economists and game theorists as the main, if not the only, solution to the bargaining problem. This preeminence is explainable by the fact that Nash developed a natural strategic model yielding exactly the same outcomes at equilibrium, as well as by his elegant characterization. In spite of the lack of unanimous agreement on some of the specific axioms that he used (in fact, one of them, the independence axiom, was subjected to a significant amount of criticism early on), the appeal of the axiomatic methodology is such that the revival of the theory can be dated to the new characterizations developed in the mid-1970s.

In order to facilitate the transition to the rest of this book, in all of which the domain is Σ, we will present this survey on the domain Σ^n. This choice will also permit us to simplify some of the proofs.

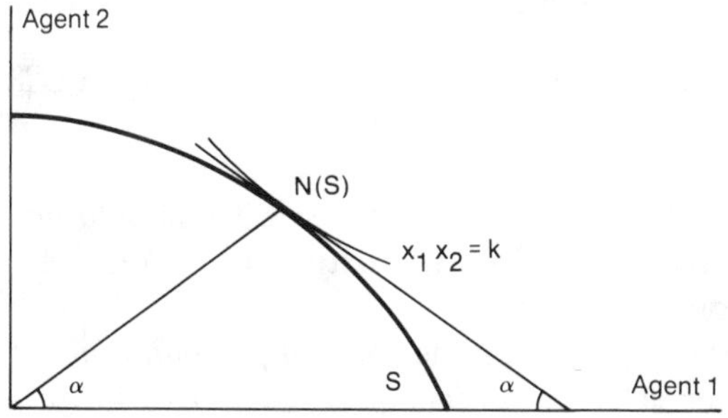

Figure 2.1. The Nash solution.

2.2.1 *The Nash solution*

Before presenting Nash's theorem in detail, we give a formal definition of the Nash solution on the domain Σ^n, and we illustrate the solution for $n=2$ (see Figure 2.1).

In what follows, e^n is the vector in $\mathbb{R}^n$ of coordinates all equal to 1.

> ***Definition.*** *The Nash solution N is defined by setting, for all $S \in \Sigma^n$, $N(S)$ equal to the maximizer in $x \in S$ of the "Nash product" $\prod x_i$.*

For $n=2$, the Nash solution can be described in two other ways. First, $N(S)$ is the undominated point x of S at which S has a line of support whose slope is equal to the negative of the slope of the line segment $[0,x]$. The point $N(S)$ is also the point of contact of the highest rectangular hyperbola touching S having the axes as asymptotes. (These geometric definitions easily extend to arbitrary n.)

Nash's theorem is based on the following axioms, abbreviated with lowercase letters. All of the axioms formulated in this chapter for solutions defined on Σ^n have counterparts for solutions defined on Σ, where population may vary. In order to keep clear the conceptual distinction between solutions defined on a fixed-population domain and solutions defined on a variable-population domain, we will abbreviate the latter with capital letters. (For example, the counterpart of *p.o,* imposed on F defined on Σ^n, is denoted *P.O.*)

Pareto-optimality (p.o): For all $S \in \Sigma^n$, for all $x \in \mathbb{R}^n$, if $x \geq F(S)$, then $x \notin S$.

A slightly weaker condition is

Weak Pareto-optimality (w.p.o): For all $S \in \Sigma^n$, for all $x \in \mathbb{R}^n$, if $x > F(S)$, then $x \notin S$.

According to *p.o,* the alternative that is selected should not be semi-strictly dominated by any feasible alternative; *w.p.o* requires only that no strict domination be possible.

Let $\Pi^n: \{1, \ldots, n\} \to \{1, \ldots, n\}$ be the *class of permutations of order n.* Given $\pi \in \Pi^n$, and $x \in \mathbb{R}^n$, let $\pi(x) \equiv (x_{\pi(1)}, \ldots, x_{\pi(n)})$. Also, given $S \subset \mathbb{R}^n$, let $\pi(S) \equiv \{x' \in \mathbb{R}^n \mid \exists x \in S \text{ with } x' = \pi(x)\}$.

Symmetry (sy): For all $S \in \Sigma^n$, if for all $\pi \in \Pi^n$, $\pi(S) = S$, then $F_i(S) = F_j(S)$ for all i, j. [Note that $\pi(S) \in \Sigma^n$.]

This says that if all agents are interchangeable in the geometric description of a problem, they should receive the same amount.

Let $\Lambda^n: \mathbb{R}^n \to \mathbb{R}^n$ be the class of *positive, independent person-by-person, and linear, transformations of order n.* Each $\lambda \in \Lambda^n$ is characterized by n positive numbers a_i such that given $x \in \mathbb{R}^n$, $\lambda(x) = (a_1 x_1, \ldots, a_n x_n)$. Now, given $S \subset \mathbb{R}^n$, let $\lambda(S) \equiv \{x' \in \mathbb{R}^n \mid \exists x \in S \text{ with } x' = \lambda(x)\}$.

Scale invariance (s.inv): For all $S \in \Sigma^n$, for all $\lambda \in \Lambda^n$, $F(\lambda(S)) = \lambda(F(S))$. [Note that $\lambda(S) \in \Sigma^n$.]

In Nash's formulation, utilities are of the von Neumann–Morgenstern type, that is, they are invariant only up to arbitrary positive affine transformations; it is therefore natural to require of solutions that they be invariant under the same class of transformations. Each such transformation has an additive component and a multiplicative component. Since we have chosen $d = 0$, we do not have to require invariance under addition to the utilities of arbitrary constants. Instead, we only require invariance under multiplication of the utilities by arbitrary positive constants.

Independence of irrelevant alternatives (i.i.a): For all $S, S' \in \Sigma^n$, if $S' \subset S$ and $F(S) \in S'$, then $F(S') = F(S)$.

This says that if the solution outcome of a given problem remains feasible for a new problem obtained from it by contraction, then it should also be the solution outcome of this new problem.

Nash showed that, for $n = 2$, only one solution satisfies these four requirements. His result extends directly to arbitrary n.

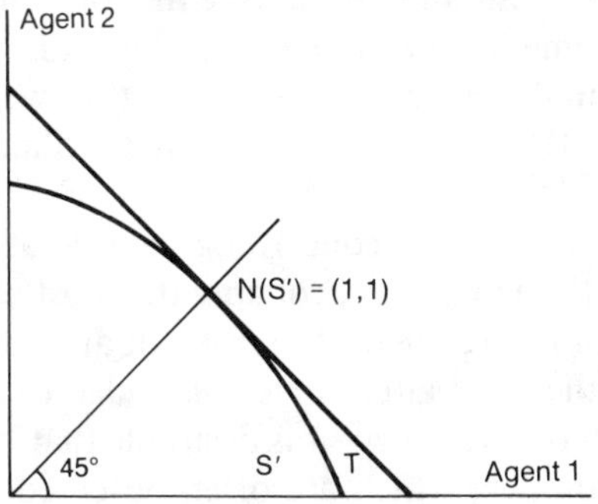

Figure 2.2. Theorem 2.1. Characterization of the Nash solution.

Theorem 2.1. *A solution on* Σ^n *satisfies p.o, sy, s.inv, and i.i.a if and only if it is the Nash solution.*

Proof. It is easy to see that N satisfies the four axioms. Conversely, to show that if a solution F on Σ^n satisfies the four axioms then $F=N$, let $S \in \Sigma^n$ be given. Note that $N(S)>0$ (since there exists $x \in S$ with $\prod x_i > 0$ the maximum of $\prod x_i$ for $x \in S$ is also positive); therefore, the transformation $\lambda: \mathbb{R}^n \to \mathbb{R}^n$ associating with every $x \in \mathbb{R}^n$ the point $\lambda(x) \equiv (x_1/N_1(S), \ldots, x_n/N_n(S))$ is a well-defined element of Λ^n. We have that $\lambda(N(S)) = (1, \ldots, 1) \equiv e^n$. Also, by definition of N, S is supported at $N(S)$ by the hyperplane of equation $\sum (x_i'/N_i(S)) = n$. Therefore, $S' \equiv \lambda(S)$ is supported at $\lambda(N(S))$ by the hyperplane of equation $\sum x_i' = n$ (Figure 2.2). By *s.inv,* it suffices to show that $F(S') = N(S') = e^n$. To establish this, let $T \in \Sigma^n$ be defined by $T \equiv \{x' \in \mathbb{R}^n_+ \mid \sum x_i' \leq n\}$. Note that $e^n \in \mathrm{PO}(S) \equiv \{x \in S \mid \text{if } x' \geq x, \text{ then } x' \notin S\}$ and that T is invariant under all exchanges of agents. Therefore, by *p.o* and *sy,* $F(T) = e^n$. Also, $S' \subset T$ and $F(T) \in S'$. By *i.i.a,* $F(S') = F(T) = e^n$. Q.E.D.

This theorem constitutes the foundation of the axiomatic theory of bargaining. It shows that a *unique* point can be identified for each problem, representing an equitable compromise. In the mid-1970s, Nash's result became the object of a considerable amount of renewed attention, and the role played by each axiom in the characterization was scrutinized by several authors. Some of the axioms were shown to be of marginal importance in that their removal made admissible only very few additional solutions whereas the removal of the others made admissible unmanageably large families of solutions. A variety of other axioms were then formulated and substituted for Nash's axioms, and other appealing lists of axioms were shown to characterize other solutions. We devote the following pages to an account of these developments and, in particular, we discuss four other solutions that will be fundamental to the theory that we exposit later: the Kalai–Smorodinsky, Egalitarian, Leximin, and Utilitarian solutions.

We start with Roth's early contribution concerning the role of Pareto-optimality in Theorem 2.1. Although *p.o* is probably the most easily acceptable condition when solutions are meant to represent an arbitrator's choice, to the extent that the theory is alternatively intended to describe how agents reach compromises on their own, it is desirable that it be able to explain nonoptimal compromises, which are often observed in practice. But if optimality is violated, how is it violated? Can the theory help predict the sort of violations that will occur? This is the question addressed by Roth (1977a). The statement of the conclusion he reached requires the formulation of one more axiom.

Strong individual rationality (st.i.r): For all $S \in \Sigma^n$, $F(S) > 0$.

This says that all agents should strictly gain from the agreement. Note that on our domain, the weaker condition $F(S) \geqq 0$ is automatically satisfied since $S \subset \mathbb{R}^n_+$. (This is one of the disadvantages of our choice of domains. It obscures the significance of the individual rationality axioms. However, the requirement is natural, and the loss of generality due to this choice is limited.)

> ***Theorem 2.2.*** *A solution on Σ^n satisfies st.i.r, sy, s.inv, and i.i.a if and only if it is the Nash solution.*

Proof. We have already pointed out that N satisfies *sy, s.inv,* and *i.i.a,* and the fact that N satisfies *st.i.r* was noted and used in the proof of Theorem 2.1. Conversely, let F be a solution on Σ^n satisfying the four axioms. The desired conclusion, that $F = N$, will follow from Theorem 2.1 and the fact that *s.inv, i.i.a,* and *st.i.r* together (*sy* is not needed) imply *p.o,* as shown next: Let $S \in \Sigma^n$ be given and suppose, by way of contradiction, that $F(S) \notin \mathrm{PO}(S)$, that is, that there exists $x \in S$ with $x \geq F(S)$. Without loss of generality, suppose that $x_1 > F_1(S)$. Let $\lambda: \mathbb{R}^n \to \mathbb{R}^n$ be defined by $\lambda(x') = ((F_1(S)/x_1)x'_1, x'_2, \ldots, x'_n)$. Note that $\lambda \in \Lambda^n$ since $F_1(S) > 0$, by *st.i.r,* and since $x_1 > 0$. Therefore, $S' \equiv \lambda(S) \in \Sigma^n$. We have $\lambda(x) = F(S)$. Therefore, $F(S) \in S'$. Also, $S' \subset S$. By *i.i.a,* $F(S') = F(S)$. Also, by *s.inv,* $F(S') = \lambda(F(S)) \neq F(S)$ since $F_1(S) > 0$. This contradiction between our last two conclusions establishes the claim. Q.E.D.

A straightforward corollary of Theorem 2.2 is that if *st.i.r* is not used at all, only one additional solution becomes admissible.

Definition. *The **Disagreement solution 0** is defined by setting, for all $S \in \Sigma^n$, $0(S) \equiv 0$.*

Corollary 2.1. *A solution on Σ^n satisfies sy, s.inv, and i.i.a if and only if it is the Nash solution or it is the Disagreement solution.*

If *sy* is dropped from the list of axioms of Theorem 2.1, a somewhat wider but still small family of additional solutions become admissible. Let Δ^{n-1} be the $(n-1)$-dimensional simplex.

Definition. *Given $\alpha \in \text{rel. int. } \Delta^{n-1}$, the **asymmetric Nash solution with weights** α, N^α, is defined by setting, for all $S \in \Sigma^n$, $N^\alpha(S) \equiv \text{argmax} \prod x_i^{\alpha_i}$ for $x \in S$.*

These solutions were introduced by Harsanyi and Selten (1972).

Theorem 2.3. *A solution on Σ^n satisfies st.i.r, s.inv, and i.i.a if and only if it is an asymmetric Nash solution.*

Proof. It is easy to see that all N^α satisfy the three properties. The proof of the converse is very similar to that of Theorem 2.2. Given a solution F on Σ^n satisfying the three axioms, we first note, as in Theorem 2.2, that F in fact satisfies *p.o*. Let $\alpha \equiv F(\text{cch}\{\Delta^{n-1}\})$. By *p.o* and *st.i.r*, $\alpha \in \text{rel. int. } \Delta^{n-1}$. Given $S \in \Sigma^n$, let $\lambda \in \Lambda^n$ be such that $\lambda(S)$ be supported at α by Δ^{n-1}. This λ exists uniquely. Then the proof concludes as in Theorem 2.2. Q.E.D.

If *st.i.r* is not used, a few other solutions become available.

Definition. *Given $i \in \{1, \ldots, n\}$, the **ith Dictatorial solution D^i** is defined by setting, for all $S \in \Sigma^n$, $D^i(S)$ equal to the maximal point of S in the direction of the ith unit vector.*

Note that all D^i satisfy *s.inv* and *i.i.a*, but only *w.p.o* (instead of *p.o*). To recover full optimality, one may proceed as follows. First, select an ordering π of the n agents. Then given $S \in \Sigma^n$, pick $D^{\pi(1)}(S)$ if this point belongs to $\text{PO}(S)$; otherwise, among the points whose $\pi(1)$th coordinate is equal to $D^{\pi(1)}_{\pi(1)}(S)$, find the maximal point in the direction of the unit vector pertaining to agent $\pi(2)$. Pick this point if it belongs to $\text{PO}(S)$;

otherwise, repeat the operation with $\pi(3)\ldots$. This algorithm is summarized in the following definition.

> ***Definition.*** *Given an ordering π of $\{1, \ldots, n\}$, the **Lexicographic Dictatorial solution relative to π, D^π**, is defined by setting, for all $S \in \Sigma^n$, $D^\pi(S)$ to be the lexicographic maximizer over $x \in S$ of $x_{\pi(1)}, x_{\pi(2)}, \ldots, x_{\pi(n)}$.*

All of these solutions satisfy *p.o, s.inv,* and *i.i.a,* and there are no others if $n=2$. For them, the violations of symmetry are in a sense "maximal." The characterization of all solutions satisfying *w.p.o* (or *p.o*), *s.inv,* and *i.i.a* was accomplished by Peters, Tijs, and de Koster (1983) for $n=2$ and Peters (1983) for arbitrary n. (If $n>2$, other solutions exist defined by lexicographic maximization of certain Nash products involving subgroups of the agents.)

Omitting either *s.inv* or *i.i.a* from Theorem 2.1 makes admissible very large classes of solutions, some of which will be discussed in what follows. Roth (1977b) reformulated *i.i.a* by replacing the hypothesis that the problems have the same disagreement point (this hypothesis is part of the formulation of *i.i.a* for solutions defined on $\bar{\Sigma}^n$) by the hypothesis that they have the same "ideal point" (this point enters in a fundamental way in the definition of the Kalai–Smorodinsky solution, studied next). He showed the incompatibility of this version of *i.i.a* with the other three requirements of Theorem 2.1. However, if $n=2$ and the hypothesis of equal disagreement points is replaced by the hypothesis of equal points of "minimal expectations" [the point whose ith coordinate is $D_j^i(S)$ where $j \neq i$], then the resulting axiom together with the other three axioms of Theorem 2.1 characterize a Nashlike solution defined by maximizing in the feasible set the product of utility gains not from the origin but from this point of minimal expectations. Thomson (1981a) proposes other choices of such "reference points" and similarly characterizes corresponding variants of the Nash solution.

2.2.2 The Kalai–Smorodinsky solution

A new impetus was given to the axiomatic theory of bargaining when Kalai and Smorodinsky (1975) provided a characterization of the following solution, illustrated in Figure 2.3.

> ***Definition.*** *The **Kalai–Smorodinsky solution K** is defined by setting, for all $S \in \Sigma^n$, $K(S)$ to be the maximal point of S on the*

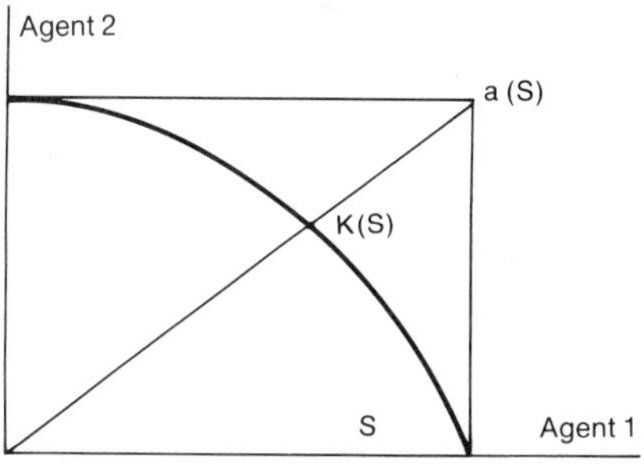

Figure 2.3. The Kalai–Smorodinsky solution.

segment connecting the origin to $a(S)$, the ***ideal point of S,*** *defined by $a_i(S) \equiv \max\{x_i \mid x \in S\}$ for each i.*

This solution has been mainly studied for $n=2$, a case in which it satisfies a greater number of appealing properties than for arbitrary n. Consequently, we will limit our attention to that case in the next few paragraphs. An important distinguishing feature between the Nash solution and the Kalai–Smorodinsky solution is that the latter responds much more satisfactorily to expansions and contractions of the feasible set. In particular, it satisfies the following axiom.

Individual monotonicity (i.mon): For all $S, S' \in \Sigma^2$, for all i, if $a_j(S) = a_j(S')$ and $S' \supset S$, then $F_i(S') \geqq F_i(S)$.

For each utility level attainable by agent j, the maximal utility level achievable by agent i increases, whereas the range of utility levels attainable by agent j remains the same. It therefore seems natural to require that agent i not be negatively affected by the expansion. It is on this property that the characterization offered by Kalai and Smorodinsky mainly rests.

Theorem 2.4. *A solution on Σ^2 satisfies p.o, sy, s.inv, and i.mon if and only if it is the Kalai–Smorodinsky solution.*

Proof. It is easily verified that K satisfies the four properties. Conversely, let F be a solution on Σ^2 satisfying the four properties and $S \in \Sigma^2$ be given. Let $\lambda \in \Lambda^2$ be such that $\lambda(a(S)) = (1,1)$ and $S' \equiv \lambda(S)$ (see Figure 2.4). Note that $\lambda(K(S)) = K(S') \equiv x$ is a point of equal coordinates. Let $T \equiv$ cch$\{(1,0), x, (0,1)\}$. Note that T is a symmetric element of Σ^2. Therefore,

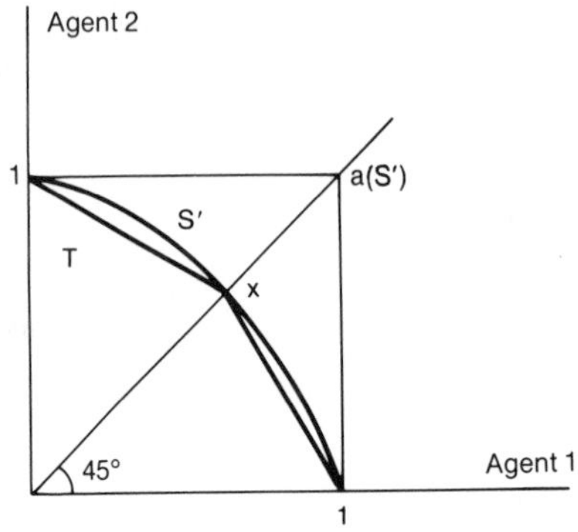

Figure 2.4. Theorem 2.4. Characterization of the Kalai–Smorodinsky solution.

by *p.o* and *sy*, $F(T)=x=K(T)$. Also, $T\subset S'$, $a_1(T)=a_1(S')$ and $a_2(T)=a_2(S')$. By *i.mon* applied twice, $F(S')\geqq F(T)=x$. Because $x\in \mathrm{PO}(S')$, $F(S')=x$ and the desired conclusion follows by *s.inv*. Q.E.D.

By deleting *p.o* from the axioms of Theorem 2.4, a one-parameter family of solutions obtained by scaling down $K(S)$ by some number $\lambda\in[0,1]$ becomes admissible. Note that the locus of $K(S)$ as S varies in Σ^2 subject to the condition $a(S)=(1,1)$ is the segment $[(\frac{1}{2},\frac{1}{2}),(1,1)]$. More generally, given any monotone path with one endpoint on the segment $[(1,0),(0,1)]$ and the other $(1,1)$, let the solution outcome of any S normalized so that $a(S)=(1,1)$ be the intersection of the path with $\mathrm{PO}(S)$, and that of an arbitrary S be obtained by an application of *s.inv*. Any solution constructed in this way satisfies all the axioms of Theorem 2.4 except *sy*. Peters and Tijs (1984, 1985) show that there are no others.

The removal of either *s.inv* or *i.mon* permits many additional solutions. In particular, if *s.inv* is dropped, *i.mon* can be considerably strengthened, as we will see in our discussion of the Egalitarian solution. Salonen (1985) proposed a slight reformulation of *i.mon*, which leads to a characterization of a variant of the Kalai–Smorodinsky solution.

Although the extension of the definition of the Kalai–Smorodinsky solution to the n-person case itself causes no problem, the generalization of the preceding results to the n-person case is not as straightforward as was the case of the extensions of the results concerning the Nash solution from $n=2$ to arbitrary n. First of all, for $n>2$, the n-person Kalai–Smorodinsky solution satisfies *w.p.o* only. (As noted by Roth, 1979d, if comprehensiveness of the feasible sets were not assumed, the solution could even

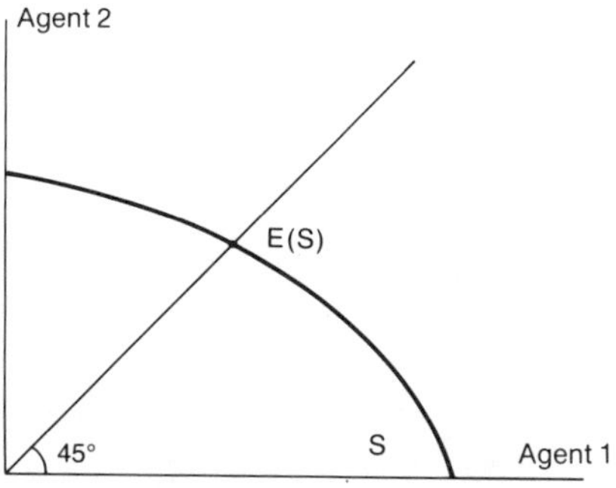

Figure 2.5. The Egalitarian solution.

select the origin.) This is not a serious limitation since, for most problems S, $K(S)$ in fact is (fully) Pareto optimal. In addition, Pareto-optimality can be recovered by a lexicographic operation that we will more extensively discuss in connection with the Egalitarian solution. Imai (1983), who proposed this extension, showed that the resulting solution could also be characterized by a suitable reformulation of the axioms of Theorem 2.4 together with the addition of a weak version of the independence axiom.

The weakening of *p.o* to *w.p.o* is not the only change that has to be made in the axioms of Theorem 2.4 to extend the characterization of the Kalai–Smorodinsky solution to the case $n > 2$. Indeed, several natural ways exist of generalizing the individual monotonicity condition, as discussed by Segal (1980) and Thomson (1980). One extension that will work for that purpose is: For all $S, S' \in \Sigma^n$, for all i, if $S \subset S'$ and $a_j(S) = a_j(S')$ for all $j \neq i$, then $F_i(S') \geqq F_i(S)$. This axiom is however less appealing than the two-person version since the range of utility vectors attainable by the agents different from i has not been left unaffected by the expansion.

2.2.3 *The Egalitarian solution*

We now turn to a third solution, whose main distinguishing feature from the previous two is that it involves interpersonal comparisons of utility.

> ***Definition.*** *The* ***Egalitarian solution E*** *is defined by setting, for all* $S \in \Sigma^n$, $E(S)$ *to be the maximal point of* S *of equal coordinates.*

The definition is illustrated in Figure 2.5.

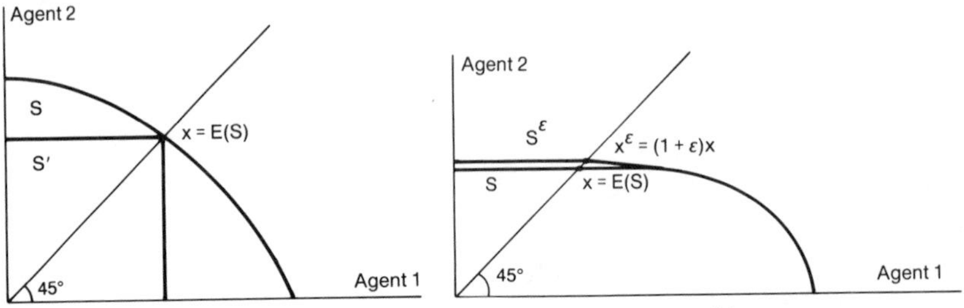

(a) (b)

Figure 2.6. Theorem 2.5. Characterization of the Egalitarian solution. (a) $E(S) \in \text{PO}(S)$; (b) $E(S) \in \text{WPO}(S) \setminus \text{PO}(S)$.

The most striking feature of this solution is that it satisfies the following monotonicity condition, which is very strong, since no restrictions are imposed in its hypotheses on the sort of expansions that take S into S'. In fact, this axiom can serve to provide an easy characterization of the solution.

Strong monotonicity (st.mon): For all $S, S' \in \Sigma^n$, if $S \subset S'$, then $F(S) \leqq F(S')$.

The following characterization result is a variant of a theorem due to Kalai (1977b).

Theorem 2.5. *A solution on Σ^n satisfies w.p.o, sy, and st.mon if and only if it is the Egalitarian solution.*

Proof. It is easily verified that E satisfies the three properties. Conversely, let F be a solution on Σ^n satisfying the three properties. Given any symmetric S, it follows from *w.p.o* and *sy* that $F(S) = E(S)$. Given any other $S \in \Sigma^n$, let $x \equiv E(S)$ and $S' \equiv \text{cch}\{x\}$ (Figure 2.6a). By the previous step, $F(S') = E(S')$, and since $S' \subset S$, it follows from *st.mon* that (i) $F(S) \geqq F(S') = E(S') = E(S) = x$. We are done if $E(S) \in \text{PO}(S)$. If not, for each $\epsilon > 0$, let $x^\epsilon \equiv (1+\epsilon)x$ and $S^\epsilon \in \Sigma^n$ be defined by $S^\epsilon \equiv \text{cch}\{S, x^\epsilon\}$ (Figure 2.6b). Note that $x^\epsilon = E(S^\epsilon) \in \text{PO}(S^\epsilon)$ so that, by the preceding argument, $F(S^\epsilon) = x^\epsilon$. Also $S^\epsilon \supset S$, so that by *st.mon*, $F(S^\epsilon) \geqq F(S)$. Since $x^\epsilon \to x$ as $\epsilon \to 0$, (ii) $F(S) \leqq x$. The desired conclusion follows from (i) and (ii).
Q.E.D.

Without *w.p.o*, the one-parameter family of *solutions of proportional character* introduced by Roth (1979a) become admissible. This family

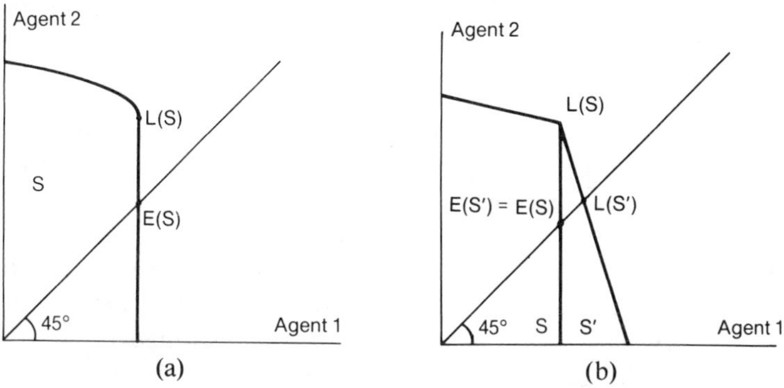

Figure 2.7. The Leximin solution L. (a) Definition of L; (b) L does not satisfy *st.mon*.

includes scaled-down versions of the Egalitarian solution obtained by choosing $\lambda \in [0,1]$ and setting the solution outcome of S equal to $\lambda E(S)$.

Conversely, one might wonder about the price of strengthening *w.p.o* to *p.o*. A lexicographic extension of the Egalitarian solution, which coincides with it on the class of strictly comprehensive problems, can be defined as follows:

Given $x \in \mathbb{R}^n$, let $\gamma(x) \in \mathbb{R}^n$ be obtained by rewriting the coordinates of x in increasing order: $\gamma_1(x) \leqq \gamma_2(x) \leqq \cdots \leqq \gamma_n(x)$. Given $x, y \in \mathbb{R}^n$, say that x is lexicographically greater than y, written as $x >_L y$, if $\gamma_1(x) > \gamma_1(y)$ or $[\gamma_1(x) = \gamma_1(y)$ and $\gamma_2(x) > \gamma_2(y)]$ or more generally if [for some $k \leqq n$, $\gamma_i(x) = \gamma_i(y)$ for all $i < k$ and $\gamma_k(x) > \gamma_k(y)$].

Definition. *The **Leximin solution L** is defined by setting, for all $S \in \Sigma^n$, $L(S)$ equal to the maximizer over S of $\gtrsim_L$.*

The definition is illustrated in Figure 2.7a for $n = 2$.

It is straightforward to verify that this solution is well defined and satisfies *p.o* and *sy*. However, it does not satisfy *st.mon* as illustrated by the example of Figure 2.7b: There $S \subset S'$ and yet $L_2(S') < L_2(S)$.

The properties of a normalized version of this solution were extensively studied by Imai (1983).

The family of Monotone Path solutions, defined next, is obtained by dropping *sy* from Theorem 2.5.

Definition. *Given a continuous, unbounded, and monotone path in $\mathbb{R}^n$ starting at the origin, the **Monotone Path Solution relative***

to G, E^G is defined by setting, for all $S \in \Sigma^n$, $E^G(S)$ equal to the maximal point of S on that path.

Any solution defined in this way satisfies *w.p.o* and *st.mon*. For the solution to be continuous, the path should be strictly increasing, except perhaps initially. These solutions are discussed in Myerson (1977) and Thomson and Myerson (1980). See also Kalai (1977b).

Theorem 2.5 shows that *st.mon* is a very strong condition indeed (in fact, Luce and Raiffa (1957) had long ago noted the incompatibility of *st.mon* and *w.p.o* on domains of nonnecessarily comprehensive problems). However, other conditions can be substituted for it in Theorem 2.5 without affecting the conclusion. For instance, Kalai (1977b) proposed the following condition.

Decomposability (dec): For all $S, S', S'' \in \Sigma^n$, if $S'' = \{x \in \mathbb{R}^n_+ \mid \exists x' \in S' \text{ s.t. } x' = x + F(S)\}$, then $F(S') = F(S) + F(S'')$.

This axiom says that the solution outcome of an expanded problem can be indifferently obtained directly or in stages by first computing the solution outcome of the initial problem and then solving the problem derived from the expanded problem by taking as disagreement point this initial solution outcome. It follows directly from Kalai that *w.p.o, sy,* and *dec* still characterize the Egalitarian solution. Other characteristics of the Egalitarian solution have been obtained by Myerson (1981) and Peters (1986).

2.2.4 The Utilitarian solution

We close this review with a short discussion of the Utilitarian solution. This solution has played a fundamental role in the theory of social choice in general but a marginal role in bargaining theory because it has the serious disadvantage of being independent of the disagreement point (this fact is the second one to be obscured by our choice of domain Σ^n). In spite of this limitation, we often refer to the Utilitarian solution for the purpose of comparison and because it is a limit case, permitting the most utility substitution.

The Utilitarian solution is obtained by maximizing the sum of utilities over the feasible set. Since we required solutions to associate with each problem a single point, we should specify what to do in case the sum of utilities is maximized at more than one point (having to include a tie-breaking rule in its definition is a second drawback of the solution). In the two-person case, selecting the midpoint of the segment of maximizers may be a natural choice. However, there is no equally natural choice for

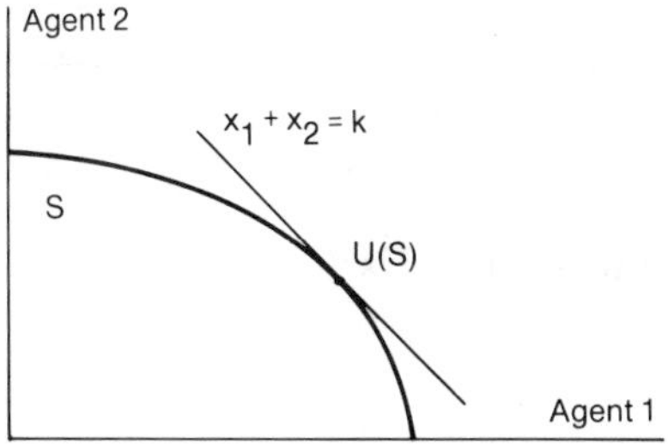

Figure 2.8. The Utilitarian solution.

more than two persons. Because of the various ways of making selections, we will sometimes use the phrase *utilitarian solutions*. (Another way to obtain a single point is of course to restrict the domain to problems with a strictly convex Pareto-optimal boundary.)

> ***Definition.*** *A* ***Utilitarian solution*** *U is defined by choosing, for each $S \in \Sigma^n$, $U(S)$ among the maximizers of $\sum x_i$ for $x \in S$.*

The definition is illustrated in Figure 2.8.

Obviously, all Utilitarian solutions satisfy *p.o.* They also satisfy *sy* if appropriate selections are made. However, no Utilitarian solution satisfies *s.inv* (even on the class of problems with a strictly convex Pareto-optimal boundary). Also, no Utilitarian solution satisfies *cont* or *i.i.a* because of the impossibility of performing appropriate selections.

The Utilitarian solution has been characterized by Myerson (1981) (see also Thomson, 1981b, c).

2.3 Other solutions

Other solutions have been discussed in the literature by Raiffa (1953), Luce and Raiffa (1957), and Perles and Maschler (1981). These solutions will not play a role in our exposition of the theory of bargaining with a variable number of agents.

CHAPTER 3

Population Monotonicity and the Kalai–Smorodinsky solution

3.1 Introduction

In this chapter we present our first example of an axiom relating solution outcomes across cardinalities, and we use it in conjunction with several familiar axioms to characterize the Kalai–Smorodinsky solution.

The axiom expresses a form of solidarity among agents in circumstances in which their number varies while the opportunities available to them remain unchanged. Imagine that a solution has been selected and consider a particular problem involving some group of agents. After the solution has been applied to the problem, a new agent enters the scene and is recognized to have claims as legitimate as everyone else's. Accommodating these claims will typically require sacrifices from some of the agents originally present. However, at the new solution outcome, some others could be better off. It is this possibility that the axiom will prohibit: All agents should share in the new responsibilities of the group, thus the term *solidarity.* If a solution satisfies it, it will be said to be *population monotonic.*

The axiom, which will be called the *Population Monotonicity* axiom, is illustrated in Figure 3.1. There S is a problem involving the group $P \equiv \{1, 2\}$, and T is the problem faced by the enlarged group $Q \equiv \{1, 2, 3\}$. The problem has the particular feature that its projection onto (or equivalently, since we consider only comprehensive problems, its intersection with) the coordinate subspace relative to P coincides with S. What agent 1 gets in S is compared to what he gets in T; we demand that agent 1 should not be better off when he is part of the large group than when he is part of the small group. The same condition is imposed on agent 2. Together, these conditions imply that the projection of the solution outcome for T onto the coordinate subspace pertaining to P is weakly dominated by the solution outcome for S.

To require that the problem S faced by P coincides with the projection T_P of the problem T faced by Q onto $\mathbb{R}^P$ implies that the arrival of the new agent is not accompanied by external effects. In general, the mere presence of new agents could affect, positively or negatively, the welfare of the agents originally present. Then the projection of T onto $\mathbb{R}^P$ would

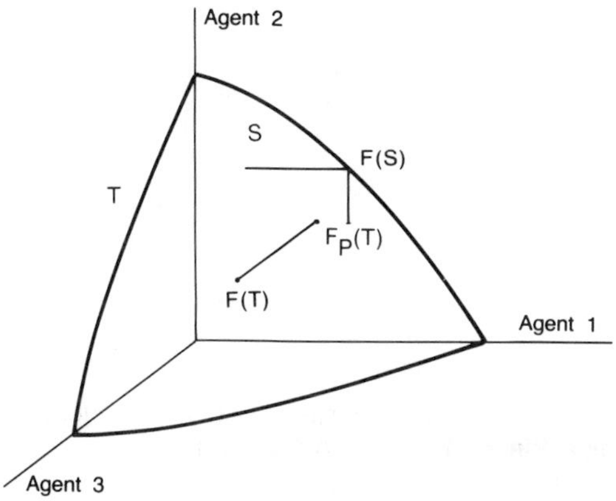

Figure 3.1. The axiom of Population Monotonicity: $F_P(T) \leqq F(T_P)$.

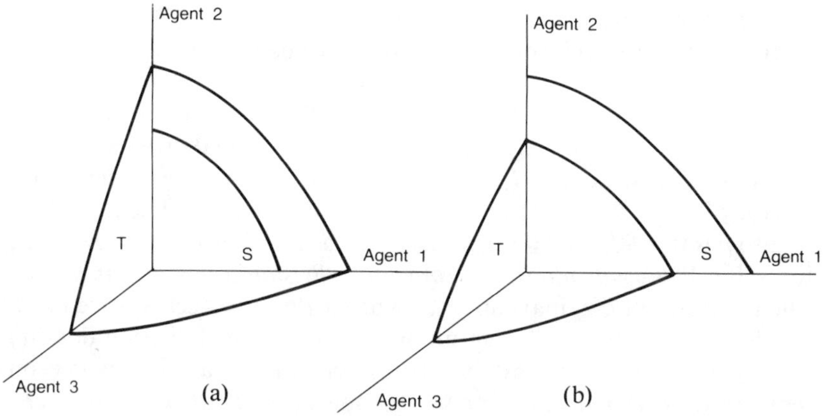

Figure 3.2. Arrival of agent 3 accompanied by external effects. (a) Positive external effects; (b) negative external effects.

strictly contain S in the first case or be strictly contained in S in the second case. These two possibilities are illustrated in Figures 3.2a and 3.2b.

As a concrete illustration of the axiom, imagine that the choice problem under study is the economic problem of distributing a fixed bundle of goods. Our requirement is that the arrival of an extra agent should not lead to a reshuffling of bundles that makes one (or more) of the original agents better off. Conversely, if an agent were to leave the economy, the

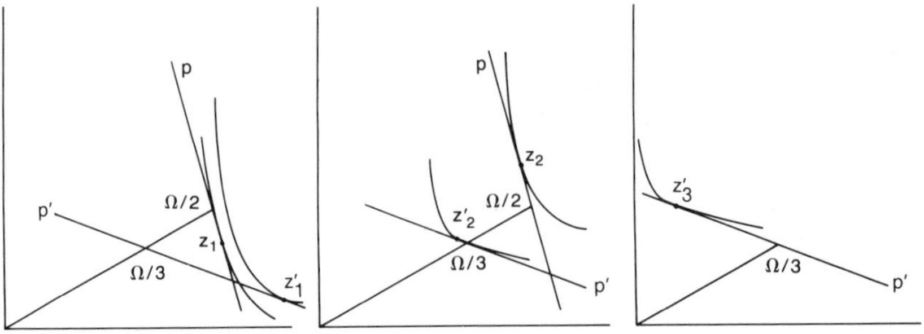

Figure 3.3. The Walrasian mechanism operated from equal division does not satisfy the axiom of Population Monotonicity.

resources freed by his departure should be used to improve (perhaps not strictly) the lot of the remaining agents. In response to increases (or decreases) in the size of the population, all of the original (or remaining) agents should lose (or gain) together.

It may be worthwhile pursuing further the analysis of this example and to show that one of the most natural (at least to economists) division principles fails to satisfy the Population Monotonicity axiom. This mechanism is the Walrasian mechanism operated from equal division. It is defined as follows: Let $e=(l,\Omega,u)$ be an n-person economy. Given a price vector $p\in\Delta^{l-1}$, the $(l-1)$-dimensional simplex, agent i's budget set relative to p is $\{z_i'\in\mathbb{R}^l_+ \mid pz_i'\leqq p\Omega/n\}$. Now, a feasible allocation $z=(z_1,\ldots,z_n)$ for e is a *Walrasian allocation from equal division* if there exists $p\in\Delta^{l-1}$ such that for all i, z_i maximizes u_i in agent i's budget set relative to p.

The fact that the Walrasian mechanism from equal division does not satisfy the axiom is now established by constructing a two-person economy $e=(l,\Omega,u)$ and a three-person economy $e'=(l',\Omega',u')$ such that $l=l'=2$, $\Omega=\Omega'$, $u_1=u_1'$, $u_2=u_2'$, and such that at a Walrasian allocation of e' from $(\Omega/3,\Omega/3,\Omega/3)$ agent 1 is better off than he was in e at a Walrasian allocation from $(\Omega/2,\Omega/2)$. The example is represented in Figure 3.3. Each of the three graphs depicts sample indifference curves of one of the three agents. Assuming first that only agents 1 and 2 are present and that each starts out with $\Omega/2$, the Walrasian equilibrium (p,z), where $p\in\Delta^1$ and $z=(z_1,z_2)\in\mathbb{R}^4_+$, is achieved. When agent 3 joins agents 1 and 2, each of the three agents starts out with $\Omega/3$, and the Walrasian equilibrium (p',z'), where $p'\in\Delta^1$ and $z'=(z_1',z_2',z_3')\in\mathbb{R}^6_+$, results, with $u_1(z_1')>u_1(z_1)$.

This undesirable feature of the Walrasian mechanism bears a certain relation to the phenomenon known in international trade theory as the transfer paradox. The fact that it can happen in otherwise well-behaved economies is discussed in Chichilnisky and Thomson (1987), and a detailed investigation of its relation to the transfer paradox appears in Jones (1987).

This example was discussed at some length because of its importance to economics. However, strictly speaking, it is not directly relevant to the situation under study in this book since the problems under investigation here are subsets of utility space and not of allocation space.

We conclude this introduction by noting that the general idea of Population Monotonicity itself is of course not new. Related requirements have for instance been found quite powerful in the axiomatic characterization of apportionment methods (see Balinski and Young, 1982).

The rest of the chapter is organized as follows. Section 2 contains a formal statement of the axiom of Population Monotonicity and of several familiar axioms. These axioms are then shown to jointly characterize the Kalai–Smorodinsky solution. This is the main result of this chapter. Variants are presented in Section 3.3, and Section 3.4 contains some concluding comments. This chapter is based on Thomson (1983c).

3.2 Characterization of the Kalai–Smorodinsky solution

We will make use of the following axioms:

Weak Pareto-Optimality (W.P.O): For all $P \in \mathcal{P}$, for all $S \in \Sigma^P$, for all $y \in \mathbb{R}^P_+$, if $y > F(S)$, then $y \notin S$.

Pareto-Optimality (P.O): For all $P \in \mathcal{P}$, for all $S \in \Sigma^P$, for all $y \in \mathbb{R}^P_+$, if $y \geq F(S)$, then $y \notin S$.

W.P.O says that it is not feasible to simultaneously increase all agents' utilities from what they are at the solution outcome. *P.O* is a slightly stronger condition which says that it is not feasible to increase any agent's utility from what it is at the solution outcome without decreasing some other agent's utility. *W.P.O* and *P.O* are often seen as minimal requirements of collective rationality.

Anonymity (AN): For all $P, P' \in \mathcal{P}$ with $|P| = |P'|$, for all one-to-one functions $\gamma: P \to P'$, for all $S \in \Sigma^P$, for all $S' \in \Sigma^P$, if $S' = \{x' \in \mathbb{R}^{P'} \mid \exists x \in S$ s.t. $\forall i \in P,\ x'_{\gamma(i)} = x_i\}$, then for all $i \in P$, $F_{\gamma(i)}(S') = F_i(S)$.

AN says that two groups of agents of same cardinalities would solve two problems with the same geometric structures in the same way: The names of the agents do not matter. All the information needed to solve a problem is contained in its mathematical description, and there is no reason to treat differently two problems that have the same description. Applied to a given group P of agents, this axiom says that a permutation of their names would be accompanied by an identical permutation of the coordinates of the solution outcome. But the axiom also applies when some of the agents are replaced by new agents. *AN* is therefore a strengthening of the axiom of Symmetry, which says that if a problem involving a given group of agents is invariant under arbitrary permutations of all the agents, its solution outcome should have equal coordinates. Symmetry was encountered in Chapter 2 for the fixed-population case and will be used again in several of the following chapters in its variable-population formulation:

Symmetry (SY): For all $P \in \mathcal{P}$, for all $S \in \Sigma^P$, if for all one-to-one functions $\gamma: P \to P$, $S = \{x' \in \mathbb{R}^P \mid \exists x \in S \text{ s.t. } \forall i \in P,\ x'_{\gamma(i)} = x_i\}$, then for all $i, j \in P$, $F_i(S) = F_j(S)$.

Given $P \in \mathcal{P}$, let Λ^P be the class of transformations λ from $\mathbb{R}^P_+$ into $\mathbb{R}^P_+$ defined as follows: For each $i \in P$, there exists a positive real number α_i such that for all $x \in \mathbb{R}^P_+$, $\lambda_i(x) = \alpha_i x_i$. Given $S \in \Sigma^P$, $\lambda(S)$ is defined to be $\{y \in \mathbb{R}^P_+ \mid \exists x \in S \text{ with } y = \lambda(x)\}$. Note that $\lambda(S)$ is also in Σ^P.

Scale Invariance (S.INV): For all $P \in \mathcal{P}$, for all $S \in \Sigma^P$, for all $\lambda \in \Lambda^P$, $F(\lambda(S)) = \lambda(F(S))$.

S.INV says that subjecting a problem to a positive linear transformation acting independently on each coordinate leads to a new problem that should be solved at the image under this transformation of the solution outcome of the original problem.

There has been a fair amount of debate as to whether this is a reasonable axiom. On the one hand, if the agent's utility functions are of the von Neumann–Morgenstern type, then *S.INV* is a natural reflection of the fact that such utility functions are unique only up to positive affine transformations. On the other hand, if the utility functions are of the classical variety, which measure intensities of preferences, then *S.INV* must be interpreted as a condition that precludes certain types of interpersonal comparisons of utility. Although no consensus exists in the literature as to how such comparisons should and could be made, the fact is that they are often made in the real world, and it certainly would be desirable to develop theories permitting them. This objective will be partially achieved in some later chapters devoted to the analysis of the Egalitarian and Leximin solutions, but for now we will impose Scale Invariance.

Continuity (CONT): For all $P \in \mathcal{P}$, for all sequences $\{S^k\} \subset \Sigma^P$ converging in the Hausdorff topology to some $S \in \Sigma^P$, $F(S^k) \to F(S)$.

CONT says that small changes in problems lead to small changes in solution outcomes. It guarantees that minor perturbations in the data defining the problem, due to errors of measurement, for example, do not lead to radical changes in the solution outcomes.

CONT as well as *W.P.O, P.O,* and *S.INV* are of course familiar axioms already formulated in Chapter 2 for the fixed-population case, but they had to be appropriately rewritten to apply to the variable-population case.

Population Monotonicity (MON): For all $P, Q \in \mathcal{P}$ with $P \subset Q$, for all $S \in \Sigma^P$, for all $T \in \Sigma^Q$, if $S = T_P$, then $F(S) \geqq F_P(T)$.

MON, which is the only axiom in this chapter to relate solution outcomes across cardinalities, was informally described in the introduction. The problem T is the problem faced by the large group Q and S is the problem that the members of the subgroup P of Q would face if they disregarded the agents in $Q \backslash P$ (i.e., attributed to them a zero utility). The requirement is that none of the members of P should end up better off after the rights of the agents in $Q \backslash P$ have been recognized. Note that it could have been written differently, by requiring that the cardinalities of P and Q differ by 1 only. However, a repeated application of this alternative axiom would yield the axiom given in the preceding.

We are now ready to turn to the results.

Proposition 3.1. *The Kalai–Smorodinsky solution satisfies W.P.O, AN, S.INV, CONT, and MON.*

Proof. That K satisfies *W.P.O, AN, S.INV,* and *CONT* is easily verified. To show that K also satisfies *MON,* let P, Q, S, T be as in the statement of that axiom. We have to establish that $K(S) \geqq K_P(T)$. To see this, note that for all $i \in P$, $a_i(S) = a_i(T)$. Therefore, the projection of $a(T)$ onto $\mathbb{R}^P$ is $a(S)$. Since $K(T) \in [0, a(T)]$, it then follows that $K_P(T) \in [0, a(S)]$. Since, in addition, $S = T_P$, then $K_P(T)$ is in fact weakly dominated by the intersection of $[0, a(S)]$ with the boundary of S. But this intersection is just $K(S)$, so the desired conclusion follows. Q.E.D.

Proposition 3.2. *A solution F satisfies W.P.O, AN, S.INV, and MON only if $F \geqq K$. [That is, for all $P \in \mathcal{P}$ and for all $S \in \Sigma^P$, $F(S) \geqq K(S)$.]*

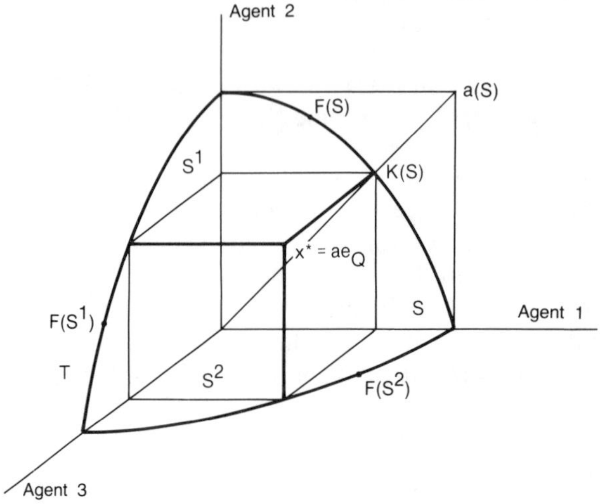

Figure 3.4. Proposition 3.2.

Proof. Let $P \in \mathcal{P}$ and $S \in \Sigma^P$ be given. By *S.INV*, S can be assumed to be normalized so that $a(S) = e_P$. Let $x \equiv K(S)$; x is the only point of $\text{WPO}(S)$ with equal coordinates, say $x = ae_P$. Let $y \equiv F(S)$, and suppose by way of contradiction that it is not the case that $y \geqq x$. Then for some $i \in P$, $F_i(S) < a$. Let $b \equiv F_i(S)$.

The proof consists in constructing a problem T involving the original members of P as well as some new agents and such that every agent faces one subproblem identical to that faced by i in S.

Because this construction is not obvious, two versions of it will be presented. The first version, which concerns the case $|P| = 2$, lends itself to a simple geometric representation. The other concerns the general case.

First, note that because F satisfies *AN*, the components of F depend on the P's only through their cardinalities.

First construction: the case $|P| = 2$. (See Figure 3.4.) Without loss of generality, we take $P \equiv \{1, 2\}$ and $i = 1$. We introduce a third agent who, also without loss of generality, we take to be agent 3. Let $Q \equiv \{1, 2, 3\}$. Now we construct a problem $T \in \Sigma^Q$. The first step of the construction of T consists in replicating S in $\mathbb{R}^{\{2,3\}}$ and $\mathbb{R}^{\{3,1\}}$ with agents 2 and 3, respectively, playing the role played by agent 1 in S. These copies of S will be the intersections of T with $\mathbb{R}^{\{2,3\}}$ and $\mathbb{R}^{\{3,1\}}$, respectively. Formally, let

$$S^1 \equiv \{(y_2, y_3) \in \mathbb{R}^{\{2,3\}} \mid \exists (x_1, x_2) \in S \text{ with } y_2 = x_1 \text{ and } y_3 = x_2\},$$
$$S^2 \equiv \{(y_3, y_1) \in \mathbb{R}^{\{3,1\}} \mid \exists (x_1, x_2) \in S \text{ with } y_3 = x_1 \text{ and } y_1 = x_2\}.$$

Let now $x^* \equiv ae_Q$ and finally let $T \subset \mathbb{R}^Q$ be given by

$$T \equiv \text{cch}\{S, S^1, S^2, x^*\}.$$

It is clear that $T \in \Sigma^Q$, $S = T_P$, $S^1 = T_{\{2,3\}}$, and $S^2 = T_{\{3,1\}}$.

By *AN*, we have $F_2(S^1) = F_3(S^2) = F_1(S) = b$.

Now, we apply *MON* to compare what agent 1 gets in T, which is $F_1(T)$, to what she gets in $S = T_P$, which is b. *MON* requires $F_1(T) \leqq b$. Since T is invariant under rotations of the agents, it also follows that $F_2(T) \leqq b$ and $F_3(T) \leqq b$. These three inequalities together yield $F(T) \leqq be_Q$. However, $x^* = ae_Q \in T$ and, therefore, $F(T) < x^*$, in contradiction with *W.P.O.* This completes the proof for the case $|P| = 2$.

Second construction: the general case. Without loss of generality, we take $P \equiv \{1, \ldots, n\}$ and $i = 1$. Let $P^1 \equiv P \backslash 1$ and P^2 and P^3 be two elements of $\mathcal{P}$ disjoint from each other as well as disjoint from P and such that $|P^2| = |P^3| = |P^1| = n - 1$. Also, let $Q \equiv P \cup P^2 \cup P^3$. Note that $\bigcup_{j=1}^3 P^j = Q \backslash 1$. Now, we construct $T \in \Sigma^Q$ by first specifying its intersections with various subspaces of $\mathbb{R}^Q$ of dimension n.

First, let γ^1 be a one-to-one function from P^1 to P^2. For each $i \in P^1$, let $S^i \subset \mathbb{R}_+^{P^2 \cup \{i\}}$ be defined by $S^i \equiv \{x \in \mathbb{R}_+^{P^2 \cup \{i\}} \mid \exists y \in S \text{ s.t. } x_i = y_1 \text{ and } \forall j \in P^1, x_{\gamma^1(j)} = y_j\}$. The problem S^i is a replica of S in which agent i plays the role played in S by agent 1, and the agents in P^2 play the roles played in S by the agents in P^1.

The operation that we just performed for each of the members of P^1 in relation to the set P^2 is then successively carried out for each of the members of P^2 in relation to the set P^3 and for each of the members of P^3 in relation to the set P^1. More precisely, let γ^2 be a one-to-one function from P^2 to P^3, and for each $i \in P^2$, let $S^i \subset \mathbb{R}_+^{P^3 \cup \{i\}}$ be defined by

$$S^i \equiv \{x \in \mathbb{R}_+^{P^3 \cup \{i\}} \mid \exists y \in S \text{ s.t. } x_i = y_1 \text{ and } \forall j \in P^1, x_{\gamma^2 \circ \gamma^1(j)} = y_j\}.$$

Also, for each $i \in P^3$, let $S^i \subset \mathbb{R}_+^{P^1 \cup \{i\}}$ be defined by

$$S^i \equiv \{x \in \mathbb{R}_+^{P^1 \cup \{i\}} \mid \exists y \in S \text{ s.t. } x_i = y_1 \text{ and } \forall j \in P^1, x_j = y_j\}.$$

Now let $x^* \equiv ae_Q$ and finally let $T \subset \mathbb{R}^Q$ be given by $T \equiv \text{cch}\{S, S^i \text{ for } i \in Q \backslash 1, x^*\}$.

Let P_i denote $P^2 \cup \{i\}$ for $i \in P^1$, $P^3 \cup \{i\}$ for $i \in P^2$, and $P^1 \cup \{i\}$ for $i \in P^3$.

It can be verified that $T \in \Sigma^Q$, $S = T_P$, and $S^i = T_{P_i}$ for each $i \in Q \backslash 1$.

Obviously, for each $i \in Q \backslash 1$, $S^i \in \Sigma^{P_i}$, and by *AN*, $F_i(S^i) = F_1(S) = b$.

Now, we apply *MON* to compare what agent 1 gets in T, which is $F_1(T)$, to what she gets in $S = T_P$, which is b. *MON* requires that $F_1(T) \leqq b$. Similarly, applying *MON* to each agent $i \in Q \backslash 1$ to compare what she gets in T to what she gets in $S^i = T_{P_i}$, we obtain $F_i(T) \leqq F_i(S^i) = b$.

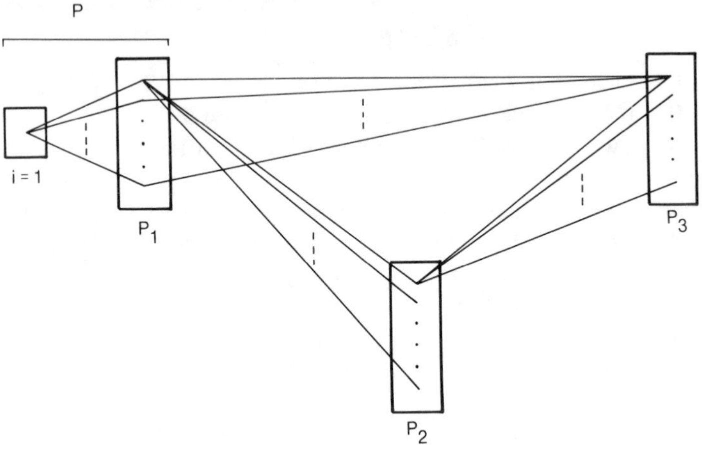

Figure 3.5. The relationships between the members of Q.

These inequalities together yield $F(T) \leqq be_Q$. However, $x^* = ae_Q \in T$, and since $a > b$, a violation of *W.P.O* results. Q.E.D.

Remark: It should be pointed out that the general construction applies to the case $|P| = 2$ as well but does not coincide with the one given for that case. This first argument is simpler.

These operations are illustrated in Figures 3.5 and 3.6. In Figure 3.5 we indicate schematically with which group each agent is associated so as to face a problem identical to that faced by agent 1 in S.

In Figure 3.6 the case $|P| = 3$ is illustrated somewhat more precisely, with $P = \{1, 2, 3\}$, $P^1 = \{2, 3\}$, $P^2 = \{4, 5\}$, $P^3 = \{6, 7\}$, and $Q = \{1, \ldots, 7\}$. The problem to be replicated involves agent $i = 1$ and agents 2 and 3. We indicate it by its three intersections with the three coordinate planes and its completion in the third dimension, represented by the arrow. Agents 2 and 3 are each to the group $\{4, 5\}$ as agents 4 and 5 are each to the group $\{6, 7\}$; agents 6 and 7 are each to the group $\{2, 3\}$ and as agent 1 is to the group $\{2, 3\}$. This means that agent 2 is to agent 3 as agent 4 is to agent 5 and as agent 6 is to agent 7. The proof first specifies the intersections S^i of T with the following subspaces of $\mathbb{R}^Q$: $\mathbb{R}^{\{1,2,3\}}$, $\mathbb{R}^{\{2,4,5\}}$, $\mathbb{R}^{\{3,4,5\}}$, $\mathbb{R}^{\{4,6,7\}}$, $\mathbb{R}^{\{5,6,7\}}$, $\mathbb{R}^{\{6,2,3\}}$, $\mathbb{R}^{\{7,2,3\}}$. (Only four of them are represented in Figure 3.6.) The construction of T is completed by adding the point x^* of coordinates all equal to a and taking the convex and comprehensive hull of S, the S^i for $i = 2, \ldots, 7$, and x^*.

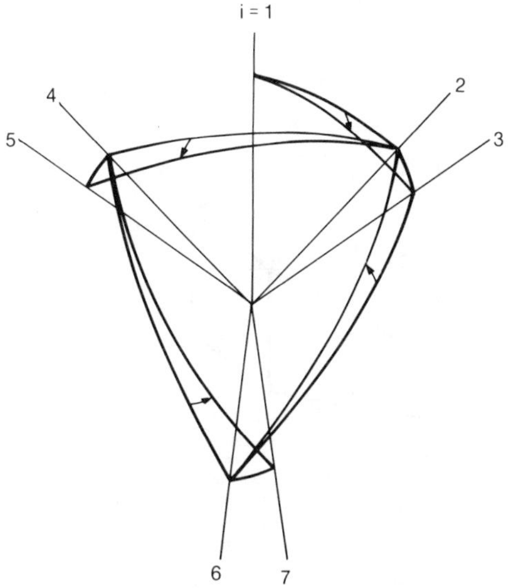

Figure 3.6. A schematic representation of T for the case $|P| = 3$.

Corollary 3.1. *If a solution F satisfies W.P.O, AN, S.INV, and MON, then for all* $P \in \mathcal{P}$, $F = K$ *on* $\tilde{\Sigma}^P$.

Proof. The proof is a straightforward consequence of Proposition 3.2 and of the fact that for each $P \in \mathcal{P}$ and for each $S \in \tilde{\Sigma}^P$, $x \in S$ can satisfy $x \geqq K(S)$ only if $x = K(S)$. Q.E.D.

It also follows from Proposition 3.2 that Pareto-Optimality (instead of Weak Pareto-Optimality) cannot be satisfied on the unrestricted domain Σ in conjunction with *AN, S.INV,* and *MON.*

Corollary 3.2. *There is no solution satisfying P.O, AN, S.INV, and MON.*

Proof. The proof is by way of the following example (see Figure 3.7): $P \equiv \{1,2\}$, $Q \equiv \{1,2,3\}$, and $T \equiv \text{cch}\{(2,1,1),(0,2,0),(0,0,2)\}$. It is easy to check that $K(T) = e_Q$. Moreover, by Proposition 3.2 and *P.O,* $F(T) = (2,1,1)$. Also, $K(S) = K(T_P) = K(\text{cch}\{(2,1),(0,2)\}) = (\frac{4}{3}, \frac{4}{3})$. This point is in fact Pareto optimal for S, and therefore, applying Proposition 3.2 again, it coincides with $F(S)$. But then $F_1(T) = 2 > \frac{4}{3} = F_1(T_P)$, in violation of *MON.* Q.E.D.

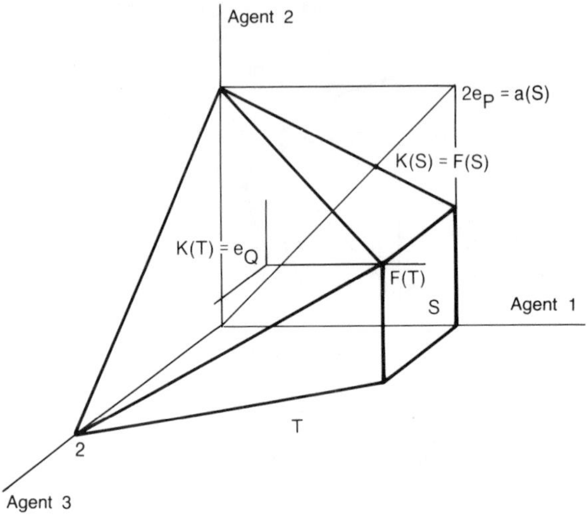

Figure 3.7. Corollary 3.2.

In view of Corollary 3.2, it is natural to return to the weak form of the optimality axiom. Proposition 3.1 implies that the Kalai–Smorodinsky solution satisfies *W.P.O, AN, S.INV,* and *MON,* and Proposition 3.2 indicates that there may be other solutions satisfying these four axioms. The existence of such solutions is formally established in the next lemma.

Lemma 3.1. *The Kalai–Smorodinsky solution is not the only one to satisfy W.P.O, AN, S.INV, and MON.*

Proof. The proof is by way of an example of a solution F that satisfies the four axioms but differs from the Kalai–Smorodinsky solution (see Figure 3.8): Let $\bar{P} \equiv \{1,2,3\}$ and $\bar{S} \in \Sigma^{\bar{P}}$ be given by $\bar{S} \equiv \text{cch}\{(1,0,1),(0,1,1)\}$. Let $F(\bar{S}) \equiv (\frac{1}{2},\frac{1}{2},1)$. Given any $S' \in \Sigma^{\bar{P}}$ that can be obtained from $\bar{S}$ by a positive linear transformation, let $F(S')$ be the image of $(\frac{1}{2},\frac{1}{2},1)$ under this transformation. Given any $P' \in \mathcal{P}$ with $|P'|=3$, define F on $\Sigma^{P'}$ from F on $\Sigma^{\bar{P}}$ by applying *AN*. Given any other $P'' \in \mathcal{P}$ with $|P''| \neq 3$, choose F to coincide with K on $\Sigma^{P''}$. It is immediate to verify that the solution so constructed satisfies the four axioms, but it differs from K since $F(\bar{S}) \neq K(\bar{S})$. Q.E.D.

The solution constructed in the proof of Lemma 3.1 is not very attractive because it is not continuous. At this point, therefore, we appeal to the Continuity axiom, and we obtain the following result.

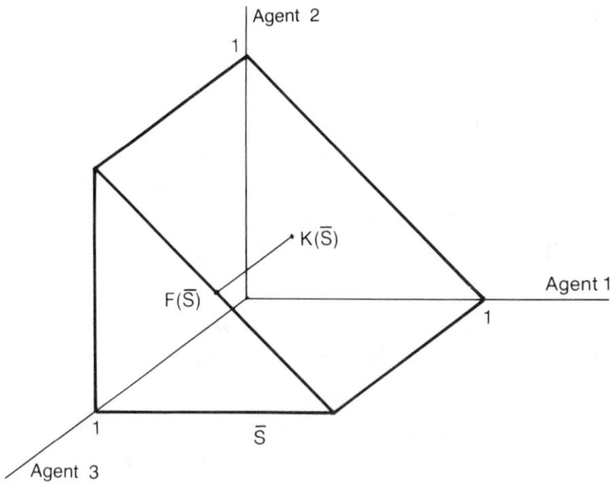

Figure 3.8. Lemma 3.1. A solution $F \neq K$ that satisfies *W.P.O, AN, S.INV,* and *MON.*

Proposition 3.3. *If a solution satisfies W.P.O, AN, S.INV, MON, and CONT, then it is the Kalai–Smorodinsky solution.*

Proof. The proof is a direct consequence of Corollary 3.1 and of the fact that for each $P \in \mathcal{P}$, any element of Σ^P can be approximated by a sequence of elements of the restricted domain $\tilde{\Sigma}^P$. Q.E.D.

Propositions 3.1 and 3.3 imply directly the main result of this chapter.

Theorem 3.1. *A solution satisfies W.P.O, AN, S.INV, CONT, and MON if and only if it is the Kalai–Smorodinsky solution.*

3.3 Variants

In this section we investigate how the conclusions reached in Section 3.2 would be affected by changing in various ways the domain over which solutions are defined. We also study the consequences of dropping one axiom at a time from the list of axioms leading to the characterization of the Kalai–Smorodinsky solution.

These variants are very useful in testing the robustness of Theorem 3.1 and in throwing light on the role played by each axiom.

3.3.1 Alternative domains

(i) Adding the requirement of strict comprehensiveness: This is the requirement that for all $x, y \in S$, if $y \geq x$, then there exists $z \in S$ with $z > x$ [requirement (c) given in Definition 1.2]. If (c) holds, then an alternative is weakly Pareto optimal for S if and only if it is Pareto optimal.

Imagine now that solutions are required to be defined only on this restricted domain. Then the following result holds.

Theorem 3.2. *A solution on $\tilde{\Sigma}$ satisfies P.O, AN, S.INV, and MON if and only if it is the Kalai–Smorodinsky solution.*

Note that this result differs from Theorem 3.1 in that *W.P.O* is strengthened to *P.O* whereas *CONT* is not used at all. The "only if" part of Theorem 3.2 is not implied by Corollary 3.1 since elements of $\Sigma^P \setminus \tilde{\Sigma}^P$ are used in the proof of Proposition 3.2, from which Corollary 3.1 is derived. However, the proof of Theorem 3.2 is closely related to that of Proposition 3.2.

Proof. The only adjustment needed for the first construction given in Proposition 3.2 consists in defining x^* equal to ce_Q with $c = (a+b)/2$ instead of $x^* = ae_Q$. After verifying that $T \equiv \text{cch}\{S^0, S^1, S^2, x^*\}$ belongs to $\tilde{\Sigma}^Q$, the argument concludes as originally.

The adjustment needed for the second construction is in the same spirit, although more complicated to describe. After S has been replicated (as before), the family $\mathcal{P}^*$ of subsets of Q different from P, all the P_i, and any subset of these is introduced. For each $\tilde{P} \in \mathcal{P}^*$, let $x^{\tilde{P}}$ be the point of $\mathbb{R}^{\tilde{P}}$ that has all of its coordinates equal to $c + (a-c)(|Q| - |\tilde{P}|)/(|Q| - |P|)$ if $|\tilde{P}| \geq |P|$ and $a + (1-a)(|P| - |\tilde{P}|)/(|P| - 1)$ if $|\tilde{P}| \leq |P|$. Note that $x^Q = x^*$ of the original construction.

Then $T \subset \mathbb{R}^Q$ is defined by $T \equiv \text{cch}\{S,\ S^i \text{ for } i \in Q \setminus 1,\ x^{\tilde{P}} \text{ for } \tilde{P} \in \mathcal{P}^*\}$.

The tedious verification that T satisfies all the desired properties is omitted. The argument concludes as originally. Q.E.D.

(ii) Removing the comprehensiveness requirement: As pointed out in (i), Pareto-Optimality may not be satisfied by the n-person Kalai–Smorodinsky solution if $n \geqq 3$ for problems in $\Sigma \setminus \tilde{\Sigma}$. The case $n = 2$ being an important special case, it is worthwhile recalling that the Kalai–Smorodinsky solution satisfies Pareto-Optimality on $\tilde{\Sigma}^2$, and even on $\bar{\Sigma}^2$, the domain obtained from $\tilde{\Sigma}^2$ by dropping the comprehensiveness requirement.

For each $P \in \mathcal{P}$, let $\bar{\Sigma}^P$ be obtained from Σ^P in the same way $\bar{\Sigma}^2$ was obtained from Σ^2, and let $\bar{\Sigma} \equiv \bigcup_{P \in \mathcal{P}} \bar{\Sigma}^P$. On $\bar{\Sigma}$ the Kalai–Smorodinsky solution does not satisfy *MON* rewritten with the condition $S = T_P$ replaced by $S = T \cap \{y \in \mathbb{R}^Q_+ \mid y_{Q \setminus P} = 0\}$, and this can even be seen by setting P and Q, as they appear in the statement of *MON*, equal to $\{1\}$ and to $\{1, 2\}$, respectively. Let, for instance, $T \in \bar{\Sigma}^{\{1,2\}}$ be defined by $T \equiv \text{co}\{(0,0), (1,0), (2,2), (0,1)\}$. Then, $K(T) = (2,2)$, but

$$K_1(T \cap \{y \in \mathbb{R}^2_+ \mid y_2 = 0\}) = K_1([0,1]) = 1 < K_1(T) = 2.$$

(iii) Removing the convexity requirement: Consider now the case in which the problems faced by the agents of any $P \in \mathcal{P}$ are the comprehensive hulls of compact subsets of $\mathbb{R}^P_+$ containing at least one strictly positive vector. Then, on this domain, the Kalai–Smorodinsky solution remains well defined, although the problems may fail to be convex. It still satisfies the five axioms listed in Theorem 3.1. Clearly, any solution satisfying the five axioms on this large domain coincides with the Kalai–Smorodinsky solution on the original domain. In fact, there is a unique extension to the large domain satisfying the five axioms; it is the Kalai–Smorodinsky solution. This can be proved by a simple adaptation of the proof of Theorem 3.1.

(iv) Removing the requirement that the set of potential agents be infinite: Instead of assuming that the number of potential agents is infinite, suppose that there is some maximal number n of agents among whom a division is ever to be considered. Then the universe of potential agents is $I = \{1, \ldots, n\}$. The question is whether the Kalai–Smorodinsky solution can still be characterized as the only solution to satisfy *W.P.O, AN, S.INV, CONT,* and *MON.*

The sufficiency (Proposition 3.1) would not be affected of course by this domain restriction. But the necessity would. The general proof of Proposition 3.2 relies on being able to construct for each $P \in \mathcal{P}$ and each problem $S \in \Sigma^P$ a certain problem involving $3|P| - 2$ agents; therefore, if *F is a solution satisfying W.P.O, AN, S.INV, and MON, then for all* $P \in \mathcal{P}$ *such that* $3|P| - 2 \leqq n$, $F \geqq K$ *on* Σ^P. But in that proof no attempt was made to minimize the number of additional agents, and tighter bounds could perhaps be found. Indeed, we already know from the first construction of the proof of Proposition 3.2 that in order to be able to conclude that $F \geqq K$ on Σ^P for $|P| = 2$, it suffices to have the option to introduce only one additional agent; a different construction, not reproduced here, shows similarly that in order to be able to conclude that $F \geqq K$ on Σ^P for $|P| = 3$, two additional agents suffice.

It is clear, however, that if the number of agents is bounded, the Kalai–Smorodinsky solution is *not* the only solution to satisfy the five axioms. Another example is obtained by setting $F=K$ on Σ^P for all $P \in \mathcal{P}$ different from I, whereas the component of F relative to I is defined to associate with every $S \in \Sigma^I$ the maximizer of the Nash product $\prod x_i$ over the points of S satisfying the inequalities required by *MON* and the selection just made of the other components of F. This solution is well defined as it involves the maximization of a continuous function over a compact set, which is nonempty since $K(S)$ belongs to it. We omit the verification that it satisfies the five axioms.

3.3.2 *Removing the axioms one at a time*

We study here the additional solutions that would be made possible by removing in turn each of the axioms listed in Theorem 3.1.

(i) Removing the axiom of Weak Pareto-Optimality: The trivial solution associating, for every $P \in \mathcal{P}$ and with every $S \in \Sigma^P$, the origin of $\mathbb{R}^P_+$ satisfies *AN, S.INV, MON,* and *CONT*. This solution is of course not of great interest.

More generally, let $\alpha \equiv \{\alpha^P \mid P \in \mathcal{P}\}$ be a list of nonnegative real numbers such that $\alpha^i \leqq 1$ for all $i \in I$ and $\alpha^P \geqq \alpha^Q$ for all $P, Q \in \mathcal{P}$ with $P \subset Q$, and let G^α be the solution such that for every $P \in \mathcal{P}$ and for each $S \in \Sigma^P$, $G^\alpha(S) = \alpha^P K(S)$: Given $S \in \Sigma^P$, $G^\alpha(S)$ is obtained by scaling down the $|P|$-person Kalai–Smorodinsky solution outcome of S by the factor α^P, with the restriction that if two sets of agents are ordered by inclusion, the larger group is assigned a smaller scaling factor. The Kalai–Smorodinsky solution is obtained by choosing $\alpha^P = 1$ for all $P \in \mathcal{P}$. Each of the members of the infinite family G^α so defined satisfies *SY, S.INV, MON,* and *CONT*. *AN* holds if $\alpha^P = \alpha^{P'}$ whenever $|P| = |P'|$.

Another infinite family of solutions satisfying these axioms is the following: Let $f = \{f^P \mid P \in \mathcal{P}\}$ be a list of solutions $f^P: \Sigma^P \to \mathbb{R}^P_+$. Assume that for each $P \in \mathcal{P}$, f^P satisfies *sy* and *s.inv*. Then for each $P \in \mathcal{P}$ and for each $S \in \Sigma^P$, let $G^f(S) \equiv f^P(\{x \in S \mid \forall i \in P, \forall P' \subset P \text{ with } |P'| = |P|-1, x_i \leqq G^f(S_{P'})\})$. The Kalai–Smorodinsky solution is obtained by choosing f^P to be the $|P|$-person Kalai–Smorodinsky solution for all $P \in \mathcal{P}$. The G^f are constructed recursively from low dimensionalities. They all satisfy *SY, S.INV, CONT,* and *MON*. *AN* holds if $f^P = f^{P'}$ whenever $|P| = |P'|$. This is straightforward to verify for *AN* and *CONT*. *S.INV* follows from the fact that for each $P \in \mathcal{P}$ and for each $S \in \Sigma^P$, $G^f(S)$ is obtained by applying a function satisfying *s.inv* (f^P) to a set whose definition is invariant under positive affine transformations. *MON* follows directly from the construction of these constraints.

(ii) Removing the axiom of Anonymity: Let $\phi = \{\phi_i \mid i \in I\}$ be a list of functions from $\mathbb{R}_+$ to $\mathbb{R}_+$ indexed by the members of I with the following properties for all i: $\phi_i(0)=0$, ϕ_i is increasing, $\phi_i(t) \to \infty$ as $t \to \infty$. Then for each $P \in \mathcal{P}$, let G^P be the graph of the function ϕ^P: $\mathbb{R}_+ \to \mathbb{R}^P_+$ defined by $\phi_i^P = \phi_i$ for all $i \in P$.

Now, given $S \in \Sigma^P$, let λ: $\mathbb{R}^P \to \mathbb{R}^P$ be the unique positive linear transformation such that $a_i(\lambda(S))=1$ for all $i \in P$. Then, $G^\phi(S)$ is defined to be the inverse image under λ of the unique point of intersection of WPO(S) with G^P. Each of the members of the infinite family G^ϕ so constructed satisfies *W.P.O, S.INV, MON,* and *CONT.*

We note that K is obtained by choosing ϕ to be any list of identical functions.

(iii) Removing the axiom of Scale Invariance: The Egalitarian solution satisfies *W.P.O, AN, MON,* and *CONT*. See the next chapter for details.

(iv) Removing the axiom of Continuity: An example of a solution satisfying *W.P.O, AN, S.INV,* and *MON* is given in Lemma 3.1. Other such examples could easily be constructed.

(v) Removing the axiom of Monotonicity: Since this axiom is the only one to place constraints on how solution outcomes should be related across cardinalities, independent choices of the components of F can now be made for each cardinality of P. For instance, the solution F, where for each P of even cardinality F is the $|P|$-person Nash solution on Σ^P and for each P of odd cardinality F is the $|P|$-person Kalai–Smorodinsky solution on Σ^P, satisfies *W.P.O, AN, S.INV,* and *CONT.*

3.4 Concluding comment

Because of the importance of the n-person Nash solution in bargaining theory, it is useful to provide an example of a problem showing that the Nash solution does not satisfy *MON*. This negative result is a consequence of Theorem 3.1 since the Nash solution satisfies all the other axioms listed in the statement of that theorem [the fact that the Nash solution satisfies *P.O* (and therefore *W.P.O*), *S.INV,* and *AN* is well known from Nash's paper; it is also discussed in Chapter 2]; because the example is particularly simple, it may throw further light on Theorem 3.1, which essentially

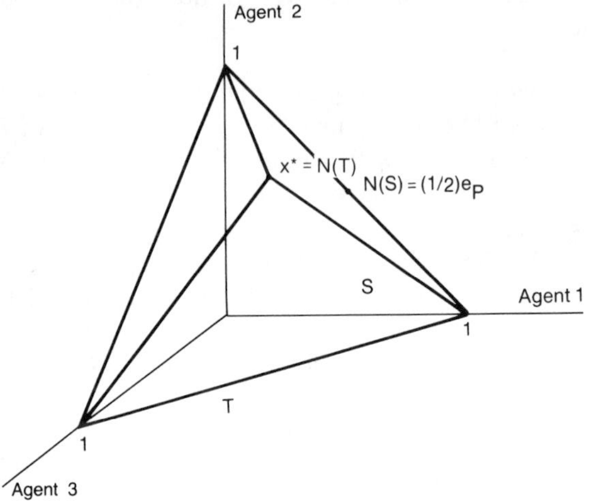

Figure 3.9. The Nash solution does not satisfy *MON*.

says that no substitution among the agents' utilities is permitted by any solution satisfying the five axioms. In a sense, it is because the Nash solution does allow for such substitution that it fails to satisfy *MON*.

Let $Q \equiv \{1,2,3\}$ and $T \subset \mathbb{R}^Q_+$ be defined by $T \equiv \text{cch}\{e_1, e_2, e_3, x^*\}$ with $x^* \equiv (\frac{5}{12}, \frac{7}{12}, \frac{5}{12})$. One checks that $N(T) = x^*$ and that $N(T_{\{1,2\}}) = (\frac{1}{2}, \frac{1}{2})$. But then $N_2(T) = \frac{7}{12} > \frac{1}{2} = N_2(T_{\{1,2\}})$, in contradiction with *MON* (see Figure 3.9).

CHAPTER 4

Population Monotonicity and the Egalitarian solution

4.1 Introduction

In this chapter we offer a characterization of the Egalitarian solution based on the axiom of Population Monotonicity introduced in Chapter 3 as well as on several familiar axioms. Specifically, we show that the Egalitarian solution is the only solution to satisfy Weak Pareto-Optimality, Symmetry, Independence of Irrelevant Alternatives, Continuity, and Population Monotonicity. This list of axioms differs from the list used in Chapter 3 to characterize the Kalai–Smorodinsky solution only in that the independence axiom replaces the invariance axiom. The independence axiom has already been briefly encountered in Chapter 2. The present chapter opens with its detailed evaluation.

First, recall that the independence axiom originally introduced by Nash (his property 7 on p. 159 in 1950, his axiom V on p. 137 in 1953) states that restricting a problem without eliminating the alternative chosen as best for that problem should leave this best alternative unaffected. Since there are fewer alternatives with which the originally chosen alternative is competing, this should strengthen its appeal. The axiom has been the object of a large amount of attention, and it has been adapted to a number of other contexts. In the social choice literature, it is now known under a variety of names, such as *Property* α, *contraction consistency,* and the *Chernoff condition.* [See, for instance, Sen (1979), who discusses it and relates it to similar axioms.] Here we will keep the phrase *independence of irrelevant alternatives,* which seems to have remained standard in bargaining theory (see Roth, 1979b), with a warning that the axiom should not be confused with the condition of the same name used by Arrow (1951).

The axiom is illustrated in Figure 4.1. Starting from some problem S solved at x, the opportunities open to the agents shrink to S' but x remains feasible. The requirement is that S' should also be solved at x.

The motivation offered by Nash for this axiom in his 1950 paper differs somewhat from the one he gave in his 1953 paper. We first quote from Nash (1950, p. 159) using our notation:

If two rational individuals would agree that $F(T)$ would be a fair bargain if T were the set of possible bargains, then they should be willing to make an agreement, of

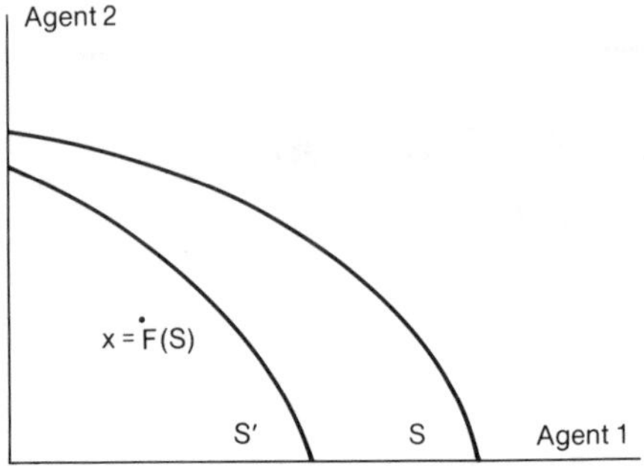

Figure 4.1. The axiom of independence of irrelevant alternatives: if $S \supset S'$ and $x = F(S) \in S'$, then $x = F(S')$.

lesser restrictiveness, not to attempt to arrive at any bargains represented by points outside of the set S if S contained $F(T)$. If S were contained in T this would reduce their situation to one with S as the set of possibilities. Hence, $F(S)$ should equal $F(T)$.

This is essentially the argument with which we opened this section. However, Nash offered a somewhat different motivation (1953, p. 138):

> This axiom is equivalent to an axiom of "localization" of the solution point on the shape of the set S. The location of the solution point on the upper-right boundary of S is determined only by the shape of any small segment of the boundary that extends to both sides of it. It does not depend on the rest of the boundary curve.
>
> Thus there is no "action at a distance" in the influence of the shape of S on the location of the solution point. Thinking in terms of bargaining, it is as if a proposed deal is to compete with small modifications of itself and that ultimately the negotiation will be understood to be restricted to a narrow range of alternative deals and to be unconcerned with more remote alternatives.

This interpretation is particularly appealing when the set of feasible alternatives is known with precision only locally, although no attempt will be made here to model the informational considerations that would provide a full justification for it.

Next we offer a third motivation based on the work of Shapley (1969) and pursued in Thomson (1981a). Given a two-person solution F defined on Σ^2 and an element S of Σ^2_{dif}, the subclass of Σ^2 of problems having a differentiable boundary, assume that $F(S)$ is Pareto-optimal. Shapley argues that utility comparisons are implicitly made in two ways in the determination of $F(S)$. (i) First, $F(S)$ can be seen as resulting from the maximization of some welfare function over S; at $F(S)$, marginal transfers of utility are possible at a ratio equal to the negative of the slope of the line of

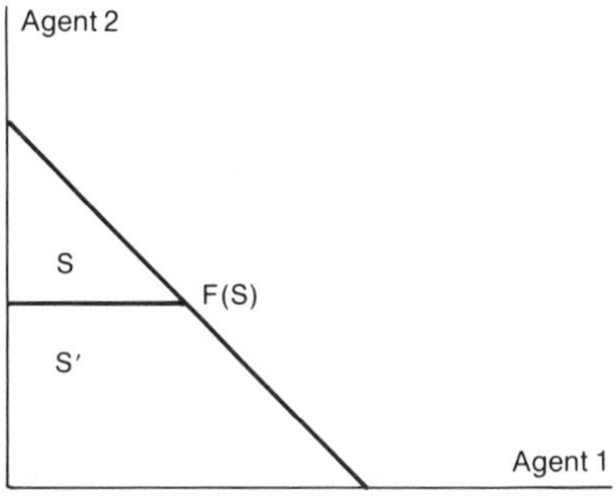

Figure 4.2. An objection to the axiom of independence of irrelevant alternatives.

support of S at $F(S)$. This yields a first set of comparison weights. (ii) The ratio of the agents' utility gains, measured from the origin to $F(S)$, yields another set of comparison weights. Shapley requires that the two sets of weights, the first one providing a guide to the "maximization of social welfare" and the second one to the "sharing of the social surplus," be equal: "An outcome is (declared) acceptable if there exist scaling factors for the individual (cardinal) utilities under which the outcome is both equitable and efficient" (p. 259).

Slightly more generally, a solution can be interpreted as establishing for each problem a certain relation between efficiency and equity weights. If the two sets of weights are appropriately related for some S at x so that $x=F(S)$, then for any $S'\in\Sigma^2_{\text{dif}}$ such that $S'\subset S$ and $x\in S'$, the same relationship will exist between efficiency and equity weights, and x should be the solution outcome for S' also.

Finally, the assumption that S be in Σ^2_{dif}, made to simplify the exposition, can be dropped without any damage to this interpretation.

On the negative side, mention should be made of the fact that a fair amount of criticism has been addressed at this axiom, starting with Luce and Raiffa (1957), who based their objection to it on the following example. Let F be a two-person solution defined on Σ^2 and satisfying independence; let $S\equiv \text{cch}\{e_1, e_2\}$ and $x\equiv F(S)$ (see Figure 4.2). If F satisfies weak Pareto-optimality and symmetry as well, then $x=(\frac{1}{2},\frac{1}{2})$. Now, let $S'\equiv\text{cch}\{x, e_1\}$. By independence, $F(S')=F(S)$, but this is unappealing since S' is obtained from S by eliminating alternatives that are all unambiguously favorable to agent 2 and unfavorable to agent 1 *when compared to the alternative originally chosen as best*. It seems that agent 2's claims are weakened by this change and that he should lose. The problem

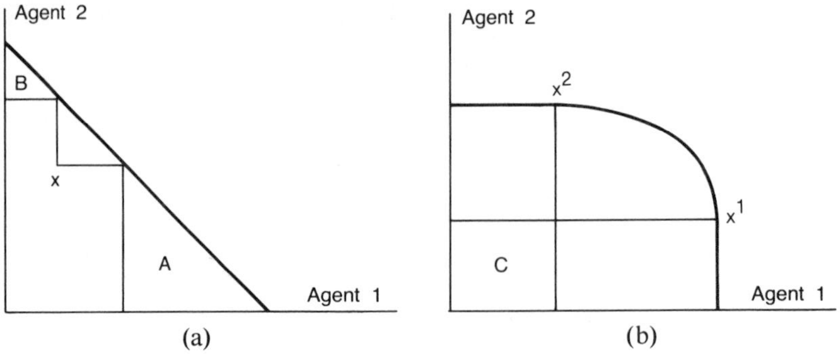

Figure 4.3. A further objection of the axiom of independence of irrelevant alternatives. (a) Triangular problem; (b) arbitrary problem.

with the independence axiom is that it specifically *precludes* that agent 2 loses.

One could of course say that this argument constitutes an objection not to independence itself but to the three axioms of weak Pareto-optimality, symmetry, and independence together since all three were involved. It is indeed illegitimate to blame the undesirable result described in the preceding on only one of the several axioms that have been used to derive it. Technically, the three axioms are jointly responsible for it.

In response to that and in defense of the Luce and Raiffa position, we note that we usually, and in particular in this chapter, make use of weak Pareto-optimality and symmetry. In addition, the last two of the arguments that we presented in favor of the axiom make sense only for solutions required to satisfy optimality anyway.

More importantly, however, we claim that any solution that is required *only* to satisfy independence can behave in the way described by Luce and Raiffa unless it essentially always selects the origin, a hardly interesting case.

Indeed, as noted earlier, the essential feature of the truncation used by Luce and Raiffa in their example is that *each of the eliminated alternatives is better for one agent and worse for the other than the alternative selected as best for the original problem*. This is really what makes the example appealing and why the independence axiom seems unreasonable.

Suppose now that F is not required to satisfy either weak Pareto-optimality or symmetry. Then the solution outcome of the symmetric triangle may be a point such as x in Figure 4.3a. By drawing lines parallel to the axes through x, we determine a zone A of points that are all better than x for agent 1 and worse than x for agent 2 and a zone B where the opposite holds. If F satisfies independence, F is *precluded* from responding to the

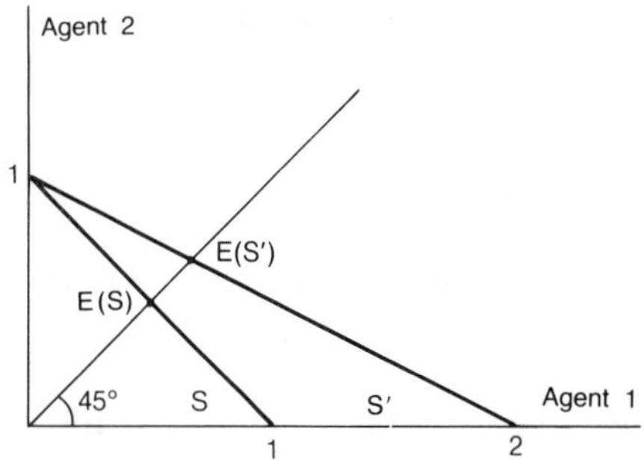

Figure 4.4. The two-person egalitarian solution does not satisfy scale invariance.

truncation of A only or B only, and this creates the same difficulty as in the Luce and Raiffa example. If x were on the vertical axis, zone B would be degenerate, and if x were on the horizontal axis, zone A would be degenerate. To prevent the possibility of any truncation leading to an undesirable conclusion, x can only be at the origin for this example.

More generally, for problems that are not triangles, x should satisfy $x_1 \leqq x_1^2$ and $x_2 \leqq x_2^1$ where x^1 and x^2 are the Pareto-optimal points most favorable to agents 1 and 2, respectively. For the example represented in Figure 4.3b, x should be in area C. If S is strictly comprehensive, this area collapses to the origin. Since most problems are of this kind, it follows that a solution can simultaneously satisfy independence and yet not give rise to the undesirable phenomenon pointed out by Luce and Raiffa only if it selects the origin for essentially all problems.

Our discussion of the merits and demerits of the independence axiom will conclude here. Later chapters will help us understand the extent to which the axiom can be replaced by other axioms perhaps less vulnerable to the criticisms raised in the preceding.

Let us now go back to the egalitarian solution and observe that it does not satisfy the axiom of scale invariance. This is illustrated in Figure 4.4. Starting from the two-person problem $S \equiv \text{cch}\{e_1, e_2\}$, agent 1's utility scale is multiplied by 2, which yields the problem $S' = \text{cch}\{2e_1, e_2\}$. Scale Invariance requires that the solution outcome for S' be obtained from the solution outcome for S by the same transformation, yielding $(1, \frac{1}{2})$. But the Egalitarian solution outcome of S' is $(\frac{2}{3}, \frac{2}{3})$.

The rest of the chapter is organized as follows. Section 4.2 presents a formal statement of the independence axiom appropriate for the context of variable population as well as the main characterization result. Section 4.3 contains variants of the main result.

This chapter is based on Thomson (1983d).

4.2 Characterization of the Egalitarian solution

All but one of the axioms that will be needed here have already been formally stated in Chapter 3. It remains to formulate the independence axiom in the context of a variable number of agents.

Independence of Irrelevant Alternatives (I.I.A): For all $P \in \mathcal{P}$, for all $S, S' \in \Sigma^P$, if $S' \subset S$ and $F(S) \in S'$, then $F(S') = F(S)$.

This says that the outcome declared the best compromise for any problem S should still be judged best after the deletion from S of alternatives to which it was originally found superior.

Our characterization of the Egalitarian solution can now be presented. The results leading to it are similar in their structure to those of the preceding chapter, but their proofs differ markedly.

Proposition 4.1. *The Egalitarian solution satisfies W.P.O, SY, I.I.A, CONT, and MON.*

Proof. That E satisfies *W.P.O, SY, CONT,* and *I.I.A* is easily established. That E satisfies *MON* would be proved in a way similar to the way it was proved for the Kalai–Smorodinsky solution (in Proposition 3.1).

Q.E.D.

The proof, that if a solution satisfies the five axioms it is the Egalitarian solution, is in several steps.

Lemma 4.1. *If a solution F satisfies W.P.O, SY, I.I.A, MON, and CONT, then for all $P \in \mathcal{P}$ with $|P| = 2$ and for all $S \in \Sigma^P$ with* $\max\{x_i \mid i \in P, x \in S\} \leqq 2E_j(S)$ *(where j is either one of the members of P), $F(S) = E(S)$.*

Proof. (See Figure 4.5.) Without loss of generality, we assume that $P = \{1,2\}$ and that $E(S) = e_P$. We introduce agent 3, and we define $Q \equiv \{1,2,3\}$ and $T \in \Sigma^Q$ by $T \equiv \text{cch}\{3e_i \mid i \in Q\}$. By *W.P.O* and *SY*, $F(T) = e_Q$.

Next, we define $T' \in \Sigma^Q$ by $T' \equiv \text{cch}\{S, e_Q\}$. Since $E(S) = e_P$, it follows from the hypothesis on S that $\max\{x_i \mid i \in P, x \in S\} \leqq 2$, and these two facts imply that $\max\{\sum_P x_i \mid x \in S\} \leqq 3$. Consequently, $T_P \supset S$, which together with $e_Q \in T$ implies that $T \supset T'$. But $e_Q = F(T)$, so that by *I.I.A*, $F(T') = F(T) = e_Q$. After noting that $S = T'_P$, we apply *MON* to compare what each member of P obtains in T' to what she obtains in S. This gives $1 = F_1(T') \leqq F_1(T'_P) = F_1(S)$ and similarly $1 \leqq F_2(S)$; therefore, $F(S) \geqq e_P = E(S)$.

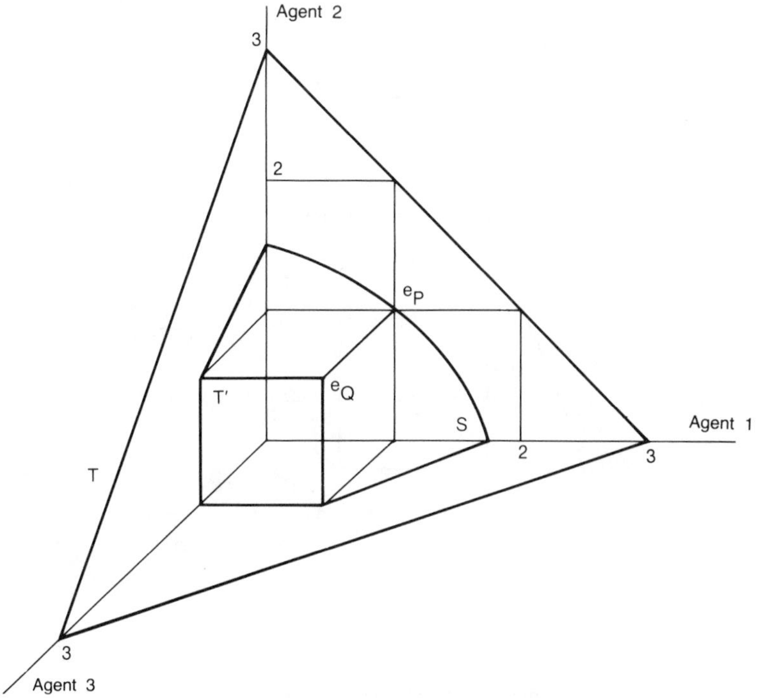

Figure 4.5. Lemma 4.1. $P=\{1,2\}$, $Q=\{1,2,3\}$.

Note that if $S \in \tilde{\Sigma}^P$, $F(S)=E(S)$ since then $E(S) \in \mathrm{PO}(S)$. The desired conclusion, that $F(S)=E(S)$ for all $S \in \Sigma^P$, follows from *CONT* and the fact that any $S \in \Sigma^P$ can be approximated by a sequence in $\tilde{\Sigma}^P$. Q.E.D.

Lemma 4.2. *If a solution F satisfies I.I.A and CONT and for all $P \in \mathcal{P}$ with $|P|=2$, for all $S \in \Sigma^P$ with* $\max\{x_i \mid i \in P, x \in S\} \leqq 2E_j(S)$ *(where j is either one of the members of P)*, $F(S)=E(S)$, *then for all $P \in \mathcal{P}$ with $|P|=2$, $F=E$ on Σ^P.*

Proof. Let $P \in \mathcal{P}$ with $|P|=2$ and $S \in \Sigma^P$ be given. Without loss of generality, we assume that $P=\{1,2\}$ and that $E(S)=e_P$. First note that if $F(S) \leqq 2E(S)$, then in fact, $F(S)=E(S)$. Indeed, let $S' \in \Sigma^P$ be defined by $S' \equiv \{x \in S \mid x \leqq 2e_P\}$. Clearly, $S \supset S'$ and $F(S) \in S'$ so that by *I.I.A*, $F(S')=F(S)$. Also, $E(S')=E(S)$. Because $\max\{x_i \mid i \in P, x \in S'\}=2 \leqq 2E_j(S')$ (where j is either one of the members of P), it follows from the hypotheses of the lemma that $F(S')=E(S')$. The equalities of the last three sentences imply that $F(S)=E(S)$.

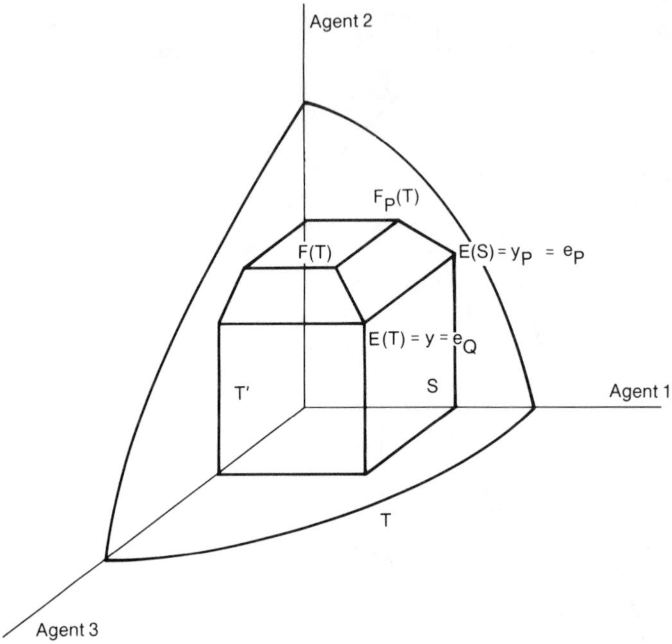

Figure 4.6. Lemma 4.2. $P=\{1,2\}$, $Q=\{1,2,3\}$.

Next, we suppose that $F_i(S)>2$ for some $i \in P$, say, $i=1$. We define the continuous function h: $[2, a_1(S)] \rightarrow \Sigma^P$ by $h(t) \equiv \{x \in S \mid x_1 \leqq t\}$. We note that $E(h(t))=e_P$ for all t; that $\max\{x_i \mid i \in P, x \in h(2)\}=2 \leqq 2E_1(h(2))=2$ so that by the hypotheses of the lemma, $F(h(2))=E(h(2))=e_P$; and finally that $h(a_1(S))=S$. These facts are in contradiction with the conclusion of the previous paragraph and *CONT*. Q.E.D.

Proposition 4.2. *If a solution F satisfies W.P.O, SY, I.I.A, MON, and CONT, then $F=E$.*

Proof. (See Figure 4.6.) We have to show that $F=E$ on Σ^P for all $P \in \mathcal{P}$. If $|P|=1$, the result follows from *W.P.O,* and if $|P|=2$, it follows from Lemmas 4.1 and 4.2. Now, given $Q \in \mathcal{P}$ with $|Q|>2$ and $T \in \tilde{\Sigma}^Q$, we assume, by way of contradiction, that $F(T) \neq E(T)$. Then, by *W.P.O,* there are $i, j \in Q$ with $F_i(T)<E_i(T)=E_j(T)<F_j(T)$. Without loss of generality, assume that $Q \supset \{1,2\}$, $i=1$, $j=2$, and $y \equiv E(T)=e_Q$ (in Figure 4.6, $Q=\{1,2,3\}$).

Define $T' \in \Sigma^Q$ by $T' \equiv \text{cch}\{y, F(T)\}$. Since $y, F(T) \in T$, we have $T \supset T'$. Then, by *I.I.A*, $F(T') = F(T)$.

Now, let $P \equiv \{1, 2\}$ and $S \equiv T'_P$. Clearly, $S = \text{cch}\{y_P, F_P(T)\}$. Also, $E(S) = y_P$ and $y_P \in \text{PO}(S)$. Since $|P| = 2$, $F(S) = y_P$, as already noted. However, $F_2(T') > 1 > F_2(S) = F_2(T'_P)$, in contradiction with *MON*.

The case where $T \in \Sigma^Q \backslash \tilde{\Sigma}^Q$ is dealt with by appealing to *CONT*.

Q.E.D.

The announced characterization of the Egalitarian solution follows from Propositions 4.1 and 4.2.

Theorem 4.1. *A solution satisfies W.P.O, SY, I.I.A, MON, and CONT if and only if it is the Egalitarian solution.*

4.3 Variants

4.3.1 Alternative domains

(i) Adding the requirement of strict comprehensiveness: If solutions are only required to be defined on the small domain $\tilde{\Sigma} \equiv \bigcup_P \tilde{\Sigma}^P$, then Theorem 4.1 becomes

Theorem 4.2. *A solution defined on $\tilde{\Sigma}$ satisfies P.O, SY, I.I.A, and MON if and only if it is the Egalitarian solution.*

Note that on this smaller domain, *CONT* is *implied* by the other axioms. This is puzzling since we made repeated use of *CONT* in the proof of Theorem 4.1. We used *CONT,* first, to extend certain conclusions from various dense subdomains to their closures and, second, to extend to highly skewed problems a conclusion established for problems that are not too skewed. If the domain is $\tilde{\Sigma}$, extensions of the first kind do not have to be carried out anymore, whereas the extension of the second kind can be done by adapting an argument presented later (Section 4.3.2). That argument is an induction on the "degree of skewedness" on the problems under consideration.

The proof, which would closely follow that of Proposition 4.4 of Section 4.3.2, is omitted.

(ii) Removing the comprehensiveness requirement: It can easily be shown, by adapting the proof (Section 3.3.1) that the Kalai–Smorodinsky solution does not satisfy *MON* on $\hat{\Sigma}$ (the class of problems obtained from Σ by dropping the comprehensiveness requirement), that the Egalitarian solution also fails to meet this requirement on $\hat{\Sigma}$.

(iii) Removing the convexity requirement: The Egalitarian solution is the only solution to satisfy our five axioms on the domain of problems obtained from Σ by dropping the convexity requirement. We omit the proof of this statement.

(iv) Infinite number of potential agents: To prove Theorem 4.1, we only needed the number of potential agents to be at least 3. Note that this is the minimal cardinality for which *MON* has any power. The remarkable fact that this cardinality actually suffices for the proof is the reason we presented that result as the main theorem of this chapter. However, by using the fact that the number of agents involved in any problem is allowed to be arbitrarily large, a simpler argument can be given, generalizing that of Lemma 4.1.

Proposition 4.3. *If a solution F satisfies W.P.O, SY, I.I.A, and MON, then* $F \geqq E$.

Proof. Let $P \in \mathcal{P}$ and $S \in \Sigma^P$ be given. Without loss of generality, assume that $P = \{1, 2, \ldots, m\}$ for some positive integer m and that $E(S) = e_P$. Let n be an integer such that $n \geqq 1 + \max\{\Sigma_P x_i \mid x \in S\}$. Note that $n > m$. Let $Q \equiv \{1, 2, \ldots, n\}$ and $T \equiv \{y \in \mathbb{R}^Q_+ \mid \Sigma_Q y_i \leqq n\}$. Note that T is a symmetric element of Σ^Q and that $e_Q \in \mathrm{PO}(T)$. By *W.P.O* and *SY*, $F(T) = e_Q$. By the choice of n, $T_P \supset S$. Let now $T' \in \Sigma^Q$ be defined by $T' \equiv \mathrm{cch}\{S, e_Q\}$. Clearly, $T \supset T'$ and $F(T) \in T'$. By *I.I.A*, $F(T') = F(T)$. Also, $T'_P = S$, and by *MON*, $F(S) = F(T'_P) \geqq F_P(T') = e_P = E(S)$. Q.E.D.

4.3.2 *Removing the axioms one at a time*

In order to better understand the role played by each axiom in the main characterization proof, we investigate here what additional solutions would be made possible by its removal.

(i) Removing the axiom of Weak Pareto-Optimality: Let $\alpha \equiv \{\alpha^P \mid P \in \mathcal{P}\}$ be a list of nonnegative and possibly infinite real numbers such that $\alpha^P \geqq \alpha^Q$ for all $P, Q \in \mathcal{P}$ with $P \subset Q$. Given $P \in \mathcal{P}$ and $S \in \Sigma^P$, let $F^\alpha(S)$ be equal to $\alpha^P e_P$ if this point belongs to S and equal to $E(S)$ otherwise. All solutions F^α so defined satisfy *SY, I.I.A, CONT,* and *MON.* The Egalitarian solution is obtained by choosing $\alpha^P = \infty$ for all $P \in \mathcal{P}$. However, there are solutions satisfying the four axioms that are not of this type. These additional solutions differ from the F^α only in that they permit some utility substitution in the two-person case. See the next chapter for details.

(ii) Removing the axiom of Symmetry: Let $\phi \equiv \{\phi_i \mid i \in I\}$ be a sequence of continuous functions from $\mathbb{R}_+$ to $\mathbb{R}_+$ with the following additional properties for each $i \in I$: $\phi_i(0) = 0$, ϕ_i is increasing, $\phi_i(t) \to \infty$ as $t \to \infty$. Then, for each $P \in \mathcal{P}$, let G^P be the graph of the function ϕ^P: $\mathbb{R}_+ \to \mathbb{R}_+^P$ defined by $\phi_i^P = \phi_i$ for each $i \in P$, and for all $S \in \Sigma^P$, let $F^\phi(S)$ be the intersection of G^P with WPO(S). It is easily verified that this intersection exists and is unique. All solutions F^ϕ so defined satisfy *W.P.O, I.I.A, MON,* and *CONT*. These solutions generalize the *monotone path solutions* of Chapter 2. The Egalitarian solution is obtained by choosing $\phi_i = \phi_j$ for all $i, j \in I$. However, there are solutions satisfying the four axioms that are not of this type. As in (i), the additional solutions permit some limited utility substitution in the two-person case. See the next chapter for details.

(iii) Removing the axiom of Independence of Irrelevant Alternatives: Without this axiom, it becomes possible to impose the requirement that the solution be independent of the units of measurements of the utility functions, that is, satisfy the axiom of Scale Invariance. In fact, the Kalai–Smorodinsky solution can be so characterized, as discussed in Chapter 3.

(iv) Removing the axiom of Monotonicity: Since *MON* is the only axiom to relate solution outcomes across cardinalities, independent choices of the components of F for each cardinality are now permitted. The resolution of problems involving n agents for each fixed n can be performed by using any n-person solution satisfying the remaining axioms, and there need be no connection between these n-person solutions for different n. An example of a solution F satisfying *W.P.O, SY, I.I.A,* and *CONT* is obtained by choosing F to coincide on Σ^P with the Nash solution if $|P|$ is odd and with the Egalitarian solution if $|P|$ is even.

(v) Removing the axiom of Continuity: The role played by continuity was briefly discussed in Section 4.3.1. We show here that without this axiom, the important conclusion that the solution should *dominate* the Egalitarian solution can still be derived. In order to do this, we proceed by induction on the "degree of skewedness" of the problems under consideration, as detailed in Lemma 4.3. The techniques of proof developed in that lemma will be used in other parts of this book, notably in Chapter 9.

As a by-product of that analysis, we will show that even if a solution is not required to satisfy *CONT* at all, it still cannot be required to satisfy *P.O* (instead of just *W.P.O*) in the presence of *SY, I.I.A,* and *MON* (Corollary 4.2).

Lemma 4.3. If a solution F satisfies W.P.O, SY, I.I.A, and MON, then for all $P \in \mathcal{P}$ *with* $|P| = 2$ *and for all* $S \in \Sigma^P$ *with* $\max\{x_i \mid i \in P, x \in S\} \leqq 2E_j(S)$ *(where j is either one of the members of P),* $F(S) \geqq E(S)$.

Proof. The proof is the same as that of Lemma 4.1 except for the last paragraph, which should be deleted. Q.E.D.

The result of Lemma 4.3, that F weakly dominates E for two-person problems that are not too skewed, is now extended to problems with a greater and greater degree of skewedness. The proof is by induction on a parameter k measuring this degree of skewedness.

Lemma 4.4. If a solution F satisfies W.P.O, SY, I.I.A, and MON, then for all $P \in \mathcal{P}$ *with* $|P| = 2$, $F \geqq E$ *on* Σ^P.

Proof. Without loss of generality, we assume that $P = \{1, 2\}$ and that $E(S) = e_P$. Let $a \equiv a_1(S)$ and $b \equiv a_2(S)$. We observe that a and b cannot both be greater than 2, and without loss of generality, we assume that $b \leqq 2$. Let k be the smallest integer such that $k \leqq a \leqq k+1$. If $k = 1$, S satisfies the hypotheses of Lemma 4.3, and we are done. Assume then that the desired conclusion holds up to $k-1$ for $k \geqq 2$. To prove it for k, we distinguish two cases.

(i) If $F_1(S) \leqq k$, we define $S' \in \Sigma^P$ by $S' \equiv \{x \in \mathbb{R}^P \mid x_1 \leqq k\}$, and we observe that $S \supset S'$ and that $F(S) \in S'$. By *I.I.A*, $F(S') = F(S)$. But the induction hypothesis applies to S', so that $F(S') \geqq E(S') = E(S) = e_P$. Therefore, $F(S) \geqq E(S)$.

(ii) If $F_1(S) > k$, we distinguish two subcases. If $F_2(S) = 1$, then again $F(S) \geqq E(S)$. If $F_2(S) < 1$, we introduce agent 3, and we define $Q \equiv \{1, 2, 3\}$, $P^1 \equiv \{2, 3\}$, $P^2 \equiv \{1, 3\}$, and $T \in \Sigma^Q$ by $T \equiv \text{cch}\{S + \{be_3\}, ke_{P^2}\}$. (See Figure 4.7.) Note that $S = T_P$. Let $S^1 \equiv T_{P^1}$ and $S^2 \equiv T_{P^2}$.

Observe that $a_2(S^1) = b$ and that $a_3(S^1) = k$. Also, $E(S^1) = be_{P^1}$. Therefore, $\max\{x_i \mid i \in P^1, x \in S^1\} \leqq kE_2(S^1)$ so that by the induction hypothesis, $F(S^1) \geqq E(S^1) = be_{P^1}$. Since $be_{P^1} \in \text{PO}(S^1)$, it follows that $F(S^1) = be_{P^1}$.

Similarly, we note that $a_1(S^2) = a \leqq k+1$ and that $a_3(S^2) = k$. Also, $E(S^2) = ke_{P^2}$. Therefore, $\max\{x_i \mid i \in P^2, x \in S^2\} \leqq 2E_1(S^2)$, and by Lemma 4.3, $F(S^2) \geqq ke_{P^2}$. Since $ke_{P^2} \in \text{PO}(S^2)$, it follows that $F(S^2) = ke_{P^2}$.

Now we apply *MON* twice and obtain

$$F_1(T) \leqq F_1(T_{P^2}) = F_1(S^2) = k,$$

$$F_3(T) \leqq F_3(T_{P^1}) = F_3(S^1) = b.$$

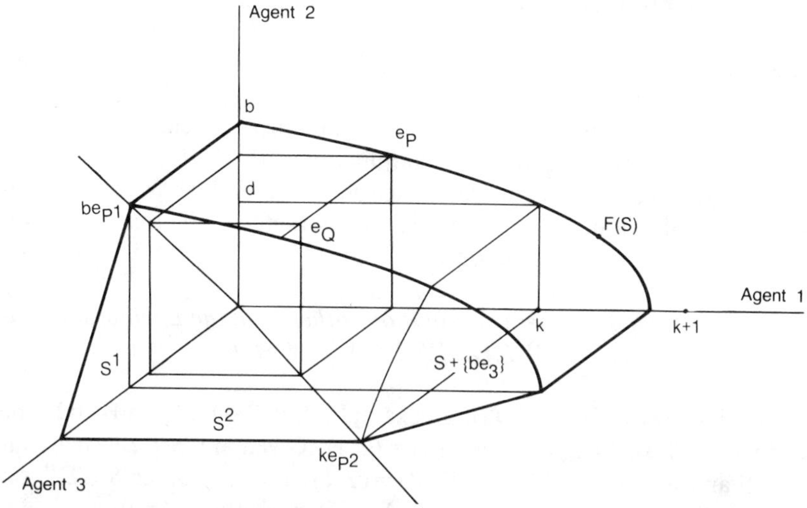

Figure 4.7. Lemma 4.4. $P=\{1,2\}$, $P^1=\{2,3\}$, $k=2$.

The points of WPO(T) satisfying these constraints all project on $\mathbb{R}^P$ somewhere on the subset of WPO(S) with endpoints (k,d) and be_2, d being such that $(k,d)\in$ WPO(S). By *W.P.O*, $F_P(T)$ belongs to that curvilinear segment.

Since $F_1(S)>k$ and $F_2(S)<1$, no point of that segment is weakly dominated by $F(S)$, but this is in contradiction with *MON*, which requires $F_P(T)\geqq F(T_P)=F(S)$. Q.E.D.

Proposition 4.4. *If a solution F satisfies W.P.O, SY, I.I.A, and MON, then* $F\geqq E$.

Proof. The proof is the same as that of Proposition 4.2, except for the last paragraph, which should be deleted. Q.E.D.

Corollary 4.1. *If a solution F satisfies W.P.O, SY, I.I.A, and MON, then* $F=E$ *on* $\tilde{\Sigma}$.

This is the main step, which says that any solution satisfying the four axioms coincides with the Egalitarian solution for most problems.

The next corollary states a disappointing result.

Corollary 4.2. *There is no solution satisfying P.O, SY, I.I.A, and MON.*

Proof. The proof is based on the same example as the one used in the proof of Corollary 3.2 of the previous chapter. Indeed, the problem T constructed there and the subproblem S of T used to derive the desired conclusion happen to be normalized problems, and therefore their Egalitarian and Kalai–Smorodinsky solution outcomes coincide.

Since *P.O* cannot be satisfied in conjunction with *SY, I.I.A,* and *MON,* it is natural to use *W.P.O* instead. The following result shows that the resulting list of axioms is now too weak to characterize the Egalitarian solution. *CONT* cannot be dispensed with. Q.E.D.

Lemma 4.5. *There are solutions other than the Egalitarian solution satisfying W.P.O, SY, I.I.A, and MON.*

Proof. The proof is by way of an example. Let $P \equiv \{1,2\}$ and $S \in \Sigma^P$ be defined by $S \equiv \text{cch}\{(2,1)\}$. Set $F(S) \equiv (2,1)$. Given any $S' \in \Sigma^P$ such that $S' \supset S$ and $e_P \in \text{WPO}(S')$, set $F(S') \equiv (2,1)$. For any other $S' \in \Sigma^P$, set $F(S') \equiv E(S')$. Finally, set $F \equiv E$ on $\Sigma^{P'}$ for any other $P' \in \mathcal{P}$.

It can be checked that the solution so constructed satisfies the four axioms (the only axiom for which this requires some work is *I.I.A*).

Q.E.D.

Clearly, many other such solutions could be constructed. Note also that the example could easily be adapted so as to satisfy *AN* instead of just *SY*.

CHAPTER 5

Truncated Egalitarian and Monotone Path solutions

5.1 Introduction

In the preceding chapter we proved that the Egalitarian solution is the only solution to jointly satisfy Weak Pareto-Optimality, Symmetry, Independence of Irrelevant Alternatives, Population Monotonicity, and Continuity. The purpose of the present chapter is to pursue this characterization further by determining what additional solutions would be made admissible by removing from this list of axioms Weak Pareto-Optimality on the one hand and Symmetry on the other.

Each of the two previous chapters concluded with the sort of "sensitivity analysis" that consists in successively dropping each of the axioms from a list previously shown to characterize a solution. The following chapters will contain similar exercises whenever relevant. In most cases it will be possible to give a complete description of all solutions satisfying the shorter list of axioms, and in the process important insights into the power and the significance of each of the axioms will be gained. Sometimes, interesting new families of solutions will be encountered, and these cases will be treated at greater length. This is the situation when either Weak Pareto-Optimality or Symmetry are deleted from the list of Chapter 4 characterizing the Egalitarian solution.

Apart from the technical interest of the sensitivity analysis discussed here, there are important conceptual reasons for it. Once a solution has been characterized, it is indeed natural to investigate how much freedom would be gained by sacrificing each of the axioms involved in the characterization and to find out what alternative axioms are compatible with the remaining ones. One would often like to impose more axioms than can be jointly satisfied, and analyzing "trade-offs" among axioms is an important part of the axiomatic study of solutions. The best way to evaluate the "power" of an axiom is to determine whether removing it yields a "large" or a "limited" class of additional solutions – for instance, these solutions may be described in terms of a finite list of parameters or they may constitute a complicated space – and whether they share the same essential features. Of course, what is meant by *essential* is somewhat subjective. In the case of the Egalitarian solution, though, one such feature is certainly that it permits no trade-off across the agents' utilities, that is, it precludes arguments of the kind: Agent i should give up α units of utility so as to permit agent j to gain β units of utility. By analogy with demand theory, where one speaks of the "degree of substitutability" between two commodities in a consumer's preferences to describe the extent to which the consumer would be willing to give up some of one commodity in order to consume more of another commodity, it is natural to speak here of the "degree of substitutability" between the utilities of two agents. According to this terminology, the Egalitarian solution permits no utility substitution.

In addition, no axiom is ever fully convincing in all situations in which one would like to impose it. This is certainly the case for the two on which we focus here. (What can be achieved by dropping the others is discussed at the end of Chapter 4.)

Let us first discuss Weak Pareto-Optimality. Although it does not seem too restrictive to impose this requirement on an arbitrator's choice, non-arbitrated disputes result in strictly dominated outcomes quite often.

But what kind of violations of optimality do occur? In our setting, it is natural to expect violations to be more and more severe as the number of agents involved grows, reflecting the greater difficulty of reaching a consensus in large groups. In a sense made precise later on, this expectation is confirmed by our analysis.

The case for dropping Symmetry is equally strong and involves interesting conceptual issues: First, an arbitrator may want to solve a symmetric problem at a nonsymmetric point in order to compensate for some inequities not explicitly described in the model. Alternatively, an agent who is a "better bargainer" may be able to impose a nonsymmetric outcome as compromise to a symmetric problem. Of course, it can be argued that such possibilities can arise only if all relevant variables are not properly taken into account to start with. But identifying these variables and explicitly incorporating them into a model may not be an easy task. An alternative approach is simply to summarize their effects on representative "test problems" and deduce from this information, taken exogenously, how the solution behaves everywhere. This requires that a "sufficient" family of test problems be discovered, sufficient in that it permits such an extension. A well-known illustration of this methodology is the characterization of the asymmetric Nash solutions, each of which can be completely determined from the knowledge of how it solves one triangular problem. In that case, one test problem suffices to identify a particular solution. (See Chapter 2 for a more extensive discussion of this example.)

Another reason for being interested in deleting the Symmetry axiom from the list of axioms characterizing the Egalitarian solution is that it is the only one of that list not to be invariant under ordinal transformations of the utilities, in the sense that if a problem satisfies the hypotheses of an axiom, then the problem obtained from it by subjecting the agents' utilities to independent ordinal transformations does not typically satisfy the same hypotheses: If a problem is symmetric initially, it will not remain symmetric under such a transformation. Because we consider only solutions defined on domains of convex problems and convexity is not a property that is invariant under all ordinal transformations of utilities, it may be natural to allow only concave transformations of utilities (then, convexity will be unaffected). However, these transformations still constitute a very large class, under which the symmetry of a problem is usually not preserved. The only way to preserve symmetry is to subject all utilities to a common transformation, but this implies a large degree of interpersonal comparability of utilities. Therefore, dropping the symmetry axiom considerably weakens the informational assumptions implicit in the analysis. The remaining axioms being all ordinal, it would be striking if they could be jointly satisfied only by solutions that are both invariant only under common transformations of utilities and in addition permit no utility substitutions. As it turns out, however, this is "almost" what happens.

A summary of the results is now presented.

It is easy to demonstrate the existence of solutions satisfying the list of axioms shown in Chapter 4 to characterize the Egalitarian solution except for Weak Pareto-Optimality on the one hand and Symmetry on the other, and permitting utility substitutions. An example of a solution satisfying *SY, I.I.A, CONT,* and *MON* is the solution that selects the Nash solution outcome for problems involving two agents and the origin otherwise. An example of a solution satisfying *W.P.O, I.I.A, CONT,* and *MON* is obtained as follows: First order the agents in some arbitrary way; then solve any problem faced by any group containing the group made up of the first two agents at the two-person Nash solution outcome of the intersection of the problem with the coordinate subspace corresponding to these two agents; finally, solve any problem faced by any other group at the alternative that is the most favorable to the agent with the highest rank in that ordering, and that yields zero utility to all the others.

These examples show that possibilities of utility substitutions arise whenever *MON* is made ineffectual by a strong enough violation of *W.P.O* or *SY*. The question is how extensive they can be.

The first main result is that possibilities of utility substitutions are in fact fairly limited and in particular never involve more than two agents in a nontrivial way. In establishing this result, we are led to introduce two families of solutions generalizing the Egalitarian solution in two different directions.

We name the members of the first family *Truncated Egalitarian* solutions. They can be informally defined by describing how a typical Truncated Egalitarian solution solves a problem "expanding" away from the origin: Initially, the solution outcome is the Egalitarian outcome, but beyond a certain "size," the solution outcome remains fixed at some maximal Egalitarian point. In addition, the common value of the coordinates of this maximal point for a given group is never greater than the corresponding value for any subgroup, and it is in this sense that the conjecture that violations of optimality should be less severe in small groups than in large groups is confirmed. All Truncated Egalitarian solutions satisfy *SY, I.I.A, CONT,* and *MON* and prohibit utility substitutions. As illustrated earlier, there are other solutions that satisfy these axioms and do permit utility substitutions. But the possibilities of utility substitutions are limited to the two-person case. Of course, even these limited possibilities are of significance because of the important role played by the two-person case both in the theory of bargaining and in many concrete situations, labor management conflicts being a prominent example.

The second family is the family of *Monotone Path* solutions, generalizing the n-person solutions by the same names that we discussed in Chapter 2: Each of the components of such a solution is described by a continuous, strictly monotone, and unbounded path in the utility space pertaining to the corresponding group of agents, starting at the origin, the solution outcome of a given problem involving that group being the intersection of its weak Pareto-optimal boundary with the path. This is as in the fixed-population case. In addition, the projection of the path relative to any group of agents onto the subspace pertaining to any one of its subgroups is the path relative to that subgroup. All Monotone Path solutions satisfy *W.P.O, I.I.A, CONT,* and *MON* and prohibit utility substitutions. Here too, however, there are other solutions satisfying the four axioms, but these other solutions permit nontrivial utility substitutions only for two-person groups. (The qualifier *nontrivial* is added because a component pertaining to a group of cardinality greater than 2 could coincide with the component pertaining to a group of cardinality 2 that does happen to permit utility substitutions.) However, under two mild additional conditions limiting the extent to which an agent can be discriminated against, only Monotone Path solutions remain acceptable.

This section closes with a restatement, as Theorem 5.1, of the characterization of the Egalitarian solution of the preceding chapter. This result will be our point of departure.

This chapter is based on Thomson (1983a, 1984a).

Theorem 5.1. *A solution satisfies W.P.O, SY, I.I.A, CONT, and MON if and only if it is the Egalitarian solution.*

5.2 Removing the axiom of Weak Pareto-Optimality

We investigate here what solutions other than the Egalitarian solution satisfy the list of axioms of Theorem 5.1 after the deletion of Weak Pareto-Optimality.

The trivial solution 0, where for each $P \in \mathcal{P}$ and for each $S \in \Sigma^P$, $0(S)$ is the origin of $\mathbb{R}^P_+$, obviously satisfies *SY, I.I.A, CONT,* and *MON*. More generally, let $\alpha \in \mathbb{R}_+$ be given and for each $P \in \mathcal{P}$ and $S \in \Sigma^P$, choose the solution outcome of S equal to $E(S)$ if αe_P does not belong to S and equal to αe_P otherwise. Any solution obtained in this way also satisfies the four axioms. These solutions can be further generalized by letting α depend on P provided that the α that pertains to each group is never greater than the α that pertains to any of its subgroups, as specified in the following definition.

Definition. *Given a list $\alpha = \{\alpha^P \mid P \in \mathcal{P}\}$ of nonnegative and possibly infinite real numbers such that for all $P, Q \in \mathcal{P}$ with $P \subset Q$, $\alpha^P \geqq \alpha^Q$, the associated* **Truncated Egalitarian solution** *(or* **TE solution***) E^α is defined by setting for all $P \in \mathcal{P}$ and for all $S \in \Sigma^P$, $E^\alpha(S) = E(S)$ if $\alpha^P e_P$ does not belong to S and $E^\alpha(S) = \alpha^P e_P$ otherwise.*

All TE solutions satisfy *SY, I.I.A, CONT,* and *MON*. The Egalitarian solution itself is a particular member of the family, obtained by choosing $\alpha^P = \infty$ for all P. The distinguishing features of the TE solutions have a natural interpretation. The fact that for each $P \in \mathcal{P}$ a TE solution is fully responsive to "expansions of opportunities" over some initial range and then totally unresponsive reflects the fact that negotiations are likely to lead to a satisfactory agreement if not too much is at stake and to stall if the problem at hand becomes really important. Note that we do not find that the difficulty of negotiations increases progressively, a feature of the solutions that may be puzzling. On the other hand, the monotonicity of the α^P is easy to interpret: It means that it is relatively harder to reach a satisfactory agreement in large groups than in small groups.

We prove in what follows that any solution satisfying the four axioms coincides with some TE solution E^α except perhaps on Σ^P for some P with $|P| = 2$ for probems $S \in \Sigma^P$ such that $\alpha^Q e_P \leqq E(S) \leqq \alpha^P e_P$ for all $Q \in \mathcal{P}$ with $Q \supset P$. In that range, utility substitutions are possible. As a simple example, consider the solution F defined by setting $F(S)=0(S)$ for all $S \in \Sigma^P$ whenever $|P| \geqq 2$ and $F(S)=N(S)$ otherwise (N designates the Nash solution). Note that the specification of F on Σ^P for $|P| \geqq 3$ essentially deprives *MON* of all power.

It is worthwhile comparing the components of the Truncated Egalitarian solutions to the solutions of "proportional character" discovered by Roth (1979a) in analogous circumstances (see Chapter 2). Recall that Roth asked what n-person solutions other than the n-person Egalitarian solution would satisfy a list of axioms previously shown to characterize that solution but from which the optimality axiom had been removed. The additional solutions include a one-parameter family F^k indexed by $k \in [0,1]$: Given some n-person problem S, $F^k(S)$ is obtained by scaling down the Egalitarian outcome $E(S)$ by the factor k, that is, $F^k(S)=kE(S)$. These are the solutions of proportional character, which obviously do not satisfy Independence of Irrelevant Alternatives.

The ways in which the components of the E^α and the F^k fail to reach optimality are interestingly different. The solution outcomes recommended by all elements of both families are always in the direction of the Egalitarian outcome. They coincide with it or with some fixed point for the elements of the first family. They fail to reach it by a constant factor for the elements of the second family.

We now present our characterization of all solutions satisfying *SY*, *I.I.A*, *MON*, and *CONT*.

> ***Lemma 5.1.*** *If a solution F satisfies I.I.A and CONT, then for all $P \in \mathcal{P}$ there exists a point $\bar{x} \in \mathbb{R}^P_+$ of coordinates possibly infinite such that for all $S \in \Sigma^P$, $F(S)=\bar{x}$ if $\bar{x} \in S$ and $F(S) \in WPO(S)$ otherwise.*

Proof. Suppose that for some $P \in \mathcal{P}$ and for some $\bar{S} \in \Sigma^P$, $F(\bar{S}) \notin WPO(\bar{S})$. Let $\bar{x} \equiv F(\bar{S})$. Let now $S \in \Sigma^P$ be given and $x \equiv F(S)$.

(i) *First we show that if* $\bar{x} \in$ rel.int. S, *then* $x=\bar{x}$. We prove this under the assumption that $x \in \bar{S}$, and subsequently, we prove that indeed $x \in \bar{S}$.

Supposing then that $x \in \bar{S}$, define $S' \in \Sigma^P$ by $S' \equiv \text{cch}\{\bar{x}+\epsilon e_P, x\}$, where $\epsilon > 0$ is chosen sufficiently small to guarantee that $\bar{x}+\epsilon e_P \in \bar{S} \cap S$ (this is possible since $\bar{x} \in$ rel.int. $\bar{S} \cap S$). (See Figure 5.1.) Observe that $\bar{S} \supset S'$ and that $F(\bar{S}) \in S'$. By *I.I.A*, $F(S')=F(\bar{S})=\bar{x}$. Also, $S \supset S'$ and $F(S) \in S'$. By *I.I.A*, $F(S')=F(S)=x$. Therefore $x=\bar{x}$.

We prove that $x \in \bar{S}$ by contradiction. Define a continuous function h: $[0,1] \to \Sigma^P$ such that $h(0)=S$, $h(1)=\bar{S}$, and $\bar{x} \in$ rel.int. $h(t)$ for all t. For any $t \in [0,1]$, if $F(h(t)) \in \bar{S}$, then $F(h(t))=\bar{x}$, by the preceding paragraph. The path of $F(h(t))$ is continuous by *CONT;* it starts outside of

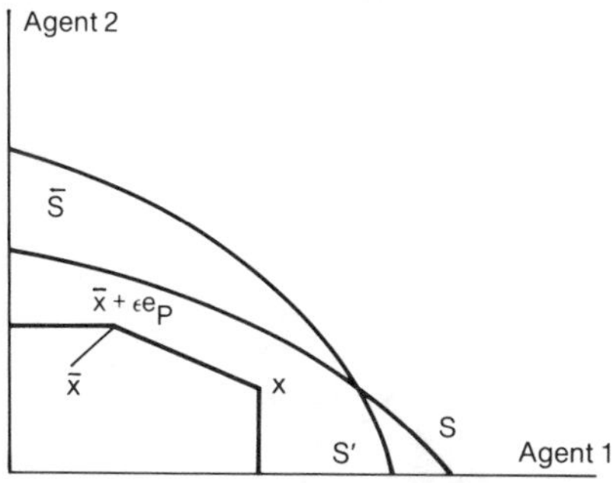

Figure 5.1. Lemma 5.1. Step (i).

$\bar{S}$ and ends at $\bar{x}$, but $F(h(t))$ cannot be in $\bar{S}$ unless it coincides with $\bar{x}$. This is impossible since $\bar{x} \in$ rel.int. $\bar{S}$.

(ii) *Next, we show that if* $\bar{x} \notin$ rel.int. S, $x \in \mathrm{WPO}(S)$. Suppose not, and let $S' \in \Sigma^P$ containing both $\bar{S}$ and S in its interior be given. Since both $\bar{x}$ and $x \in$ rel.int. S', we conclude by applying (i) twice that $F(S') = \bar{x}$ and that $F(S') = x$. Therefore $x = \bar{x}$, in contradiction with the assumptions that $\bar{x} \in$ rel.int. S and that $x \notin \mathrm{WPO}(S)$.

To take care of the possibility that there is no $\bar{S} \in \Sigma^P$ such that $F(\bar{S}) \notin \mathrm{WPO}(\bar{S})$, it suffices to choose $\bar{x}$ with at least one infinite coordinate.

Q.E.D.

On the basis of Lemma 5.1, we can conclude that with each solution F satisfying *SY* as well as *I.I.A* and *CONT* can be associated a list $\alpha = \{\alpha^P \mid P \in \mathcal{P}\}$, where each α^P is a nonnegative and possibly infinite real number such that for all $P \in \mathcal{P}$ and for all $S \in \Sigma^P$, $F(S) = \alpha^P e_P$ if this point belongs to S and $F(S) \in \mathrm{WPO}(S)$ otherwise.

Note that so far no use has been made of *MON*.

Lemma 5.2. *If a solution F satisfies SY, I.I.A, CONT, and MON, then its associated list* α *is such that for all* $P, Q \in \mathcal{P}$ *with* $P \subset Q$, $\alpha^P \geqq \alpha^Q$.

Proof. Suppose by way of contradiction that for some $P, Q \in \mathcal{P}$ with $P \subset Q$, $\alpha^Q > \alpha^P$. Let $T \in \Sigma^Q$ be defined by $T \equiv \mathrm{cch}\{\alpha^Q e_Q\}$. It follows from the definition of the list α that $F(T) = \alpha^Q e_Q$, and because $\alpha^P e_P \in S \equiv T_P = \mathrm{cch}\{\alpha^Q e_P\}$, $F(S) = \alpha^P e_P$. But this is in contradiction with *MON*.

Q.E.D.

Lemma 5.3. *If a solution F satisfies SY, I.I.A, CONT, and MON, then for all* $P, Q \in \mathcal{P}$ *with* $|P| = 2$ *and* $P \subset Q$ *and for all* $S \in \Sigma^P$ *such that* $\alpha^Q e_P \in S$, $F(S) \geqq \alpha^Q e_P$.

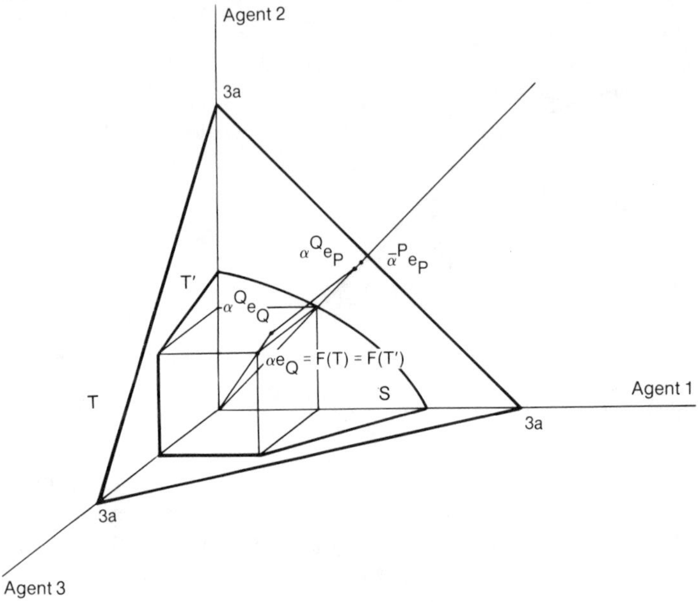

Figure 5.2. Lemma 5.4.

Proof. Let $T \in \Sigma^Q$ be given such that $\alpha^Q e_Q \in T$ and $S = T_P$. By definition of the sequence α, $F(T) = \alpha^Q e_Q$, and by *MON*, $F(S) \geqq F_P(T) = \alpha^Q e_P$. Q.E.D.

Given $P \in \mathcal{P}$ with $|P| = 2$, let $\bar{\alpha}^P \equiv \sup\{\alpha^Q \mid Q \in \mathcal{P}, P \subset Q\}$. (In this definition the requirement $|Q| = 3$ could be imposed; this is in view of Lemma 5.2.)

Lemma 5.4. *If a solution F satisfies SY, I.I.A, CONT, and MON, then for all $P \in \mathcal{P}$ with $|P| = 2$ and for all $S \in \Sigma^P$ such that $\bar{\alpha}^P e_P \notin S$, $F(S) \geqq E(S)$.*

Proof. (See Figure 5.2.) Let $a \in \mathbb{R}_+$ be such that $E(S) = a e_P$, and assume that $\max\{\Sigma_P x_i \mid x \in S\} \leqq 3a$. Let $Q \in \mathcal{P}$ with $|Q| = 3$ be such that $P \subset Q$ and $\alpha^Q > a$ (that Q exists follows from the fact that $a < \bar{\alpha}^P$ and the definition of $\bar{\alpha}^P$). Let $T \in \Sigma^Q$ be defined by $T \equiv \{x \in \mathbb{R}^Q_+ \mid \Sigma_Q x_i \leqq 3a\}$. Since $\alpha^Q e_Q \notin T$, $F(T) \in \mathrm{WPO}(T)$ by Lemma 5.1. This, in addition to *SY*, implies that $F(T) = a e_Q$. Also, $S \subset T_P$. Then, let $T' \in \Sigma^Q$ be defined by $T' \equiv \mathrm{cch}\{S, a e_Q\}$. Clearly, $T \supset T'$ and $F(T) \in T'$. By *I.I.A*, $F(T') = F(T)$. Because $S = T'_P$, it follows from *MON* that $F_P(T') = a e_P = E(S) \leqq F(S)$, the desired conclusion. If the inequality $\max\{\Sigma_P x_i \mid x \in S\} \leqq 3a$ were not satisfied, conclude by applying *CONT* (the argument would be as in Lemma 5.1). Q.E.D.

Lemma 5.5. *If a solution F satisfies SY, I.I.A, CONT, and MON, then for all $P \in \mathcal{P}$ with $|P| \geqq 3$ and for all $S \in \Sigma^P$ such that $\alpha^P e_P \notin S$, $F(S) \geqq E(S)$.*

Proof. Let $Q \in \mathcal{P}$ be given with $|Q| \geqq 3$ and suppose, by way of contradiction, that for some $T \in \Sigma^Q$ such that $\alpha^Q e_Q \notin T$, it is not the case that $F(T) \geqq E(T)$. This means that for some $i \in Q$, $\epsilon \equiv E_i(T) - F_i(T) > 0$. Because $\alpha^Q e_Q \notin T$, conclude by Lemma 5.1 that $F(T) \in \text{WPO}(T)$; therefore, for some $j \in Q$, $F_j(T) - E_j(T) \geqq 0$. Then, let $y \equiv (1-\epsilon/2)E(T)$, $T' \in \Sigma^Q$, be defined by $T' \equiv \text{cch}\{y, F(T)\}$, $P \equiv \{i, j\}$, and $S \equiv T'_P$. Clearly, $S = \text{cch}\{y_P, F_P(T)\}$ and $E(S) = y_P$. Since $\alpha^P e_P \notin S$, which results from the fact that $E_i(S) = (1-\epsilon/2)E_i(T) < E_i(T) \leqq \alpha^Q \leqq \alpha^P$, it follows from Lemma 5.3 that $F(S) \geqq E(S) = y_P$. But $y_P \in \text{PO}(S)$, and therefore $F(S) = y_P$.

On the other hand, $T \supset T'$ and $F(T) \in T'$. By *I.I.A*, $F(T') = F(T)$. Then, we apply *MON* to compare what agent j gets in T' and in $S = T'_P$. This yields $F_j(T) \leqq F_j(S) = E_j(S) = (1-\epsilon/2)E_j(T) < E_j(T) \leqq F_j(T)$, a contradiction. Q.E.D.

All of the preceding results are summarized in the following theorem.

Theorem 5.2. *A solution F satisfies SY, I.I.A, CONT, and MON if and only if*

(i) *it coincides with a Truncated Egalitarian solution E^α except perhaps when $|P| = 2$ on the subclass Σ^P_α of Σ^P of problems S such that $\alpha^P e_P \geqq E(S) \geqq \bar{\alpha}^P e_P$ where $\bar{\alpha}^P \equiv \sup\{\alpha^Q \mid Q \in \mathcal{P}, P \subset Q\}$;*

(ii) *for each $P \in \mathcal{P}$ with $|P| = 2$, it coincides on Σ^P_α with a solution $\tilde{F}$ satisfying SY, I.I.A, and CONT such that $\tilde{F}(S) \geqq \bar{\alpha}^P e_P$ for all $S \in \Sigma^P_\alpha$; and*

(iii) *for all $i \in I$, $\alpha^i \geqq \sup\{x_i \mid x = F(S), P \in \mathcal{P}, i \in P, S \in \Sigma^P\}$.*

Proof. Necessity follows directly from Lemmas 5.1–5.4. Note that *CONT* has to be used to strengthen the statements $F(S) \geqq E(S)$ of Lemmas 5.4 and 5.5 to $F(S) = E(S)$. Also, (iii) is imposed to ensure that *MON* is satisfied when groups of cardinalities 1 and 2 are compared. Sufficiency is straightforward. Q.E.D.

The following remarks should help to clarify the significance of Theorem 5.2.

(a) First, note that the solutions described in Theorem 5.2 do not satisfy the axiom of Anonymity (*AN*); that is, their components pertaining to two groups of the same cardinality may differ. In order for Anonymity to hold, one should impose the additional requirements that $\alpha^P = \alpha^{P'}$ whenever $|P| = |P'|$ and that the two-person solutions $\tilde{F}$ mentioned in (ii) be identical.

(b) A characterization of all solutions satisfying *SY, I.I.A, CONT,* and *MON* as well as *S.INV* can be obtained as a simple corollary of Theorem 5.2.

> ***Corollary 5.1.*** *A solution F satisfies SY, I.I.A, CONT, MON, and S.INV if and only if either* $F = 0$ *or, for all* $P \in \mathcal{P}$ *with* $|P| \geqq 3$, *F coincides with 0 on* Σ^P *and otherwise F coincides with N.*

Proof. It follows directly from Theorem 5.2 that for all $P \in \mathcal{P}$ with $|P| \geqq 3$, F coincides with 0 on Σ^P. If $|P| = 2$, apply the theorem of Roth (1977a, see Chapter 2), which says that *SY, I.I.A,* and *S.INV* are simultaneously satisfied on Σ^P only by the trivial solution 0 or by the Nash solution N. A straightforward appeal to (iii) of Theorem 5.2 yields the desired conclusion for $|P| = 1$. Q.E.D.

(c) A significantly weaker condition than Scale Invariance is Homogeneity (*HOM*): *HOM* says that the solution outcome should be invariant under *common* positive linear transformations of the utilities (when the λ_i appearing in the statement of *S.INV* are independent of i).

> ***Corollary 5.2.*** *A solution F satisfies AN, I.I.A, CONT, MON, and HOM if and only if:* (i) *for some* $k > 3$, *F coincides with* 0 *on* Σ^P *whenever* $|P| \geqq k$ *and F coincides with E on* Σ^P *whenever* $|P| < k$; *or* (ii) *F coincides with* 0 *on* Σ^P *whenever* $|P| \geqq 3$ *and F coincides with some nonzero solution* $\tilde{F}$ *on* Σ^P *satisfying SY, I.I.A, CONT, and HOM whenever* $|P| = 2$ *and with E on* $\Sigma^{\{i\}}$ *for all i.*

Proof. Simply note that if for some $P \in \mathcal{P}$ with $|P| = 3$ and some $S \in \Sigma^P$, $F(S) \geqq 0$, then F should coincide with E on Σ^P. Then it follows from Theorem 5.2 that F coincides with E on Σ^P for all $P \in \mathcal{P}$ with $|P| \leqq 2$.

Q.E.D.

(d) Utility substitutions are impossible as soon as for all $P \in \mathcal{P}$ with $|P| = 2$, $\bar{\alpha}^P = \alpha^P$.

(e) This section concludes with an example of a nontrivial solution of the form described in Theorem 5.2 (see Figure 5.3).

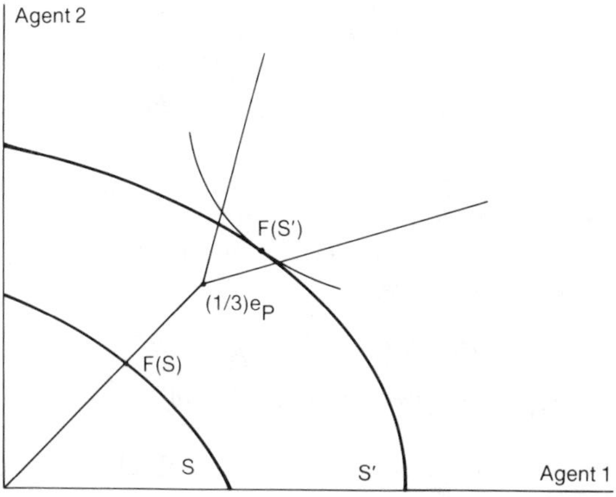

Figure 5.3. Example 1.

Example 1. For all $P \in \mathcal{P}$ with $|P| \geqq 2$, let $\alpha^P \equiv 1/|P|$, and for all $P \in \mathcal{P}$ with $|P| \geqq 3$ and $S \in \Sigma^P$, let $F(S) \equiv \alpha^P e_P$ if $\alpha^P e_P \in S$ and $F(S) \equiv E(S)$ otherwise. For all $P \in \mathcal{P}$ with $|P| = 2$ and $S \in \Sigma^P$, let $F(S) \equiv \frac{1}{2} e_P$ if $\frac{1}{2} e_P \in S$, $E(S)$ if $\frac{1}{3} e_P \notin S$, and $\text{argmax}\{x_i x_j \mid x \in S;\ 4x_i - x_j \geqq 1;\ -x_i + 4x_j \geqq 1\}$ otherwise, where i and j are the two members of P. An example of a problem to which the third case applies is presented in Figure 5.3 for $P = \{1, 2\}$. The set of points of S that satisfy the constraints is the small triangle having $\frac{1}{3} e_P$ as one of its vertices.

The solution so defined satisfies *SY* (in fact, *AN*), *I.I.A*, *MON*, and *CONT* and presents all the essential characteristics of any solution satisfying these four axioms.

5.3 Removing the axiom of Symmetry

5.3.1 Characterization of Monotone Path solutions

We investigate here what solutions other than the Egalitarian solution satisfy the list of axioms of Theorem 5.1 after the deletion of Symmetry.

First, we describe a family of solutions that generalize in a natural way the Egalitarian solution and that satisfy *W.P.O*, *I.I.A*, *MON*, and *CONT*. We refer to these solutions as *Monotone Path solutions.*

> ***Definitions.*** *A* ***monotone path*** *in* $\mathbb{R}^P_+$ is the range G^P *of a function* $\phi^P = \{\phi^P_i \mid i \in P\}$ *from* $\mathbb{R}_+$ *to* $\mathbb{R}^P_+$ *where each* ϕ^P_i *is continuous, increasing, and onto* $\mathbb{R}_+$. *A* ***monotone path solution*** *on* Σ^P

is a function from Σ^P to $\mathbb{R}^P_+$ such that there exists a monotone path G^P in $\mathbb{R}^P_+$ with the property that for all $S \in \Sigma^P$, the solution outcome of S is the intersection of G^P with $WPO(S)$. With a slight abuse of notation, the resulting solution is also denoted G^P.

Definition. *A **Monotone Path,** or **MP, solution G** is such that for each $P \in \mathcal{P}$, G coincides on Σ^P with a monotone path solution G^P, and furthermore,*

$$\text{for all } P, Q \in \mathcal{P} \text{ with } P \subset Q,\ G^P = G^Q_P \tag{1}$$

(recall that G^Q_P is the projection of G^Q on $\mathbb{R}^P_+$).

Note that condition (1) implies that a solution obtained by arbitrarily choosing for each $P \in \mathcal{P}$ the corresponding component of F to be a monotone path solution on Σ^P is not an MP solution, and that if F is an MP solution, then for all i and for all P, P' containing i, ϕ_i^P may be chosen equal to $\phi_i^{P'}$.

Monotone path solutions on related classes of n-person problems are discussed in Thomson and Myerson (1980) and Myerson (1981) (see Chapter 2). The proportional solutions studied by Kalai (1977b) are monotone path solutions obtained by taking the ϕ_i^P to be proportional to each other. The Egalitarian solution is the monotone path solution obtained by choosing the ϕ_i^P to be identical functions. As all proportional solutions, the MP solutions prohibit utility substitutions.

It is easy to see that all MP solutions satisfy *W.P.O, I.I.A, MON,* and *CONT,* as claimed earlier. We show in what follows that there are other solutions with these four properties. However, the MP solutions are the only ones to satisfy the four properties as well as two mild additional conditions whose effect is to limit the extent to which a solution can discriminate against an individual. If either one of these properties is not met, other solutions exist that permit utility substitutions, but utility substitutions remain limited; as in Section 5.3, they essentially concern only two-person components. If neither one of these properties is met, possibilities of substitutions, although still limited to two-person components, expand significantly for that case. In fact, the two-person components cannot be given a simple characterization anymore. We will instead illustrate the range of possibilities by way of examples.

The two conditions mentioned in the preceding are now formally defined. The first one is familiar (see Chapter 2).

Strong Individual Rationality (ST.I.R): For all $P \in \mathcal{P}$ and for all $S \in \Sigma^P$, $F(S) > 0$.

This says that all agents gain something from their cooperation. This condition ensures the willing participation of all of them.

Unbounded Payoffs (U): For all $P \in \mathcal{P}$, for all $i \in P$, and for all $M \in \mathbb{R}$, there exists $t > 0$ such that $F_i(\{x \in \mathbb{R}^P_+ \mid \Sigma_P x_i \leqq t\}) \geqq M$.

The most an individual can be discriminated against is when he is always assigned utility zero independently of the problem at hand. Condition U prevents this and a bit more: The utility that each individual obtains on the class of simplicial problems should not be bounded from above.

Our next theorem can now be presented.

> ***Theorem 5.3.*** *A solution satisfies W.P.O, I.I.A, MON, and CONT as well as ST.I.R and U if and only if it is an MP solution.*

Proof. (i) Let $Q \in \mathcal{P}$ with $|Q| = 3$ and $t > 0$ be given and let $T \in \Sigma^Q$ be defined by $T \equiv \{x \in \mathbb{R}^Q_+ \mid \Sigma_Q x_i \leqq t\}$. By *ST.I.R*, conclude that for each $t > 0$, $y \equiv F(T) > 0$. Let $P \in \mathcal{P}$ with $P \subset Q$ and $|P| = 2$ be given and let $x \equiv y_P$. Clearly, $\Sigma_P x_i < t$. Let now $T' \in \Sigma^Q$ be such that $T \supset T'$, $y \in T'$, and $x \in \mathrm{PO}(S')$, where $S' \equiv T'_P$. By *I.I.A*, $F(T') = y$, and by *MON*, $F(S') = x$. This equality holds for any S' obtained in this way, and since $x \in \text{rel.int.}\, T_P$, *CONT* and *I.I.A* imply that for all $S \in \Sigma^P$ such that $x \in \mathrm{WPO}(S)$, $F(S) = x$.

(ii) Let now t vary in $]0, \infty[$ and let G^P be the path traced out by x. By *CONT*, G^P is a continuous path. To show that G^P is monotone, suppose by way of contradiction that there exist x and $x' \in G^P$ with $x \neq x'$ such that neither $x > x'$ nor $x' > x$. Then both x and $x' \in \mathrm{WPO}(S)$ where $S \in \Sigma^P$ is defined by $S \equiv \mathrm{cch}\{x, x'\}$, and by the conclusion of the preceding paragraph applied twice, it follows that $F(S) = x$ and that $F(S) = x'$, two contradictory statements. By U, both coordinates of x go to infinity as t goes to infinity. Therefore, for each $P \in \mathcal{P}$ with $|P| = 2$, the component of F relative to P is a monotone path solution on Σ^P.

(iii) Next we show that the two-person paths are consistent in the sense that they are obtained by projecting higher order paths (Figure 5.4). To see this, let $Q \in \mathcal{P}$ be given with $|Q| = 3$. Without loss of generality, assume that $Q = \{1, 2, 3\}$. Let $P \equiv \{1, 2\}$, $P^1 \equiv \{2, 3\}$, and $P^2 \equiv \{1, 3\}$. Now, let (a_1, a_2) be a point of G^P. By U, there exists $a_3 > 0$ such that $(a_2, a_3) \in G^{P^1}$. We claim that $(a_1, a_2, a_3) \in G^Q$ and that $(a_1, a_3) \in G^{P^2}$. To see this, let $T \in \Sigma^Q$ be defined by $T \equiv \mathrm{cch}\{(a_1, a_2, a_3)\}$. To conclude that $(a_1, a_2, a_3) \in G^Q$, first observe that by feasibility, $F(T) \leqq (a_1, a_2, a_3)$. Suppose then, by way of contradiction, that the inequality is strict for one coordinate. By *W.P.O*, equality holds for at least one of the other coordinates. Without loss of generality, assume that $F_1(T) < a_1$ and that $F_2(T) = a_2$. Then, let $T' \in \Sigma^Q$ be defined by $T' \equiv \{x \in T \mid x_1 + x_2 \leqq F_1(T) + F_2(T)\}$. Since $T \supset T'$

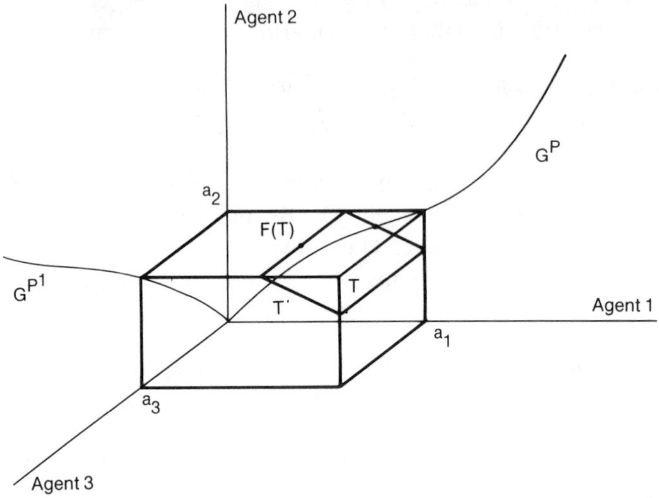

Figure 5.4. Theorem 5.3.

and $F(T) \in T'$, it follows from *I.I.A* that $F(T') = F(T)$. Also, by (i), $F(T'_P)$ is the point of intersection of G^P with WPO(T'_P). This point is strictly dominated by (a_1, a_2). Then $a_2 = F_2(T') > F_2(T'_P)$, in contradiction with *MON*. This argument shows that $F(T) = (a_1, a_2, a_3)$ and, applying *MON* again, that $F_{P2}(T) \leqq F(T_{P2}) = F(\text{cch}\{(a_1, a_3)\})$, that is, that $F(\text{cch}\{(a_1, a_3)\}) = (a_1, a_3)$, so that $(a_1, a_3) \in G^{P^2}$.

(iv) This argument can be easily generalized to show that for all $Q \in \mathcal{P}$, there exists a Monotone Path G^Q such that for all $P \in \mathcal{P}$ with $P \subset Q$ and $|P| = 2$, $G^Q_P = G^P$. By an argument similar to the one of (iii), it can then be proved that for all $T \in \Sigma^Q$, $F(T) = G^Q(T)$. Q.E.D.

In order to further illustrate Theorem 5.3, examples are now presented that show how relaxing *either ST.I.R* or *U* generates new solutions that can exhibit utility substitutions. (For simplicity, the examples are specified for the case $|I|$ finite.) The form that these utility substitutions can take is also discussed. Finally, we show that relaxing both *ST.I.R* and *U* permits yet additional utility substitutions.

To facilitate description of these results, we introduce the following:

Definition. *Given $P \in \mathcal{P}$ and $i \in I$, the* **ith Dictatorial solution** D^i *is the solution associating with each $S \in \Sigma^P$ the alternative that gives maximal utility to agent i and zero utility to all others.*

5.3.2 Relaxing the Unboundedness condition

First, we offer a slight generalization of the MP solution. For each $P \in \mathcal{P}$, the requirement previously imposed on the list $\{\phi_i^P \mid i \in P\}$ defining G^P, that each ϕ_i^P be onto $\mathbb{R}_+$, is weakened to the requirement that, for *at least one* $i \in P$, ϕ_i^P be onto $\mathbb{R}_+$. This guarantees the unboundedness of the path G^P and the existence of a point of intersection of G^P with WPO(S) for any $S \in \Sigma^P$. Then a *MP*[1] *solution* G is defined to be such that, for each $P \in \mathcal{P}$, G coincides with some G^P as just generalized, and the consistency condition (1) between the graphs of the G^P is replaced by

$$\text{for all } P, Q \in \mathcal{P} \text{ with } P \subset Q, \; G^P \supset G_P^Q. \tag{1'}$$

The next example is constructed to show that the relaxation of the requirements imposed on the ϕ_i^P, as one generalizes the family of MP solutions to the family of MP[1] solutions, introduces possibilities of utility substitutions. The example exhibits all the essential features of any solution satisfying *W.P.O, I.I.A, MON, CONT,* and *ST.I.R.*

Example 2. (See Figure 5.5.) Here, $I = \{1, 2, 3\}$. On Σ^I, F coincides with a monotone path G^I in $\mathbb{R}^I$ approximating $[0, e_I] \cup \{e_I + \lambda e_3 \mid \lambda > 0\}$. On $\Sigma^{\{2,3\}}$, $F \equiv G^I_{\{2,3\}}$, and on $\Sigma^{\{1,3\}}$, $F \equiv G^I_{\{1,3\}}$. Given $S \in \Sigma^{\{1,2\}}$, $F(S) \equiv E(S)$ if $e_{\{1,2\}} \notin$ rel. int. S; otherwise, for $\epsilon < 0$ and $|\epsilon|$ small,

$$F(S) \equiv \operatorname{argmax}\{x_1 x_2 \mid x \in S, x_1 + \epsilon x_2 \geqq 1 + \epsilon, \epsilon x_1 + x_2 \geqq 1 + \epsilon\}.$$

(The path $[0, e_I] \cup \{e_I + \lambda e_3 \mid \lambda > 0\}$ is only weakly increasing and therefore does not define a monotone path solution on Σ^I, which is why we take an "approximation" to it. Similar approximations will be used in the forthcoming examples. We choose ϵ negative to guarantee *CONT.*)

In no three-person problem are agents 1 and 2 ever allocated more than 1 so that the constraints imposed by *MON* on F for the pair $\Sigma^I, \Sigma^{\{1,2\}}$ are automatically satisfied whenever $F(S)$, for $S \in \Sigma^{\{1,2\}}$, can be chosen to dominate $e_{\{1,2\}}$.

By generalizing this observation, the following characterization theorem is obtained.

Theorem 5.4. *A solution F satisfies W.P.O, I.I.A, MON, CONT, and ST.I.R if and only if there is an MP*[1] *solution with which it coincides except perhaps for one $P \in \mathcal{P}$ with $|P| = 2$ and for all $S \in \Sigma^P$ not containing $\bar{\beta}^P \equiv \sup\{x_P \mid x \in G^I\}$. On that subclass of possible exceptions, F should coincide with some solution $\tilde{F}$ satisfying W.P.O, I.I.A, CONT, and $\tilde{F}(S) \geqq \bar{\beta}^P e_P$ for all S in the subclass.*

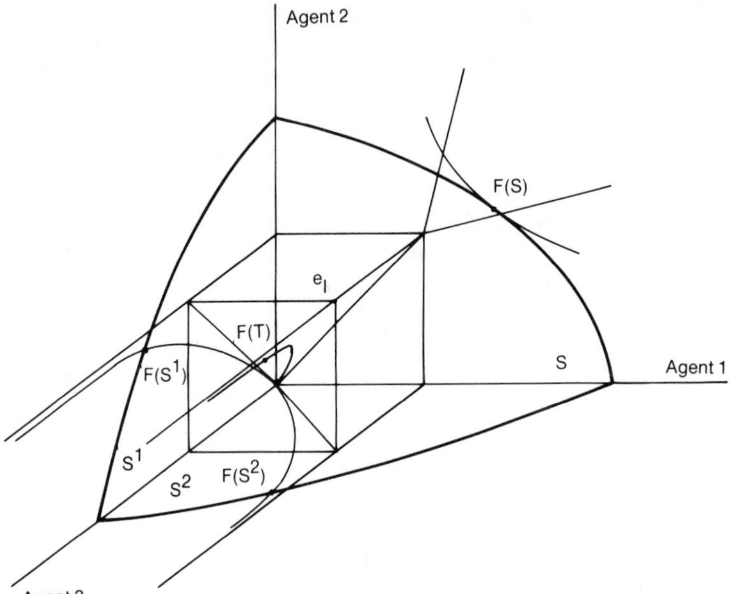

Figure 5.5. Example 2.

Proof. The proof is obtained by a simple adaptation of the proof of Theorem 5.3. Q.E.D.

5.3.3 *Relaxing the Strong Individual Rationality condition*

First, a second trivial generalization of the MP solutions is offered. Each component path is now permitted to be *initially* nondecreasing and then increasing (instead of being increasing throughout), that is, initially to lie in a subspace of smaller dimensionality than the space to which the component pertains and to successively enter subspaces of greater and greater cardinalities. Such a solution will be referred to as an MP^2 *solution*. Formally, this is achieved by letting each ϕ_i^P be equal to 0 on some nondegenerate interval $[0, \gamma_i]$ (but still increasing on $[\gamma_i, \infty]$). The next example is constructed so as to show that the relaxation of the requirements imposed on the ϕ_i^P, as one generalizes the family of MP solutions to the family of MP^2 solutions, also introduces possibilities of utility substitutions. The example exhibits all the essential features exhibited by any solution satisfying *W.P.O, I.I.A, MON, CONT,* and *U.*

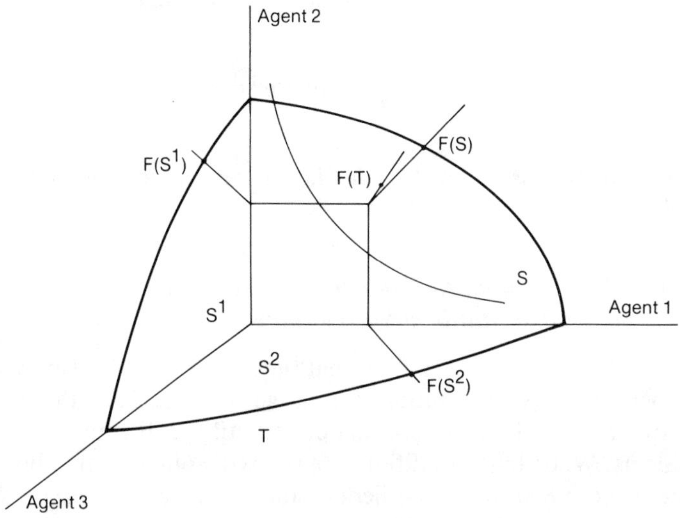

Figure 5.6. Example 3.

Example 3. (See Figure 5.6.) Let $I = \{1,2,3\}$. Given $S \in \Sigma^{\{1,2\}}$, $F(S) \equiv \text{argmax}\{x_1x_2 \mid x \in S, x \leqq e_{\{1,2\}}\}$ if $e_{\{1,2\}} \notin S$ and $E(S)$ otherwise. On $\Sigma^{\{2,3\}}$ and $\Sigma^{\{1,3\}}$, F coincides with some MP^2 solution G such that $G_{\{2,3\}} \equiv [0,e_2] \cup \{e_2 + \lambda e_{\{2,3\}} \mid \lambda > 0\}$ and $G_{\{1,3\}} \equiv [0,e_1] \cup \{e_1 + \lambda e_{\{1,3\}} \mid \lambda > 0\}$. Given $S \in \Sigma^I$, $F(S) \equiv F(S_{\{1,2\}})$ if $\text{WPO}(S) \cap \{e_{\{1,2\}} + \lambda e_1 \mid \lambda > 0\} = \emptyset$ and that point of intersection otherwise.

What is interesting about this example is that for problems "large enough," the solution coincides with an MP solution. Only one two-person component permits utility substitutions, in some domain of the form $[0,\gamma_1] \times [0,\gamma_2]$, and there, it coincides with the three-person component. The next theorem shows that this is the general situation in the three-person case and that if there are more than three agents, it remains true that only one two-person component can permit utility substitutions. Otherwise, the solution coincides with an MP^2 solution.

Theorem 5.5. *A solution F satisfies W.P.O, I.I.A, MON, CONT, and U if and only if there is an MP^2 solution with which it coincides, except that if γ denotes the maximal point of G^I that belongs to a two-dimensional subspace and P the corresponding two-person group, then for all $Q \in \mathcal{P}$ with $Q \supset P$ and for all T in the subclass of Σ^Q of problems not containing γ_Q, $F(T) = \tilde{F}(T_P)$,* *where $\tilde{F}$ is a solution satisfying W.P.O, I.I.A, CONT, and $\tilde{F}(S) \leqq \gamma_P$ for all S in the subclass.*

Proof. The proof is obtained by a simple adaptation of the proof of Theorem 5.3. Q.E.D.

This theorem says that *ST.I.R* plays a very minor role indeed in preventing utility substitutions.

5.3.4 *Relaxing both the Unboundedness and the Strong Individual Rationality conditions*

Sections 5.3.2 and 5.3.3 showed that the relaxation of *U* yields solutions that permit utility substitutions for "large" problems and that the relaxation of *ST.I.R* yields solutions that permit utility substitutions for "small" problems. When both conditions are relaxed, solutions are obtained that combine both features, but other possibilities arise. Because the solutions that satisfy *W.P.O, I.I.A, MON,* and *CONT* do not constitute a simple family, no characterization will be offered; instead, we will provide illustrative examples.

Example 4. *Lexicographic Dictatorial solutions:* There is one such solution for each possible ordering of the agents.

> ***Definition.*** *Given an ordering π of the members of I, the associated* **Lexicographic Dictatorial solution D^π** *is such that given any $P \in \mathcal{P}$ and any $S \in \Sigma^P$, $D_i^\pi(S) = a_i(S)$ where i is the maximal element of π in P and $D_j^\pi(S) = 0$ for all $j \in P \backslash i$.*

Note that these solutions select only weakly Pareto-optimal points. Solutions in the same spirit but selecting Pareto-optimal points can be obtained as follows.

> ***Definition.*** *Given an ordering π of the members of I, the associated* **Sequential Lexicographic Dictatorial solution $D^{*\pi}$** *is such that given any $P \in \mathcal{P}$ and any $S \in \Sigma^P$, $D_{i_1}^{*\pi}(S) = a_{i_1}(S)$ where i_1 is the maximal element of π in P, $D_{i_2}^{*\pi}(S) = a_{i_2}(S')$ where i_2 is the second maximal element of π in P, $S' \equiv \{x \in S \mid x_{i_1} = a_{i_1}(S)\}, \ldots,$ $D_{i_k}^{*\pi}(S) = a_{i_k}(S^{k-1})$ where i_k is the* kth *maximal element of π in P and $S^{k-1} \equiv \{x \in S^{k-2} \mid x_{i_{k-1}} = a_{i_{k-1}}(S^{k-2})\}$, and so on.*

These generalizations of the D^π are provided for completeness only. Indeed, they are discontinuous, and *CONT* will remain one of our requirements.

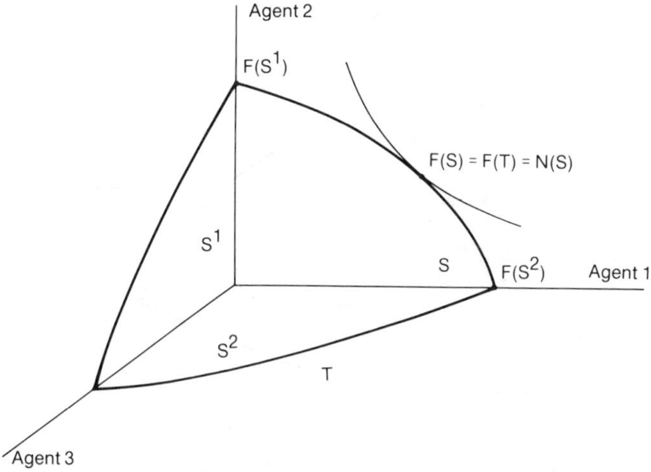

Figure 5.7. Example 5.

It is fairly clear that violations of *SY* are "the worst" for the D^π solutions. These solutions do not allow *any* utility substitutions, but there are related solutions that satisfy *W.P.O, I.I.A, MON,* and *CONT* and do allow utility substitutions. Indeed, the MP^2 solutions can be generalized by permitting the component path relative to any Q to totally lie in a subspace $\mathbb{R}^P_+$ of $\mathbb{R}^Q_+$. This is illustrated by the following example.

Example 5. (See Figure 5.7.) Let $I = \{1, 2, 3\}$. Given $T \in \Sigma^I$, $F(T) = F(T_{\{1,2\}}) = N(T_{\{1,2\}})$; on $\Sigma^{\{1,2\}}$, $F = N$; on $\Sigma^{\{2,3\}}$, $F = D^2$; and on $\Sigma^{\{1,3\}}$, $F = D^1$.

In Example 5, *ST.I.R* is violated in the worst way for one agent (agent 3) since he is always ignored by all components relative to groups containing him. Utility substitutions are permitted over the whole of $\mathbb{R}^{\{1,2\}}$ to solve any problem involving both agents 1 and 2.

In the next example, the opposite occurs. One agent (agent 3) always gets his preferred alternative. The components of the solution relative to any group containing him coincide with D^3. Utility substitutions remain possible over the whole of $\mathbb{R}^{\{1,2\}}$ to solve any two-person problem involving both agents 1 and 2.

Example 6. (See Figure 5.8.) Let $I = \{1, 2, 3\}$. Given $T \in \Sigma^I$, $F(T) = F(T_{\{2,3\}}) = F(T_{\{1,3\}}) = D^3(T)$; on $\Sigma^{\{1,2\}}$, $F = N$.

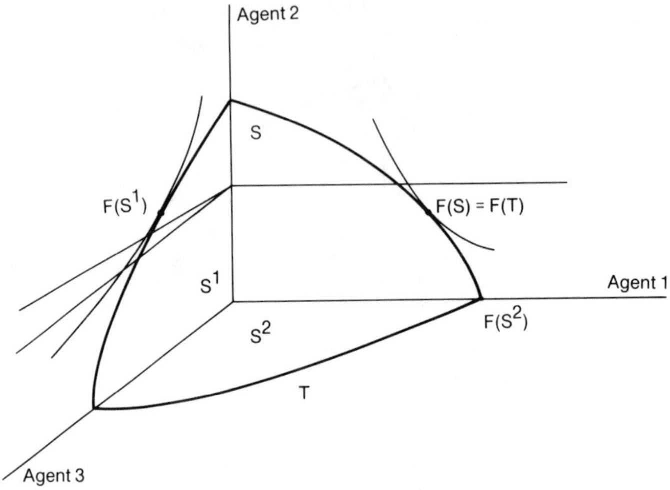

Figure 5.8. Example 6.

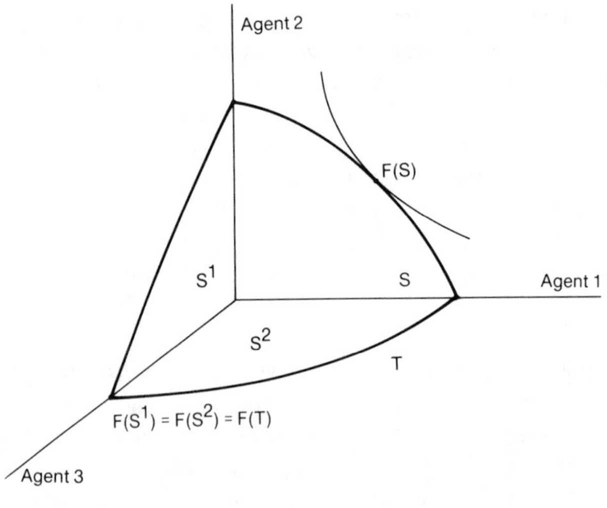

Figure 5.9. Example 7.

The next example shows that the components of a solution relative to two different two-person groups may both permit utility substitutions provided that the domains over which this possibility arises satisfy certain compatibility conditions; in the example, F coincides on $\Sigma^{\{1,2\}}$ with N in $\mathbb{R}_+ \times [0, 1]$ whereas F coincides on $\Sigma^{\{2,3\}}$ with N in a subset of $[1, \infty[\times \mathbb{R}_+$.

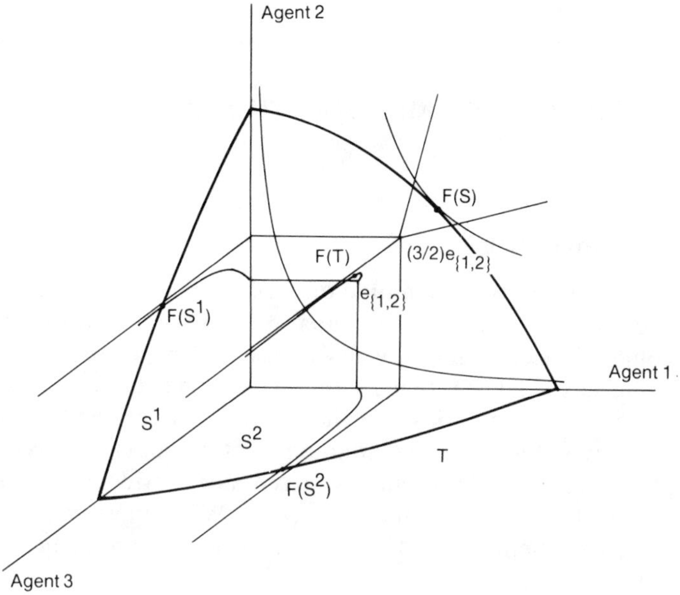

Figure 5.10. Example 8.

Example 7. (See Figure 5.9.) Let $I=\{1,2,3\}$. Given $S\in\Sigma^{\{1,2\}}$, $F(S)\equiv \operatorname{argmax}\{x_1x_2 \mid x\in S,\ x_2\leqq 1\}$. Given $S\in\Sigma^{\{2,3\}}$, $F(S)\equiv D^2(S)$ if $\max\{x_2 \mid x\in S\}<1$ and $\operatorname{argmax}\{x_2x_3 \mid x\in S, x_2+\epsilon x_3\geqq 1+\epsilon\}$ where $\epsilon<0$ and $|\epsilon|<1$ otherwise. On $\Sigma^{\{1,3\}}$, $F=D^1$. Given $T\in\Sigma^I$, $F(S)=F(T_{\{1,2\}})$.

The final example shows that for a given component the domain over which utility substitutions are possible may be made up of two separate subdomains; in the example, F coincides with E for "small" members of $\Sigma^{\{1,2\}}$ and with N for larger elements of $\Sigma^{\{1,2\}}$.

Example 8. (See Figure 5.10.) Let $I=\{1,2,3\}$. Given $S\in\Sigma^{\{1,2\}}$, $F(S)\equiv \operatorname{argmax}\{x_1x_2 \mid x\in S, x\leqq e_{\{1,2\}}\}$ if $e_{\{1,2\}}\notin S$; $F(S)\equiv \operatorname{argmax}\{x_1x_2 \mid x\in S, x_1+\epsilon x_2\geqq 1+\epsilon, \epsilon x_1+x_2\geqq 1+\epsilon\}$ for some $\epsilon<0$ and $|\epsilon|$ small if $\frac{3}{2}e_{\{1,2\}}\in S$ and $F(S)\equiv E(S)$ in all other cases. Given $T\in\Sigma^I$, $F(T)\equiv F(T_{\{1,2\}})$ if $e_{\{1,2\}}\notin T$ and F coincides with an MP^2 solution G^I whose graph contains $[0, e_{\{1,2\}}]$ and approximates $[0, \frac{3}{2}e_{\{1,2\}}]\cup\{\frac{3}{2}e_{\{1,2\}}+\lambda e_3 \mid \lambda>0\}$. Finally, $F=G^I_{\{1,3\}}$ on $\Sigma^{\{1,3\}}$ and $F=G^I_{\{2,3\}}$ on $\Sigma^{\{2,3\}}$.

CHAPTER 6

Guarantees and opportunities

6.1 Introduction

We focus here on the magnitude of the losses and of the gains that an agent originally present may experience upon the arrival of a group of newcomers unaccompanied by an expansion of opportunities. We investigate the maximal losses that a solution may inflict on the old agents and the opportunities for gains that the solution may provide them in such circumstances. We argue that solutions that do not cause large drops in the utilities of the agents originally present nor provide them with opportunities for large gains are more desirable. We propose ways of quantifying these phenomena, and we compare solutions on the basis of these quantitative measures.

First, we examine the issue of guarantees. Let a solution be given as well as some group P of agents, some member i of P, and some group $\bar{P}$ of agents disjoint from P. When $\bar{P}$ joins P, the recognition of the claims of its members typically will necessitate that some of the agents originally present lose. In order to measure the "protection" offered by the solution to agent i, we determine the greatest number α such that agent i's final utility is guaranteed to be at least α times his original utility. The *guarantee structure* of the solution is then defined as the list of all of the α's so obtained for all choices of P, i, and $\bar{P}$ satisfying the conditions listed in the preceding.

Solutions that offer high guarantees are of course more appealing. If each term of the guarantee structure of some solution is no smaller than the corresponding term of the guarantee structure of some other solution, we say that the former *weakly dominates* the latter. Of course, given two arbitrary solutions, their guarantee structures may or may not be comparable in this way.

A number of natural questions arise. What are the guarantee structures of the most commonly used solutions? Is there a greatest element in the set of guarantee structures associated with solutions satisfying minimal requirements? Does any one of the well-known solutions offer this greatest guarantee structure (if it exists)?

The answers to these questions are given in this chapter. (i) The most commonly used solutions can be ranked as follows: The Egalitarian and

Utilitarian solutions fare the worst. In fact, they offer no guarantees at all. Then comes the Nash solution, and finally comes the Kalai–Smorodinsky solution. (ii) There is a greatest guarantee structure in the set of guarantee structures associated with solutions satisfying Weak Pareto-Optimality and Anonymity. (iii) This greatest guarantee structure is achieved by the Kalai–Smorodinsky solution. (iv) Is the Kalai–Smorodinsky solution the only one satisfying Weak Pareto-Optimality and Anonymity and achieving the greatest guarantee structure? No, not even in the set of solutions satisfying other appealing properties, such as Scale Invariance and Continuity. Other solutions with these five properties can in particular be constructed by perturbing the Kalai–Smorodinsky solution.

Note that the guarantees discussed in the preceding are *individual* guarantees. The extent to which *group* interests have to be sacrificed in order to offer high guarantees to *individuals* is investigated next. The notion of a *collective guarantee structure* is proposed to measure the protection offered to groups, and a parallel series of results based on this notion is developed. (i) Not surprisingly, the Egalitarian and Utilitarian solutions still offer no guarantees, but the ranking of the Nash and Kalai–Smorodinsky solutions is now reversed. (ii) There is a greatest collective guarantee associated with solutions satisfying Weak Pareto-Optimality and Anonymity. (iii) This greatest collective guarantee is achieved by the Nash solution. (iv) However, the Nash solution is not the only solution with that property also to satisfy Scale Invariance and Continuity.

The notions of guarantee structures proposed in the foregoing are meant to formalize intuitive concepts of "protection" and to allow quantitative comparisons of solutions. There is, however, a natural counterpart to the notion of guarantee structures that is worth studying too. Recall that when new agents enter the scene, some solutions, such as the Nash solution, sometimes recommend that the payoff of some of the original agents be increased even if the arrival of the newcomers is not accompanied by an expansion of opportunities. We argued earlier that this opportunity for gain that a solution may offer to agents is contrary to fairness. We now suggest that solutions should also be evaluated on the basis of the extent to which they permit such opportunities.

In order to measure the opportunity for gain offered by a solution to some agent i originally part of some group P upon the arrival of some group $\bar{P}$, we determine the greatest number γ with the property that agent i's final utility may be equal to γ times his original utility. The numbers so obtained for all choices of i, P, and $\bar{P}$ as described in the preceding constitute the *opportunity structure* of the solution. This concept also permits a partial ordering of solutions. Is there agreement between the orderings based on opportunities and the orderings based on guarantees?

Yes and no. We find that the Kalai–Smorodinsky and Egalitarian solutions perform equally well this time and that both dominate all solutions satisfying Weak Pareto-Optimality and Anonymity. In particular, they perform strictly better than the Nash solution, which in turn performs strictly better than the Utilitarian solution.

When the opportunities for gain that solutions give to the initial group seen as a whole are used as a basis of comparison, we find that the Kalai–Smorodinsky, Egalitarian, and Nash solutions become equivalent and that no solution satisfying Weak Pareto-Optimality and Anonymity can do better.

The notion of opportunity structure therefore does not permit us to discriminate between solutions as finely as the notion of guarantee structure, although the rankings the two notions yield are roughly consistent with one another either when individuals are considered or when groups are considered.

Overall, the results presented in this chapter reinforce the appeal of the Kalai–Smorodinsky and Nash solutions and strengthen our intuition about their relative merits.

The rest of the chapter is organized as follows. Sections 6.2 and 6.3 concern individual and collective guarantees, respectively, whereas Sections 6.4 and 6.5 are devoted to individual and collective opportunities, respectively. Section 6.6 contains some concluding comments.

This chapter is based on Thomson and Lensberg (1983) and Thomson (1983b, 1987a). Further results appear in Chun and Thomson (1988).

6.2 Individual guarantees

Let F be a solution. Let $i \in I$, $P \in \mathcal{P}$ with $i \in P$, and $Q \in \mathcal{P}$ with $P \subset Q$ be given. Assume that for some $\alpha \in \mathbb{R}_+$, the following is true:

$$\text{for all } S \in \Sigma^P \text{ and } T \in \Sigma^Q \text{ with } S = T_P, \; F_i(T) \geqq \alpha F_i(S). \tag{1}$$

The solution outcome of the problem S faced by the group P to which agent i belongs is first determined. Then new agents come in, while opportunities as seen from the perspective of the group P do not expand. By this we mean that the intersection of the problem T faced by the enlarged group Q with the subspace pertaining to the initial group is equal to S. The solution outcome of T is computed. As we discussed in the previous chapters, depending upon which solution F is used, agent i may or may not lose. However, if he does lose, the inequality appearing in (1) means that his final utility level will be least the fraction α of his initial utility level. Let

$$\alpha_F^{iPQ} \equiv \inf\{F_i(T)/F_i(S) \mid S \in \Sigma^P, T \in \Sigma^Q, S = T_P\}.$$

In this definition as well as in the definitions of the following sections, we find it convenient to limit our attention to pairs S, T giving rise to well-defined ratios of utilities. (Since all but one of the solutions that we will examine in detail satisfy Strong Individual Rationality, this is a minor restriction.)

The number α_F^{iPQ} represents the guarantee offered by the solution F to agent i in group P upon the arrival of group $Q \backslash P$. If F satisfies Anonymity, this number depends only on the cardinalities m and n of P and $Q \backslash P$, and it can be written as α_F^{mn}. We will limit our attention to anonymous solutions and consequently define the ***individual guarantee structure of F*** as

$$\alpha_F \equiv \{\alpha_F^{mn} \mid m, n \in \mathbb{N}\}.$$

Note that this definition is meant to capture how a *single individual* is affected by the arrival of new agents. In Section 6.3, we will study how groups are affected. Until then, we will use the phrase *guarantee structure* to keep our language simple.

Given two solutions F and G, we say that $\boldsymbol{\alpha_F}$ ***weakly dominates*** $\boldsymbol{\alpha_G}$ if for all $m, n \in \mathbb{N}$, $\alpha_F^{mn} \geqq \alpha_G^{mn}$. The domination relation provides a partial ordering on the set of guarantee structures.

In order to illustrate the concept of a guarantee structure and to motivate properties of guarantee structures that are of interest, we turn to the study of a few examples.

Example 1. *The Egalitarian and Utilitarian solutions.*

> ***Theorem 6.1.*** *The guarantee structures α_E and α_U of the Egalitarian and Utilitarian solutions are given by $\alpha_E^{mn} = \alpha_U^{mn} = 0$ for all $m, n \in \mathbb{N}$.*

Proof. Let $P \equiv \{1, \dots, m\}$ and $Q \equiv \{1, \dots, n\}$. Given $\epsilon > 0$, let $T^\epsilon \in \Sigma^Q$ be defined by $T^\epsilon \equiv \text{cch}\{e_P, \epsilon e_{Q \backslash P}\}$. We have $E(T^\epsilon) = [\epsilon/(1+\epsilon)]e_Q$. Since $T_P^\epsilon = \text{cch}\{e_P\}$, we have $E(T_P^\epsilon) = e_P$. Therefore, $E_1(T^\epsilon)/E_1(T_P^\epsilon) = \epsilon/(1+\epsilon) \to 0$ as $\epsilon \to 0$, and $\alpha_E^{mn} = 0$.

The proof that $\alpha_U = 0$ is similar, and we omit it. Q.E.D.

The zero guarantee structure is of course the worst possible one.

Example 2. *The transferable utility case.* Let us assume for a moment that utility is transferable among the agents in the sense that the undominated boundary of the admissible problems for any group $P \in \mathcal{P}$ is the intersection with $\mathbb{R}_+^P$ of a hyperplane normal to e_P. This amounts to saying that there is a fixed amount of "utility" that can be freely transferred among the agents. On this restricted domain, there is only one solution satisfying *W.P.O* and *AN*: It consists in giving to the agents equal shares of whatever amount is available. The guarantee structure α of this solution is such that $\alpha^{mn} = m/(m+n)$ for all $m, n \in \mathbb{N}$. It is of particular interest since the proportional loss incurred by an agent upon the addition of a fixed number of agents goes to zero as the number of agents originally present goes to infinity. It seems legitimate to conjecture that this asymptotic property will hold for other solutions even if the domain is not restricted as in the present example. However, we show next that the Nash solution does not enjoy the property, and we then turn to a general examination of the conjecture.

Example 3. *The Nash solution.*

> ***Theorem 6.2.*** *The guarantee structure α_N of the Nash solution is given by*
>
> $$\alpha_N^{mn} = \frac{m(n+2) - \sqrt{mn(mn+4m-4)}}{2(m+n)} \quad \text{for all } m, n \in \mathbb{N}.$$

Proof. Let $P \equiv \{1, \ldots, n\}$ and $Q \equiv \{1, \ldots, m+n\}$; we want to solve the following problem:

Problem 1: Find the infimum of $N_1(T)/N_1(T_P)$ for $T \in \Sigma^Q$. (The focus on agent 1 is without loss of generality.)

Appealing to the fact that N satisfies *S.INV*, we can assume that $N(T_P) = e_P$. Let $y \equiv N(T)$. Since N satisfies *ST.I.R*, $y > 0$. Let $T' \equiv \text{cch}\{y, e_P\}$. Since N satisfies *I.I.A*, then $N(T') = y$ and $N(T'_P) = e_P$, so that $N_1(T)/N_1(T_P) = N_1(T')/N_1(T'_P) = y_1$. Therefore, we can limit our search among $T' \in \Sigma^Q$ of the form $T' \equiv \text{cch}\{y, e_P\}$ provided $N(T') = y$ and $N(T'_P) = e_P$. (See Figure 6.1, where $P \equiv \{1, 2\}$ and $Q \equiv \{1, 2, 3\}$.) For $N(T'_P) = e_P$ to hold, it is necessary and sufficient that $T'_P \equiv \text{cch}\{y_P, e_P\}$ be supported at e_P by the hyperplane in $\mathbb{R}^P$ normal to e_P, a condition that can be expressed as $\sum_P y_i \leqq m$. Similarly, for $N(T') = y$ to hold, it is necessary and sufficient that T' be supported at y by the hyperplane of support at y to the set $\{y' \in \mathbb{R}^Q_+ \mid \prod_Q y'_i \geqq \prod_Q y_i\}$. This is ensured by choosing e_P below this hyperplane, a condition that can be expressed as

$$y_1 \geqq \frac{1}{m+n-\sum_{P'}(1/y_i)} \equiv g(y_{P'}), \quad \text{where } P' \equiv P \backslash 1.$$

Therefore, Problem 1 is equivalent to Problem 2:

Problem 2: Find the infimum of x_1 for $x \in \mathbb{R}^P_{++}$ such that (i) $\sum_P x_i \leqq m$ and (ii) $x_1 \geqq g(x_{P'})$.

This problem takes place entirely in $\mathbb{R}^P_+$.

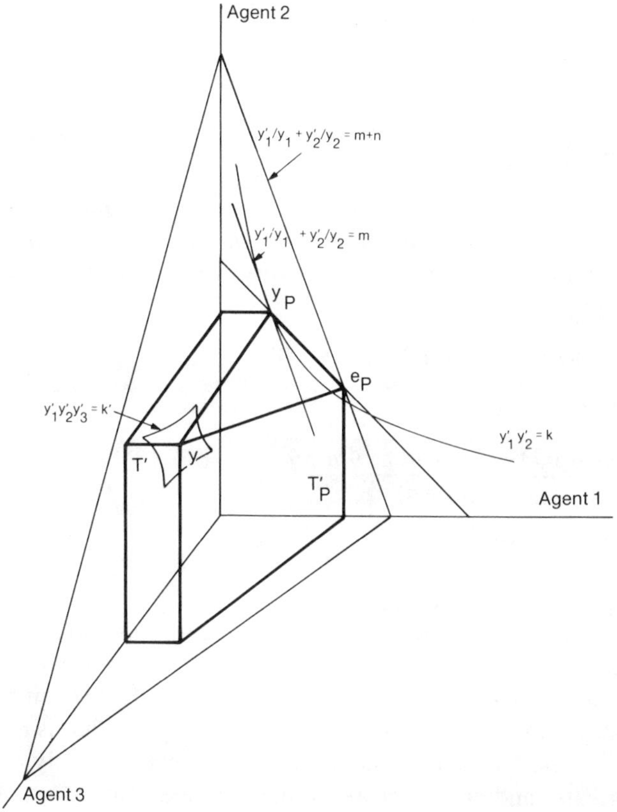

Figure 6.1. Theorem 6.2.

It is easy to show that because g is continuous and decreasing in x_i for each $i \in P'$, we can limit our search among $x \in \mathbb{R}^P_+$ such that (i) and (ii) hold as equalities. (In Figure 6.1, the hyperplanes of support to $\{y' \in \mathbb{R}^Q_+ \mid \prod_Q y'_i = \prod_Q y_i\}$ at y and to $\{x' \in \mathbb{R}^P_+ \mid \prod_P x'_i = 1\}$ at e_P are shown to contain e_P and y_P, respectively.) Finally, we claim that we can choose $x_i = x_j$ for all $i, j \in P'$. To see this, let $x \in \mathbb{R}^P_{++}$ satisfying (i) and (ii) as equalities. We show that there exists $\bar{x} \in \mathbb{R}^P_{++}$ with $\bar{x}_i = \bar{x}_j$ for all $i, j \in P'$ also satisfying (i) and (ii) and achieving the same value of the objective function. Indeed, let $\bar{x}_1 \equiv x_1$ and $\bar{x}_i \equiv \sum_{P'} x_k/(m-1)$ for all $i \in P'$. Clearly, $\bar{x}$ satisfies (i). To show that $\bar{x}$ satisfies (ii) also, we write (ii) as

$$\frac{1}{\bar{x}_1} + \sum_{P'} \frac{1}{\bar{x}_i} \leqq m+n,$$

which, since

$$\frac{1}{x_1}+\sum_{P'}\frac{1}{x_i}=m+n \quad \text{and} \quad x_1=\bar{x}_1,$$

is equivalent to

$$\frac{1}{\sum_{P'} x_i/(m-1)} \leqq \frac{\sum_{P'}(1/x_i)}{m-1},$$

an inequality that follows from the convexity of the function $h(t)=1/t$. Thus, in Problem 2, we can choose $x_i=(m-x_1)/(m-1)$ for all $i\in P'$. Substituting in (ii), written as an equality, we obtain the quadratic expression in x_1,

$$(m+n)x_1^2-m(n+2)x_1+m=0$$

whose smallest root is

$$\frac{m(n+2)-\sqrt{mn(mn+4m-4)}}{2(m+n)},$$

the desired expression. Q.E.D.

It is easy to check that the Nash guarantee structure does not satisfy the asymptotic property discussed in connection with the transferable utility problems. In fact, $\alpha_N^{mn}\leqq 1/(n+1)$ for all $m,n\in\mathbb{N}$. Somewhat more disturbingly, α_N^{mn} is a decreasing function of m for each n (we omit the computations); as $m\to\infty$, $\alpha_N^{mn}\to[n+2-\sqrt{n(n+4)}\,]/2$. What is disturbing, of course, is the fact that as the number of agents originally present increases, greater and greater proportional sacrifices may be required of at least one of them upon the addition of a group of fixed size. Note, however, that α_N^{mn} is a decreasing function of n for each fixed m, as seems desirable.

Are there solutions satisfying the asymptotic property? The answer is that no solution satisfying *W.P.O* (in addition to *AN*, which is imposed throughout in this chapter) does. In fact, a much stronger result holds:

Theorem 6.3. *The guarantee structure of any solution satisfying W.P.O and AN is weakly dominated by* $\bar{\alpha}$ *defined by* $\bar{\alpha}^{mn}\equiv 1/(n+1)$ *for all* $m,n\in\mathbb{N}$.

Proof. Let F be a solution satisfying *W.P.O* and *AN*. Let $P',Q\in\mathcal{P}$ with $P'\subset Q$, $|P'|=m-1$, $|Q|=m+n$ be given, and let $P''=Q\backslash P'$. Also, let $T\in\Sigma^Q$ be defined by $T\equiv\{x\in\mathbb{R}_+^Q \mid x_{P'}\leqq e_{P'} \text{ and } \sum_{P''}x_i\leqq 1\}$. It follows from *AN* that $F_{P''}(T)$ has equal coordinates. This, in conjunction with feasibility, implies that $F_i(T)\leqq 1/|P''|=1/(n+1)$ for all $i\in P''$. Given some arbitrary $k \in P''$, let now $P \equiv P' \cup \{k\}$ and $S \equiv T_P$. We note that $S = \text{cch}\{e_P\}$. By *W.P.O* and *AN*, $F(S) = e_P$. Thus, $F_k(T) \leqq F_k(S)/(n+1)$. Because $|P| = m$ and $|Q \backslash P| = n$, we conclude that $\alpha_F^{mn} \leqq 1/(n+1)$.

Q.E.D.

It is instructive to provide an explicit example of an exchange economy whose associated feasible set in utility space is the problem T used in the proof of Theorem 6.3. The complementaries and incompatibilities exhibited by the agents' preferences in relation to the bundle available to them may shed some light on the significance this result has for the application to economics of the abstract theory developed here.

Assume that there are m goods indexed by the members of P, that each agent $i \in P$ cares only about good i, and that each of the agents in $Q \backslash P$ cares only about good k. This is achieved by the following choice of utility functions: Given an arbitrary consumption bundle z in the m-dimensional commodity space $\mathbb{R}_+^P$, set $u_i(z) \equiv z_i$ for all $i \in P$ and $u_i(z) \equiv z_k$ for all $i \in Q \backslash P$. Finally, assume that there is one unit of each good available for distribution. It is easy to check that

$$T = \{x \in \mathbb{R}_+^Q \mid \forall i \in Q, \exists z^i \in \mathbb{R}_+^P \text{ s.t. } \textstyle\sum_Q z_i \leqq e_P \text{ and } \forall i \in Q, u_i(z_i) = x_i\}.$$

We first distribute the aggregate bundle among the members of P whose preferences do not conflict; each of them ends up with one unit of the good she likes, and this distribution results in a utility of 1 for agent k. The larger group Q is then formed by introducing n agents whose preferences are identical to that of agent k. The only compromise at which the $n+1$ identical agents are treated symmetrically is obtained by giving them equal amounts of the commodity they care about; this brings agent k's utility down to $1/(n+1)$.

The result described in Theorem 6.3 certainly is a disappointment since it says that even if there are already a large number of agents, the addition of only one agent (more generally a *fixed* number n of agents) may require that at least one of the original agents loses a full $\frac{1}{2}$ [more generally, a full $n/(n+1)$] of what she was getting.

At this point, we do not even know whether there are any solutions offering the guarantee structure $\bar{\alpha}$. Things could be even worse. Fortunately, we have

Theorem 6.4. *The guarantee structure of the Kalai–Smorodinsky solution is* $\bar{\alpha}$.

Proof. Let $P, Q \in \mathcal{P}$ with $P \subset Q$, $|P| = m$, and $|Q| = m+n$ as well as $i \in P$, $S \in \Sigma^P$, and $T \in \Sigma^Q$ with $S = T_P$ be given. We will show that $K_i(T)/K_i(S) \geqq 1/(n+1)$; the desired conclusion will then follow from Theorem 6.3 and the fact that K satisfies *W.P.O* and *AN*. Since K satisfies *S.INV*, we can assume that $a(T)=e_Q$. This implies that $a(S)=e_P$ and consequently $K(S)=\lambda e_P$ for some $\lambda \in]0,1]$. Since the points λe_P and e_j for all $j \in Q \backslash P$ belong to T, their convex combination that has equal coordinates also does. This is the point $\lambda e_Q/(n\lambda+1)$. Since $K(T)$ also has equal coordinates, it follows from *W.P.O* that $K_i(T) \geqq \lambda/(n\lambda+1)$. Therefore, $K_i(T) \geqq K_i(S)/(n\lambda+1) \geqq K_i(S)/(n+1)$. Q.E.D.

Theorem 6.4 describes a remarkable property of the Kalai–Smorodinsky solution, which distinguishes it favorably from other solutions and in particular from the Nash solution.

An intuitive explanation of how the four solutions that we have explicitly considered compare may be useful at this point. The somewhat disappointing behavior of the Nash solution is due to the fact that this solution allows for substitutions among the agents' utilities. As the number of additional agents increases, the problem pertaining to the larger group has more freedom to "stretch out" in a direction unfavorable to a given one of the original agents. By contrast, the Kalai–Smorodinsky solution keeps all utilities tied together and prevents a given agent from being "exploited" for the benefit of the others. The poor performance of the Egalitarian and Utilitarian solutions can be understood by noting that these solutions involve interpersonal comparisons of utilities. If one of the new agents is a very bad "pleasure machine," he will force everyone's utility down if utilities have to be kept equal, as required by the Egalitarian solution. On the other hand, if one of the new agents is a very good "pleasure machine," he will force everyone down if it is only the sum of utilities that matters, as is the case for the Utilitarian solutions.

In view of Theorems 6.3 and 6.4, we will refer to $\bar{\alpha}$ as the *greatest guarantee structure*.

A natural question is whether the Kalai–Smorodinsky solution is the only solution to satisfy *W.P.O* and *AN* and to offer the greatest guarantee structure. The next theorem shows this not to be the case even if two additional appealing requirements, *S.INV* and *CONT*, are imposed. Solutions other than the Kalai–Smorodinsky solution and satisfying all five properties can be obtained by perturbing it.

It may be useful to compare this nonuniqueness result to the characterization of the Kalai–Smorodinsky solution provided in Chapter 3. Recall that this solution is shown there to be the only one to satisfy *W.P.O*, *AN*, *S.INV*, *CONT*, and the axiom of Population Monotonicity (*MON*), which says that in order to accommodate the claims of new agents, sacrifices (in the weak sense) should be required of every agent originally present. *MON* is a sort of dual of the requirement that the solution offer the

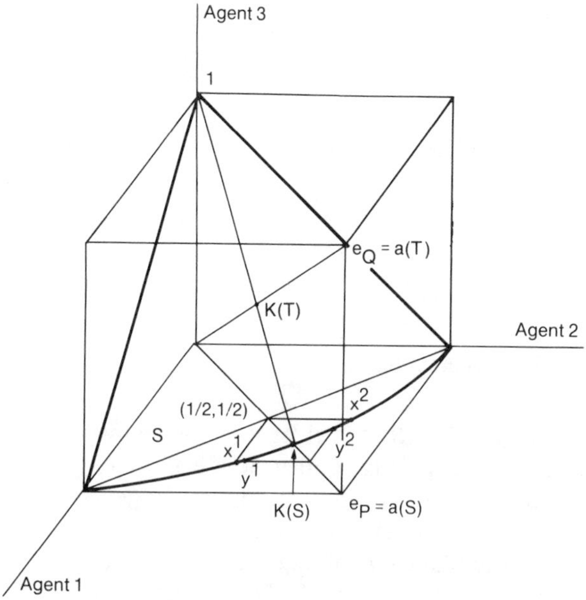

Figure 6.2. Theorem 6.5. $l_1(S)$ = curvilinear segment $[x^1, x^2]$, $l_2(S)$ = curvilinear segment $[y^1, y^2]$.

greatest guarantees, limiting agents' gains instead of their losses. This "duality" suggests that a parallel characterization of the solution could be obtained by substituting the requirement for *MON* in the list characterizing it. But this is not the case, as is now formally established.

Theorem 6.5. *There are solutions other than the Kalai–Smorodinsky solution that satisfy W.P.O, AN, S.INV, and CONT and offer the greatest guarantees.*

Proof. The proof consists in constructing a solution F that satisfies all the axioms but differs from K. To do this, we first set $P \equiv \{1, 2\}$, and we define F on the subset of Σ^P of problems S that are normalized by the condition that $a(S) = e_P$. The definition of F on Σ^P is completed by an appeal to *S.INV*. Then, F is extended to all $\Sigma^{P'}$ with $|P'| = 2$ by applying *AN*. Finally, given any $Q \in \mathcal{P}$ with $|Q| \neq 2$, F is chosen to coincide with K on Σ^Q.

The specification of F for the normalized members of Σ^P is illustrated in Figures 6.2 and 6.3. Let $S \in \Sigma^P$ be such that $a(S) = e_P$. We first determine the arc $l_1(S)$ of points in WPO(S) that weakly dominate $\frac{1}{2}e_P$. This arc

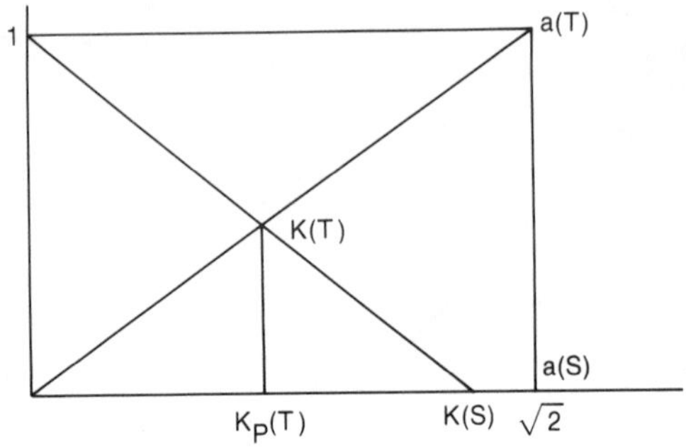

Figure 6.3. Theorem 6.5.

contains $K(S)$. Unless $\text{PO}(S)$ coincides with the segment connecting the two unit vectors in Σ^P, $l_1(S)$ is nondegenerate and $K(S) \in \text{rel.int.}\, l_1(S)$.

Next, we introduce a third agent (without loss of generality, we can assume that it is agent 3). We set $Q \equiv \{1,2,3\}$ and $T \equiv \text{cch}\{S, e_3\}$. The intersection of T with the plane containing the third axis and $K(S)$ is represented in Figure 6.3. It is easily checked there that $K_P(T)$ is not less than halfway from the origin toward $K(S)$. This implies that the arc $l_2(S)$ of points in $\text{WPO}(S)$ that are weakly dominated by $2K_P(T)$ is nonempty. This arc contains $K(S)$. Unless $S = \text{cch}\{e_P\}$, $l_2(S)$ is nondegenerate, and $K(S) \in \text{rel.int.}\, l_2(S)$.

We note that $l_1(S) \cap l_2(S) \neq \emptyset$ for any normalized $S \in \Sigma^P$. We now define F on Σ^P to be a continuous single-valued selection from $l_1(S) \cap l_2(S)$ that picks a symmetric point if S is symmetric. [As an example, $F(S)$ could be the maximizer of the Nash product $x_1 x_2$ over all points x of $l_1(S) \cap l_2(S)$.] This completes the specification of F.

Clearly, F satisfies *W.P.O, AN, S.INV,* and *CONT*. To prove that F offers the greatest guarantees, we first observe that by definition of F, $\alpha_F^{mn} = \alpha_K^{mn} = \bar{\alpha}^{mn}$ for all $m, n \in \mathbb{N}$ with $m = 1$ and $n \geqq 2$ or with $m \geqq 3$. To show that $\alpha_F^{11} = \frac{1}{2}$, we set $P \equiv \{1,2\}$, and we observe that for all $S \in \Sigma^P$, $F_1(S) \geqq \frac{1}{2} F_1(S_{\{1\}}) = \frac{1}{2} K_1(S_{\{1\}}) = \frac{1}{2}$. This is because $F(S) \in l_1(S)$. Finally, to show that $\alpha_F^{2n} = 1/(n+1)$, we let $P, Q \in \mathcal{P}$ with $P \subset Q$, $|P| = 2$, $|Q| = 2+n$ be given as well as $S \in \Sigma^P$, $T \in \Sigma^Q$ with $S = T_P$. Since F satisfies *S.INV*, we can assume that $a(T) = e_Q$. Then $K(S) = \lambda e_P$ for some $\lambda \in]0,1]$, and $F(T) = K(T) = \mu e_Q$ for some $\mu \in]0,1]$. Given S, the minimal μ is obtained for $T \equiv \text{cch}\{S;\, e_j \text{ for } j \in Q \backslash P\}$. Then, $\mu = \lambda/(1+\lambda n)$. (This is as in the proof of Theorem 6.4.) Therefore, given $i \in P$ and $u_i \equiv F_i(S)$, we want

$$\frac{\lambda}{1+\lambda n} \cdot \frac{1}{u_i} \geqq \frac{1}{n+1} \quad \text{or} \quad u_i \leqq \frac{(1+n)\lambda}{1+\lambda n} \quad \text{for all } n \in \mathbb{N}.$$

If $n=1$, the inequality is equivalent to $u_i \leqq 2K_i(T)$, which holds because $F(S) \in l_2(S)$. Since the function $f(n) \equiv (1+n)/(1+\lambda n)$ is nondecreasing, the inequality is in fact satisfied for all n. Q.E.D.

Note that there is nothing pathological about F. Theorem 6.5 shows that in order for a solution to satisfy the five properties, it need not prohibit utility substitutions altogether as the Kalai–Smorodinsky solution does. However, it is intuitive from its construction that F permits only limited substitutability.

6.3 Collective guarantees

The extent to which *group* interests have to be sacrificed in order to offer high guarantees to *individuals* is the object of this section. Protecting any one agent against large losses may indeed be very costly to the group to which he belongs in the sense that large contributions or sacrifices may be required of the other members of the group. We propose here a way of measuring the protection offered by solutions to original groups, and as earlier with individual guarantees, we compare solutions on that basis. We obtain a series of results parallel to those of Section 6.2; this time, it is the Nash solution that comes out best. Indeed, our main result is that the Nash solution weakly dominates any weakly Pareto-optimal and anonymous solution and in fact strictly dominates the Kalai–Smorodinsky solution.

One way to evaluate the guarantee offered by a solution to an initial group would be to take the minimal ratio of the sum of the final utilities of its members to the sum of their initial utilities. However, such a procedure would not be invariant under scale changes of the utilities. For that reason, we will average over the members of the original group the ratios of their final to initial utilities.

Formally, given $P, Q \in \mathcal{P}$ with $P \subset Q$, we determine

$$\beta_F^{PQ} \equiv \inf\{(1/|P|)\Sigma_P[F_i(T)/F_i(S)] \mid S \in \Sigma^P, T \in \Sigma^Q, S = T_P\}.$$

If F satisfies Anonymity, as we will again assume from here on in this section, then each β_F^{PQ} depends only on the cardinalities m and n of P and $Q \backslash P$ and can be denoted β_F^{mn}. Finally, the ***collective guarantee structure of F*** is defined to be

$$\beta_F \equiv \{\beta_F^{mn} \mid m, n \in \mathbb{N}\}.$$

Two elementary properties of collective guarantees in relation to individual guarantees are that $\beta_F \geqq \alpha_F$ and that $\beta_F^{1n} = \alpha_F^{1n}$ for all $n \in \mathbb{N}$.

Next, we have

Theorem 6.6. *The collective guarantee structures β_E and β_U of the Egalitarian and Utilitarian solutions are given by*

$$\beta_E^{mn} = \beta_U^{mn} = 0 \quad \text{for all} \ m, n \in \mathbb{N}.$$

The proof is omitted.

This result certainly is not a surprise. Our earlier intuitive explanation of the behavior of these solutions from the viewpoint of individual guarantees (after Theorem 6.4) applies here as well. Next, we investigate how well the Kalai–Smorodinsky solution performs.

Theorem 6.7. *The collective guarantee structure β_K of the Kalai–Smorodinsky solution is given by $\beta_K^{mn} = 1/(n+1)$ for all $m, n \in \mathbb{N}$.*

Proof. Since $\beta_K \geqq \alpha_K$ and $\alpha_K^{mn} = 1/(n+1)$ for all $m, n \in \mathbb{N}$ (Theorem 6.4), it is enough to show that given $P, Q \in \mathcal{P}$ with $P \subset Q$, $|P| = m$ and $|Q| = m+n$, there exist $S \in \Sigma^P$ and $T \in \Sigma^Q$ with $S = T_P$ and $\Sigma_P [K_i(T)/K_i(S)]/m = 1/(n+1)$, which will hold if $K_i(T)/K_i(S) = 1/(n+1)$ for all $i \in P$.

Indeed, let $T \equiv \text{cch}\{e_P; e_j \text{ for } j \in Q \backslash P\}$. We have $S \equiv T_P = \text{cch}\{e_P\}$ and $K(S) = e_P$. Also, $a(T) = e_Q$ so that $K(T)$ has equal coordinates. The point $K(T)$ can be written as $\lambda e_P + \Sigma_{Q \backslash P}(1-\lambda)e_j/n$ for some $\lambda \in [0,1]$, equal coordinates being achieved for $\lambda = 1/(n+1)$. Then $K_i(T)/K_i(S) = 1/(n+1)$ for each $i \in P$. Q.E.D.

Although the Kalai–Smorodinsky solution guarantees that the proportional loss incurred by an agent originally part of some group of m agents upon the arrival of some incremental group of n agents will never be more than $1/(n+1)$, it cannot prevent the proportional losses incurred by *all* m agents to simultaneously reach this upper bound, and this independently of n, even if m is large compared to n.

Here, too, we exhibit an exchange economy that yields the problem T used in the preceding. Assume that there are m goods, indexed by the members of P, that each agent i in P cares only about good i, and that each of the agents in $Q \backslash P$ cares about all the goods provided they come in equal amounts. This is achieved by the following choice of the utility functions: Given an arbitrary consumption bundle z in the m-dimensional commodity space $\mathbb{R}^P_+$, set $u_i(z) \equiv z_i$ for all $i \in P$ and $u_i(z) \equiv \min\{z_k \mid k \in P\}$ for all $i \in Q \backslash P$. Finally, assume that there is one unit of each good available for distribution. It is easy to check that

$$T = \{x \in \mathbb{R}^Q_+ \mid \forall i \in Q, \exists z_i \in \mathbb{R}^P_+ \text{ s.t. } \Sigma_Q z_i \leqq e_P \text{ and } \forall i \in Q, u_i(z_i) = x_i\}.$$

In the original group P, there is no conflict among the agents' preferences, and each of them ends up with one unit of the good he likes. The only way the utilities of the new agents can be equalized without waste is to give each of them equal amounts of each of the commodities. Equality of utilities for all agents is achieved when each agent i in P has given up the proportion $n/(n+1)$ of what he originally consumed. This leaves him with utility $1/(n+1)$. In the aggregate, the bundle $ne_P/(n+1)$ is released, and each of the agents in $Q \backslash P$ ends up with $e_P/(n+1)$, which gives him utility $1/(n+1)$.

Theorem 6.8. *The collective guarantee structure of any solution satisfying W.P.O and AN is weakly dominated by $\bar{\beta}$ defined by $\bar{\beta}^{mn} = m/(m+n)$ for all $m, n \in \mathbb{N}$.*

Proof. Let $P, Q \in \mathcal{P}$ with $P \subset Q$, $|P| = m$ and $|Q| = m+n$ be given. Also, let F be a solution satisfying *W.P.O* and *AN*. Finally, let $T \in \Sigma^Q$ be defined by $T \equiv \text{cch}\{e_i \mid i \in Q\}$. Let $S \equiv T_P$. We have $S = \text{cch}\{e_i \mid i \in P\}$. By *W.P.O* and *AN*, $F(T) = e_Q/(m+n)$ and $F(S) = e_P/m$, so that for each $i \in P$, $F_i(T)/F_i(S) = m/(m+n)$. Therefore, $\beta_F^{mn} \leqq m/(m+n)$. Q.E.D.

The next theorem shows that $\bar{\beta}$ is achieved by the Nash solution.

Theorem 6.9. *The collective guarantee structure β_N of the Nash solution is $\bar{\beta}$.*

Proof. By Theorem 6.8, we already know that $\beta_N \leqq \bar{\beta}$ since N satisfies *W.P.O* and *AN*. It remains to show that given $P, Q \in \mathcal{P}$ with $P \subset Q$, $|P| = m$ and $|Q| = m+n$, and given any $S \in \Sigma^P$ and $T \in \Sigma^Q$ with $S = T_P$, we have

$$\sum_P \frac{N_i(T)/N_i(S)}{m} \geqq \frac{m}{m+n}.$$

Since N satisfies *S.INV*, we can assume that T is normalized so that $N(T) = e_Q$. Let $x \equiv N(S)$. Since T is supported at $N(T)$ by a hyperplane normal to e_Q and $S = T_P$, it follows that (i) $\sum_P x_i \leqq m+n$. Since $x = N(S)$ and N satisfies *I.I.A*, then (ii) $x = N(\text{cch}\{x, e_P\})$. The quantity we are evaluating is therefore no smaller than the minimum of $\sum_P (1/x_i)/m$ where $x \in \mathbb{R}_+^P$ is chosen so as to satisfy (i) and (ii). This minimum is achieved when $\sum_P x_i = m+n$ and $x_i = x_j$ for all $i, j \in P$. Then $N_i(T)/N_i(S) = m/(m+n)$ for each $i \in P$ and $\beta_N^{mn} = m/(m+n)$. Q.E.D.

Theorems 6.8 and 6.9 together show that the Nash solution weakly dominates any solution satisfying *W.P.O* and *AN*. A particularly appealing property of $\beta_N = \bar{\beta}$ is that for each fixed n, $\beta_N^{mn} \to 1$ as $m \to \infty$, so that a group of new agents of fixed size inflict vanishing losses on an original group of increasing size.

We now ask whether the Nash solution is the only solution satisfying *W.P.O* and *AN* and offering the greatest collective guarantees. The answer is no even if *S.INV* and *CONT* are required as well.

> ***Theorem 6.10.*** *There are solutions other than the Nash solution that satisfy W.P.O, AN, S.INV, and CONT and offer the greatest collective guarantees.*

Proof. The proof is by way of an example. Let F be defined by setting $F=K$ on Σ^P whenever $|P|=2$ and $F=N$ on Σ^P for any other $P \in \mathcal{P}$. It is immediate that F satisfies *W.P.O* and *AN*. To see that $\beta_F = \bar{\beta}$, we observe that in view of Theorem 6.9, we need compute only β_F^{11} and β_F^{2n} for all $n \in \mathbb{N}$. That $\beta_F^{11} = \frac{1}{2}$ is easily verified. To show that $\beta_F^{2n} = 2/(2+n)$ for all $n \in \mathbb{N}$, let $P, Q \in \mathcal{P}$ with $|P|=2$ (by *AN*, we can assume that $P=\{1,2\}$) and $|Q|=2+n$ be given; it is enough to exhibit $S \in \Sigma^P$, $T \in \Sigma^Q$, with $S=T_P$ and $\Sigma_P[F_i(T)/F_i(S)]/2 = 2/(2+n)$. Let then $T \equiv \text{cch}\{e_Q, (2+n)e_P/2\}$. Because T is supported at e_Q by the hyperplane in $\mathbb{R}^Q$ normal to e_Q, we conclude that $N(T)=e_Q$. Also, $S = \text{cch}\{(2+n)e_P/2\}$, and consequently, $K(S)=(2+n)e_P/2$. Therefore,

$$\frac{1}{2}\left[\frac{F_1(T)}{F_1(S)} + \frac{F_2(T)}{F_2(S)}\right] = \frac{1}{2}\left[\frac{N_1(T)}{K_1(S)} + \frac{N_2(T)}{K_2(S)}\right]$$

$$= \frac{1}{2}\left[\frac{1}{K_1(S)} + \frac{1}{K_2(S)}\right] = \frac{2}{2+n} \qquad \text{Q.E.D.}$$

6.4 Individual opportunities

The concepts developed in the next two sections are counterparts of those developed in the previous two.

First, we will evaluate solutions on the basis of the opportunity for gain that they give to an agent originally present in spite of increases in the number of claimants. Given some initial group P containing some agent i and given some final group Q containing P, we consider the quantity

$$\gamma_F^{iPQ} \equiv \sup\{F_i(T)/F_i(S) \mid S \in \Sigma^P, T \in \Sigma^Q, S = T_P\},$$

which is the greatest possible ratio of agent i's final to initial utilities in such circumstances. If F satisfies Anonymity, this number only depends on the cardinalities m and n of P and $Q \backslash P$ and can be written as γ_F^{mn}.

As earlier, we will limit our attention to anonymous solutions and consequently define the ***individual opportunity structure of F*** as

$$\gamma_F \equiv \{\gamma_F^{mn} \mid m, n \in \mathbb{N}\}.$$

We first determine the opportunity structure of the Nash solution. The reader will note the close similarity of this proof with the proof of Theorem 6.2.

Theorem 6.11. *The opportunity structure of the Nash solution is given by*

$$\gamma_N^{mn} = \frac{2m}{m(n+2) - \sqrt{mn(mn+4m-4)}} \quad \textit{for all } m, n \in \mathbb{N}.$$

Proof. Let $P \equiv \{1, \ldots, m\}$ and $Q \equiv \{1, \ldots, m+n\}$; we have to solve the following problem:

Problem 1: Find the supremum of $N_1(T)/N_1(T_P)$ for $T \in \Sigma^Q$. (The focus on agent 1 is without loss of generality.)

Since N satisfies *S.INV*, we can assume that $N(T) = e_Q$. Let $x \equiv N(T_P)$ and $T' \equiv \text{cch}\{e_Q, x\}$. Because N satisfies *I.I.A*, $N(T') = e_Q$ and $N(T'_P) = x$ so that $N_1(T)/N_1(T_P) = N_1(T')/N_1(T'_P) = 1/x_1$. For $N(T') = e_Q$ to hold, it is necessary and sufficient that T' be supported at e_Q by the hyperplane of support to $\{y' \in \mathbb{R}^Q_+ \mid \prod_Q y'_i = 1\}$, that is, that x be below this hyperplane, a condition that can be written as $\sum_P x_i \leqq m + n$. Similarly, for $N(T'_P) = N(\text{cch}\{e_P, x\}) = x$ to hold, it is necessary and sufficient that T'_P be supported at x by the hyperplane of support to $\{x' \in \mathbb{R}^P_+ \mid \prod_P x'_i = \prod_P x_i\}$, that is, that e_P be below this hyperplane, a condition that can be written as $x > 0$ and $\sum_P (1/x_i) \leqq m$. Therefore, Problem 1 is equivalent to Problem 2.

Problem 2: Find the supremum of $1/x_1$ for $x \in \mathbb{R}^P_+$ such that (i) $\sum_P x_i \leqq m+n$ and (ii) $x > 0$ and $\sum_P (1/x_i) \leqq m$.

This problem takes place entirely in $\mathbb{R}^P_+$.

We claim now that we can limit our search to $x \in \mathbb{R}^P_+$ satisfying the additional constraint $x_i = x_j$ for all $i, j \neq 1$. Indeed, given x satisfying (i) and (ii), we can construct x' with $1/x'_1 = 1/x_1$ and satisfying (i) and (ii) as well as this additional constraint: Let $x'_1 \equiv x_1$ and $x'_k \equiv [1/(m-1)] \sum_{P\backslash 1} x_i$ for each $k \in P\backslash 1$. Clearly, $\sum_P x'_i = \sum_P x_i \leqq m+n$. Also, $x' > 0$ and $\sum_P (1/x'_i) = 1/x_1 + \sum_{P\backslash 1} (1/x'_k) = 1/x_1 + (m-1)^2/\sum_{P\backslash 1} x_i \leqq 1/x_1 + \sum_{P\backslash 1} (1/x_i) \leqq m$, where the penultimate inequality follows from the convexity of the function $h(t) = 1/t$. From here on, we assume that $x_i = x_j$ for all $i, j \neq 1$.

Finally, we can assume that (i) and (ii) are met as equalities. Indeed, if x satisfies the constraints in Problem 2 with $x_1 + (m-1)x_2 < m+n$ then x'

defined by $x_1' \equiv x_1$ and $x_2' \equiv x_2 + \epsilon/(m-1)$ where $\epsilon \equiv m+n-x_1-(m-1)x_2$ achieves the same value of the supremand and satisfies the constraints in Problem 2 with $x_1'+(m-1)x_2' = m+n$. Furthermore, if x satisfies the constraints in Problem 2 with $1/x_1+(m-1)/x_2 < m$ then x' defined by $x_1' \equiv 1/[m-(m-1)/x_2]$ and $x_i' \equiv x_i$ for all $i \neq 1$ achieves a greater value of the supremand and satisfies the constraints in Problem 2 with $1/x_1' + (m-1)/x_2' = m$.

Then, the elimination of x_2 from (i) and (ii) gives rise to a quadratic expression in $1/x_1$ whose greatest root is the desired expression. (We omit the computations, which are analogous to the ones appearing in the proof of Theorem 6.2. In fact, we end up with the very same equation.)

Q.E.D.

There is a simple relation between γ_N^{mn} and the corresponding expression α_N^{mn} obtained in our examination of individual guarantee structures: $\gamma_N^{mn}\alpha_N^{mn} = m/(m+n)$. Also, for each fixed n, γ_N^{mn} is an increasing function of m: As the number of agents originally present increases, the opportunity for gain of any one of them upon the arrival of a group of newcomers of fixed size n increases. However, the proportional gains are bounded from above by the quantity $[n+2+\sqrt{n(n+4)}\,]/2$. Finally, for each fixed m, γ_N^{mn} is an increasing function of n, and $\gamma_N^{mn} \to m$ as $n \to \infty$.

Theorem 6.12. *The opportunity structure γ_U of the Utilitarian solutions is given by $\gamma_U^{mn} = \infty$ for all $m, n \in \mathbb{N}$.*

Proof. Let $P \equiv \{1, \ldots, m\}$ and $Q \equiv \{1, \ldots, m+n\}$. Let $S \in \Sigma^P$ and $T \in \Sigma^Q$ be defined by $S \equiv \text{cch}\{e_1, e_1/\nu + 2e_2, e_3, \ldots, e_m\}$ for all $\nu \in \mathbb{N}$ and $T \equiv \text{cch}\{S, y\}$, where $y \in \mathbb{R}_+^Q$ is such that $y_1 = 1$, $y_i = 0$ for all $i \in P\backslash 1$ and $y_i = 2$ for all $i \in Q\backslash P$. Then $U(S) = e_1/\nu + 2e_2$ and $U(T) = y$, implying that $U_1(T)/U_1(S) = \nu$. The desired conclusion follows by letting $\nu \to \infty$.

Q.E.D.

This bad performance of the Utilitarian solutions with regard to opportunities is of course fairly intuitive, as it was for guarantees.

Theorem 6.13. *The opportunity structures γ_K and γ_E of the Kalai-Smorodinsky and Egalitarian solutions are given by $\gamma_K^{mn} = \gamma_E^{mn} = 1$ for all $m, n \in \mathbb{N}$.*

Proof. Let $P \equiv \{1, \ldots, m\}$ and $Q \equiv \{1, \ldots, m+n\}$. Let $S \in \Sigma^P$ and $T \in \Sigma^Q$, with $S = T_P$, be given. As we know from Chapter 3, $K_P(T) \leqq K(S)$. Therefore, $\gamma_K^{mn} \leqq 1$. To show that in fact $\gamma_K^{mn} = 1$, let $T \in \Sigma^Q$ be defined by $T \equiv \text{cch}\{e_Q\}$ and let $S \equiv T_P$. Then $K(T) = e_Q$, $S = \text{cch}\{e_P\}$, $K(S) = e_P$, and $K_i(T)/K_i(S) = 1$ for all $i \in P$.

The reasoning is the same for E. Q.E.D.

The last lines of this proof also show

Theorem 6.14. *If a solution F satisfies W.P.O and AN, then* $\gamma_F^{mn} \geqq 1$ *for all* $m, n \in \mathbb{N}$.

Therefore, Theorems 6.13 and 6.14 establish that the Kalai–Smorodinsky and Egalitarian solutions are the best in terms of opportunity structures among a very large class of solutions of interest. In conjunction with Theorem 6.11, Theorem 6.13 shows that they strictly dominate the Nash solution.

6.5 Collective opportunities

Examining the opportunity for gains that a solution gives to individuals is not the only way to look at the question. It is also of interest to know how many of the originally present individuals can simultaneously be given large opportunities to benefit from the arrival of the newcomers.

In order to evaluate the opportunities offered to initial groups by a solution F, we define, for all $P, Q \in \mathcal{P}$ with $P \subset Q$,

$$\delta_F^{PQ} \equiv \sup(1/|P|)\{\Sigma_P[F_i(T)/F_i(S)] \mid S \in \Sigma^P, T \in \Sigma^Q, S = T_P\}.$$

If F satisfies Anonymity, as we will again assume, each δ_F^{PQ} depends only on the cardinalities m and n of P and $Q \backslash P$ and can be denoted δ_F^{mn}. Finally, the ***collective opportunity structure of F*** is defined to be

$$\delta_F \equiv \{\delta_F^{mn} \mid m, n \in \mathbb{N}\}.$$

The quantity δ_F^{mn} measures the maximal extent to which an initial group of m agents can take advantage of the arrival of an additional group of n agents.

Recall that the parallel notion of collective guarantees reversed the ordering of the Nash and Kalai–Smorodinsky solutions obtained from an examination of individual guarantees. Will such a reversal occur here as well?

Before computing the collective opportunity structures of the four solutions we examined earlier, we note that for any F, $\delta_F \leqq \gamma_F$. This follows directly from the definitions.

Next, we have

Theorem 6.15. *The collective opportunity structure* δ_N *of the Nash solution is given by* $\delta_N^{mn} = 1$ *for all* $m, n \in \mathbb{N}$.

Proof. Let $P \equiv \{1, \ldots, m\}$ and $Q \equiv \{1, \ldots, m+n\}$; we must solve the following problem:

Problem 1: Find the supremum of $(1/m)\sum_P [N_i(T)/N_i(T_P)]$ for $T \in \Sigma^Q$.

Since N satisfies *S.INV,* we can assume that $N(T) = e_Q$. Let $x \equiv N(T_P)$. Because N satisfies *I.I.A,* we can assume that $T = \text{cch}\{x, e_Q\}$. Then, $T_P = \text{cch}\{x, e_P\}$ and $(1/m)\sum_P [N_i(T)/N_i(T_P)] = (1/m)\sum_P (1/x_i)$. For $N(T) = e_Q$ to hold, it is necessary and sufficient that $\sum_P x_i \leqq m+n$, whereas for $N(\text{cch}\{x, e_P\}) = x$ to hold, it is necessary and sufficient that $x > 0$ and that $\sum_P (1/x_i) \leqq m$.

Therefore, Problem 1 is equivalent to Problem 2:

Problem 2: Find the supremum of $(1/m)\sum_P (1/x_i)$ for $x \in \mathbb{R}^P_+$ such that (i) $\sum_P x_i \leqq m+n$ and (ii) $x > 0$ and $\sum_P (1/x_i) \leqq m$.

This problem takes place entirely in $\mathbb{R}^P_+$.

Since the expression whose supremum we are searching also appears (multiplied by m) on the left side of the second inequality constraint of (ii), we will be done if we can show that the other constraints can be satisfied when this second inequality is met with equality. To show this, it suffices to select $x = e_P$. Then $(1/m)\sum_P (1/x_i) = 1$. Q.E.D.

Remark: In fact, the supremum is reached at all points of the set $\{x' \in \mathbb{R}^P_+ \mid \exists p \in \mathbb{R}^P_+ \text{ with } \sum_P p_i = 1, \prod_P x'_i \geqq \prod_P x''_i \; \forall x'' \in \mathbb{R}^P_+ \text{ with } px \leqq 1, \sum x'_i \leqq m\}$.

Theorem 6.16. *The collective opportunity structure δ_U of the Utilitarian solutions is given by $\delta_U^{mn} = \infty$ for all $m, n \in \mathbb{N}$.*

Proof. This follows directly from Theorem 6.12. Q.E.D.

Theorem 6.17. *The collective opportunity structures δ_K and δ_E of the Kalai–Smorodinsky and Egalitarian solutions are given by $\delta_K^{mn} = \delta_E^{mn} = 1$ for all $m, n \in \mathbb{N}$.*

Proof. The proof is obtained by a straightforward adaptation of that of Theorem 6.13. Q.E.D.

Theorem 6.18. *If a solution F satisfies W.P.O and AN, then $\delta_F^{mn} \geqq 1$ for all $m, n \in \mathbb{N}$.*

Proof. The proof is the same as that of Theorem 6.16. Q.E.D.

These results indicate that no strict reversal of the rankings of the main solutions takes place when collective opportunities instead of individual opportunities are examined, although then the Nash solution does become just as good as the Kalai–Smorodinsky and Egalitarian solutions.

They also show that the concept of collective opportunity is less powerful in differentiating among solutions than the concept of individual opportunities and the concepts of individual and collective guarantees. But there is a rough agreement between the two individual rankings as well as between the two collective rankings.

6.6 Concluding comment on expected losses and gains

We argued here that it is of interest to an agent, in her evaluation of a solution, to compare what she has initially to what she ends up with in circumstances in which more agents turn out to have claims on the fixed resources available to society. There are several ways in which such comparisons could be made, and the methods we have adopted embody a strong degree of pessimism since they are based on focusing on the worst possible changes. We believe that such behavior is not infrequent in the real world: People do demand guarantees and take steps to protect themselves against changes in their situations, an attitude not in contradiction with their expectation, usually realized, that they will do better than their minimum.

However, we certainly do not want to claim that our approach is the only one of interest. In some specific contexts, more may be known about the relation between initial and final problems (some domain restriction may apply) or about the frequency with which they will arise. Then an agent could be interested in the weighted average of the proportional losses she would incur. Solutions could be compared on the basis of the corresponding notions of guarantees. We will not attempt such comparisons here, as the interest of our conclusions would too intimately depend on the underlying domain restrictions and probability structures that would have to be chosen. We note, however, that such conclusions would be the counterpart of those reached by O'Neill (1982) in his comparisons of two-person solutions based on similar probabilistic assumptions.

The preceding comments would of course apply *mutatis mutandis* to collective guarantees and to individual and collective guarantees.

CHAPTER 7

Stability and the Nash solution

7.1 Introduction

The focus of this chapter is on the Nash solution. We offer a new characterization of this solution based on several standard axioms already introduced and discussed in previous chapters and a new axiom, similar to the Population Monotonicity axiom, that concerns the behavior of solutions across cardinalities. Loosely speaking, this axiom says that the outcome selected for a particular problem should be best not only for that problem but also for the subproblem faced by any subgroup, consisting of all the feasible alternatives at which the utilities of all the agents not in the subgroup are kept at the levels specified by the proposed outcome.

The characterization offered here differs from the classic characterization of the Nash solution (see Chapter 2) in that no use is made of the axiom of Independence of Irrelevant Alternatives, whose role is played by this new axiom.

The characterization of the two-person Nash solution, given by Nash in his original paper, has indeed been criticized for its reliance on the independence axiom. Although there are good reasons why one may want to impose it (recall our discussion of the axiom in Chapter 4), it would be of interest to develop results that do not rely on it. It is in that spirit that another axiom will be used instead. This axiom will turn out to play a role very similar to that played by the independence axiom, but its normative significance is quite different.

The axiom was originally introduced by Harsanyi (1959) under the name *Bilateral Equilibrium,* also in the context of bargaining and also in connection with the Nash solution. Harsanyi was interested in reducing the question of solving n-person bargaining problems to the simpler one of solving two-person problems. He argued that a particular payoff vector "will represent the equilibrium outcome of bargaining among the n players only if no pair of players i and j has any incentive to *redistribute* their payoffs between them, as long as the other players' payoffs are kept constant" (Harsanyi, 1977, p. 196).

In order to formalize such a condition, which we will designate here by a different name, an additional piece of notation is needed. Given $P, Q \in \mathcal{P}$

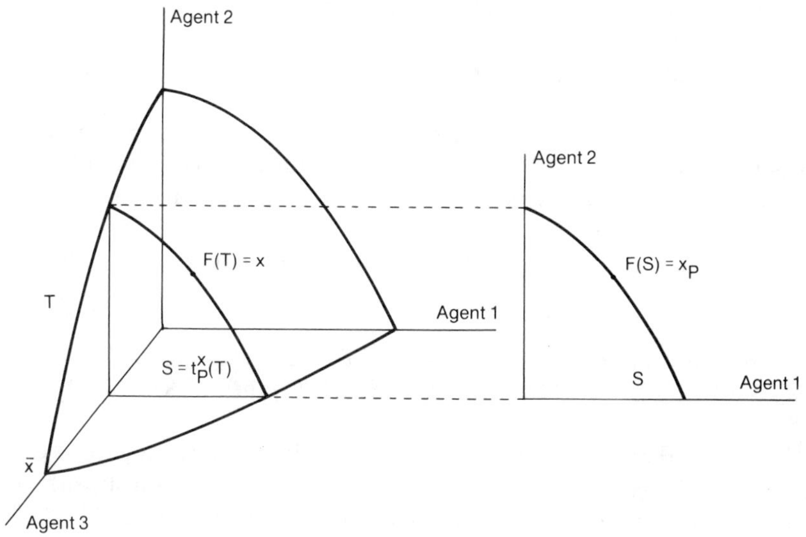

Figure 7.1. The axiom of Bilateral Stability. $P=\{1,2\}$, $Q=\{1,2,3\}$.

with $P \subset Q$, a subset A of $\mathbb{R}^Q$, and a point x of A, $t_P^x(A)$ is the intersection of A with the hyperplane through x parallel to $\mathbb{R}^P$, seen as a subset of $\mathbb{R}^P$, that is, $t_P^x(A) \equiv \{x' \in \mathbb{R}_+^P \mid (x', x_{Q \setminus P}) \in A\}$.

The new axiom can now be formally stated.

Bilateral Stability (B.STAB): For all $P, Q \in \mathcal{P}$ with $P \subset Q$ and $|P|=2$, for all $S \in \Sigma^P$, for all $T \in \Sigma^Q$, if $S = t_P^x(T)$ where $x = F(T)$, then $F(S) = x_P$.

The axiom is illustrated in Figure 7.1 for $P=\{1,2\}$ and $Q=\{1,2,3\}$. Here, T is a three-person problem solved at x, and S is the two-person problem involving agents 1 and 2 obtained from T by keeping agent 3's utility constant at x_3. The requirement is that the solution outcome of S be (x_1, x_2).

In other words, a utility allocation x is the solution of a problem T involving some group of players Q only if x "agrees" with the solution outcomes of all the two-person subproblems obtained from T by keeping the payoffs to all but two of the players at the levels specified by x. [This axiom differs from Harsanyi's condition of Bilateral Equilibrium only in that here account is taken of the fact that the subproblems $t_P^x(T)$ may not be well defined; it is the requirement that there be a point of $t_P^x(T)$ strictly dominating the origin that could be violated, as illustrated in Figure 7.1 by supposing that $F(T)$ is the point denoted $\bar{x}$.]

Harsanyi motivates the condition by pointing out that a rational player i will not accept a tentative agreement for the bargaining problem T if he has reason to believe that he could successfully force or convince some other player j to make a concession in his favor. If simultaneous challenges against more than one player are not permitted, then i can base his beliefs concerning j's willingness to concede only on the principles that would guide them in solving two-person problems involving just the two of them.

We will also consider the following straightforward generalization of *B.STAB*.

Multilateral Stability (M.STAB): For all $P, Q \in \mathcal{P}$ with $P \subset Q$, for all $S \in \Sigma^P$, for all $T \in \Sigma^Q$, if $S = t_P^x(T)$ where $x = F(T)$, then $F(S) = x_P$.

This says that there should be consistency in the sense described earlier, not only with respect to two-person subproblems but also with respect to subproblems involving any subset of the original group. Although *M.STAB* is logically stronger than *B.STAB*, it may be a more natural condition, since there appears to be no a priori reason why a dissatisfied player should limit herself to challenging only one player at a time for concessions if she believes that she may gain by entering into multilateral renegotiations.

It will sometimes be convenient to use the following alternative definitions of the stability axioms: Let F be a solution and let $Q \in \mathcal{P}$ and $T \in \Sigma^Q$ be given. We will say that a point x of T is *F multilaterally stable* if for all $P \subset Q$ with $P \neq Q$ such that $S \equiv t_P^x(T)$ is a well-defined member of Σ^P, it is true that $F(S) = x_P$. Letting $M_F(T)$ denote the set of F multilaterally stable points of T, observe that *M.STAB* is equivalent to the requirement that $M_F(T)$ be nonempty and contain $F(T)$. The definition of the set $B_F(T)$ of *F bilaterally stable* points of T is identical, except that the restriction $|P| = 2$ is added. Clearly, *B.STAB* says that $F(T) \in B_F(T)$.

It should be noted that the appeal of the stability requirement goes beyond its application to bargaining. The axiom says that the point selected as solution outcome should be best not only for the original problem but also for all the subproblems obtained by keeping the utilities of an arbitrary group of agents constant at their proposed levels. Various versions of such a principle have recently been used to characterize the *nucleolus* of a characteristic function game (Sobolev, 1975), the *core* (Peleg, 1985), and the *prekernel* (Peleg, 1986). Balinski and Young (1982) have used an axiom in the same spirit in their development of a theory of *apportionment,* for example, for allocating seats in a parliament in agreement with the populations of different states. Other interesting applications have been made by Aumann and Maschler (1985), Moulin (1985a, b, 1987), and Young (1984, 1987, 1988) in studies of cost allocation, surplus sharing, and taxation problems, and Thomson (1988) studied its implications for the problem of fair division in exchange economies. Finally, an extension of the principle was used by Hart and Mas-Colell (1987) in their characterization of the Shapley value.

As an example to illustrate the nature of the stability argument, consider a bricklayer, a carpenter, and a painter, who have the option of building a house for a certain amount of money. Suppose that they reach an agreement on how to share the money. The contract is signed and the work proceeds in the obvious sequence; the bricklayer does his part of the work, collects his share of the money and leaves the scene. Now suppose that the carpenter refuses to carry out her part of the deal unless there is a redistribution of the remaining funds in her favor. It is this kind of situation that a solution satisfying Multilateral Stability will prevent, as no agent can then expect to gain anything by threatening to break an agreement that has been partially fulfilled. The axiom can thus be interpreted as stating a condition of *stability with respect to partial implementation of the solution outcome*.

The normative content of the axiom is perhaps best brought out by the next example. Consider the distribution among all men and women of the resources available on earth. The fairness of the distribution can be evaluated by examining what the distribution is not only in the whole world but also in each continent, each country, each city, each family: If restricting one's attention to any such subgroup never reveals any inequities, then the distribution could be considered fair. This again is the axiom of Multilateral Stability, which here can be interpreted as a condition of *group fairness* [see the literature on equity criteria that arose out of Foley's (1967) work].

In that context, it may be useful to point out that the Walrasian mechanism from equal division, which as noted in Chapter 3 is often proposed as a solution to the problem of fair division, does satisfy the axiom of Multilateral Stability. See Thomson (1988) for a discussion of this and other notions of stability in economic contexts.

This chapter is based on Lensberg (1988).

7.2 Characterization of the Nash solution

We now present the announced characterization of the Nash solution.

> ***Proposition 7.1.*** *The Nash solution satisfies P.O, AN, S.INV, and M.STAB.*

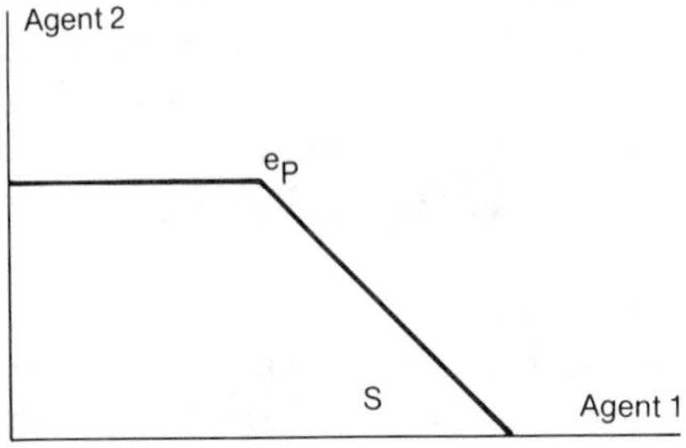

Figure 7.2. The problem S whose solution outcome is to be determined.

Proof. We only show that N satisfies $M.STAB$ since we have already seen in Chapter 2 that it satisfies $P.O$ and $S.INV$, whereas the proof that it satisfies AN is straightforward. Then let $P, Q \in \mathcal{P}$ with $P \subset Q$ and $T \in \Sigma^Q$ be given. Let $y \equiv N(T)$. By definition of N, $\prod_Q y_i \geqq \prod_Q x_i$ for all $x \in T$, and since T contains a strictly positive vector (one of the properties required of the elements of Σ^Q), it follows that $y > 0$. This fact and the definition of Σ^Q imply that $S \equiv t_P^y(T)$ is an element of Σ^P. Since $\prod_Q y_i \geqq \prod_Q x_i$ for all $x \in T$, then $\prod_Q y_i \geqq \prod_Q x_i$ for all x in any subset of T and in particular for all $x \in S$. Any such x has $x_i = y_i$ for all $i \in Q \backslash P$, so that after canceling out the positive quantity $\prod_{Q \backslash P} y_i$ from both sides of the last inequality, it follows that $\prod_P y_i \geqq \prod_P x_i$ for all $x \in S$, or equivalently that $y_P = N(S)$, the desired conclusion. Q.E.D.

Since $M.STAB$ implies $B.STAB$, a direct consequence of Proposition 7.1 is that the Nash solution satisfies $B.STAB$ also.

We show next that if a solution F satisfies the four axioms, it is the Nash solution. The proof is in two main steps, the first one of which consists in showing that F coincides with the Nash solution for two-person problems whereas the second step extends this conclusion to any number of agents.

First we will give the spirit of the proof of the first step by treating an explicit example of a two-person problem S and describing a natural attempt at showing that $F(S) = N(S)$. The main idea is to introduce a third agent and to construct a three-person problem T with the following properties: (i) Its solution outcome y can be determined by an application of $P.O$ and AN and (ii) slicing T through y by a plane parallel to $\mathbb{R}^P$ yields S.

If the attempt were successful, we could deduce from $B.STAB$ the solution outcome of S. We specified the example so as to illustrate that (ii) need not be satisfied, however, so that the argument will have to be

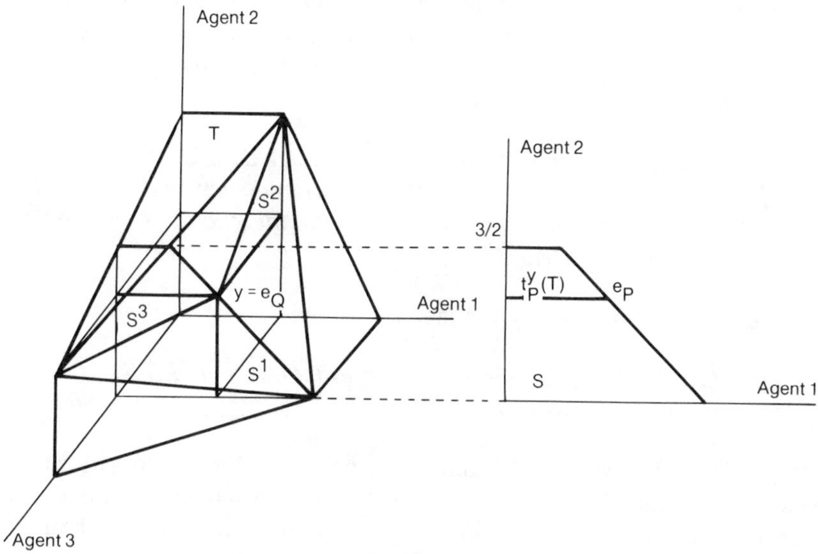

Figure 7.3. The construction of T.

modified. Typically, we will have to introduce more than one additional agent and generalize the construction of T accordingly.

The example S is depicted in Figure 7.2. Let $P \equiv \{1, 2\}$, and let $S \equiv \text{cch}\{2e_1, e_P\}$. The construction of T is illustrated in Figure 7.3.

Introduce agent 3, set $Q \equiv \{1, 2, 3\}$, define

$$S^1 \equiv \{x \in \mathbb{R}^Q_+ \mid x_P \in S \text{ and } x_3 = 1\},$$

S^2 and S^3 being obtained from S^1 by rotating the agents by one position and two positions, respectively, and finally define $T \equiv \text{cch}\{S^1, S^2, S^3\}$.

Since T is invariant under arbitrary rotations of the agents, *AN* implies that $F(T)$ should have equal coordinates. Also, T contains e_Q and is supported there by the hyperplane normal to e_Q. Therefore, by *P.O*, $F(T) = e_Q \equiv y$. If it were the case that $t^y_P(T) = S$, we could conclude, by *B.STAB*, that $F(S) = e_P = N(S)$. Unfortunately, $t^y_P(T) = \text{cch}\{2e_1, (\frac{1}{2}, \frac{3}{2})\} \neq S$. The reason why $t^y_P(T) \neq S$ is that S is very asymmetric; in fact, S could not be worse in that respect, which explains why the difference between S and $t^y_P(T)$ is large. [Note, in particular, that $a_2(t^y_P(T)) = \frac{3}{2} a_2(S) = \frac{3}{2}$.]

It is essentially the same construction that we will use in what follows except that more agents will be involved. We will show that the difference between S and $t^y_P(T)$ goes to zero as the number of additional agents increases. Moreover, if the boundary of S contains a nondegenerate line segment centered at its Nash solution outcome, then for some finite number of additional agents, S is just equal to $t_P^y(T)$. This motivates the following definition:

> ***Definition.*** *Given $P \in \mathcal{P}$ with $|P| = 2$, let $\Sigma_1^P \subset \Sigma^P$ be the family of problems S such that $N(S) = E(S)$ and such that the Pareto-optimal boundary of S contains a nondegenerate line segment centered at $N(S)$.*

The ground is now ready for the first lemma.

> ***Lemma 7.1.*** *If a solution F satisfies P.O, AN, and B.STAB, then for all $P \in \mathcal{P}$ with $|P| = 2$, $F = N$ on Σ_1^P.*

Proof. Let $P \in \mathcal{P}$ with $|P| = 2$ and $S \in \Sigma_1^P$ be given. Without loss of generality, assume that $P = \{1, 2\}$ and that $N(S) = e_P$. Then by definition of Σ_1^P, the segment $[(1+\delta, 1-\delta), (1-\delta, 1+\delta)]$ lies in the Pareto-optimal boundary of S for some $\delta > 0$. If $\delta = 1$, then S is a symmetric triangle, and the desired conclusion follows directly from $P.O$ and AN. Otherwise, let $n \in \mathbb{N}$ be such that $n \geqq 1 + 1/\delta$, let $Q \equiv \{1, \dots, n\}$ and $P' \equiv Q \backslash P$. Also, for each $j \in Q$, let $\gamma^j : Q \to Q$ be the permutation such that for each $i \in Q$, $\gamma^j(i) = i \hat{+} (j-1)$, where $\hat{+}$ denotes sum modulo n. For each $x \in \mathbb{R}_+^Q$, let $\gamma^j(x)$ be the vector $y \in \mathbb{R}_+^Q$ such that $y_k = x_i$ for all $i \in Q$, where $k \equiv \gamma^j(i)$. Let $S^1 \equiv \{x \in \mathbb{R}_+^Q \mid x_P \in S, x_{P'} = e_{P'}\}$; for all $j \in Q \backslash 1$, $S^j \equiv \gamma^j(S^1)$ and $T \equiv \text{cch}\{\bigcup_Q S^j\}$. Similarly, let $\bar{S} \equiv \{x \in \mathbb{R}_+^P \mid \sum_P x_i \leqq 2\}$, $\bar{S}^1 \equiv \{x \in \mathbb{R}_+^Q \mid x_P \in \bar{S}, x_{P'} = e_{P'}\}$; for all $j \in Q \backslash 1$, $\bar{S}^j \equiv \gamma^j(\bar{S}^1)$ and $\bar{T} \equiv \text{cch}\{S^1 \cup (\bigcup_{Q \backslash 1} \bar{S}^j)\}$. Note that $T \subset \bar{T}$ since $S \subset \bar{S}$. Let $y \equiv e_Q$.

Claim (i): $F(T) = y$. First, we show that $y \in \text{PO}(T)$. Indeed, since S is supported at e_P by the hyperplane $\{x \in \mathbb{R}^P \mid \sum_P x_i = 2\}$, it follows that for each $j \in Q$, S^j is supported at e_Q by the hyperplane $\{x \in \mathbb{R}^Q \mid \sum_Q x_i = n\}$, and therefore T, which is the convex and comprehensive hull of the S^j's, is also supported at e_Q by that hyperplane. Since all the members of Q play the same role in the construction of T, AN implies that $F(T)$ has equal coordinates. This fact, the Pareto-optimality of y, and $P.O$ imply that $F(T) = y$.

Claim (ii): $t_P^y(T) = S$. Since $S \subset t_P^y(T)$ by construction of T and since $T \subset \bar{T}$, it is sufficient to show that $t_P^y(\bar{T}) \subset S$, that is, that $x_P \in S$ for all $x \in \bar{T}$ with $x_{P'} = e_{P'}$. Let such an x be given. Then x is dominated by a convex combination of points $\{z^1, z^2, \dots, z^n\}$ where $z^1 \in \text{PO}(S^1)$ and $z^j \in \text{PO}(\bar{S}^j)$ for $j \in \{2, \dots, n\}$, that is, $x \leqq \sum_Q \alpha_j z^j$ for some α in the unit simplex of $\mathbb{R}^Q$. Since $z^1 \in S^1$, then $z_{P'}^1 = x_{P'} = e_{P'}$. For all $j \in Q \backslash 1$, since $z^j \in \text{PO}(\bar{S}^j)$, then $z^j = e_Q + \beta_j(e_{j\hat{+}1} - e_j)$ for some β_j in the interval $[-1, 1]$. The system $x \leqq \sum_Q \alpha_j z^j$ may then be written more explicitly as follows:

$$\begin{aligned}
&(1) \quad x_1 \leqq 1 + (z_1^1 - 1)\alpha_1 \qquad\qquad\qquad\qquad + \alpha_n\beta_n \\
&(2) \quad x_2 \leqq 1 + (z_2^1 - 1)\alpha_1 - \alpha_2\beta_2 \\
&(3) \quad 0 \leqq \qquad\qquad \alpha_2\beta_2 - \alpha_3\beta_3 \\
&\qquad \vdots \\
&(n) \quad 0 \leqq \qquad\qquad\qquad\qquad \alpha_{n-1}\beta_{n-1} - \alpha_n\beta_n
\end{aligned}$$

Let $c \equiv [1/(n-1)]\sum_{Q\setminus 1} \alpha_j\beta_j$. Since $\beta_j \in [-1, 1]$ for $j \in Q\setminus 1$ and since $\sum_{Q\setminus 1} \alpha_j = 1 - \alpha_1$ and $n \geqq 1 + 1/\delta$, we have that $c \in [-\delta(1-\alpha_1), \delta(1-\alpha_1)]$. From inequalities (3)-(n), it follows that $\alpha_2\beta_2 \geqq \alpha_3\beta_3 \geqq \cdots \geqq \alpha_n\beta_n$, which by definition of c implies that $\alpha_n\beta_n \leqq c$ and $-\alpha_2\beta_2 \leqq -c$. Therefore, by inequalities (1) and (2), $(x_1, x_2) = x_P \leqq \alpha_1 z_P^1 + (1-\alpha_1)e_P + (c, -c)$, which since $c \in [-\delta(1-\alpha_1), \delta(1-\alpha_1)]$ implies that $x_P \leqq \alpha_1 z_P^1 + (1-\alpha_1)v$, where v is a vector in the segment $[(1+\delta, 1-\delta), (1-\delta, 1+\delta)]$.

By hypothesis, this segment is a subset of S. But then x_P is dominated by a convex combination of z_P^1 and v, which both belong to S, so by convexity and comprehensiveness of S, $x_P \in S$ as well, which proves claim (ii).

That $F(S) = y_P = e_P$ now follows from (i), (ii), and *B.STAB*. Q.E.D.

Lemma 7.2. *If a solution F satisfies P.O, S.INV, and M.STAB and if for all $P \in \mathcal{P}$ with $|P| = 2$, $F = N$ on Σ_1^P, then $F = N$.*

Proof. Let $P \in \mathcal{P}$ and $S \in \Sigma^P$ be given. Because F satisfies *S.INV*, we can assume that S has been subjected to a positive linear transformation such that $N(S) = e_P$. (This is as in Nash's characterization of his solution; see Chapter 2.) Let k be an agent who is not a member of P, and define $Q \equiv P \cup \{k\}$ and $n \equiv |Q|$. We will construct a problem $T \in \Sigma^Q$ such that $F(T) = y \equiv e_Q$ and $t_P^y(T) = S$. It will follow from *M.STAB* that $F(S) = y_P = N(S)$. In Figure 7.4, T is depicted for $|P| = 2$. Let $S^1 \equiv S + \{e_k\}$, $H \equiv \{x \in \mathbb{R}_+^Q \mid \sum_Q x_i = n$ and $x_k \leqq 1\}$, and for $\epsilon > 0$, let C^ϵ be the cone with vertex $(1+\epsilon)e_k$ spanned by S^1. If ϵ is not too large, $ne_i \in$ rel.int. C^ϵ for all $i \in P$. Let such an ϵ be given. Finally, let $T \equiv C^\epsilon \cap \text{cch}\{H\}$.

Note that $T \in \Sigma^Q$ and that the open line segment $\sigma^i \equiv \,]ne_i, y[$ lies in rel.int. $H \cap \text{PO}(T)$ for all $i \in P$. Moreover, $t_P^y(T) = S$. It remains to show that $F(T) = y$. Two cases will be distinguished.

(i) $|P| = 2$. Let $z \equiv F(T)$. Suppose, by way of contradiction, that $z \neq y$. Since $\max\{x_k \mid x \in T\} = 1$, *P.O* implies that for some $j \in P$, $z_j > 1$. Assume first that $n > z_j$. Let i be the other member of P, and let $P' \equiv \{i, k\}$ and $S' \equiv t_{P'}^z(T)$. We show that $S' \in \Sigma_1^{P'}$. Indeed, since $n > z_j > 1$, there is a point

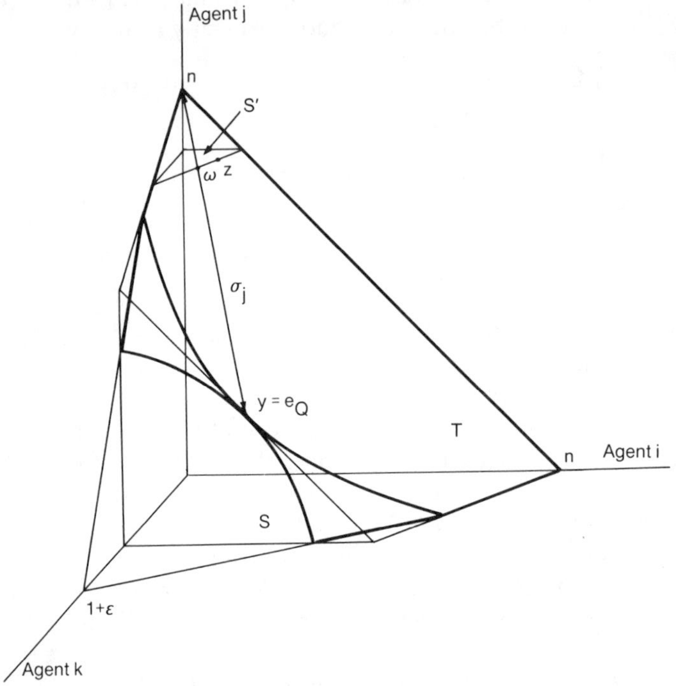

Figure 7.4. Lemma 7.2. $P=\{i,j\}$, $Q=\{i,j,k\}$, $P'=\{i,k\}$.

$w\in\sigma^j$ such that $(w_i,w_j)\in S'$. Since $\sigma^j\subset\text{rel.int.}\,H\cap\text{PO}(T)$, $\text{PO}(S')$ contains a nondegenerate line segment normal to e_P centered at w. Therefore, $S'\in\Sigma_1^{P'}$, and by the hypothesis of the lemma, $F(S')=N(S')$, a point with equal ith and kth coordinates. By *B.STAB*, $z_i=z_k$. Thus $z\in\sigma^j$ and $z_k<1$. By a similar argument as the one used to prove that $S'\in\Sigma_1^{P'}$, we can prove that $t_P^z(T)\in\Sigma_1^P$, which implies similarly that $z_i=z_j$. Hence $z_i=z_j=z_k<1$, in contradiction with *P.O*.

It would be in direct contradiction with *B.STAB* and the hypothesis of the lemma to suppose that $z_j=n$, since then $t_P^z(T)$ would be a symmetric triangle.

(ii) $|P|>2$. Observe first that by construction, T is such that for all $i\in P$ and for all $z\in T$, the point x defined by $x_k=0$, $x_i=z_i+z_k$, and $x_j=z_j$ for all $j\in Q\backslash\{i,k\}$ is also in T.

Let $z\equiv F(T)$. We show that $z_i\geqq z_k$ for all $i\in P$. To see this, let $i\in P$ be given and let $S'\equiv t_{P'}^z(T)$, where $P'\equiv\{i,k\}$. By convexity of S' and the previous paragraph, it follows that the segment $\sigma\equiv[(z_i,z_k),(z_i+z_k,0)]$

is a subset of S'. By $B.STAB$ and (i), $F(S') = N(S') = (z_i, z_k)$. Consequently, given any $(x_i, x_k) \in \sigma$, $z_i z_k \geqq x_i x_k$. Thus for all $\alpha \in [0,1]$ it follows that $z_i z_k \geqq (\alpha z_i + (1-\alpha)(z_i + z_k)) \cdot (\alpha z_k + (1-\alpha)0)$, that is, $(1-\alpha) z_i \geqq \alpha(1-\alpha) z_k$. By taking α arbitrarily close to 1, it follows that $z_i \geqq z_k$.

Since $z_i \geqq z_k$ for all $i \in P$, it follows from $P.O$ that

$$z \in A \equiv \text{co}\{e_Q, (ne_i)_{i \in P}\},$$

which is a subset of $H \cap \text{PO}(T)$. Moreover, $z \in B_N(T)$ by $B.STAB$ and part (i) of the proof. To show that $z = y$, suppose, by way of contradiction, that $z \neq y$. Then $z_k < 1$ since $z \in A$. This means that $z \in \text{rel.int.}\, H \cap \text{PO}(T)$, which implies that $z \in B_N(\bar{T})$ as well, where $\bar{T} \equiv \text{cch}\{H\}$. But $B_N(\bar{T}) = \{y\}$, and so $z = y$ after all. Since $t_P^y(T) = S$, $M.STAB$ implies that $F(S) = y_P = N(S)$. Q.E.D.

Collecting the results of Proposition 7.1 and Lemmas 7.1 and 7.2, the announced characterization of the Nash solution results.

Theorem 7.1. *A solution satisfies P.O, AN, S.INV, and M.STAB if and only if it is the Nash solution.*

The relationship of this result with the result of Harsanyi's mentioned earlier can now be clarified. Harsanyi established part (ii) of Lemma 7.2. The improvement of our theorem over Harsanyi's is Lemma 7.1, which shows that one need not require that two-person problems be solved by the Nash solution, an unnatural assumption. Instead, by imposing the axioms used by Nash (with the exception of the independence axiom, which is replaced by our stability condition), we *show* that all problems, including those involving two persons only, have to be solved by the Nash solution.

7.3 Variants

7.3.1 Alternative domains

(i) Removing the requirement that the number of potential agents be infinite: In the proofs of Lemmas 7.1 and 7.2, which led to Theorem 7.1, we used the assumption that the number of potential agents is infinite. Can this assumption be dispensed with? We show here that the answer is negative by constructing a solution that satisfies the four axioms of Theorem 7.1 but differs from the Nash solution. Then we show how a fifth axiom of continuity could be used instead.

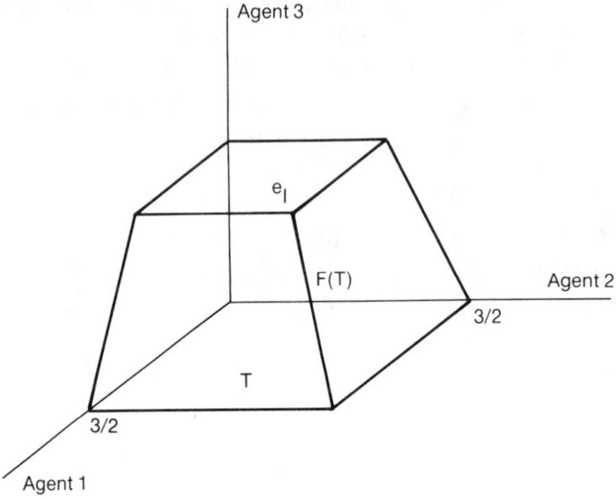

Figure 7.5. Proposition 7.2. Construction of F for $I=\{1,2,3\}$.

From here on suppose that $I=\{1,\ldots,n\}$.

Proposition 7.2. *Assume $|I|$ is finite. The Nash solution is not the only one to satisfy P.O, AN, S.INV, and M.STAB.*

Proof. If $|I|\leqq 2$, then any solution satisfying *P.O* (e.g., the Kalai–Smorodinsky solution) also satisfies *M.STAB*. The proof for $|I|\geqq 3$ is by way of an example, illustrated in Figure 7.5 for the case $I=\{1,2,3\}$. Let $P\equiv\{1,2\}$ and $\bar{T}\in\Sigma^I$ be defined by $\bar{T}\equiv \mathrm{cch}\{e_I, z\}$ where $z\equiv\frac{3}{2}e_P$. Set $F(\bar{T})\equiv(e_I+z)/2$. For any $T\in\Sigma^I$ that can be obtained from $\bar{T}$ by a relabeling of the agents and/or a positive linear transformation, define $F(\bar{T})$ by an application of *AN* or *S.INV*. For any other $T\in\Sigma^I$, set $F(T)=N(T)$. For any $Q\in\mathcal{P}$ with $Q\neq I$ and any $S\in\Sigma^Q$, set $F(S)=N(S)$.

It is straightforward to verify that the point $(e_I+z)/2$ is N multilaterally stable for $\bar{T}$. However, $F\neq N$ since $F(\bar{T})\neq e_I=N(\bar{T})$. The proof that F satisfies all the desired axioms is omitted. Q.E.D.

Note that the solution so constructed is not continuous. It is a consequence of the next lemma that the addition of *CONT* to the four axioms of Theorem 7.1 yields a characterization of the Nash solution provided $|I|\geqq 3$. The proof of that lemma involves the construction of a problem that bears a close resemblance to that used in the proof of Lemma 7.2.

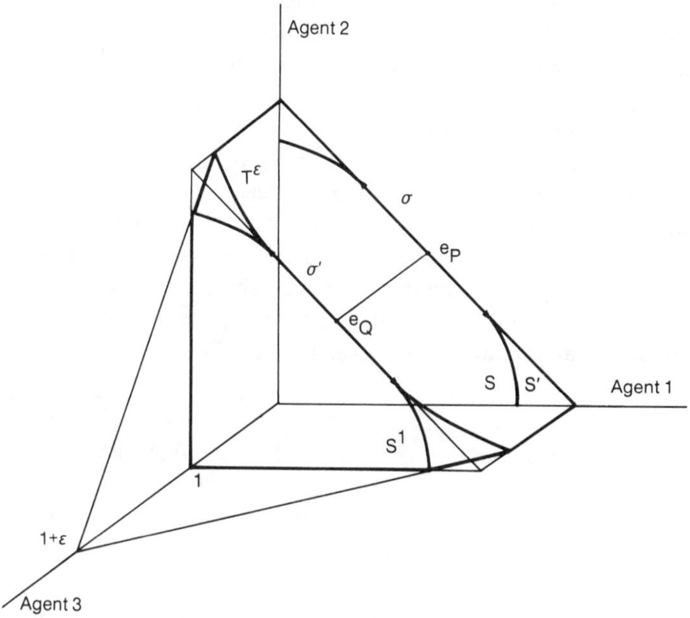

Figure 7.6. Lemma 7.3.

Lemma 7.3. *Assume $|I| \geqq 3$. If a solution F satisfies P.O, AN, S.INV, CONT, and B.STAB, then for all $P \in \mathcal{P}$ with $|P|=2$, $F=N$ on Σ^P.*

Proof. Let $P \in \mathcal{P}$ with $|P|=2$ and $S \in \Sigma^P$ be given (see Figure 7.6). Because F satisfies *S.INV*, we can assume that S has been subjected to a positive linear transformation such that $N(S)=y \equiv e_P$. We have to show that $y=F(S)$. To do this, first assume that $S \in \Sigma_1^P$.

Let σ be the nondegenerate segment centered at $N(S)$, let i and j denote the two members of P, and let $S' \equiv \text{cch}\{2e_i, 2e_j\}$. By *P.O* and *AN*, $F(S')=y$.

Now introduce an agent k who is not a member of P and define $Q \equiv \{i,j,k\}$ and $S^1 \equiv S+\{e_k\}$. For $\epsilon>0$, let C^ϵ be the cone with vertex $(1+\epsilon)e_k$ spanned by S^1. Set

$$T^\epsilon \equiv C^\epsilon \cap \{x \in \mathbb{R}_+^Q \mid x_P \in S'\}, \qquad T^0 \equiv \lim_{\epsilon \to 0} T^\epsilon = \text{cch}\{S'+\{e_k\}\},$$

and $\sigma^1 \equiv \sigma + \{e_k\}$, and note that for all $\epsilon \geqq 0$, $\sigma^1 \subset \text{PO}(T^\epsilon)$ and $T^\epsilon \in \Sigma^Q$.

Let now $x \equiv F(T^0)$. We will show that $z = e_Q$. Indeed, note that whatever z is, it follows from the construction of T^0 that $t_P^z(T^0) = S'$. By *B.STAB*, $z_P = y = e_P$. Since e_Q is the only point of $\mathrm{PO}(T^0)$ projecting on $\mathbb{R}_+^P$ at e_P, *P.O* implies that $z = e_Q$.

Consider now $z^\epsilon \equiv F(T^\epsilon)$ as $\epsilon \to 0$. By *CONT*, the path traced out by z^ϵ is continuous. It starts at z for $\epsilon = 0$, and if it moves away from z at all, it has to be along the segment σ^1 because of *P.O*. Let $\bar{\epsilon} > 0$ be such that $z^\epsilon \in \sigma^1$ for all $\epsilon \in [0, \bar{\epsilon}]$. Note that for all $\epsilon \in]0, \bar{\epsilon}]$, $S^\epsilon \equiv t_P^{z^\epsilon}(T^\epsilon) = S$, and therefore, by *B.STAB*, $F(S^\epsilon)$ is constant for all $\epsilon \in]0, \bar{\epsilon}]$ and equal to $F(S^0) = e_P$. This is the desired conclusion.

Finally, if $S \notin \Sigma_1^P$, note that S can be approximated by a sequence of elements from Σ_1^P, and again, conclude by *CONT*. Q.E.D.

Lemma 7.4. *Assume $|I| \geqq 3$. If a solution F satisfies P.O, CONT, and B.STAB and if $F = N$ on Σ^P for all $P \in \mathcal{P}$ with $|P| = 2$, then $F = N$.*

Proof. We have to show that for all $Q \in \mathcal{P}$, F coincides with N on Σ^Q. If $|Q| = 1$ this follows from *P.O*, and if $|Q| = 2$ it is true by hypothesis. Suppose that $|Q| \geqq 3$ and let Σ_{dif}^Q be the subset of Σ^Q of problems admitting of a unique hyperplane of support at all points in the relative interior of their weakly Pareto-optimal boundary. Let $\tilde{\Sigma}_{\text{dif}}^Q \equiv \tilde{\Sigma}^Q \cap \Sigma_{\text{dif}}^Q$.

Let $T \in \tilde{\Sigma}_{\text{dif}}^Q$ be given and $y \equiv F(T)$. We prove that $y > 0$. Otherwise, for some $i \in Q$, $y_i = 0$. Then by *P.O* and the fact that $T \in \Sigma^Q$, there exists $j \in Q$ such that $y_j > 0$. Let $P \equiv \{i, j\}$ and $S \equiv t_P^y(T)$. Because S contains a semipositive vector and $T \in \tilde{\Sigma}^Q$, then $S \in \tilde{\Sigma}^P$. Also, $|P| = 2$, so that by hypothesis, $F(S) = N(S) > 0$, in contradiction with *B.STAB* and the fact that $y_i = 0$.

Since $y > 0$ and $T \in \Sigma_{\text{dif}}^Q$, there is a unique hyperplane H_F supporting T at y. Let $G \equiv \{x \in \mathbb{R}_+^Q \mid \prod_Q x_i \geqq \prod_Q y_i\}$ and H_N be the unique hyperplane supporting G at y. That $y = N(T)$ will follow if we can show that $H_F = H_N$, since then H_F separates T and int. G, or equivalently, y maximizes $\prod_Q x_i$ on T.

Suppose, by way of contradiction, that $H_F \neq H_N$. Then for some $P \subset Q$ with $|P| = 2$, $t_P^y(H_F) \neq t_P^y(H_N)$. Since $T \in \Sigma_{\text{dif}}^Q$ and $S \in \tilde{\Sigma}^P$, then in fact $S \in \tilde{\Sigma}_{\text{dif}}^P$ and $t_P^y(H_F)$ is the only line of support of S at y_P. Finally, since $F = N$ on Σ^P by hypothesis, *B.STAB* requires that $y_P = N(S)$, which in turn implies that S is supported at y_P by $t_P^y(H_N)$, a contradiction. Hence, $H_F = H_N$ and $y = N(T)$. The proof of the lemma is completed by observing that any element of Σ^Q can be approximated by a sequence of elements of $\tilde{\Sigma}_{\text{dif}}^Q$ and by applying *CONT*. Q.E.D.

The next theorem is a consequence of Proposition 7.1, Lemmas 7.3 and 7.4, and the fact that the Nash solution satisfies *CONT*.

> ***Theorem 7.2.*** *Assume $|I| \geqq 3$. A solution satisfies P.O, AN, S.INV, CONT, and B.STAB if and only if it is the Nash solution.*

A comparison of Theorems 7.1 and 7.2 shows that the assumption of an infinite number of potential agents serves the same purpose as a continuity requirement. Theorem 7.1 requires that $|I|$ be infinite but does not involve *CONT,* whereas it is the opposite with Theorem 7.2. Also, *B.STAB* is used in Theorem 7.2, but *M.STAB* is used in Theorem 7.1.

A further result on this issue appears in Thomson (1985b).

(ii) Removing the comprehensiveness requirement: The question of whether the Nash solution is then uniquely characterized by the list of axioms in Theorem 7.1 is open. It can, however, be shown that the Nash solution is the only *continuous* solution to satisfy that list of axioms. Observe that the Nash solution yields Pareto-optimal outcomes even when comprehensiveness is not assumed, in favorable contrast with both the Kalai–Smorodinsky and the Egalitarian solutions.

(iii) Removing the convexity requirement: Without convexity, the Nash solution is not well defined because there may be several maximizers of the product $\prod_P x_i$ over $x \in S$. Solution *correspondences* may then be of interest. Since allowing for multiplicities of *solution outcomes* often leads to multiplicities of *solutions* in situations where a requirement of single-valuedness leads to a unique solution, it is natural to search for *minimal* multivalued solution correspondences when single-valuedness is not possible. The first task in such a search is to reformulate the axioms so that they can be applicable to solution correspondences. The question can then be asked whether the Nash solution correspondence is the minimal solution correspondence to satisfy the appropriately rewritten axioms of Theorem 7.1 on the wider domain obtained from Σ by dropping the convexity requirement. This question is open.

7.3.2 Removing the axioms one at a time

This exercise will be particularly fruitful in the case of Pareto-optimality and Anonymity.

(i) Removing the axiom of Pareto-optimality: The removal of Pareto-optimality altogether leads to the study of a one-parameter family

of multivalued solutions of great interest, both in themselves and with respect to the interpretation and understanding of the Nash solution, which is their limit. This study is the object of the next chapter.

Here we show that a considerable weakening of Pareto-optimality still permits a characterization of the Nash solution. This new axiom simply says that one-person problems should be solved optimally. This in fact is not an axiom of *collective* rationality, in contrast with Pareto-optimality.

Individual Optimality (I.O): For all $P \in \mathcal{P}$ with $|P| = 1$, for all $S \in \Sigma^P$, $F(S) = \max\{x \mid x \in S\}$.

In conjunction with *M.STAB,* this says that an outcome will be considered undesirable if it is possible to increase some agent's utility without hurting the other agents. This is precisely the requirement of Pareto-optimality.

> ***Lemma 7.5.*** *If a solution satisfies I.O and M.STAB, then it satisfies P.O.*

The proof is straightforward and is omitted.

It is clear why *M.STAB* is needed here. *B.STAB* says nothing about one-person subproblems. Then we have

> ***Theorem 7.3.*** *A solution satisfies I.O, AN, S.INV, and M.STAB if and only if it is the Nash solution.*

Proof. The proof is a straightforward adaptation of that of Theorem 7.1 together with Lemma 7.5. Q.E.D.

(ii) Removing the axiom of Anonymity: First note that *AN* may be replaced in Theorem 7.2 by the weaker axiom of Symmetry. Indeed, *AN* was applied in the proof of Lemma 7.3 to a symmetric triangle only.

Moreover, *AN* is a consequence of *SY* together with two of the other axioms that are used.

> ***Proposition 7.3.*** *If a solution satisfies SY, B.STAB, and CONT, then it satisfies AN.*

Proof. Anonymity says that a solution is invariant under arbitrary renaming of the agents. This property will be shown to hold when only one agent is renamed. The desired conclusion will then follow from an iteration of the argument.

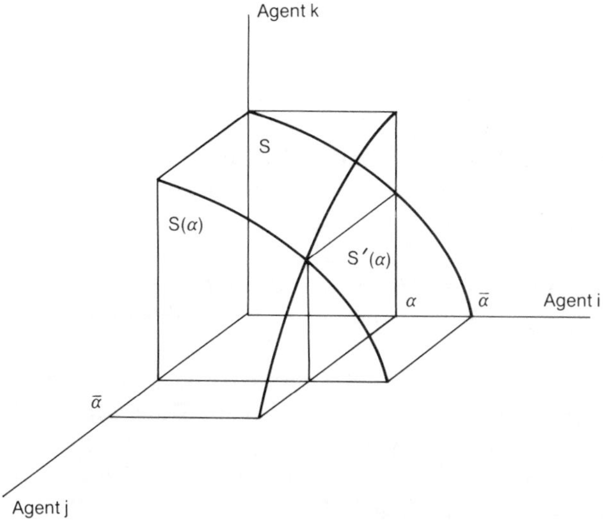

Figure 7.7. Proposition 7.3. $P=\{i,k\}$, $P'=\{j,k\}$, $Q=\{i,j,k\}$.

Let $P\in\mathcal{P}$, $i\in P$, and $j\in I\backslash P$ be given (see Figure 7.7). Let P' be obtained from P by replacing i by j and $Q\equiv P\cup P'$. Also, given $S\in\Sigma^P$, let $S'\in\Sigma^{P'}$ be such that

$$S'=\{x\in\mathbb{R}_+^{P'}\mid \exists y\in S \text{ with } y_i=x_j \text{ and } \forall k\in P\backslash i,\ y_k=x_k\}.$$

We must show that $F_j(S')=F_i(S)$ and that $F_k(S')=F_k(S)$ for all $k\in P\cap P'$.

To this end, let $\bar{\alpha}\equiv a_i(S)$ and for each $\alpha\in[0,\bar{\alpha}]$, define $S(\alpha)\equiv\{x\in\mathbb{R}_+^Q\mid x_P\in S,\ x_j=\alpha\}$, $S'(\alpha)\equiv\{x\in\mathbb{R}_+^Q\mid x_{P'}\in S',\ x_i=\alpha\}$, and finally $T(\alpha)\equiv \text{cch}\{S(\alpha),S'(\alpha)\}$.

Since $T(\alpha)$ is invariant under exchanges of i and j, it follows that for all $x\in T(\alpha)$, $t^x_{\{i,j\}}(T(\alpha))$ is a symmetric element of $\Sigma^{\{i,j\}}$. Therefore, by *SY* and *B.STAB*, $F_i(T(\alpha))=F_j(T(\alpha))\equiv d(\alpha)$. Since for all $\alpha\in[0,\bar{\alpha}]$, $T(\alpha)\subset\{x\in\mathbb{R}_+^Q\mid\forall k\in\{i,j\},\ 0\leqq x_k\leqq\bar{\alpha}\}$, it follows that d is a function from $[0,\alpha]$ to itself. It is continuous by *CONT* and therefore for some $\hat{\alpha}\in[0,\bar{\alpha}]$, $d(\hat{\alpha})=\hat{\alpha}$. Let $y\equiv F(T(\hat{\alpha}))$. Then clearly $t^y_P(T(\hat{\alpha}))=S(\hat{\alpha})$ and $t^y_{P'}(T(\hat{\alpha}))=S'(\hat{\alpha})$. Since $S(\hat{\alpha})$ and $S'(\hat{\alpha})$ are copies of S and S', we conclude by *B.STAB* that for all $k\in P\cap P'$,

$$\begin{aligned}F_k(S)&=F_k(S(\hat{\alpha}))=F_k(t^y_P(T(\hat{\alpha})))=F_k(T(\hat{\alpha}))=F_k(t^y_{P'}((T(\hat{\alpha})))\\&=F_k(S'(\hat{\alpha}))=F_k(S').\end{aligned}$$

Since $F_i(T(\hat{\alpha}))=F_j(T(\hat{\alpha}))$, *B.STAB* also implies that $F_i(S)=F_j(S')$.

Q.E.D.

If AN is removed altogether, the whole family of *asymmetric Nash solutions* becomes admissible. This family is defined as follows: Let $\alpha = \{\alpha_i \mid i \in I\}$ be a list of positive real numbers, and let $\mathcal{A}$ be the set of all such α's. Then given $\alpha \in \mathcal{A}$, $P \in \mathcal{P}$, and $S \in \Sigma^P$, let $N^\alpha(S)$ be the unique maximizer of the product $\prod_P x_i^{\alpha_i}$ over S. Note that the Nash solution is obtained by choosing α such that $\alpha_i = \alpha_j$ for all $i, j \in I$. It is natural to ask whether the solutions in this family are the only ones to satisfy *P.O*, *S.INV*, and *M.STAB*. The next result shows the answer to be negative.

Proposition 7.4. *There exists a solution satisfying P.O, S.INV, and M.STAB that is not an asymmetric Nash solution.*

Proof. Let $\gtrsim$ be a lexicographic ordering of $\mathbb{R}^I$ and for each $P \in \mathcal{P}$, let $\gtrsim_P$ be the restriction of $\gtrsim$ to $\mathbb{R}^P$. For each $P \in \mathcal{P}$ and for each $S \in \Sigma^P$, define $F(S)$ to be the unique maximizer of $\gtrsim_P$ over S. It is clear that F is not an asymmetric Nash solution and that it satisfies *P.O* and *S.INV*. To see that it satisfies *M.STAB*, observe that for all $P, Q \in \mathcal{P}$ with $P \subset Q$, the restriction of $\gtrsim_Q$ to any hyperplane parallel to $\mathbb{R}^P$ coincides with $\gtrsim_P$. Thus, if x maximizes $\gtrsim_Q$ over $T \in \Sigma^Q$, then x_P maximizes $\gtrsim_P$ over $t_P^x(T)$ also, which is the requirement of *M.STAB*. Q.E.D.

Observe that the "lexicographic" solution F is not continuous. In fact, by adding *CONT* to the list of axioms in Proposition 7.3, a complete characterization of the family of asymmetric Nash solutions results.

Theorem 7.4. *Assume* $|I| \geqq 3$. *A solution F satisfies P.O, S.INV, CONT, and B.STAB if and only if* $F = N^\alpha$ *for some* $\alpha \in \mathcal{A}$.

A proof of Theorem 7.4 can be given along the lines of that of Theorem 7.2. It is omitted here, as Theorem 7.4 will turn out to be a special case of a more general result that will be presented in Chapter 11.

(iii) Removing the axiom of Scale Invariance: Other solutions can then be found. In particular, the Leximin solution, which violates *S.INV*, can be characterized by a list of axioms closely related to that used in Theorem 7.1, with *S.INV* being replaced by Individual Monotonicity. This result is presented in Chapter 9.

(iv) Removing the axiom of Stability: Since this axiom is the only one to relate solution outcomes across cardinalities, the components of F can now be selected independently for P's of different cardinalities. This is as in Chapters 3 and 4, and there is no need to elaborate.

CHAPTER 8

Stability without Pareto-Optimality

8.1 Introduction

Our point of departure here is the characterization of the Nash solution offered in the previous chapter. Our objective is to elucidate the role played by Pareto-Optimality in deriving it.

It may be worthwhile recalling (see Chapter 2) that the usual characterization of the Nash solution for a fixed number of agents involves the following axioms: pareto-optimality, symmetry, scale invariance, and independence of irrelevant alternatives. However, as shown by Roth (1977a), pareto-optimality can be replaced by strong individual rationality. Indeed, this axiom together with scale invariance and independence of irrelevant alternatives implies pareto-optimality. Since the satisfaction of strong individual rationality seems to require much less cooperation than the satisfaction of pareto-optimality (although obviously pareto-optimality does not logically imply strong individual rationality), Roth's result has considerable appeal. The same question will be addressed here, whether Pareto-Optimality can be replaced by Strong Individual Rationality in the characterization of the Nash solution of Chapter 7.

The answer will also turn out to be positive.

However, this conclusion will be derived in a considerably more roundabout way than Roth's result.

This chapter is based on Lensberg and Thomson (1988).

8.2 The results

We start with a short summary of our results, for which we will need the following important definition: Given $P \in \mathcal{P}$, $i \in P$, $x \in \mathbb{R}^P$, and $\lambda \in]0,1]$, the ith *λ-extension of* x, denoted $\chi^i(\lambda, x)$, is the point $y \in \mathbb{R}^P$ such that $x_i = \lambda y_i$ and $x_j = y_j$ for all $j \in P$ with $j \neq i$.

Recall that *HOM* is obtained from *S.INV* by requiring that all utilities be subjected to the same transformation. (It states invariance of the solution under *radial* contractions or expansions.)

First, we show that if a solution satisfies *AN, HOM,* and *B.STAB,* then it satisfies *P.O,* or it is the disagreement solution, or there exists $\lambda \in]0,1[$

such that for all $P \in \mathcal{P}$ and for all $S \in \Sigma^P$, if x is the solution outcome of S, then for all $i \in P$, the $|P|$ λ-*extensions of* x all belong to the weak Pareto-optimal boundary of S.

Given $S \in \Sigma^P$ and $\lambda \in]0,1[$, let then $N^\lambda(S)$ be the *set* of points whose $|P|$ λ-extensions all belong to WPO(S). If $|P|=2$, $N^\lambda(S)$ is always a singleton so that the necessary conditions lead to well-defined two-person component solutions. As λ increases from 0 to 1, the path of this point is a continuous curve that has the origin and the Nash solution outcome of S as endpoints. Therefore, this one-parameter family of *Nashlike solutions* N^λ may be interpreted as modeling a progressive negotiation process leading to the Nash solution.

If $|P| \geqq 3$, it remains true that $N^\lambda(S) \neq \emptyset$ for all $S \in \Sigma^P$. However, complications arise. Indeed, for every $\lambda \in]0,1[$ there exist some problems S for which $N^\lambda(S)$ is not a singleton. Are there single-valued selections from the *correspondence* N^λ that satisfy *CONT*? The answer is negative. This is somewhat disappointing since continuity certainly is a desirable property. However, the property that is of most interest to us here is *M.STAB*. Are there single-valued selections that satisfy *M.STAB*? Again, the answer is negative. This dashes our hopes of finding solutions satisfying *AN, HOM,* and *M.STAB*.

But this negative result is what gives us our characterization of the Nash solution. Indeed, the only values of λ left are then $\lambda=0$ and $\lambda=1$. If $\lambda=0$, the disagreement solution obtains. If $\lambda=1$, *P.O* holds and then the result of Chapter 7 becomes applicable, when *HOM* is strengthened to *S.INV,* leading to the Nash solution. Again, by requiring that at least one problem be solved at a point different from the origin, only the Nash solution remains admissible.

It will be convenient to extend the definition of the family N^λ of Nashlike solution correspondences to include the boundary cases $\lambda=0$ and $\lambda=1$. Formally, for all $P \in \mathcal{P}$ and all $S \in \Sigma^P$, we define

$$N^\lambda(S) \equiv \begin{cases} \{0\} & \text{if } \lambda=0, \\ \{x \in S \mid \forall i \in P, \chi^i(\lambda,x) \in \mathrm{WPO}(S)\} & \text{if } \lambda \in]0,1[, \\ \mathrm{PO}(S) & \text{if } \lambda=1. \end{cases}$$

We are now ready to present the details of the proof. Recall that our objective is to characterize all solutions satisfying *AN, S.INV,* and *M.STAB,* but we will be able to derive workable necessary conditions by using *HOM* instead of *S.INV* and *B.STAB* instead of *M.STAB*. We develop the necessary conditions first. Let F be a solution satisfying *AN, HOM,* and *B.STAB*. Our first result is based only on the first two of these axioms.

Lemma 8.1. *There exists* $\lambda \in [0,1]$ *such that for all* $P \in \mathcal{P}$ *with* $|P|=2$ *and all* $\alpha \in \mathbb{R}_{++}$, $F(\mathrm{cch}\{\alpha e_P\}) = \lambda \alpha e_P$.

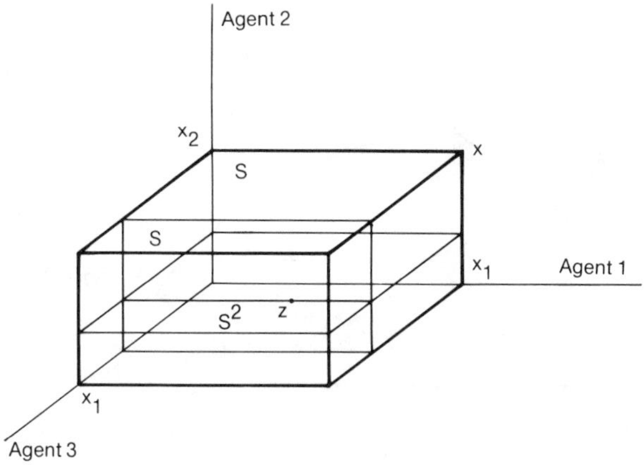

Figure 8.1. Lemma 8.2.

Proof. Let $P \equiv \{1,2\}$ and $S \equiv \text{cch}\{e_P\}$. By *SY* (implied by *AN*), it follows that $F(S) = \lambda e_P$ for some $\lambda \in [0,1]$. By *HOM,* for all $\alpha \in \mathbb{R}_{++}$, $F(\alpha S) = \lambda \alpha e_P$. The proof concludes by appealing to *AN*. Q.E.D.

Lemma 8.2. *For all $P \in \mathcal{P}$ with $|P| = 2$ and for all $x \in \mathbb{R}^P_{++}$, $F(\text{cch}\{x\}) = \lambda x$, where λ is the parameter identified in Lemma 8.1.*

Proof. The proof is illustrated in Figure 8.1. Let $P \equiv \{1,2\}$ and $S \equiv \text{cch}\{x\}$ where $x \in \mathbb{R}^P_{++}$. We introduce agent 3, and we set $Q \equiv \{1,2,3\}$ and $T \equiv \text{cch}\{(x_1, x_2, x_1)\}$. Note that $T \in \Sigma^Q$. Let $z \equiv F(T)$, $P^2 \equiv \{1,3\}$, and $S^2 \equiv t^z_{P^2}(T)$. We have $S^2 = \text{cch}\{x_1 e_{P^2}\}$. By Lemma 8.1, $F(S^2) = \lambda(x_1, x_1)$. Since $z_{P^2} = F(S^2)$ by *B.STAB,* we conclude that $z_1 = z_3 = \lambda x_1$. Also, $S = t^z_P(T)$, and by *B.STAB* again, we conclude that $z_1 = F_1(S) = \lambda x_1$.

Next, let $T \equiv \text{cch}\{(x_1, x_2, x_2)\}$. Note that $T \in \Sigma^Q$. Let $z \equiv F(T)$. Set $P^1 \equiv \{2,3\}$ and $S^1 \equiv t^z_{P^1}(T)$. We have $S^1 = \text{cch}\{x_2 e_{P^1}\}$. By Lemma 8.1, $F(S^1) = \lambda(x_2, x_2)$. A repetition of the preceding argument yields $z_2 = F_2(S) = \lambda x_2$.

Altogether, we have shown that $F(S) = \lambda(x_1, x_2) = \lambda x$. Q.E.D.

Proposition 8.1. *For all $P \in \mathcal{P}$ and for all $S \in \Sigma^P$, $F(S) \in N^\lambda(S)$, where λ is the parameter identified in Lemma 8.1.*

Proof. We first show that the proposition holds for all $P \in \mathcal{P}$ with $|P| = 2$. The proof is illustrated in Figure 8.2. Let $P \equiv \{1,2\}$ and $S \in \Sigma^P$ be given. Let $Q \equiv \{1,2,3\}$ and $T \in \Sigma^Q$ be defined by $T \equiv \text{cch}\{S + \{ce_3\}\}$, where c is

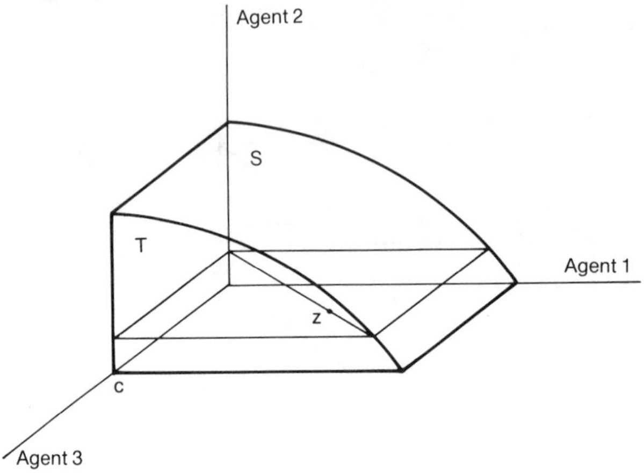

Figure 8.2. Proposition 8.1.

some arbitrary positive number. Let $z \equiv F(T)$ and $P^2 \equiv \{1,3\}$. Note that $S^2 \equiv t^z_{P^2}(T)$ is a (possibly degenerate) rectangle; that is, there exists $\alpha \geqq 0$ such that $S^2 = \text{cch}\{(\alpha, c)\}$.

Suppose first that $\lambda < 1$. We claim that $\alpha > 0$. Indeed, if $\alpha = 0$, we have $z_2 = a_2(S) = a_2(T)$. Then, let $P^1 \equiv \{2,3\}$ and observe that

$$S^1 \equiv t^z_{P^1}(T) = \text{cch}\{(a_2(S), c)\} \in \Sigma^{P^1}.$$

By Lemma 8.2, $F(S^1) = \lambda(a_2(S), c)$, and by *B.STAB*, $F(S^1) = z_{P^1}$. Therefore, $F_2(S^1) = z_2 = \lambda a_2(S)$. Since $\lambda < 1$, we obtain a contradiction with the previous equality $z_2 = a_2(S)$.

Since $\alpha > 0$, then S^2 is a nondegenerate rectangle, and it follows by Lemma 8.2 that $F(S^2) = \lambda(\alpha, c)$. Since $t^z_P(T) = S$, *B.STAB* then implies that $F_1(t^z_P(T)) = F_1(S) = \lambda\alpha$.

The same reasoning, applied to subproblems parallel to $\mathbb{R}^{P^2}$, yields that $F_2(S) = \lambda\beta$ for some $\beta > 0$ such that $t^z_{P^2}(T) = \text{cch}\{(\beta, c)\}$. Altogether, we have shown that if $x = F(S)$ then either $x = 0$ if $\lambda = 0$, or $\chi^1(\lambda, x) \in$ WPO(S) and $\chi^2(\lambda, x) \in$ WPO(S) if $\lambda \in]0,1[$. If $\lambda = 1$, it follows by a similar argument that F satisfies *P.O* on Σ^P whenever $|P| = 2$. Consequently, the proposition holds for all $P \in \mathcal{P}$ with $|P| = 2$.

Next, let $Q \in \mathcal{P}$ with $|Q| \geqq 3$ and let $T \in \Sigma^Q$ be given. If $\lambda \in [0,1[$, it follows by *B.STAB* and the first part of the proof that $F(T) \in N^\lambda(T)$. If $\lambda = 1$, suppose by way of contradiction that $y \equiv F(T) \notin N^\lambda(T) = \text{PO}(T)$. Because T contains a strictly positive vector, there exist $P \equiv \{i, j\} \subset Q$ and $x \in T$ such that $x \geqq y$, $x_i > y_i$, and $x_P > 0$. Since $x_P > 0$, the problem $S \equiv t^y_P(T)$ is well defined, which by *B.STAB* implies that $F(S) = F_P(T) = y_P$.

Since $|P|=2$, then $F(S)\in PO(S)$, in contradiction with the fact that $x_P \geq y_P$. Q.E.D.

Having thus established a necessary condition for a solution F to satisfy *AN, HOM,* and *B.STAB,* we must show next that F is well defined, that is, that $F(S)$ exists and is unique for all S. We begin with the question of existence. According to Proposition 8.1, we must show that the correspondence N^λ is nonempty valued for all λ.

To this end, we introduce the following notation and terminology. Given $P\in\mathcal{P}$ and $S\in\Sigma^P$, let $v^S\colon \mathbb{R}^P_+\to\mathbb{R}$ be a continuous and strictly increasing $[x>x' \Rightarrow v^S(x)>v^S(x')]$ function such that $v^S(x)\leqq 0$ if and only if $x\in S$. [As an example, set $v^S(0)\equiv -1$, $v^S(x)\equiv 0$ if $x\in WPO(S)$ and v^S linear on each ray.] Finally, given $\lambda\in\,]0,1[$, let $V^{S,\lambda}\colon S\to\mathbb{R}^P$ be defined by $V_i^{S,\lambda}(x)\equiv v^S(x^i(\lambda,x))$ for each $i\in P$.

Note that $V^{S,\lambda}$ defines a continuous *vector field* on S such that $V^{S,\lambda}(x)=0$ if and only if $x\in N^\lambda(S)$. Say that a vector field V on S *points out at* $x\in\partial S$ if the point $x+V(x)$ is on or above some hyperplane of support of S at x. If V points out at every $x\in\partial S$, say that *V points out on ∂S*. Clearly, $V^{S,\lambda}$ points out on ∂S. Finally, for each $P\in\mathcal{P}$, let $\Sigma^P_{\text{dif}}\equiv\{S\in\Sigma^P \mid v^S$ can be chosen to be differentiable$\}$.

Proposition 8.2. *For all* $\lambda\in[0,1]$, *the correspondence* N^λ *is nonempty valued.*

Proof. Let $P\in\mathcal{P}$ and $S\in\Sigma^P$ be given. If $\lambda=0$, then $N^\lambda(S)=\{0\}\neq\emptyset$, and if $\lambda=1$, then $N^\lambda(S)=PO(S)\neq\emptyset$. Suppose that $\lambda\in\,]0,1[$. Since $V^{S,\lambda}$ is a continuous vector field on S that points out on ∂S, there exists $x\in S$ such that $V^{S,\lambda}(S)=0$ (Varian, 1981). Any such x is in $N^\lambda(S)$. Q.E.D.

We next turn to the issue of uniqueness. This is easily dealt with if $\lambda=0$ or $\lambda=1$: Clearly, if $\lambda=0$, then F must be the Disagreement solution. If $\lambda=1$, it follows directly from Theorem 7.1 that $F=N$ if *HOM* is strengthened to *S.INV*. In either case, there is a unique solution outcome to every problem, and the necessary conditions are obviously sufficient. It remains to investigate the case $\lambda\in\,]0,1[$. First, we show that in this case N^λ is single valued on the family of two-person problems.

Proposition 8.3. *Suppose* $\lambda\in\,]0,1[$. *The correspondence* N^λ *is single valued on* Σ^P *for all* $P\in\mathcal{P}$ *with* $|P|=2$.

Proof. The argument is illustrated in Figure 8.3. Let l^1 and l^2 be the loci of the points $(\lambda x_1, x_2)$ and $(x_1,\lambda x_2)$ when x runs over $WPO(S)$. Proposition 8.2 guarantees that l^1 and l^2 intersect at some point x. We must show that x is unique.

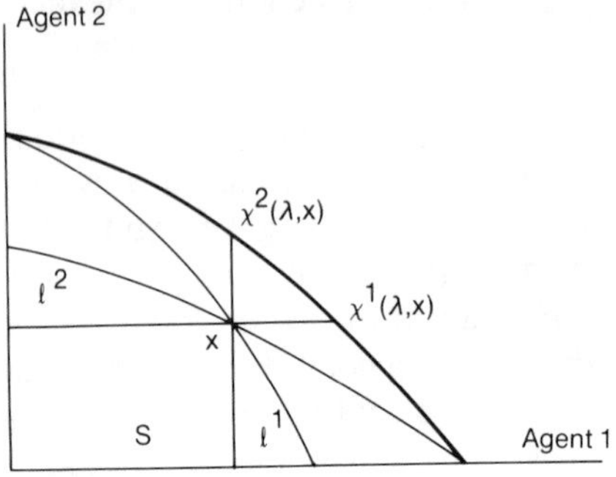

Figure 8.3. Proposition 8.3.

Suppose that l^1 and l^2 intersected more than once, at two points x and y, with $x \neq y$. Consider the two λ-extensions $x^1 \equiv \chi^1(\lambda, x)$ and $x^2 \equiv \chi^2(\lambda, x)$ of x and the two λ-extensions $y^1 \equiv \chi^1(\lambda, y)$ and $y^2 \equiv \chi^2(\lambda, y)$ of y. It is easy to check that neither one of x and y can weakly dominate the other. Without loss of generality, we can assume that $y_1 > x_1$ and $y_2 < x_2$. Therefore, x^1, x^2 and y^1, y^2 are two pairs of points of WPO(S), a concave curve, satisfying $x_1^2 \geqq y_1^2$ and $x_1^1 \geqq y_1^1$, so that the slope of the segment $[x^2, x^1]$ is smaller than the slope of the segment $[y^2, y^1]$. Since the former is equal to the negative of the slope of the segment $[0, x]$ and the latter to the negative of the slope of the segment $[0, y]$, a contradiction results with the assumed relation between x and y. Q.E.D.

The issue of single-valuedness of N^λ for problems of cardinality greater than 2 will be solved by means of an example S^0 involving a number of agents that depends on λ, but in order to simplify notation, this dependence will not be indicated. We will also write $\chi_i(x)$ for $\chi_i(\lambda, x)$.... Let n be the *smallest* integer n' such that

$$1/\lambda^2 < n'. \tag{1}$$

(Note that $n = 2$ for all $\lambda \in]1/\sqrt{2}, 1[$.)

Let $P \equiv \{1, \ldots, n+1\}$ and $a, b, c, d \in \mathbb{R}$ be defined by

$$a = [2/(n\lambda^2 + 1)]^{1/2}$$
$$b = 1 + a\lambda(1 - a)$$
$$c = (1 + \lambda)/\lambda$$
$$d = (n\lambda + 1)/\lambda$$

Then let $S^1 \equiv \{x \in \mathbb{R}_+^P \mid ax_1 + b \max_{i \neq 1}\{x_i\} \leqq c\}$, $S^2 \equiv \{x \in \mathbb{R}_+^P \mid \Sigma_P x_i \leqq d\}$, and finally $S^0 \equiv S^1 \cap S^2$. In Figure 8.4 S^0 is illustrated for $\lambda = 0.8$ (which gives $n = 2$, $a = 0.94$, $b = 1.05$, $c = 2.25$, and $d = 3.25$).

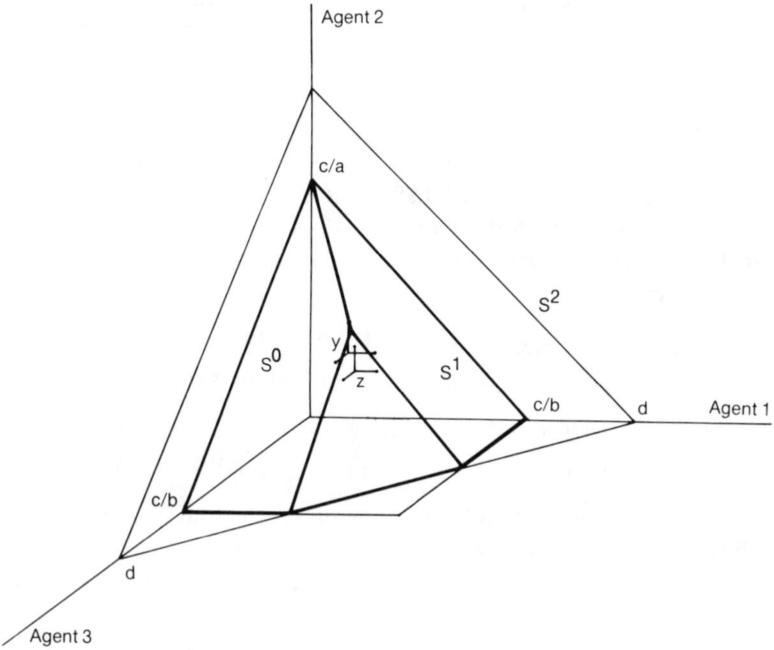

Figure 8.4. Proposition 8.4.

Proposition 8.4. *For no $\lambda \in]0,1[$ is N^λ single valued.*[1]

Proof. Let $\lambda \in]0,1[$ be given and let S^0 be the example defined in the preceding. We will show that $y \equiv (1/a, 1/b, \ldots, 1/b)$ and $z \equiv e_P$, which are distinct, both belong to $N^\lambda(S^0)$.

First, we show that $\{y\} = N^\lambda(S^1)$. It is easily checked that if a problem S' is invariant under permutations involving a subgroup of agents, then all members of the subgroup receive the same amount at any $x \in N^\lambda(S')$. Since in S^1 all agents $i \neq 1$ are interchangeable, if $x \in N^\lambda(S^1)$ then $x_i = x_j$ for all $i, j \in P \backslash 1$. In fact, $x \in N^\lambda(S^1)$ if and only if, in addition, its first two coordinates solve the following system of equations:

$$ax_1/\lambda + bx_2 = c, \qquad ax_1 + bx_2/\lambda = c.$$

Since $\lambda \in]0,1[$, this system has a unique solution. Using the equality $c = (1+\lambda)/\lambda$, we obtain $(x_1, x_2) = (1/a, 1/b)$. Thus $\{y\} = N^\lambda(S^1)$.

[1] An example establishing this fact for $n = 3$ was also constructed for us by H. Moulin (private communication).

Next, we show that $\{z\}=N^\lambda(S^2)$. Since S^2 is invariant under all permutations of agents, if $x\in N^\lambda(S^2)$ then $x_i=x_j$ for all $i\in P$. The common value of the x_i is given by solving

$$x_i/\lambda+nx_i=d,$$

and since $d=(n\lambda+1)/\lambda$, it follows that $x_i=1$. Thus $\{z\}=N^\lambda(S^2)$.

To prove that, in fact, $y,z\in N^\lambda(S^0)$, it now suffices to show that for all $i\in P$, $\chi^i(z)$ lies below $\mathrm{WPO}(S^1)$ and $\chi^i(y)$ lies below $\mathrm{WPO}(S^2)$. Appealing again to the symmetries of S^1 and S^2, it is enough to check this for $i=1,2$. This gives

$$\begin{aligned} a/\lambda+b<c&: \quad \chi^1(z) \text{ is below } \mathrm{WPO}(S^1),\\ a+b/\lambda<c&: \quad \chi^2(z) \text{ is below } \mathrm{WPO}(S^1),\\ 1/a\lambda+n/b<d&: \quad \chi^1(y) \text{ is below } \mathrm{WPO}(S^2),\\ 1/a+1/b\lambda+(n-1)/b<d&: \quad \chi^2(y) \text{ is below } \mathrm{WPO}(S^2). \end{aligned}$$

By (1), it follows that $a<1$ and $b>1$. Therefore, the four inequalities will hold if the middle two do. Given the definitions of b and c and since $a<1$, the second inequality holds. Using the definitions of b and d, the third inequality can be written as

$$A\equiv(1-a)[a^2n\lambda^2-1-a\lambda(1-a)]>0$$

and since

$$\begin{aligned} A&>(1-a)[a^2n\lambda^2-1-a(1-a)] && \text{because } \lambda<1\\ &>(1-a)(a^2n\lambda^2-2+a^2) && \text{because } a<1\\ &=(1-a)[a^2(n\lambda^2+1)-2]\\ &=0 && \text{by definition of } a, \end{aligned}$$

we are done. Q.E.D.

Remark 1: We could show by a similar argument that $N^\lambda(S^0)$ actually contains a third point x. This point is such that $\chi^1(x)\in \mathrm{PO}(S^2)$ and $\chi^i(x)\in \mathrm{WPO}(S^1)$ for all $i\in P\backslash 1$.

Remark 2: It will be useful later to note that y and z are *isolated* members of $N^\lambda(S^0)$ since $\chi^i(y)$ and $\chi^i(z)$ in fact lie *strictly* below $\mathrm{WPO}(S^2)$ and $\mathrm{WPO}(S^1)$, respectively. This is because the preceding inequalities are strict.

Remark 3: The problem S^1 used in the proof of Proposition 8.4 can be used to show that it is not in general true that $N^\lambda(S)$, as a set, converges to $N(S)$ as $\lambda \to 1$. Moreover, $N^{\lambda}(S)$ may be a singleton for all λ and still not converge to $N(S)$ as $\lambda \to 1$.

To see this, let $n=2$ and S be as S^1 above with $a=b=c=1$. Then $x \in N^{\lambda}(S)$ if and only if

$$x_1/\lambda + x_2 = 1 \quad \text{and} \quad x_1 + x_2/\lambda = 1.$$

This system of equations gives $N^{\lambda}(S) = \{[\lambda/(1+\lambda)]e_P\}$. As $\lambda \to 1$, $N^{\lambda}(S) \to \{e_P/2\}$ while $N(S) = (\frac{1}{3}, \frac{2}{3}, \frac{2}{3})$.

The reason for this lack of convergence is that the set $B_N(S)$ of points x of S such that $x_P = N(t^x_{P'}(S))$ for all $P' \subset P$ with $|P'| = 2$ is not a singleton. Indeed, $B_N(S) = [e_P/2, (0,1,1)]$. All we can say in general is that $N^{\lambda}(S)$ converges to (a subset of) $B_N(S)$. Of course, if $S \in \Sigma^P_{\text{dif}}$, then $B_N(S)$ is a singleton, as established in Chapter 7, and convergence of $N^{\lambda}(S)$ to $N(S)$ will occur. However, even if $S \in \Sigma^P_{\text{dif}}$, $N^{\lambda}(S)$ may not be a singleton. This can be seen by simply smoothing the example of Proposition 8.4.

Although N^{λ} is not single valued, we could still hope for the existence of continuous single-valued selections from N^{λ}. The next proposition dashes this hope.

Proposition 8.5. *Let $\lambda \in]0,1[$ be given. Then there is no solution F satisfying CONT such that $F(S) \in N^{\lambda}(S)$ for all $P \in \mathcal{P}$ and for all $S \in \Sigma^P$.*

Proof. Let $\lambda \in]0,1[$ and F be a single-valued subcorrespondence of N^{λ}. Also, let n, P, S^1, S^2, S^0, y, and z be as in the proof of Proposition 8.4 and let $S = S^0$. Since $y \neq z$, either $F(S) \neq y$ or $F(S) \neq z$.

Suppose first that (i) $F(S) \neq y$, and for all $\alpha \geqq 1$, let $S^{\alpha} \equiv S^1 \cap \alpha S^2$. Observe that (ii) y is an isolated member of $N^{\lambda}(S^{\alpha})$ for all $\alpha \geqq 1$ (Remark 2). Moreover, $S^{\alpha} = S^1$ for all α sufficiently large. Since $N^{\lambda}(S^1) = \{y\}$ and $F \subset N^{\lambda}$, it follows that (iii) $F(S^1) = y$. From (i), (ii), and (iii), we conclude that F does not satisfy *CONT*.

Supposing next that $F(S) \neq z$, we establish the desired conclusion by a similar argument, applied to $T^{\alpha} \equiv \alpha S^1 \cap S^2$. Q.E.D.

From this negative result and Proposition 8.1, we get the following positive one.

Theorem 8.1. *A solution satisfies AN, S.INV, B.STAB, and CONT if and only if it is either the Disagreement solution or the Nash solution.*

Theorem 8.1 shows that the axiom of Pareto-Optimality plays a very modest role in the main characterization of the Nash solution of Chapter

7. The axiom only serves to rule out one alternative solution, the Disagreement solution. Since a variant of that characterization result uses *P.O, AN, S.INV,* and *M.STAB* instead of *P.O, AN, S.INV, CONT,* and *B.STAB,* there is therefore the question of whether a similar variant to Theorem 8.1 can be obtained if *B.STAB* and *CONT* are replaced by *M.STAB*. Proposition 8.6 answers that question in the affirmative, stating that single-valued selections from N^λ are not multilaterally stable for any $\lambda \in]0,1[$.[2]

Proposition 8.6. *Let $\lambda \in]0,1[$ be given. Then there is no solution F satisfying M.STAB such that $F(S) \in N^\lambda(S)$ for all $P \in \mathcal{P}$ and for all $S \in \Sigma^P$.*

Proof. Let $\lambda \in]0,1[$ and F be single-valued subcorrespondence of N^λ. Also, let n, P, a, b, c, and d be as in the proof of Proposition 8.4. Finally, given $\rho > 1$, let $w^\rho: \mathbb{R}^P_+ \to \mathbb{R}$ be defined by

$$w^\rho(x) \equiv x_1 - \left[\left(\frac{c}{a} - \frac{b}{a}\left(\sum_{P\setminus 1} x_i^\rho\right)^{1/\rho}\right)^{-\rho} + \left(d - \sum_{P\setminus 1} x_i\right)^{-\rho}\right]^{-1/\rho}$$

The function w^ρ is strictly increasing, convex, and differentiable for all $\rho > 1$. Therefore, $S^\rho \equiv \{x \in \mathbb{R}^P_+ \mid w^\rho(x) \leqq 0\} \in \Sigma^P_{\text{dif}}$ for all $\rho > 1$. Also, for each $x \in \mathbb{R}^P$, $w^\rho(x) \to w^\infty(x)$ as $\rho \to \infty$, where

$$w^\infty(x) \equiv x_1 - \min\left[\frac{c}{a} - \frac{b}{a} \max_{P\setminus 1}\{x_i\}, d - \sum_{P\setminus 1} x_i\right],$$

and therefore $S^\rho \to S$. By Proposition 8.4, $N^\lambda(S)$ contains two distinct points y and z. These points are topologically stable as they are the unique solutions to systems of linear equations. Consequently, for sufficiently large ρ, $N^\lambda(S^\rho)$ contains two distinct points x^1 and x^2. For such a ρ, let $w \equiv w^\rho$ and $S \equiv S^\rho$.

The proof will consist in showing that if F satisfies *M.STAB,* then $F(S) = x^1$ but also $F(S) = x^2$, a contradiction to the assumption that F is a function. This conclusion will be obtained by constructing, for each $k = 1, 2$, a $|Q|$-person problem T, where $Q \supset P$ such that $N^\lambda(T)$ is a singleton y satisfying $y_P = x^k$ and $t^y_P(T) = S$, two statements that by *M.STAB* imply $F(S) = x^k$.

Choose $k = 1$ or $k = 2$. Note that, for all λ, there exists $m \in \mathbb{N}$ such that $(m-1)n/\lambda - mn > 0$. (If $\lambda < \frac{1}{2}$, the inequality is satisfied by $m = 2$.) Let $P^1 \equiv P\setminus 1 = \{2, \ldots, n+1\}$, and for all $j = 2, \ldots, m$, let $P^j \equiv \{2 + (j-1)n, \ldots, n+1+(j-1)n\}$ and $Q \equiv \{1\} \cup_{j=1}^m P^j$. Let $\gamma: \mathbb{R}^n_+ \to \mathbb{R}$ and $v^T: \mathbb{R}^Q_+ \to \mathbb{R}$ be defined by

[2] Note, however, that by definition of N^λ for $\lambda \in]0,1[$, all single-valued selections from N^λ are bilaterally stable.

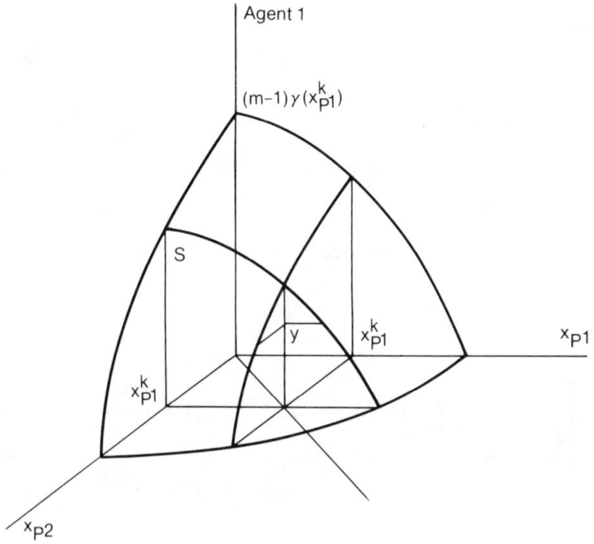

Figure 8.5. Proposition 8.6.

$$\gamma(x) \equiv w(\alpha, x) - \alpha \quad \text{where } x = (x_2, \ldots, x_{n+1}),$$

$$v^T(y) \equiv y_1 + \sum_{j=1}^{m} \gamma(y_{Pj}) - (m-1)\gamma(y^k_{P1}).$$

Finally, let T (see Figure 8.5) be defined by

$$T \equiv \{x \in \mathbb{R}^Q_+ \mid v^T(x) \leqq 0\}.$$

Note that T is symmetric in $x_{Q\setminus 1}$ since γ is symmetric in $x_{Q\setminus 1}$. Let $y \in \mathbb{R}^Q_+$ be defined by $y \equiv (x^k_1, x^k_{P1}, \ldots, x^k_{P1})$. We have $t^y_P(T) = t^y_{Pj}(T) = S$ for all $j = 1, \ldots, m$, and since $x^k \in N^\lambda(S)$, it follows that $y \in N^\lambda(T)$.

We now claim that $N^\lambda(T) = \{y\}$. To prove this, let $V^T\colon T \to \mathbb{R}^Q$ be defined by $V^T_i(x) = v^T(\chi^i(x))$ for all $i \in Q$. Then $x \in N^\lambda(T)$ if and only if $V^T(x) = 0$.

Let now $T^d \equiv T \cap \{x \in \mathbb{R}^Q \mid x_i = x_j \text{ for all } i, j \in Q\setminus 1\}$. Since T is symmetric in the coordinates $x_{Q\setminus 1}$, $N^\lambda(T) \subset T^d$, and N^λ, as a correspondence, satisfies *AN*. Thus, all the zeros of V^T belong to T^d. Also, for all $x \in T^d$, the vector $V^T(x) + x$ lies in the hyperplane in $\mathbb{R}^Q_+$ spanned by T^d. Letting $P' = \{1, 2\}$ and $T^d_{P'}$ be the projection of T^d on $\mathbb{R}^{P'}_+$, this implies that the function $V\colon T^d_{P'} \to \mathbb{R}^{P'}$ defined by $V(x_1, x_2) \equiv V^T_{P'}(x_1, x_2, \ldots, x_2)$ is a vector field on $T^d_{P'}$ such that for all $x \in T$, $V(x_1, x_2) = 0$ if and only if $V^T(x) = 0$. Moreover, V is differentiable and points out on the boundary of $T^d_{P'}$ since V^T has these properties on T.

We now show that the determinant of the Jacobian J of V is positive for all $x \in T^d_{P'}$. Then, by the Poincaré–Hopf index theorem (see, e.g., Varian, 1981), V, and hence V^T, has only one zero. Since $V(y_{P'})=0$, by the fact that $V^T(y)=0$, this will establish that $N^\lambda(T)=\{y\}$.

Now V is written as

$$V_1(x_1,x_2)=x_1/\lambda+m\gamma(x_2,\dots,x_2)-K$$

$$V_2(x_1,x_2)=x_1+\gamma(x_2/\lambda,x_2,\dots,x_2)+(m-1)\gamma(x_2,\dots,x_2)-K$$

where $K \equiv (m-1)\gamma(x^k_{P1})$. Therefore,

$$J=\begin{bmatrix} 1/\lambda & m\sum_{i=1}^{n}\gamma_i(x_2,\dots,x_2) \\ 1 & \gamma_1\left(\frac{x_2}{\lambda},x_2,\dots,x_2\right)\frac{1}{\lambda}+\sum_{i=2}^{n}\gamma_i\left(\frac{x_2}{\lambda},x_2,\dots,x_2\right) \\ & \quad +(m-1)\sum_{i=1}^{n}\gamma_i(x_2,\dots,x_2) \end{bmatrix},$$

where γ_i is the partial derivative of γ with respect to its ith argument. Since γ is symmetric and strictly increasing, $\gamma_i(x_2,\dots,x_2)=\alpha$ for some $\alpha>0$ and for all $i=1,\dots,n$. Ignoring the first two positive terms of J_{22} and dividing the second column by α, it follows that det $J>0$ because $(m-1)n/\lambda-mn>0$. Q.E.D.

From this our main result follows.

Theorem 8.2. *A solution satisfies AN, S.INV, and M.STAB if and only if it is either the Disagreement solution or the Nash solution.*

8.3 One-commodity division problems

In this section, we show that the restriction of the correspondence N^λ to the subclass of Σ of problems that are obtained from the division of a *single* commodity between agents whose utility functions satisfy standard assumptions is single valued and therefore constitutes a well-defined solution on that class.

First, the class is formally defined. Given $P \in \mathcal{P}$, let (i) U^P be the set of lists $u=(u_i)_{i\in P}$ where for each $i \in P$, $u_i: \mathbb{R}_+ \to \mathbb{R}_+$ is *agent i's utility function* and (ii) $\Omega \in \mathbb{R}_{++}$ be a social *endowment*. We assume that for each $i \in P$, u_i is strictly increasing, concave, and differentiable and satisfies $u_i(0)=0$ and $u_i(\Omega)>0$. Let $S(u,\Omega)\equiv\{x\in\mathbb{R}^P_+ \mid \exists z\in\mathbb{R}^P_+ \text{ with } \sum_P z_i \leqq \Omega \text{ and } \forall i\in P,\ u_i(z_i)=x_i\}$. Note that $S(u,\Omega)\in\Sigma^P$. Also, since for all $\alpha>0$,

$S(\hat{u}, \Omega/\alpha) = S(u, \Omega)$, where each $\hat{u}_i$ is defined by $\hat{u}_i(z_i/\alpha) = u_i(z_i)$, there is no loss of generality in taking $\Omega = 1$. Then, let Σ^{1P}, where the superscript 1 is a reference to the fact that there is a unique commodity, be the class of problems $S(u, 1) \equiv S(u)$. Finally, let $\Sigma^1 \equiv \bigcup_{P \in \mathcal{P}} \Sigma^{1P}$. Of course, if $|P| = 1$ then $\Sigma^{1P} = \Sigma^P$, but if $|P| > 1$ then Σ^{1P} is a proper subset of Σ^P. It is therefore conceivable that solutions behave better on Σ^1 than on Σ. This turns out to be the case for N^λ.

Theorem 8.3. *For all $\lambda \in [0, 1[$, for all $P \in \mathcal{P}$, N^λ is single valued on Σ^{1P}.*

Proof. Let $\lambda \in [0, 1[$ be given. If $\lambda = 0$ the proof is trivial, so let us assume that $\lambda > 0$. Let $P \in \mathcal{P}$ and $u \in U^P$ be given and $S \equiv S(u)$.

By our assumptions on the u_i, each u_i has an inverse f_i that is strictly increasing, differentiable, and convex. Then S can be alternatively described as $S \equiv \{x \in \mathbb{R}^P_+ \mid \Sigma_P f_i(x_i) \leqq 1\}$. In the notation of Section 8.2, $x \in N^\lambda(S)$ if and only if $V_i^S(x) \equiv f_i(x_i/\lambda) + \Sigma_{P \setminus i} f_j(x_j) - 1 = 0$ for all $i \in P$.

By differentiability of the f_i, it follows that the vector field V^S is smooth. To show that it vanishes at one point only, it suffices to show that its Jacobian J is positive for all $x \in S$. The Jacobian J is given by

$$J = \begin{bmatrix} (1/\lambda) f_1'(x_1/\lambda) & f_2'(x_2) & \cdots & f_n'(x_n) \\ f_1'(x_1) & (1/\lambda) f_2'(x_2/\lambda) & \cdots & f_n'(x_n) \\ \vdots & \vdots & \ddots & \vdots \\ f_1'(x_1) & f_2'(x_2) & \cdots & (1/\lambda) f_n'(x_n/\lambda) \end{bmatrix}.$$

For each $i \in P$, $f_i' > 0$; therefore, $a_i \equiv (1/\lambda) f_i'(x_i/\lambda)/f_i'(x_i)$ is well defined. Since, in addition, $\lambda < 1$ and f_i is convex, then $a_i > 1$.

To compute the sign of J, for each $i \in P$, multiply column i by $1/f_i'(x_i) > 0$ and subtract the first row from all other rows. Then for each $i \in P$, $i \neq 1$, multiply column i by the well-defined quantity $(a_1 - 1)/(a_i - 1)$ and add the sum to column 1. This yields the matrix J' with $\text{sign}|J'| = \text{sign}|J|$:

$$J' \equiv \begin{bmatrix} a_1 + \sum\limits_{i \neq 1} \dfrac{a_1 - 1}{a_i - 1} & \dfrac{a_1 - 1}{a_2 - 1} & \dfrac{a_1 - 1}{a_3 - 1} & \cdots & \dfrac{a_1 - 1}{a_n - 1} \\ 0 & a_1 - 1 & 0 & \cdots & 0 \\ 0 & 0 & a_1 - 1 & \cdots & 0 \\ \vdots & \vdots & \vdots & \ddots & \vdots \\ 0 & 0 & 0 & \cdots & a_1 - 1 \end{bmatrix}.$$

Since $\det J' > 0$, we are done. Q.E.D.

CHAPTER 9

Stability and the Leximin solution

9.1 Introduction

A characterization of the Lexicographic maximin, or *Leximin,* solution is offered in this chapter. The list of axioms it involves – Pareto-Optimality, Anonymity, *Individual Monotonicity,* and Multilateral Stability – differs from that used to characterize the Nash solution (Theorem 7.1) only in that Scale Invariance is replaced by Individual Monotonicity, an axiom requiring that if a problem is expanded in a direction favorable to an agent, then that agent should not lose. Various axioms expressing requirements in that spirit have been discussed in the literature first by Kalai and Smorodinsky (1975) and later by Kalai (1977b), Roth (1979a), Thomson and Myerson (1980), and Segal (1980). Here, Kalai's condition will be used (see Chapter 2).

Individual Monotonicity (I.MON): For all $P \in \mathcal{P}$, for all $S, S' \in \Sigma^P$, for all $i \in P$, if $S \subset S'$ and $S_{P\setminus i} = S'_{P\setminus i}$ then $F_i(S') \geqq F_i(S)$. (Recall that $P\setminus i$ means $P\setminus\{i\}$.)

The axiom is illustrated in Figure 9.1 for $P=\{1,2\}$ and $i=1$.

The motivation for this axiom is clear: The set of utility vectors attainable by the members of $P\setminus i$ is unaffected by the expansion from S to S'. Moreover, for each such vector the maximal utility attainable by agent i in S' is no smaller than the maximal utility attainable by him in S. It is in this sense that the expansion can be said to be in agent i's favor, and it is natural then to require that he should not lose.

Figure 9.2 illustrates the fact that the Nash solution does not satisfy the axiom. In the figure,

$$P \equiv \{1,2\}, \quad S \equiv \text{cch}\{e_P, (0,2)\}, \quad S' \equiv \text{cch}\{(\tfrac{8}{5},0), (\tfrac{4}{5}, \tfrac{4}{3}), (0,2)\},$$

so that $N(S) = (1, 1)$ and $N(S') = (\frac{4}{5}, \frac{4}{3})$. However, the hypothesis of *I.MON* applies to the pair $\{S, S'\}$ with $i=1$. The conclusion of that axiom, that agent 1 should not lose as a result of the expansion, is violated.

The question then is whether there are any solutions that satisfy *P.O, AN, I.MON,* and *M.STAB*. One natural candidate is the Egalitarian so-

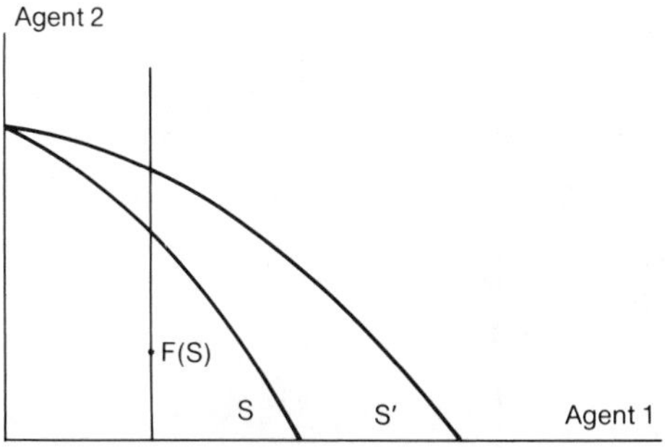

Figure 9.1. The axiom of Individual Monotonicity. The solution outcome for S' should not be to the left of the solution outcome for S.

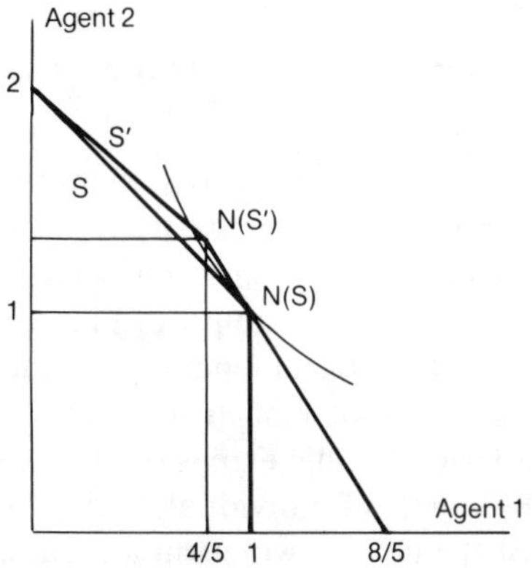

Figure 9.2. The Nash solution does not satisfy *I.MON*.

lution E since E satisfies very strong monotonicity conditions, as we saw in Chapter 2. However, E satisfies only *W.P.O* as discussed in Chapter 4, and as discussed in Chapter 7, it does not satisfy Bilateral (and a fortiori Multilateral) Stability. An example illustrating this second fact is represented in Figure 9.3, in which

$$Q \equiv \{1,2,3\}, \quad P \equiv \{2,3\}, \quad \text{and} \quad T \equiv \text{cch}\{(1,2,2)\}.$$

Note that $z \equiv E(T) = e_Q$, and therefore $t_P^z(T) = S \equiv \text{cch}\{2e_P\}$. A contradiction to Bilateral Stability is obtained by noting that $E(S) = 2e_P \neq z_P$.

We should mention here that the Egalitarian solution satisfies a slight weakening of stability; another characterization of it, based on that fact, will be provided in Chapter 10.

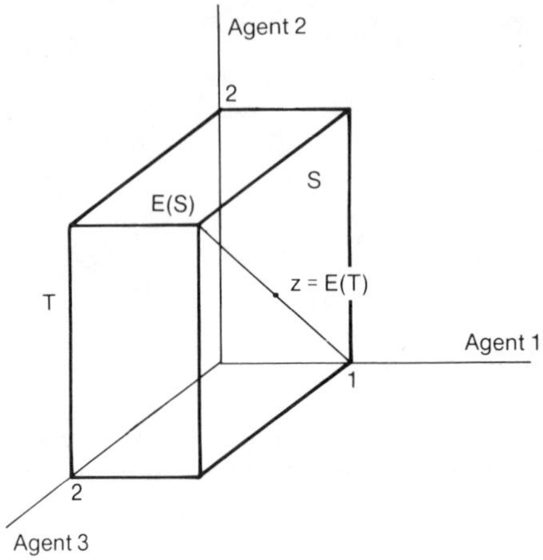

Figure 9.3. The Egalitarian solution does not satisfy Bilateral Stability.

The Egalitarian solution is closely related to the Rawlsian maximin criterion (Rawls, 1971) by always selecting a feasible alternative that maximizes the utility of the worst-off individual. In general, the set of such alternatives is not a singleton, as illustrated by the example of Figure 9.3, for which it is a square parallel to the $\{2,3\}$ coordinate plane with the points marked $E(S)$ and $E(T)$ as vertices. To resolve such multiplicities, Sen (1970) has suggested the following lexicographic extension of the criterion: First maximize the utility of the worst-off individual; then among the maximizers, maximize the utility of the next to worst-off individual, and so on, until all possibilities for increasing the utility of any individual have been exhausted. This procedure yields a well-defined solution, which will be referred to here as the Leximin solution, denoted L.

We will prove in the next section that the Leximin solution satisfies Pareto-Optimality as well as Multilateral Stability. However, it does not satisfy Continuity, as is clear from the example depicted in Figure 9.4, where $P \equiv \{1,2\}$ and $\{S^\nu\}$ is the sequence from Σ^P defined by

$$S^\nu \equiv \text{cch}\{(2, 1-1/\nu),\ e_2\} \quad \text{for each positive integer } \nu.$$

As $\nu \to \infty$, S^ν converges to $S \equiv \text{cch}\{(2,1)\}$ and $L(S^\nu)$ converges to $E(S) = e_P$, while $L(S) = (2,1)$.

It turns out that the Leximin solution does satisfy a weaker form of Continuity, which may be a more natural condition to impose on a solution already required to obey Multilateral Stability anyway. This point will be discussed in Section 9.3.

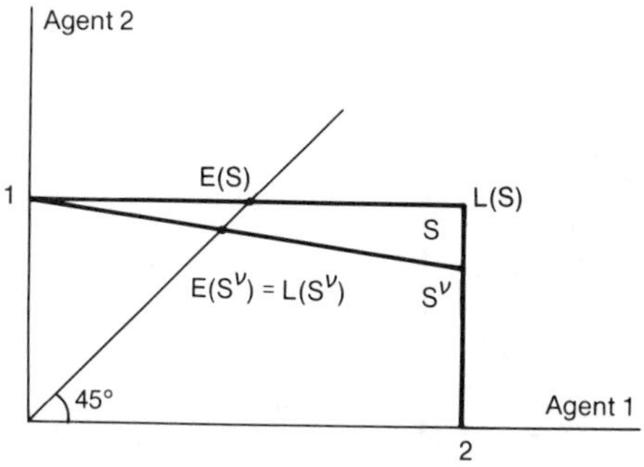

Figure 9.4. The Leximin solution does not satisfy Continuity.

In the remainder of the present section, we formally introduce the Leximin solution. In fact, we give two alternative but equivalent definitions. The first one is by way of an algorithm that generates the Leximin solution outcome.

Given $P \in \mathcal{P}$ and $S \in \Sigma^P$, first define α^1 to be the maximal positive number α such that $\alpha e_P \in S$. Clearly $\alpha^1 e_P = E(S)$. Then set $x^1 \equiv \alpha^1 e_P$ and $P^1 \equiv \{i \in P \mid \exists x \in S, x \geqq x^1, x_i > x_i^1\}$. Next define α^2 to be the maximal positive number α such that $\alpha e_{P^1} \in t_{P^1}^{x^1}(S)$ and set $x^2 \equiv x^1 + (\alpha^2 - \alpha^1) e_{P^1}$. At iteration τ define α^τ to be the maximal positive number α such that $\alpha e_{P^{\tau-1}} \in t_{P^{\tau-1}}^{x^{\tau-1}}(S)$, and set $x^\tau \equiv x^{\tau-1} + (\alpha^\tau - \alpha^{\tau-1}) e_{P^{\tau-1}}$ and $P^\tau \equiv \{i \in P^{\tau-1} \mid \exists x \in S, x \geqq x^{\tau-1}, x_i > x_i^{\tau-1}\}$. Because P^τ is a proper subset of $P^{\tau-1}$ unless $P^{\tau-1} = \emptyset$, there is a first iteration τ^* at which $P^{\tau^*} = \emptyset$. We then set $L(S) \equiv x^{\tau^*}$.

The algorithm is illustrated in Figure 9.5 for $P \equiv \{1, 2, 3\}$ and $S \equiv \text{cch}\{(1, 2, 3)\}$. For that example, $\alpha^1 = 1$, $x^1 = e_P$, $P^1 = \{2, 3\}$, $\alpha^2 = 2$, $x^2 = (1, 2, 2)$, $P^2 = \{3\}$, $\alpha^3 = 3$, $x^3 = (1, 2, 3)$, $P^3 = \emptyset$, and $L(S) = (1, 2, 3)$.

Although the preceding definition is useful as a visualization of the Leximin solution, the next one is more convenient for analytical purposes: Given $P \in \mathcal{P}$ and $x \in \mathbb{R}^P$, let $\bar{P} \equiv \{1, 2, \ldots, |P|\}$, and let $\gamma(x)$ be the vector in $\mathbb{R}^{\bar{P}}$ obtained by a relabeling of the coordinates of x so that $\gamma_1(x) \leqq \gamma_2(x) \leqq \cdots \leqq \gamma_{|P|}(x)$. Let $\succsim_P$ be the ordering of $\mathbb{R}_+^P$ such that for all $x, y \in \mathbb{R}_+^P$, $x \succ_P y$ if and only if there exists $k \in \bar{P}$ such that $\gamma_k(x) > \gamma_k(y)$ and $\gamma_i(x) = \gamma_i(y)$ for all $i \in \bar{P}$ such that $i < k$. Then $\gamma(x) = \gamma(y)$ if and only if $x \sim_P y$. For all $S \in \Sigma^P$, let $\phi(S) \equiv \{y \in S \mid y \succsim_P x \text{ for all } x \in S\}$. It follows from a simple adaptation of Lemmas 3 and 4 of Imai (1983) that $\phi(S)$ consists of the single point $L(S)$.

Let $\succsim$ be the family of orderings $\{\succsim_P \mid P \in \mathcal{P}\}$, where each $\succsim_P$ is defined as in the preceding. It is a well-known fact that the family $\succsim$ is such that

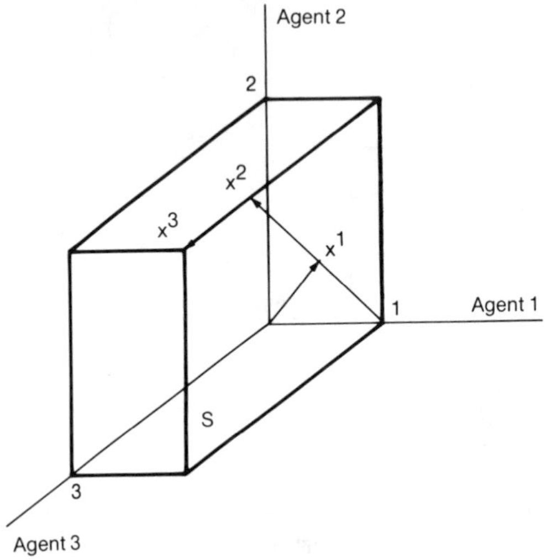

Figure 9.5. The Leximin solution outcome of a three-person example.

for all $P, Q \in \mathcal{P}$ with $P \subset Q$, for all $x, y \in \mathbb{R}^Q_+$ with $x_{Q \setminus P} = y_{Q \setminus P}$, $x \succsim_Q y$ if and only if $x_P \succsim_P y_P$ (see, e.g., d'Aspremont and Gevers, 1977, and Deschamps and Gevers, 1978). This property, due to Fleming (1952), is known in the social choice literature as *Separability*. It is closely related to Harsanyi's Bilateral Equilibrium condition and to our Multilateral Stability axiom.

The remainder of this chapter is organized as follows: Section 9.2 contains the main result and Section 9.3 some concluding comments.

This chapter is based on Lensberg (1985a).

9.2 Characterization of the Leximin solution

We show in this section that the Leximin solution is the only one to satisfy Pareto-Optimality, Anonymity, Individual Monotonicity, and Multilateral Stability. First, we have

Proposition 9.1. *The Leximin solution satisfies P.O, AN, I.MON, and M.STAB.*

Proof. That L satisfies *P.O* and *AN* is clear from the definition of the algorithm defining it. The proof that L satisfies *I.MON* follows from Imai (1983). It remains to examine *M.STAB*.

Let $P, Q \in \mathcal{P}$ with $P \subset Q$ and $T \in \Sigma^Q$ be given. Let $z \equiv L(T)$ and $S \equiv t_P^z(T)$. Since $z = L(T)$, z is the unique maximizer of the ordering $\succsim_Q$ over T. Let $S' \equiv S + \{z_{Q\setminus P}\}$. Then S' is a subset of T containing z, which implies that z is the unique maximizer of $\succsim_Q$ over S'. Since $x_{Q\setminus P} = z_{Q\setminus P}$ for all $x \in S'$, it follows from the fact that $\succsim$ satisfies Separability that z_P maximizes $\succsim_P$ over S. Thus, $z_P \in \phi(S)$, and since $\phi(S)$ consists of only $L(S)$, it follows that $z_P = L(S)$. Q.E.D.

Next, we show that if a solution satisfies the four axioms, it is the Leximin solution. The proof is organized in a sequence of lemmas. The starting point is Lemma 7.1, restated here as Lemma 9.1, which says that if a solution F satisfies *P.O, AN,* and *B.STAB,* then it coincides with the Egalitarian solution on any two-person problem whose Pareto-optimal boundary contains a nondegenerate line segment with slope -1 centered at its Egalitarian outcome. This result is then used to show that if, in addition, F satisfies *I.MON,* then F coincides with L for two-person problems that are more and more asymmetric in the sense that the maximal utility available to one of the agents is proportionally greater and greater than the maximal utility available to the other (Lemma 9.2). This argument is reminiscent of the characterization of the Egalitarian solution given in Chapter 4. Finally, this result is extended to problems involving more than two agents (Proposition 9.2).

Lemma 9.1 (Lemma 7.1 restated). *If a solution F satisfies P.O, AN, and B.STAB, then for all $P \in \mathcal{P}$ with $|P| = 2$ and for all $S \in \Sigma^P$ whose Pareto-optimal boundary contains a nondegenerate segment of slope -1 centered at $E(S)$, $F(S) = E(S)$.*

Given $P \in \mathcal{P}$ and $S \in \Sigma^P$, recall from Chapter 3 that $a(S)$, the ideal point of S, is defined by setting $a_i(S) \equiv \max\{x_i \mid x \in S\}$ for all $i \in P$.

Lemma 9.2. *If a solution F satisfies P.O, AN, I.MON, and M.STAB, then for all $P \in \mathcal{P}$ with $|P| = 2$, $F = L$ on Σ^P.*

Proof. Let $P \in \mathcal{P}$ with $|P| = 2$ and $S \in \Sigma^P$ be given. Without loss of generality, take $P = \{1, 2\}$ and assume that $a_1(S) \geqq a_2(S)$ and that $E(S) = e_P$. Let $\lambda \equiv a_1(S)$ and note that there is an integer n such that $n+1 \leqq 2\lambda < n+2$. The proof that $F(S) = L(S)$ is by induction on n.

(i) First, we prove the result for $n \leqq 2$. Given $\epsilon > 0$ but small, let $S^\epsilon \in \Sigma^P$ be defined by $S^\epsilon \equiv S \cap \{x \in \mathbb{R}_+^P \mid \Sigma_P x_i \leqq 2(1-\epsilon)\}$. Note that $\mathrm{PO}(S^\epsilon)$ contains a nondegenerate segment centered at $E(S^\epsilon)$, so that by Lemma 9.1, $F(S^\epsilon) = E(S^\epsilon)$. Since $\lambda < 2$, then for sufficiently small ϵ, $a(S^\epsilon) = a(S)$,

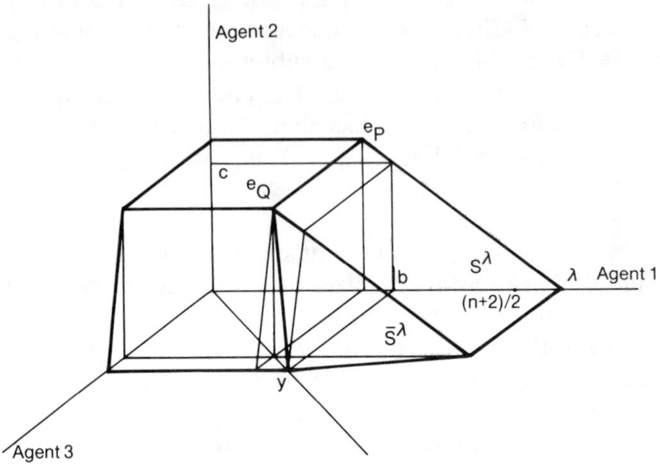

Figure 9.6. Lemma 9.2 (iia). Figure drawn for $n=2$.

and since $S^\epsilon \subset S$, it follows by *I.MON* applied twice that $E(S^\epsilon) \leqq F(S)$. Letting ϵ go to zero and observing that $E(S^\epsilon) \to E(S)$, we conclude that $F(S) \geqq E(S)$. Since $L(S)$ is the only Pareto-optimal point of S dominating $E(S)$, the desired conclusion follows from this inequality and *P.O.*

(ii) Next, given $n \geqq 2$, assume that the desired conclusion holds for all $n' \leqq n$. To prove it for $n+1$, we introduce a third agent, whom we take to be agent 3 without loss of generality, and we set $Q \equiv \{1,2,3\}$, $P^1 \equiv \{2,3\}$, and $P^2 \equiv \{1,3\}$. Define $S^\lambda \in \Sigma^P$ by $S^\lambda \equiv \text{cch}\{e_P, \lambda e_1\}$. We first prove (see Figure 9.6) that

$$F(S^\lambda) = L(S^\lambda) = E(S^\lambda). \tag{iia}$$

To see this, let $b \equiv (n+3)/(n+2)$, $y \equiv be_{P2}$, $\bar{S}^\lambda \equiv S^\lambda + \{e_3\}$, and $T \in \Sigma^Q$ be defined by $T \equiv \text{cch}\{\bar{S}^\lambda, y\}$. Given any $z \in T$, let $S^z \in \Sigma^{P^2}$ be defined by $S^z \equiv t^z_{P2}(T)$. We show that the induction hypothesis applies to all S^z. First note that for all $z \in T$, $z_2 \in [0,1]$. If $z_2 = 1$, $S^z = \text{cch}\{e_{P2}\}$ so that $a(S^z) = E(S^z) = e_{P2}$. If $z_2 = 0$, $S^z = \text{cch}\{y, (\lambda, 1)\}$ so that $a(S^z) = (\lambda, b)$ and $E(S^z) = y$. Second, we claim that for all $z \in T$, $a(S^z) < [(n+2)/2]E(S^z)$. This is obvious if $z_2 = 1$, whereas if $z_2 = 0$, it follows from the fact that $2\lambda < n+3$. If $0 < z_2 < 1$, it remains true because both $a(S^z)$ and $E(S^z)$ vary linearly with z_2. By the induction hypothesis, it follows that $F(S^z) = E(S^z)$. *M.STAB* and the fact that $[e_Q, y] \subset \text{PO}(T)$ implies that if $z = F(T)$ then $z \in [e_Q, y]$.

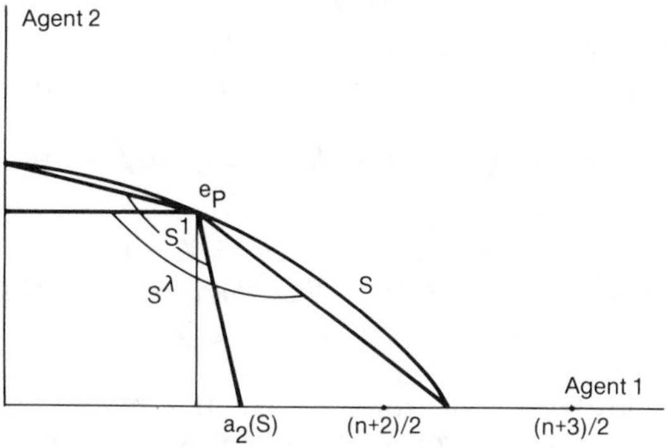

Figure 9.7. Lemma 9.2 (iib). Figure drawn for $n=2$.

Next, let $z\in[e_Q,y]$ be given and $\bar{S}^z\in\Sigma^{P^1}$ be defined by $\bar{S}^z\equiv t^z_{P1}(T)$. Note that $z_1\in[1,b]$. If $z_1=1$ then $\bar{S}^z=\text{cch}\{e_{P1},(0,b)\}$, so that $a(\bar{S}^z)\equiv(1,b)$ and $E(\bar{S}^z)=e_{P1}$. If $z_1=b$ then $\bar{S}^z=\text{cch}\{(c,1),be_3\}$, where c is such that $(b,c)\in[e_P,\lambda e_1]$, that is, $c=(\lambda-b)/(\lambda-1)$, so that $a(\bar{S}^z)=(c,b)$ and $E(\bar{S}^z)=ce_{P1}$. We now claim that $a(\bar{S}^z)<[(n+2)/2]E(\bar{S}^z)$ for all $z\in T$. As in the previous paragraph, the computations are straightforward for $z_1=1$ and $z_1=b$, and the desired conclusion for $0<z_1<b$ follows from the fact that both $a(\bar{S}^z)$ and $E(\bar{S}^z)$ vary linearly with z_1. *M.STAB* and the induction hypothesis imply that $z\in[e_Q,(b,c,1)]$ if $z=F(T)$.

It follows from the two preceding paragraphs that if $z=F(T)$, then $z\in[e_Q,y]\cap[e_Q,(b,c,1)]$. The only point in this intersection is e_Q. Therefore, $F(T)=e_Q$. To complete the proof of (iia), apply *M.STAB* to get $F(t^z_P(T))=F(S^\lambda)=e_P$. It now remains to show (see Figure 9.7) that

$$F(S)=L(S). \qquad \text{(iib)}$$

First we show that $F(S)\geqq E(S)$. To see this, let $S^1\in\Sigma^P$ be defined by $S^1\equiv\text{cch}\{e_P,a_2(S)e_1,a_2(S)e_2\}$. Note that S^1 is a symmetric problem so that by *P.O* and *AN*, $F(S^1)=e_P$. Also, $S^1\subset S$ since $a_1(S)\geqq a_2(S)$. Finally, $a_2(S^1)=a_2(S)$, and therefore, by *I.MON*, $1=F_1(S^1)\leqq F_1(S)$. Next, observe that $S^\lambda\subset S$, where $\lambda=a_1(S)$, and $a_1(S)=a_1(S^\lambda)$, so that by *I.MON* and (iia), $1=F_2(S^\lambda)\leqq F_2(S)$. Having proved that $F(S)\geqq E(S)$, conclude by applying *P.O* and noting that $L(S)$ is the only point of PO(S) dominating $E(S)$. Q.E.D.

Given a solution F and given $Q\in\mathcal{P}$ and $T\in\Sigma^Q$, recall from Chapter 7 the definition of an *F multilaterally stable point of T:* This is a point x such that for all $P \in \mathcal{P}$ with $P \subset Q$ and $P \neq Q$, if $t_P^x(T) \in \Sigma^P$ then $F(t_P^x(T)) = x_P$. The set of all these points is denoted $M_F(T)$.

The next lemma describes useful properties of the Leximin solution.

Lemma 9.3. For all $Q \in \mathcal{P}$, for all $T \in \Sigma^Q$, the following holds:

(1) $L(T) \geqq E(T)$.
(2) *If $z \in M_L(T)$ and $z \geqq E(T)$, then $z = L(T)$.*
(3) *If $z \in M_L(T)$ and $z \neq L(T)$, then there exists $k \in Q$ such that $E_k(T) > z_k$ and $E_i(T) < z_i$ for all $i \in Q \backslash k$.*

Proof. That (1) holds is obvious from the definition of L. To prove (2) and (3), let $T \in \Sigma^Q$ and $z \in M_L(T)$ be given. Let also $u \equiv E(T)$ and $y \equiv L(T)$.

First we prove (2). Suppose $z \geqq u$. By construction of L, there exists $j \in Q$ such that $y_j = u_j$. Therefore, $j \notin Q^1 \equiv \{i \in Q \mid \exists x \in T, x \geqq u, x_i > u_i\}$ and since $z \geqq u$, then $z_j = u_j$. Let $P \equiv Q \backslash j$ and $S \equiv t_P^u(T) = t_P^z(T)$. Since $u > 0$, S is a well-defined element of Σ^P, and since $z \in M_L(T)$, $z_P = L(S)$. By construction of L, $y = (u_j, L(S))$, which in conjunction with $z_j = u_j$ implies the desired conclusion.

Next we prove (3). Suppose $z \neq y$. By (2) it follows that $z \ngeqq u$, and therefore $u_k > z_k$ for some agent $k \in Q$. Suppose, by way of contradiction, that $u_j \geqq z_j$ for some $j \in Q \backslash k$. Let $P \equiv Q \backslash j$ and $S \equiv t_P^z(T)$.

Since $u_j \geqq z_j$ and T is comprehensive, then $u_P \in S$, which (since $u_P > 0$) implies that S is a well-defined member of Σ^P. Since $z \in M_L(T)$, then $z_P = L(S)$, which, by (1), implies that $z_P \geqq E(S) \geqq u_P$. Because $k \in P$ and $z_k < u_k$, this is the announced contradiction. Consequently, $u_i < z_i$ for all $i \in Q \backslash k$. Q.E.D.

Figure 9.8 represents an example showing that the set of L multilaterally stable points may be quite large. Let $Q \equiv \{1, 2, 3\}$, $P^2 \equiv \{1, 3\}$, and $T \in \Sigma^Q$ be defined by $T \equiv \text{cch}\{e_Q, 2e_{P^2}\}$. Then $M_L(T) = [e_Q, 2e_{P^2}]$. Note that for all $z \in M_L(T)$, if $z \neq L(T)$ then $z_2 < 1$ and $z_1, z_3 > 1$, in conformity with (3) of Lemma 9.3.

Proposition 9.2. If a solution satisfies P.O, AN, I.MON, and M.STAB, then it is the Leximin solution.

Proof. We have to show that F coincides with L on Σ^P for all $P \in \mathcal{P}$. The proof is by induction on $|P|$. If $|P| = 1$, *P.O* suffices to establish the result. If $|P| = 2$, the desired conclusion follows from Lemma 9.2. Let $n \geqq 3$ be given and suppose that F coincides with L on Σ^P for all $P \in \mathcal{P}$ with $|P| \leqq n-1$. Let $Q \in \mathcal{P}$ with $|Q| = n$ and $T \in \Sigma^Q$ be given, and let $z \equiv F(T)$. It follows by *M.STAB* and the induction hypothesis that $z \in M_L(T)$. Suppose,

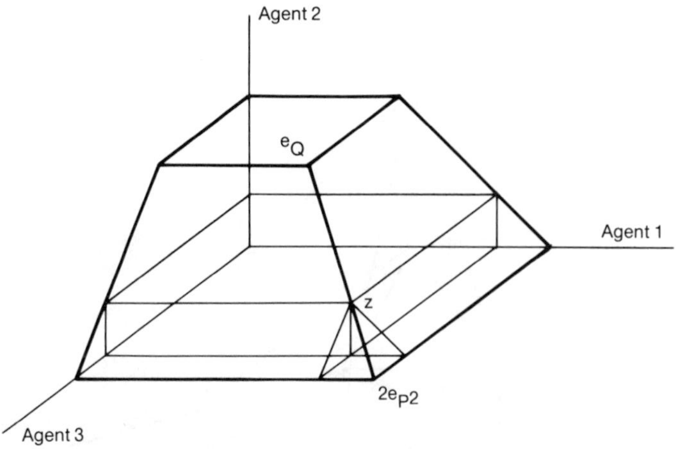

Figure 9.8. Example for which $M_L(T) \neq L(T)$.

by way of contradiction, that $z \neq L(T)$. Then by (3) of Lemma 9.3, there exists $k \in Q$ such that $z_k < E_k(T)$ and $z_i > E_i(T)$ for all $i \in P \equiv Q \backslash k$. Assume, without loss of generality, that $Q = \{1, 2, \ldots, n\}$, $k = 1$, and that $E(T) = e_Q$.

Let $T^1 \equiv \text{cch}\{e_Q, T_P\}$ and β be a real number such that

$$T^1 \subset \bar{T} \equiv \text{cch}\{e_Q, \beta e_2, \ldots, \beta e_n\}.$$

For all $i \in P$, define T^i recursively by $T^i \equiv \text{cch}\{T^{i-1}, \beta e_i\}$. Note that $T^1 \subset T$ and $T_P^1 = T_P$; $T^i \in \Sigma^Q$ and $E(T^i) = e_Q$ for all $i \in Q$; and $T^{i-1} \subset T^i$ and $T_{Q\backslash i}^{i-1} = T_{Q\backslash i}^i$ for all $i \in P$ (see Figure 9.9). For all $i \in Q$, let $z^i \equiv F(T^i)$. We claim that

$$z_1^i < 1 \quad \text{and} \quad z_P^i > 1 \quad \text{for all } i \in Q \tag{i}$$

and we prove (i) by induction on i.

For $i = 1$, it follows by *I.MON* that $z_1^1 \leqq z_1$. Since $E(T^1) = e_Q$ and $z_1^1 \leqq z_1 < 1$, then (1) of Lemma 9.3 implies that $z^1 \neq L(T^1)$. Since $z^1 \in M_L(T^1)$ by *M.STAB* and the induction hypothesis for F, and since $z_1^1 < 1$, it follows by (3) of Lemma 9.3 that $z_P^1 > e_P$, which proves (i) for $i = 1$. Next, suppose the claim holds for $i = k \in \{1, 2, \ldots, n-1\}$. To prove it for $i = k+1$, observe first that $z_i^i \geqq z_i^k$ and $z_i^k > 1$ by *I.MON* and the induction hypothesis for z^k, respectively. Since $z_i^i > 1$ and $\max\{x_i \mid x \in T^i, x_1 \geqq 1\} = 1$, then $z_1^i < 1$. Therefore, since $E(T^i) = e_Q$, (1) of Lemma 9.3 implies that $z^i \neq L(T^i)$. Since $z^i \in M_L(T^i)$ by *M.STAB* and the induction hypothesis for F and since $z_1^i < 1$, it follows by (3) of Lemma 9.3 that $z_P^i > e_P$, which proves the claim.

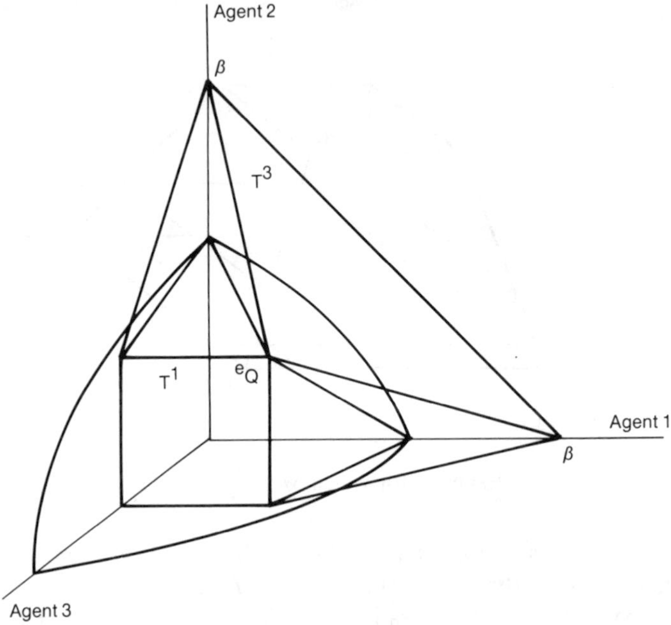

Figure 9.9. Proposition 9.2. $Q=\{1,2,3\}$.

Since $T^1 \subset \bar{T}$, then $T^n = \bar{T} = \text{cch}\{e_Q, \beta e_2, \ldots, \beta e_n\}$. Since $M_L(T^n) = \{e_Q\}$, *M.STAB* and the induction hypothesis then implies that $z^n = e_Q$, contradicting (i). This completes the proof that $F(T) = L(T)$. Q.E.D.

Combining the results of Propositions 9.1 and 9.2, the main theorem follows.

Theorem 9.1. *A solution satisfies P.O, AN, I.MON, and M.STAB if and only if it is the Leximin solution.*

Observe that the list of axioms used in Theorem 9.1 differs from the one used to characterize the Nash solution in Theorem 7.1 only in that *S.INV* has been replaced by *I.MON*. Now, *S.INV* can be interpreted as a condition that rules out interpersonal utility comparisons. Theorems 7.1 and 9.1 show that *S.INV* and *I.MON* are in a sense polar opposites when used in conjunction with the other three axioms: The Leximin solution exploits to a maximum degree the possibilities for interpersonal comparability of relative utility levels that become available when *S.INV* is dropped by permitting no trade-off between the utility levels of different agents.

9.3 Variants

We briefly examine the role played by each axiom in the proof of Theorem 9.1, and we comment on the continuity properties of the Leximin solution.

9.3.1 Removing the axioms one at a time

(i) Removing the axiom of Pareto-Optimality: We simply note here that the Truncated Egalitarian solutions of Chapter 5, which are the most natural candidates to consider, do not satisfy *M.STAB*, although they do satisfy *AN* and *I.MON*.

(ii) Removing the axiom of Anonymity: Asymmetric generalizations of the Leximin solution can be defined by weighting the agents' utilities differently. Formally, let $\alpha \equiv \{\alpha_i \mid i \in I\}$ be a sequence of positive real numbers. Then in order to solve some problem $S \in \Sigma^P$ for some $P \in \mathcal{P}$, one simply follows the sequence of operations defining L but always using E^α (the proportional solution relative to the weights α) instead of E in the computation of the intermediate steps. It is easy to verify that any solution L^α so defined satisfies *P.O, I.MON,* and *M.STAB*.

(iii) Removing the axiom of Individual Monotonicity: If *I.MON* is dropped, then the Nash solution becomes admissible.

(iv) Removing the axiom of Multilateral Stability: If *M.STAB* is dropped, then the lexicographic extension of the Kalai–Smorodinsky solution becomes admissible. Given $P \in \mathcal{P}$ and $S \in \Sigma^P$, the compromise recommended by this solution is obtained by first subjecting S to a positive linear transformation so that the ideal point of the resulting problem has equal coordinates. Then the Leximin solution outcome of the resulting problem is computed before finally taking the inverse image of that outcome under the linear transformation. This solution is discussed by Imai (1983).

This section concludes with a remark on the continuity properties of the Leximin solution.

9.3.2 A remark on continuity

In Section 9.1, we proved by way of an example that the Leximin solution does not satisfy *CONT*. However, this should not be seen as a major weakness of that solution since discontinuities occur only for sequences of problems that, although they converge in the Hausdorff topology, exhibit

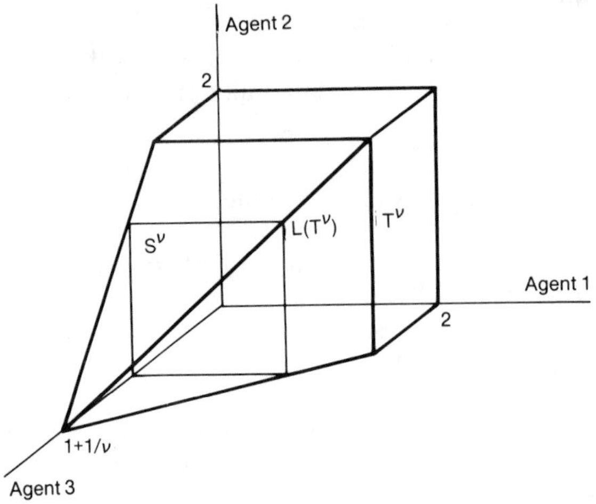

Figure 9.10. A three-person example showing that the Leximin solution does not satisfy *CONT*.

discontinuities in the subproblems obtained by taking a slice parallel to a subspace. This is clear in the example of Section 9.1 and is illustrated in the three-person example of Figure 9.10, where $Q \equiv \{1,2,3\}$ and $P \equiv \{1,2\}$, and where $T^\nu \in \Sigma^Q$ is defined for all integers ν by $T^\nu \equiv \text{cch}\{(2,2,1), (0,0,1+1/\nu)\}$. As $\nu \to \infty$, $z^\nu \equiv L(T^\nu) \to e_Q$ whereas $T^\nu \to T \equiv \text{cch}\{(2,2,1)\}$ and $L(T) = (2,2,1)$. Note, however, that the limit of $S^\nu \equiv t_P^{z^\nu}(T^\nu)$ as $\nu \to \infty$ is $\text{cch}\{e_P\}$ whereas $S \equiv t_P^{e_Q}(T) = \text{cch}\{2e_P\}$.

This example suggests that it may be unsatisfactory to impose *CONT* in conjunction with *M.STAB*. Indeed, one could argue that the violation of *CONT* exhibited in this example by the Leximin solution is an appropriate response to the discontinuity in the subproblem. If it is an appealing property of the Leximin solution that it still satisfies *M.STAB* even when sequences of subproblems exhibit discontinuities, it may be unreasonable to demand that continuity must hold in such cases. This discussion leads to the following natural weakening of *CONT* that uses a stronger notion of convergence involving subproblems.

Given $P \in \mathcal{P}$ and $A, B \subset \mathbb{R}_+^P$, let $d(A,B)$ be the Hausdorff distance of A and B. Now, given $Q \in \mathcal{P}$, $T \in \Sigma^Q$, and a sequence $\{T^\nu\}$ of elements of Σ^Q, $\{T^\nu\}$ *strongly converges* to T if $\{T^\nu\}$ itself converges to T and if, in addition, the following holds for all $\epsilon > 0$, all $z \in T$, and all sequences $\{z^\nu\}$ from $\mathbb{R}_+^Q$: If $z^\nu \in T^\nu$ for all ν and $z^\nu \to z$, then there is a $\bar{\nu}$ such that $d(t_P^z(T), t_P^{z^\nu}(T^\nu)) < \epsilon$ for all $\nu \geqq \bar{\nu}$ and all $P \subset Q$.

Weak Continuity (W.CONT): For all $Q \in \mathcal{P}$, all $T \in \Sigma^Q$, and all sequences $\{T^\nu\}$ of elements of Σ^Q, if $\{T^\nu\}$ strongly converges to T, then $F(T^\nu) \to F(T)$.

Note that in the example of Figure 9.10, $\{T^\nu\}$ does not strongly converge to T. Also consider the family of problems used in the proof of Lemma 7.3 and illustrated in Figure 7.6. In that case too, there is a discontinuity in one of the subproblems. In fact, that discontinuity is an essential part of the proof of Lemma 7.3, so the full force of *CONT* is needed for that proof.

The next result shows that the Leximin solution satisfies this weaker notion of continuity.

Proposition 9.3. *The Leximin solution satisfies W.CONT.*

Proof. We must show that L satisfies *W.CONT* on Σ^P for all $P \in \mathcal{P}$. The proof is by induction on $|P|$. If $|P| = 1$, the result follows from the Pareto-optimality of L. Suppose, by way of induction, that L satisfies *W.CONT* on Σ^P for all $P \in \mathcal{P}$ with $|P| \leqq n$ and let $Q \in \mathcal{P}$ with $|Q| = n+1$ be given. Pick $T \in \Sigma^Q$ and let $\{T^\nu\}$ be a sequence of elements of Σ^Q that strongly converges to T. For each ν, let $z^\nu \equiv L(T^\nu)$. Since the sequence $\{T^\nu\}$ converges, it is contained in some compact subset of $\mathbb{R}^Q_+$, which implies the existence of a converging subsequence of $\{z^\nu\}$. Without loss of generality, assume that $\{z^\nu\}$ itself converges to z.

Since $\{T^\nu\}$ strongly converges to T and $\{z^\nu\} \to z$, then $z \in T$, and moreover, for all $P \subset Q$, the sequence $\{t_P^{z^\nu}(T^\nu)\}$ strongly converges to $t_P^z(T)$. Since L satisfies *M.STAB,* then $L(t_P^{z^\nu}(T^\nu)) = z_P^\nu$ for all ν and all $P \subset Q$, and therefore, since $z_P^\nu \to z_P$, the induction hypothesis implies that $z_P = L(t_P^z(T))$ for all $P \subset Q$ with $P \neq Q$, that is, $z \in M_L(T)$.

Note that by (1) of Lemma 9.3, $z^\nu \geqq E(T^\nu)$ for all ν, which since $z^\nu \to z$ and $T^\nu \to T$ and E is continuous implies that $z \geqq E(T)$. Therefore, since $z \in M_L(T)$, it follows by (2) of Lemma 9.3 that $z = L(T)$. Q.E.D.

It should be noted that if $\{T^\nu\}$ is a sequence from $\tilde{\Sigma}^Q$ converging to $T \in \tilde{\Sigma}^Q$, then in fact $\{T^\nu\}$ strongly converges to T. Therefore, $L(T^\nu) \to L(T)$ since on the restricted domain $\tilde{\Sigma}^Q$ the Leximin solution coincides with the Egalitarian solution and the Egalitarian solution satisfies *CONT.* Proposition 9.3 says more, however. A simple example of a sequence $\{T^\nu\}$ covered by that proposition but not in $\tilde{\Sigma}^Q$ is given by

$$T^\nu \equiv \text{cch}\{(2, 2, 1 + 1/\nu)\}$$

for all ν.

CHAPTER 10

Population Monotonicity, Weak Stability, and the Egalitarian solution

10.1 Introduction

We come back here to the Egalitarian solution. We will show this solution to be the only solution to satisfy Weak Pareto-Optimality, Symmetry, Continuity, Monotonicity, and a weakening of the Stability condition introduced in Chapter 7, which we refer to as Weak Stability.

Recall the condition of (Multilateral) Stability. Starting from some problem T involving some group Q, consider some subgroup P and the subproblem S consisting of all the points of T at which the utilities of all the agents in $Q \backslash P$ are fixed at their values at $x \equiv F(T)$. Stability requires that S be solved at a point that coincides with the restriction of x to the subgroup P, that is, that $F(S) = x_P$. The condition of Weak Stability says that the solution outcome of S should *dominate,* instead of being equal to, the restriction of x to the subgroup P. Any solution satisfying Weak Stability and Weak Pareto-Optimality satisfies Stability (and, of course, Pareto-Optimality) on the subdomain of problems whose weak Pareto-optimal and Pareto-optimal boundaries coincide. Therefore, when used in conjunction with Weak Pareto-Optimality, as will be the case here, the two conditions of Weak Stability and Stability say nearly the same thing. In the instances in which they differ, the weaker requirement does not say, as Stability does, that no member of a subgroup would ever want to renegotiate; it simply says that renegotiations by subgroups would benefit all agents in the subgroup. This indicates that the main conflictual elements of the original problem have been solved. Whatever further moves could be recommended would be favored by everyone.

At this point, a formal statement of our condition should be given.

Weak Stability (W.STAB): For all $P, Q \in \mathcal{P}$ with $P \subset Q$, all $S \in \Sigma^P$, and all $T \in \Sigma^Q$, if $S = t_P^x(T)$, where $x = F(T)$, then $F(S) \geqq x_P$.

A counterpart of our earlier condition of Bilateral Stability (Chapter 2) would be obtained by adding the restriction $|P| = 2$. In fact, in the proof that follows, this weaker condition would suffice.

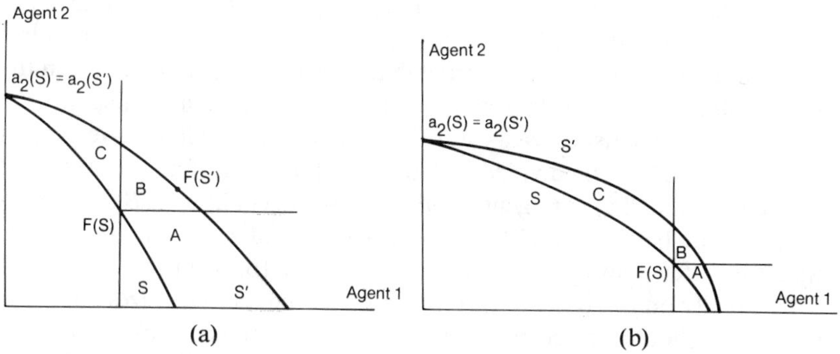

Figure 10.1. A criticism of the axiom of Individual Monotonicity.

We will show later that the Egalitarian solution satisfies this condition, but it is important to recall that it does not satisfy Stability itself, as noted in Chapter 9. On the other hand, its lexicographic extension (the Leximin solution) does satisfy Stability, as discussed in Chapter 9 as well, but it does not satisfy Monotonicity. This can easily be checked with the example used to prove Corollary 3.2. It is natural to conjecture that the Leximin solution can be characterized by Pareto-Optimality, Symmetry, Stability, and some weakening of Monotonicity. Such a theorem would be a close analogue of the one that will be proved here. This conjecture and the result proved in what follows have the particular interest of involving both considerations of Monotonicity and Stability, in contrast to our earlier results, which made use of only one of these two variable-population conditions.

It may be useful to relate the present chapter to Chapters 4 and 9, in which we offered characterizations of the Egalitarian and of the Leximin solutions, respectively.

The characterization of Chapter 4 involved the axiom of Independence of Irrelevant Alternatives, and we refer the reader to Section 4.1 for a detailed discussion of the limitations of the axiom. In Chapter 9 we used the axiom of Individual Monotonicity, and objections can certainly be raised against that axiom too, as is now explained. Consider the group made up of agents 1 and 2 and let S and S' in $\Sigma^{\{1,2\}}$ be related in the way specified in the hypotheses of the axiom: The problem S' of Figure 10.1a can be loosely described as having been obtained from S by an expansion in favor of agent 1. Individual Monotonicity says that agent 1 should not lose as a result of the expansion.

The only requirements on the relationship between S and S' are that $a_2(S)=a_2(S')$ and $S'\supset S$; however, it can be argued that these requirements are not always stringent enough to justify the demand made on the relationship between the two solution outcomes. Indeed, assuming that the solution F also satisfies Weak Pareto-Optimality, the alternatives added to S to yield S' can be divided into three sets: a set A of alternatives that are better than $F(S)$ for agent 1 and worse for agent 2; a set B of alternatives that are better than $F(S)$ for both agents; and a set C of alternatives that are better than $F(S)$ for agent 2 and worse for agent 1.

It is really on the basis of a comparison of the relative "sizes" of these sets that it should be decided how the solution outcome should move. If only A were added (ignoring, for the purposes of the conceptual issue under discussion, that this might generate a nonconvex problem), then one would certainly want to require that agent 1 gains. It is this kind of consideration that motivated Thomson and Myerson (1980) to introduce an Adding axiom with precisely this content. The effect on the solution outcome of adding B is not so clear since both agents benefit from it. But the addition of C certainly calls for a move in agent 2's favor. Altogether it is not obvious how the solution outcome should move, and a final recommendation should really depend on the relative sizes of these regions (as measured, e.g., by their areas). Figure 10.1b represents a pair S, S' satisfying the hypotheses of the axiom for which the alternatives in C outweigh the alternatives in A and B. Such a configuration appears to call for a move in agent 2's favor. (Note that comparisons of areas do not depend on which particular representatives in the von Neumann–Morgenstern families representing the agent's preferences are chosen in order to construct S. They are scale invariant.)

The chapter is organized as follows. Section 10.2 contains the main result, Section 10.3 variants of the main result, and Section 10.4 some concluding comments.

This chapter is based on Thomson (1984c).

10.2 Characterization of the Egalitarian solution

In this section we present the main result. First, we have

> ***Proposition 10.1.*** *The Egalitarian solution satisfies W.P.O, SY, CONT, MON, and W.STAB.*

Proof. That E satisfies *W.P.O, SY, CONT,* and *MON* is clear, and it has already been pointed out in Chapter 4. It remains to show that E satisfies *W.STAB*. So, let $P, Q \in \mathcal{P}$ with $P \subset Q$ and $T \in \Sigma^Q$ be given. We have $x \equiv E(T) > 0$. Therefore, $S \equiv t_P^x(T) \in \Sigma^P$. Since x has equal coordinates, the restriction x_P of x to $\mathbb{R}^P_+$ is a point of S with equal coordinates, and therefore $E(S) \geqq x_P$, the desired conclusion. Q.E.D.

The proof that if a solution satisfies the five axioms, it is the Egalitarian solution is by way of several lemmas.

Given $Q \in \mathcal{P}$, a subset A of $\mathbb{R}^Q$, and a vector t of $\mathbb{R}^Q$, first recall that $\text{Cyl}(A, t)$ designates the cylinder spanned by A with generators parallel to t.

Lemma 10.1. *If a solution F satisfies W.P.O, SY, CONT, MON, and W.STAB, then for all* $P \in \mathcal{P}$ *with* $|P| = 2$, $F = E$ *on* Σ^P.

Proof. The proof is organized in several steps in which successively larger and larger classes of problems are considered. The main steps, 1 and 3, involve the fairly laborious construction of three-person problems with certain properties. In Step 1, the three-person problem is given as a function of a parameter ϵ that has to be chosen small enough but different from 0. The problem obtained for $\epsilon = 0$ is easier to describe and represent, which we have done to facilitate the understanding of the proof. A positive but small ϵ yields an approximation to it that we have also represented. In order to simplify the notation, we write $T, U, t, \ldots$ for $T^0, U^0, t^0, \ldots$ (the values of $T^\epsilon, U^\epsilon, t^\epsilon, \ldots$ for $\epsilon = 0$).

Let $P \in \mathcal{P}$ with $|P| = 2$ and $S \in \Sigma^P$ be given.

Step 1. If $\text{WPO}(S)$ (i) contains a nondegenerate segment σ centered at $E(S)$ and normal to e_P and (ii) is supported at its points of intersection with the axes by straight lines with finite and nonzero slopes, then $F(S) = E(S)$.

Without loss of generality, we take $P = \{1, 2\}$. Assume, by way of contradiction, that for some S as just described, $F(S) \neq E(S)$. Without loss of generality, assume that $E(S) = e_P$. Let $a \equiv a_1(S)$ and $b \equiv a_2(S)$. By (i) and $E(S) = e_P$, it follows that $a \leqq 2$ and $b \leqq 2$. By (i) and *W.P.O*, either $F_1(S) > 1$ and $F_2(S) < 1$, or $F_1(S) < 1$ and $F_2(S) > 1$. Without loss of generality, assume the former.

We introduce agent 3, set $Q \equiv \{1, 2, 3\}$, $P^1 \equiv \{2, 3\}$ and $P^2 \equiv \{1, 3\}$, choose ϵ positive but small, and construct a problem $W^\epsilon \in \Sigma^Q$ as follows (see Figure 10.2; $W \equiv W^0$ is represented in Figure 10.3).

Let $y^\epsilon \equiv (1-\epsilon)e_Q$ and $T^\epsilon \equiv \mathbb{R}^Q_+ \cap \text{Cyl}(S, y^\epsilon - e_P)$.

Let $\sigma' \equiv \{x' \in \mathbb{R}^{P^2} \mid \exists x \in \sigma \text{ s.t. } x'_1 = x_1 \text{ and } x'_3 = x_2\}$, $S^2 \equiv \text{cch}\{\sigma', ae_1, ae_3\}$, and $V^\epsilon \equiv \mathbb{R}^Q_+ \cap \text{Cyl}(S^2, y^\epsilon - e_{P^2})$.

Finally, let $W^\epsilon \equiv T^\epsilon \cap V^\epsilon$. It is clear that $W^\epsilon \in \Sigma^Q$ for all ϵ.

The boundary ∂V_P of V_P is a vertical half-line emanating from ae_1. Because ∂V^ϵ_P varies continuously with ϵ and S has at ae_1 a line of support with a finite slope [assumption (ii)], it follows that for ϵ small enough,

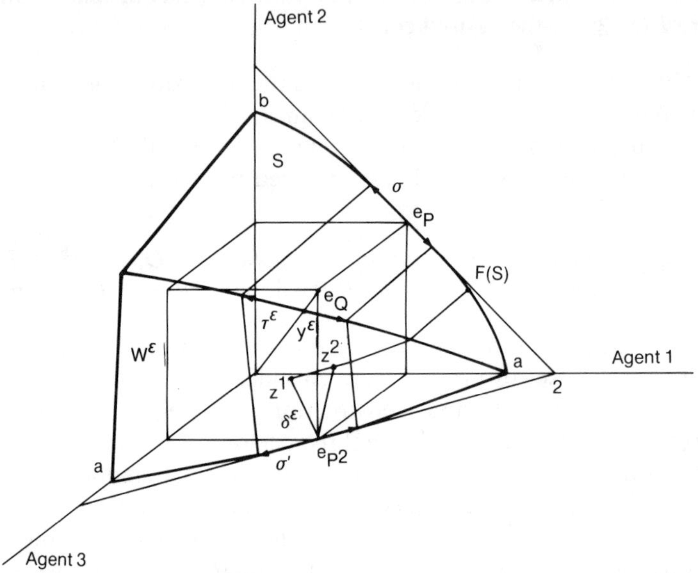

Figure 10.2. Step 1 of Lemma 10.1: W^{ϵ}.

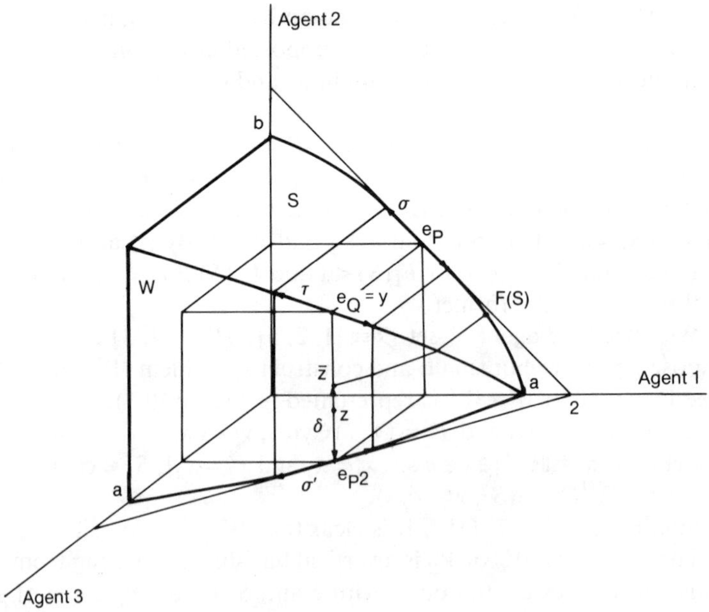

Figure 10.3. Step 1 of Lemma 10.1: W.

$S \subset V_P^\epsilon$, and therefore $W_P^\epsilon = S$. Similarly, ∂T_{P2} is a half-line parallel to e_3 emanating from ae_1. Since ∂T_{P2}^ϵ varies continuously with ϵ and S^2 has at ae_1 a line of support with a finite and nonzero slope [this is clear from (ii) and the construction of S^2], it follows that for ϵ small enough, $S^2 \subset T_{P2}^\epsilon$ and thus $W_{P2}^\epsilon = S^2$. Also, note that $\text{Cyl}(\sigma, y^\epsilon - e_P)$ and $\text{Cyl}(\sigma', y^\epsilon - e_{P2})$ are portions of planes symmetrical with respect to the plane of equation $x_2 = x_3$. They intersect along a segment denoted τ^ϵ containing y^ϵ. We have $\tau^\epsilon \subset \text{PO}(W^\epsilon)$.

Since S^2 is symmetric, we deduce from *W.P.O* and *SY* that $F(S^2) = e_{P2}$. Let $\eta \equiv 1 - F_2(S)$. By hypothesis, $\eta > 0$. Next, we apply *MON* to compare what agents 1 and 3 get in W^ϵ to what they get in $W_{P2}^\epsilon = S^2$ and what agent 2 gets in W^ϵ to what she gets in $W_P^\epsilon = S$:

$$F_1(W^\epsilon) \leqq F_1(W_{P2}^\epsilon) = F_1(S^2) = 1,$$
$$F_2(W^\epsilon) \leqq F_2(W_P^\epsilon) = F_2(S) = 1 - \eta,$$
$$F_3(W^\epsilon) \leqq F_3(W_{P2}^\epsilon) = F_3(S^2) = 1.$$

For $\epsilon = 0$, these inequalities are satisfied only by the points of a vertical segment δ with endpoints e_{P2} and $\bar{z} \equiv e_Q - \eta e_2$. For ϵ small enough, they are satisfied only by the points of a narrow triangle δ^ϵ with one vertex at e_{P2} and the other two vertices close to $\bar{z}$ (these vertices are denoted z^1 and z^2 in Figure 10.2). Let $z^\epsilon \equiv F(W^\epsilon)$.

If $\epsilon = 0$ and $z = F(W)$, then $t_{P1}^z(W) = \text{cch}\{e_{P1}\}$. For ϵ small, let $S^\epsilon \equiv t_{P1}^{z^\epsilon}(W^\epsilon)$. Note that $S^\epsilon = \text{cch}\{(1+\epsilon')e_2, (1+\epsilon')e_3, (1-\epsilon'')e_{P1}\}$ with $\epsilon' \geqq 0$ and $\epsilon', \epsilon'' \to 0$ as $\epsilon \to 0$, so that $S^\epsilon \in \Sigma^{P1}$ and $S^\epsilon \to \text{cch}\{e_{P1}\}$ as $\epsilon \to 0$.

By *W.P.O* and *SY*, $F(S^\epsilon) = (1-\epsilon'')e_{P1}$. However, $F_3(W^\epsilon) = z_3^\epsilon > 1 - \epsilon'' = F_3(S^\epsilon)$, in contradiction with $F(S^\epsilon) \geqq z_{P1}^\epsilon$, as required by *W.STAB*. This proves Step 1.

Step 2. If $\text{PO}(S)$ is supported at $E(S)$ by a straight line normal to e_P, then $F(S) = E(S)$.

This follows from the fact that any such S can be approximated by a sequence of elements of Σ^P satisfying the assumptions listed in the statement of Step 1 and *CONT*.

Step 3. Conclusion of the proof of Lemma 10.1.

As in Step 1, we assume without loss of generality that $P = \{1,2\}$. Also, appealing to *CONT*, we assume that $S \in \tilde{\Sigma}^P$. Suppose, by way of contradiction, that $F(S) \neq E(S)$ for some $S \in \tilde{\Sigma}^P$. Let $a \equiv a_1(S)$ and $b \equiv a_2(S)$. Without loss of generality, we assume that $E(S) = e_P$. Then, either $a \leqq 2$ or $b \leqq 2$. Without loss of generality, we assume the latter and distinguish two cases, supposing first that

$$a \leqq 2. \tag{i}$$

Since $S \in \tilde{\Sigma}^P$ and $F(S) \neq E(S)$, by *W.P.O* either $F_1(S) > 1$ and $F_2(S) < 1$ or $F_1(S) < 1$ and $F_2(S) > 1$. Without loss of generality, we assume the former.

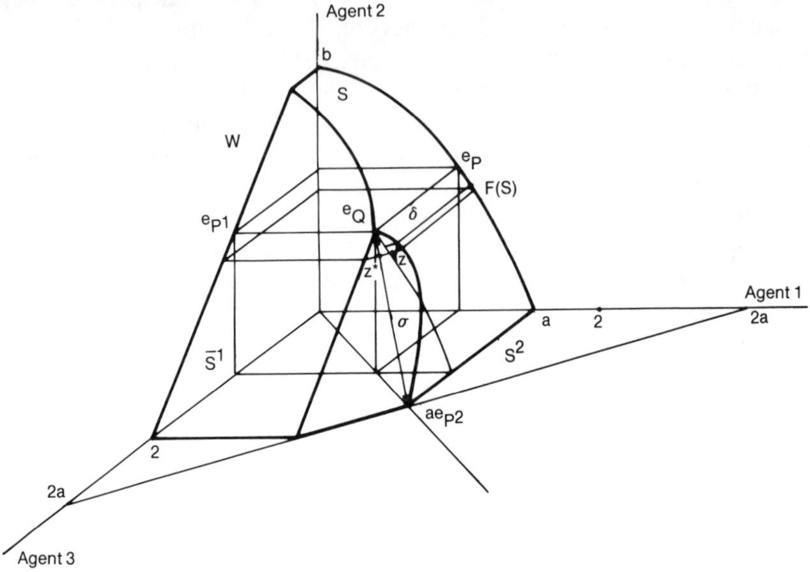

Figure 10.4. Step 3 of Lemma 10.1: $a \leqq 2$.

We introduce agent 3, set $Q \equiv \{1, 2, 3\}$, $P^1 \equiv \{2, 3\}$, and $P^2 \equiv \{1, 3\}$, and construct a problem W as follows.

Let $S^1 \equiv \text{cch}\{2e_2, 2e_3\}$ and $S^2 \equiv \text{cch}\{2ae_1, 2ae_3\}$. Let $T \equiv \text{Cyl}(S, e_3)$, $U \equiv \text{Cyl}(S^1, e_1)$, $V \equiv \text{Cyl}(S^2, e_Q - ae_{P2})$, and finally $W \equiv T \cap U \cap V$. Note that $W \in \Sigma^Q$. First, we show that $W_P = S$. It is obvious that $T_P = S$ and that $U_P \supset S$. To see that $V_P \supset S$, note that all points of S are dominated by some point of either the segment $[e_P, x^1]$, where $x^1 \equiv (a, b - a(b-1))$ (x^1 is the point on the line through be_2 and e_P which has its first coordinate equal to a), or the segment $[e_P, x^2]$, where $x^2 \equiv (a - b(a-1), b)$ (x^2 is the point on the line through ae_1 and e_P which has its second coordinate equal to b). Both of these segments lie below the line of equation $x_1/2a + [(a-1)/a]x_2 = 1$, which is the intersection with $\mathbb{R}^P$ of the plane through $2ae_1$, $2ae_2$, and e_Q determining V.

It is easy to check that $\bar{S}_1 \equiv W_{P1}$ is supported at $E^{P^1}(\bar{S}_1) = e_{P1}$ by a straight line normal to e_{P1}, that $\sigma \equiv [ae_{P2}, e_Q] \subset \text{PO}(W)$, and that for any $z' \in \sigma$, $t^z_{P2}(W)$ is supported at z' by a straight line normal to e_{P2}.

Applying *MON*, it follows that

$$F_1(W) \leqq F_1(W_P) = F_1(S),$$
$$F_2(W) \leqq F_2(W_P) = F_2(S),$$
$$F_3(W) \leqq F_3(W_{P1}) = F_3(\bar{S}^1) = 1.$$

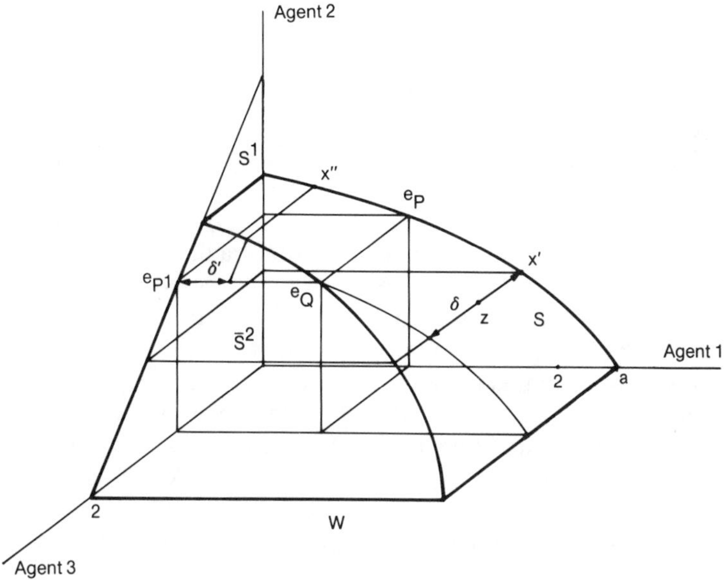

Figure 10.5. Step 3 of Lemma 10.1: $a > 2$.

These inequalities are satisfied only by the points of an area δ made up of a segment parallel to e_3 with one endpoint at $F(S)$ and of a possibly degenerate triangle contained in ∂W. [In Figure 10.4 the triangle is non-degenerate; it would be degenerate if $F(S)$ happened to be further down on $\mathrm{PO}(S)$.] No point of δ belongs to σ. Let $z \equiv F(W)$ and $\bar{S}^2 \equiv t^z_{P2}(W)$. Since $z \in \delta$, $\bar{S}^2$ intersects σ at a point z^* whose first coordinate is strictly smaller than z_1 if $F_2(S) > 0$ and $\mathrm{WPO}(S)$ does not contain $[ae_1, e_P]$. (The desired conclusion for those cases follows from *CONT*.) Also, $z^* = E(\bar{S}^2)$ and $\bar{S}^2$ is supported at z^* by a line normal to e_{P2}, as we saw earlier. Then, by Step 2, $F(\bar{S}^2) = z^*$. By *W.STAB*, $F_1(\bar{S}^2) \geqq z_1$ since $z = F(W)$. Since $z_1 > z_1^*$, a contradiction follows. This proves Step 3 when $a \leqq 2$. Now, we assume that

$$a > 2. \qquad \text{(ii)}$$

Define $T \equiv \mathrm{Cyl}(S, e_3)$, $S^1 \equiv \mathrm{cch}\{2e_2, 2e_3\}$, $U \equiv \mathrm{Cyl}(S^1, e_1)$, and finally $W \equiv T \cap U$. Note that $W \in \Sigma^{\mathcal{Q}}$.

If $F_1(S) > 1$ and $F_2(S) < 1$, the argument is as in (i) if $F_1(S)$ also satisfies $F_1(S) < 2$. (This case can be followed in Figure 10.5 by setting $F(S) = x'$.) The same inequalities are derived from *MON* to define a segment $\delta \equiv [x', x' + e_3]$ where $z \equiv F(W)$ should be. But $\bar{S}_2 \equiv t^z_{P2}(W)$ is such that

$a_1(\bar{S}_2) = z_1$ and $a_3(\bar{S}_2) = E_3(\bar{S}_2) \geqq 1$ so that $\max\{x_i \mid i = 1, 3, x \in \bar{S}_2\} \leqq 2E_3(\bar{S}_2)$, and therefore by (i), $F(\bar{S}_2) = E(\bar{S}_2)$. Since $a > 2$ implies that $E_1(\bar{S}_2) < z_1$, we obtain a violation of *W.STAB*.

If $F_1(S) \geqq 2$, a contradiction is derived by a familiar continuity argument. We define the continuous function $h: [2, a] \to \Sigma^P$ by $h(t) = \{x \in S \mid x \leqq t\}$. We note that $h(a) = S$, that $h(2)$ satisfies the hypotheses of (i), and that for all $t \in [2, a]$, $E(h(t)) = e_P$ and $a_2(h(t)) \leqq 2$. Then, $F_1(h(a)) \geqq 2$, $F_1(h(2)) = 1$ by (i), and for no $t \in [2, a]$ can $F_1(h(t))$ be in $]1, 2[$ by the preceding paragraph. These statements are in contradiction with *CONT*.

(*Note:* A proof that does not make use of *CONT* could also be developed in the spirit of the proof of Chapter 4. It proceeds by induction on k, where k is the integer such that $k < a \leqq k+1$.)

If $F_1(S) < 1$, as illustrated in Figure 10.5 by setting $F(S) = x''$, we apply an approximation argument similar to that of Step 1. We replace S^1, U, and W of (ii) by $S^{1\epsilon}$, U^ϵ, and W^ϵ defined by $S^{1\epsilon} = \text{cch}\{2(1+\epsilon)e_2, 2(1+\epsilon)e_3\}$, $U^\epsilon = \mathbb{R}^Q_+ \cap \text{Cyl}(S^{1\epsilon}, e_Q - (1+\epsilon)e_{P2})$, and $W^\epsilon \equiv T \cap U^\epsilon$. We use (i) to conclude that $F(W^\epsilon_{P1}) = E(W^\epsilon_{P1})$ and *MON* to identify a small triangle δ^ϵ of points to which $F(W)$ should belong. For $\epsilon = 0$, this triangle collapses to the segment $\delta' = [e_{P1}, e_{P1} + F(S)e_1]$ of Figure 10.5. Letting $z^\epsilon \equiv F(W^\epsilon)$ and $S^\epsilon \equiv t^{z^\epsilon}_{P2}(W^\epsilon)$, we use (i) to conclude that $F(S^\epsilon) = E(S^\epsilon)$, and after observing that $z^\epsilon_3 > E_3(S^\epsilon)$, we derive a contradiction to *W.STAB*.

Q.E.D.

Lemma 10.2. *If a solution F satisfies W.P.O, CONT, and W.STAB and if $F = E$ on Σ^P for all $P \in \mathcal{P}$ with $|P| = 2$, then $F = E$.*

Proof. Suppose, by way of contradiction, that for some $Q \in \mathcal{P}$ with $|Q| > 2$ (neglecting the case $|Q| = 1$, for which the desired conclusion follows from *W.P.O*) and for some $T \in \Sigma^Q$, $F(T) \neq E(T)$. Suppose first that $T \in \tilde{\Sigma}^Q$ (the conclusion for $T \notin \tilde{\Sigma}^Q$ would follow by *CONT*). Without loss of generality, assume that $E(T) = e_Q$. Since $F(T) \neq E(T)$, it follows from *W.P.O* that there exist $i, j \in Q$ such that $F_i(T) > 1$ and $F_j(T) < 1$. Then, let $P \equiv \{i, j\}$ and $S \equiv t^x_P(T)$, where $x \equiv F(T)$. Since S contains a semipositive vector and $T \in \tilde{\Sigma}^Q$, $S \in \tilde{\Sigma}^P$ and, by *W.STAB*, $F(S) \geqq x_P$. Since $F(S) = E(S)$ by Lemma 10.1 and since $x_P \in \text{PO}(S)$, $E_i(S) < F_i(S)$. This yields the desired contradiction. Q.E.D.

Collecting all the previous results, the announced characterization of the Egalitarian solution follows.

Theorem 10.1. *A solution satisfies W.P.O, SY, CONT, MON, and W.STAB if and only if it is the Egalitarian solution.*

10.3 Variants

10.3.1 Alternative domains

(i) Adding the requirement of strict comprehensiveness: The Egalitarian solution can be characterized on $\tilde{\Sigma}$ as the only solution to satisfy *P.O, SY, CONT, MON,* and *M.STAB,* but we will not include the proof of this statement. It can be suspected, on the basis of the fact that the variants on $\tilde{\Sigma}$ of the characterizations of the Kalai–Smorodinsky and Egalitarian solutions presented in Chapters 3 and 4 do not make use of *CONT,* that *CONT* can be dispensed with here as well.

(ii) Finite number of additional agents: In the preceding proof, no use was ever made of the unboundedness of the number of potential agents. In fact, our result holds as soon as $|I| \geqq 3$.

10.3.2 Removing the axioms one at a time

This section contains a discussion of which additional solutions would be made possible by removing one axiom at a time from the list appearing in Theorem 10.1.

(i) Removing the axiom of Weak Pareto-Optimality: Given a list $\alpha = \{\alpha^P \mid P \in \mathcal{P}\}$ of nonnegative numbers such that for all $P, Q \in \mathcal{P}$, $\alpha^P \geqq \alpha^Q$ if and only if $P \subset Q$, let F^α be defined as follows: Given $P \in \mathcal{P}$ and $S \in \Sigma^P$, $F^\alpha(S) \equiv \alpha^P e_P$ if this point belongs to S and $F(S) \equiv E(S)$ otherwise. All such F^α satisfy *SY, MON, W.STAB,* and *CONT.* These solutions are discussed in Chapter 5 under the name *Truncated Egalitarian solutions.*

(ii) Removing the axiom of Symmetry: Given a list $\phi = \{\phi_i \mid i \in I\}$ of increasing and continuous functions $\phi_i : \mathbb{R}_+ \to \mathbb{R}_+$ such that $\phi_i(0) = 0$, define F^ϕ as follows: Given $P \in \mathcal{P}$ and $S \in \Sigma^P$, $F^\phi(S)$ is the unique point of intersection with WPO(S) of the graph G^P of the function $\phi^P : \mathbb{R}_+ \to \mathbb{R}_+^P$ defined by $\phi_i^P = \phi_i$ for all $i \in P$. All such F^ϕ satisfy *W.P.O, MON, W.STAB,* and *CONT.* These solutions are discussed in Chapter 5 under the name *Monotone Path Solutions.*

(iii) Removing the axiom of Monotonicity: The Nash solution satisfies *W.P.O, SY, W.STAB,* and *CONT.* (See Chapter 7; in fact, N satisfies *P.O* and *M.STAB.*)

(iv) Removing the axiom of Weak Stability: The Kalai–Smorodinsky solution satisfies *W.P.O, SY, MON,* and *CONT* (see Chapter 3).

(v) Removing the axiom of Continuity: Many examples of solutions satisfying *W.P.O, SY, MON,* and *W.STAB* but not *CONT* can be constructed. One such example is obtained by taking F to be the Leximin solution for two agents and the Egalitarian solution otherwise.

CHAPTER 11

Stability and Collectively Rational solutions

11.1 Introduction

A major part of the theory of social choice is based on the assumption of collective rationality - that social decisions be made consistently with the maximization of some ordering on the space of alternatives, where by an *ordering* is meant a binary relation that is reflexive, transitive, and complete. For example, collective rationality is a defining property of an Arrow (1951) social welfare function (Arrow SWF), which produces social orderings of a given set of physical alternatives from profiles of individual orderings of those alternatives. Another well-known example is the family of Bergson–Samuelson social welfare functions (Bergson, 1938; Samuelson, 1947).

By a Bergson–Samuelson SWF is usually meant a real-valued function defined on utility space, representing a social ordering of all possible utility allocations for the society under consideration. As pointed out by Sen (1970, pp. 34–5), it is in general the social ordering itself that is of primary interest for social decision making. Therefore, any ordering of utility space will here be referred to as a Bergson–Samuelson SWF regardless of whether it has a real-valued representation.

Observe that the domain of definition of a Bergson–Samuelson SWF differs from that of an Arrow SWF: A Bergson–Samuelson SWF is defined on a space of *utility allocations,* whereas an Arrow SWF is defined on a space of individual orderings, for example, a space of *utility functions.*

A condition that is often imposed on the Bergson–Samuelson SWF is *Separability,* or *Independence of Unconcerned Individuals,* as it is also sometimes called. This condition (due to Fleming, 1952) says that if the utility levels for a subset of the agents of society is the same for some pair of alternatives, then the social ordering of those alternatives should not depend on the utility levels of those agents. This means that if $\succsim_Q$ is a social ordering of utility space $\mathbb{R}^Q_+$ for a group Q of agents such that $|Q| \geqq 3$, then if $P \subset Q$, the ordering $\succsim_P$ obtained from $\succsim_Q$ by restricting $\succsim_Q$ to any hyperplane parallel to $\mathbb{R}^P$ must be the same for all such hyperplanes. If, in addition, the ordering $\succsim_Q$ is continuous, then it has an additively separable numerical representation; that is, there exists a real-valued function f on $\mathbb{R}_+^Q$ such that $f(x) \geqq f(y)$ if and only if $x \gtrsim_Q y$, where f is of the form $f(x) = \Sigma_Q f_i(x_i)$ (Debreu, 1960).

The condition of Separability is indeed satisfied by most of the commonly used Bergson–Samuelson SWFs, such as the *Utilitarian SWF* (classical utilitarianism), the *Nash SWF*[1] (Nash, 1950), as well as the *Leximin SWF* (Sen, 1970), which is the symmetric lexicographic extension of the *Rawlsian (maximin) SWF* (Rawls, 1971).

Clearly, one obtains a social choice function[2] from any Bergson–Samuelson SWF, provided existence and uniqueness of the maxima for the SWF are guaranteed on the relevant domain of problems. For example, the Utilitarian solution U is derived from the ordering $\gtrsim^U$ defined by $x \gtrsim^U y$ if and only if $\Sigma x_i \geqq \Sigma y_i$, and is well defined on the domain of strictly convex problems.

On the other hand, the existence of a social ordering is not a necessary prerequisite for social decision making; it is only necessary that there be a solution outcome to every choice problem. The concept of a solution that is used here is based on this minimal requirement and thus makes no presumption about collective rationality. Nevertheless, as we discovered in previous chapters, many sets of axioms do lead to solutions that are collectively rational; thus one could look at such characterization results as being related to the *integrability problem* in demand theory, which concerns the identification of necessary and sufficient conditions for a demand function to be consistent with utility maximization.

By analogy with the integrability problem, it would be of interest to establish conditions under which a solution is (1) collectively rational, that is, consistent with the maximization of a Bergson–Samuelson SWF, and (2) consistent with the maximization of a *separable* Bergson–Samuelson SWF. An answer to the first question has been given by Richter (1971), who showed that a choice function is rational if and only if it satisfies a generalized form of Houthakker's (1950) Strong Axiom of Revealed Preference (*S.A.R.P*). The second question is the topic of this chapter.

Earlier, the axiom of Multilateral Stability (*M.STAB*) was used to characterize the Nash solution (Chapter 7) and the Leximin solution (Chapter

[1] To be precise, the Nash SWF, $\gtrsim^N$, satisfies Separability only on the strictly positive orthant of utility space: For each $P \in \mathcal{P}$, $\gtrsim_P^N$ is defined by $x \gtrsim_P^N y$ if and only if $\Pi_P x_i \geqq \Pi_P y_i$; hence, given $P, Q \in \mathcal{P}$ with $P \subset Q$ and $P \neq Q$, all points in $\mathbb{R}_+^P + \{\alpha e_{Q \setminus P}\}$ are indifferent for $\gtrsim_Q^N$ if $\alpha = 0$, whereas this is not the case if $\alpha > 0$.

[2] A *choice function* is a rule that for every set in a collection of feasible sets selects a unique element from that set. A particular choice function is obtained by (i) specifying the collection of feasible sets (the domain, e.g., convex and comprehensive subsets of $\mathbb{R}_+^n$) and (ii) specifying the rule (e.g., selecting the point of equal coordinates in the upper boundary of the feasible set). Thus, a *solution* is a particular example of a choice function.

9). As already noted, to each of these solutions there corresponds a Bergson–Samuelson SWF that happens to be separable.

This parallelism between *M.STAB* and Separability is in fact much more general: *M.STAB* implies that if two problems T and T' for a group Q of agents yield the same subproblem S for some subgroup P when intersected with hyperplanes parallel to $\mathbb{R}^P$ through their respective solution outcomes x and x', then $x_P = x'_P$. Thus, *M.STAB* seems to be the natural counterpart to Separability in the sense that it imposes on a solution much the same requirement that Separability imposes on a Bergson–Samuelson SWF. In fact, any solution obtained from a separable Bergson–Samuelson SWF can easily be shown to satisfy *M.STAB*.

What is more interesting and less obvious is that *M.STAB* imposes on a solution a fair amount of collective rationality as well. It is shown here that *M.STAB* is a necessary and sufficient condition for a Pareto-optimal and continuous solution to be consistent with the maximization of an additively separable and strictly quasi-concave Bergson–Samuelson social welfare function.[3] This is the main result of this chapter. However, it is also shown that the three axioms are independent in the sense that removing any one of them will permit solutions that are not collectively rational.

It may be worthwhile at this point to outline the basic structure of the proof of this characterization result to serve as a guide through some of the technical details involved in the argument. In particular, the proof is related to and draws heavily upon concepts and ideas from demand theory, in particular from integrability theory. The connection with demand theory is established by considering the restriction $\bar{F}$ of a solution F to the domain of linear *budget problems* known from demand theory. If the number of agents is held constant, the model then becomes formally equivalent to the standard model of demand theory, which is made up of *commodities, budget problems,* and *demand functions* instead of agents, problems, and solutions. These new terms will be used freely throughout in order to emphasize the relationship with demand theory, a relationship that will be exploited in the main part of the characterization proof, which consists in establishing sufficient conditions for a demand function $\bar{F}$ defined for a variable number of commodities to be consistent with the maximization of an additively separable *utility function*. Thus, as opposed to previous chapters where the full domain was used in all the proofs, the main part of the analysis of this chapter is conducted by considering only that subdomain that is relevant for demand theory, thereby yielding a result on the integrability of demand functions as a by-product of independent interest.

[3] The weaker version of the stability axiom (*B.STAB*) will be sufficient.

There are essentially two approaches to the integrability problem in demand theory (Chipman et al., 1971, pp. 3–6): The first one is set-theoretic and uses some version of *S.A.R.P* and some demand continuity assumption.[4] The second one is analytic and uses symmetry and negative semidefiniteness of the Slutsky matrix (direct demand function) or of the Antonelli matrix (indirect demand function).[5]

The approach followed here is analytic, based on the indirect demand function, although no explicit use is made of the Antonelli matrix – the reason being that our axioms do not imply that the indirect demand function is differentiable. In fact, the indirect demand function may even fail to be single-valued and continuous. The reason the indirect demand function is used, despite its apparent irregularity, is that *M.STAB* imposes a lot of structure on its local behavior but has little or nothing to say about the local behavior of the direct demand function. This is so because integrating an indirect demand function yields a direct utility function, whereas integrating a direct demand function yields an indirect utility function.[6] *M.STAB* is related to additive separability of the direct utility function, and it is in general not true that the indirect demand function is additively separable if the direct one has that property.

The point of departure for the characterization theorem is Lemma 11.1, which is a slight modification of Lemma 7.3, the main step in the characterization of the Nash solution that uses Continuity. The proof of Lemma 7.3 is essentially a proof that *P.O, CONT,* and *B.STAB* together imply *I.I.A* for all two-person components of F, a result that can be extended to any n-person component of F by strengthening *B.STAB* to *M.STAB*.

This result is useful for two reasons: First, it can be used to show that every strictly positive vector is the solution outcome to some budget problem. This fact allows one to restrict attention to the domain of budget problems because most problems can then be solved by applying *I.I.A* to some budget problem that contains it. Second, it turns out that the restricted solution $\bar{F}$ satisfies *W.A.R.P* (Weak Axiom of Revealed Preference) whenever F satisfies *I.I.A*. Of course, *W.A.R.P* is not a sufficiently strong condition to obtain integrability results, as the well-known counterexample by Gale (1960) has shown.[7] However, *W.A.R.P* has two other useful consequences: First, it implies that the *inverse demand correspon-*

[4] Exceptions are (1) Uzawa (1971), who uses Samuelson's (1938) Weak Axiom of Revealed Preference (*W.A.R.P*) and a regularity condition on the revealed preference relation, and (2) Hurwicz and Richter (1971), who do not assume continuity of the demand function.

[5] An exception is Hurwicz and Richter (1979), who use *W.A.R.P* and an axiom of Ville (1951).

[6] See Hurwicz (1971) for an excellent exposition and more details.

[7] See also Kihlstrom, Mas-Colell, and Sonnenschein (1976), whose results yield an infinity of demand functions that satisfy *W.A.R.P* but not *S.A.R.P*.

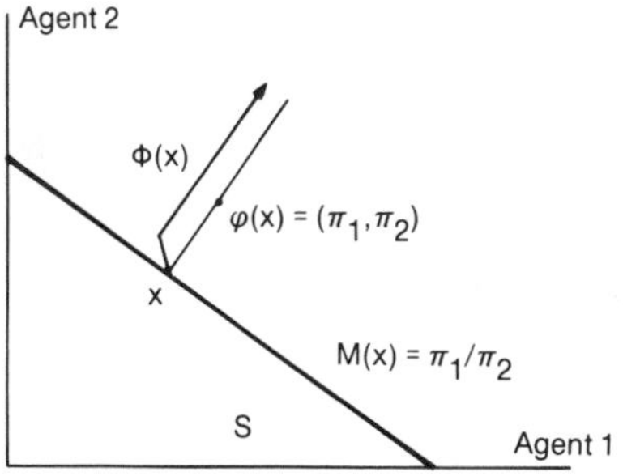

Figure 11.1. Inverse demand correspondences and the MRS.

dence (from quantities to prices) is convex-valued, which can be used to show that the *normalized* inverse demand correspondence (from quantities to prices in the unit simplex) must be single-valued except on a negligible set. Second, it implies that the real-valued representation for $\bar{F}$, if one exists, is quasi-concave.

To sum up, the main role played by the stability axiom so far is to show that *W.A.R.P* must hold for the demand function $\bar{F}$, thereby establishing properties that correspond to negative semidefiniteness of the Antonelli matrix under conditions of differentiability. What is done next is to use *M.STAB* to establish a property of the inverse demand correspondence that would imply symmetry of the Antonelli matrix under differentiability.[8]

An outline of the main idea can be given by assuming, for convenience, that the normalized inverse demand function is single-valued *everywhere* on the strictly positive orthant. The situation is illustrated in Figure 11.1, which depicts a two-dimensional budget problem S solved at $x > 0$. We denote by Φ the inverse demand correspondence, and by φ the normalized inverse demand correspondence. Thus, $\Phi(x)$ is the set of normals to all budget problems solved at x, and $\varphi(x)$ is the intersection between $\Phi(x)$ and the unit simplex. Since $x > 0$, then $\varphi(x)$ is a singleton, $\Phi(x)$ is a ray, and S is the only budget problem solved at x. The quantity $M(x) \equiv \varphi_1(x)/\varphi_2(x)$ is the price of one unit of the first commodity in terms of the second. Thus, it could be (the negative of) the slope of a level curve of some underlying utility function at x, that is, a marginal rate of substitution (MRS) at x. Note that $M(x_1, x_2) = 1/M(x_2, x_1)$.

[8] Observe the symmetry of the Antonelli matrix in the *mathematical* integrability condition; that is, it is used to prove that level curves exist, whereas negative semi-definiteness serves to give these level curves the right curvature, i.e., convexity. Again the reader is referred to Hurwicz (1971) for more details.

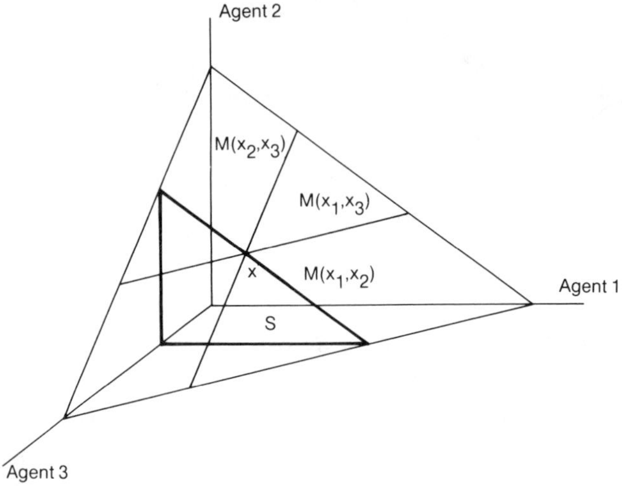

Figure 11.2. Relationship between MRS functions.

Next, let $Q \in \mathcal{P}$ with $|Q| \geqq 3$ be given. *M.STAB* implies that for all $x \in \mathbb{R}^Q_+$, if $P \subset Q$ then $\Phi_P(x) \subset \Phi(x_P)$, where (as usual) $\Phi_P(x)$ denotes the projection of $\Phi(x)$ on $\mathbb{R}^P$. In fact, this inclusion property is exactly what *M.STAB* says about the restricted solution $\bar{F}$; thus, it could serve as an alternative definition of *M.STAB* for $\bar{F}$. Note that if $x > 0$, the reverse inclusion also holds, since by assumption Φ is ray-valued on the strictly positive orthant. Hence, $\Phi_P(x) = \Phi(x_P)$ for all $P \subset Q$ and all $x \in \mathbb{R}^Q_{++}$, or equivalently, $\varphi_P(x)$ is proportional to $\varphi(x_P)$. Because $\varphi_i(x_P)/\varphi_j(x_P) = M(x_i, x_j)$ for $P = \{i, j\}$, this implies that

$$\frac{\varphi_i(x)}{\varphi_j(x)} = M(x_i, x_j) \quad \text{for all } Q \in \mathcal{P}, \text{ all } \{i, j\} \subset Q, \text{ and all } x \in \mathbb{R}^Q_{++}, \tag{i}$$

which implies that the ratio of any two components i and j of the normalized inverse demand function is independent of all but the ith and jth arguments. Setting $Q \equiv \{i, j, k\}$ and noting that

$$\frac{\varphi_i(x)}{\varphi_j(x)} = \frac{\varphi_i(x)/\varphi_k(x)}{\varphi_j(x)/\varphi_k(x)} \tag{ii}$$

identically, it follows (see Figure 11.2) that

$$M(x_i, x_j) = \frac{M(x_i, x_k)}{M(x_j, x_k)} \quad \text{for all } Q \equiv \{i, j, k\} \text{ and all } x \in \mathbb{R}^Q_{++}, \tag{iii}$$

which reveals the structure imposed by *M.STAB* on the local behavior of the indirect demand function, stating that the MRS between x_i and x_j can

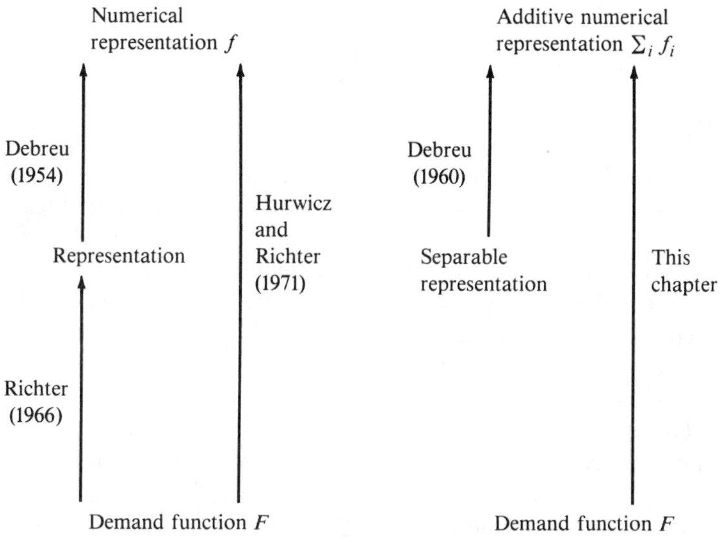

Figure 11.3. Results on the integrability of demand functions.

be written as a quotient, where the numerator does not depend on x_j and the denominator does not depend on x_i. Now fix $x_k = x_k^0$ arbitrarily and integrate the two terms on the right side of (iii) separately to obtain two functions f_i and f_j such that the left side of (iii) is (the negative of) the slope of a level curve of the function $f_i + f_j$ wherever the latter is differentiable. Continuity of the direct demand function $\bar{F}$ and single-valuedness of the indirect demand function φ, except on a negligible set, will guarantee that the MRS functions are sufficiently well behaved to be integrable.

This integrability result generalizes easily to higher dimensions by defining f_i as indicated in the previous paragraph for all $i \neq k$. It then follows by repeated use of (iii) and (i) that for all $Q \in \mathcal{P}$ that do not contain k and all $x \in \mathbb{R}^Q_{++}$, if the gradient of the function $\Sigma_Q f_i$ exists at x, then it is normal to the budget problem solved at x. It is shown in Lemma 11.12 that this result extends to all $Q \in \mathcal{P}$ by a suitable choice of the remaining function f_k. Finally, as mentioned earlier, *W.A.R.P* will guarantee that the level curves of the function $\Sigma_Q f_i$ are strictly convex for all $Q \in \mathcal{P}$.

Having outlined the main ideas in the characterization proof, we indicate in Figure 11.3 how the result in this chapter, seen as a result on the integrability of demand functions, fits in with other results in this tradition. The left part of the figure concerns representable demand functions, and the right part concerns demand functions that have additively separable representations.

The next section introduces some new notation and some new properties (axioms) that will be seen to follow from the main axioms.

This chapter is based on Lensberg (1988).

11.2 The axioms

The family of *collectively rational solutions* is first introduced. A solution F belongs to this family if there exists a list of orderings $\succsim \equiv \{\succsim_P \mid P \in \mathcal{P}\}$, where each $\succsim_P$ is defined on $\mathbb{R}^P_+$ such that for all $P \in \mathcal{P}$ and all $S \in \Sigma^P$, $F(S)$ is the unique maximal element for $\succsim_P$ in S. The list $\succsim$ will be referred to as a *representation* for F. If, for each component $\succsim_P$ of $\succsim$, there exists an extended real-valued function f^P defined on $\mathbb{R}^P_+$ with the property that $f^P(x) \geqq f^P(y)$ if and only if $x \succsim_P y$, then the list $f \equiv \{f^P \mid P \in \mathcal{P}\}$ is said to be a *numerical representation for F*.

Our concern here will be with solutions that have *additively separable* numerical representations: Let $\mathfrak{F}$ be the family of all sequences $\{f_i\}_{i \in I}$ of strictly increasing and continuous functions $f_i: \mathbb{R}^{\{i\}}_+ \to \mathbb{R}^{\{i\}} \cup \{-\infty\}$ such that for all $P \in \mathcal{P}$, the function $\Sigma_P f_i$ is strictly quasi-concave.[9] A solution F has an *additively separable numerical representation* if there exists a sequence from $\mathfrak{F}$ of functions $\{f_i\}_{i \in I}$ such that for all $P \in \mathcal{P}$ and all $S \in \Sigma^P$, $F(S) = \operatorname{argmax}\{\Sigma_P f_i(x) \mid x \in S\}$. A ***collectively rational*** solution that admits of an additively ***separable*** numerical representation will be referred to as a ***CRS solution***.

As mentioned earlier, the main part of the characterization proof consists in showing that if a solution F satisfies certain axioms, then its restriction to the family of budget problems is of the CRS type. For each $P \in \mathcal{P}$, the family of *budget problems* for the set P of agents is denoted Σ^P_Δ and consists of those $S \in \Sigma^P$ such that $S = \{x \in \mathbb{R}^P_+ \mid \pi x \leqq \pi\omega\}$ for some $(\pi, \omega) \in \mathbb{R}^P_{++} \times \mathbb{R}^P_+ \backslash \{0\}$.

It will be convenient to consider the set of such *price endowment* pairs (π, ω) as the domain of definition for the restriction $\bar{F}$ of a solution F to the family of budget problems: For all $P \in \mathcal{P}$ and all $(\pi, \omega) \in \mathbb{R}^P_+ \times \mathbb{R}^P_+$, let $b(\pi, \omega) \equiv \{x \in \mathbb{R}^P_+ \mid \pi x \leqq \pi\omega\}$; for all $(\pi, \omega) \in \mathbb{R}^P_{++} \times \mathbb{R}^P_+$, define $\bar{F}(\pi, \omega) \equiv F(b(\pi, \omega))$ if $\omega \geq 0$ and $\bar{F}(\pi, 0) \equiv 0$. The convention that $\bar{F}(\pi, 0) = 0$ is adopted for notational convenience, although strictly speaking, the set $b(\pi, 0) = \{0\}$ is not a well-defined problem as it does not contain a strictly positive vector. Thus, $\bar{F}$ is a function from $\bigcup_{P \in \mathcal{P}} \mathbb{R}^P_{++} \times \mathbb{R}^P_+$ to $\bigcup_{P \in \mathcal{P}} \mathbb{R}^P_+$ such that for all $P \in \mathcal{P}$ and all $(\pi, \omega) \in \mathbb{R}^P_{++} \times \mathbb{R}^P_+$, $\bar{F}(\pi, \omega)$ satisfies the *budget constraint* $\pi\bar{F}(\pi, \omega) \leqq \pi\omega$.

[9] An extended real-valued function h on $\mathbb{R}^n_+$ is *strictly quasi-concave* if for all $y \in \mathbb{R}^n_+$, the upper contour set $G(y) \equiv \{x \in \mathbb{R}^n_+ \mid h(x) \geqq h(y)\}$ is strictly convex in $\mathbb{R}^n_+$, meaning that for all $x, z \in G(y)$ with $x \neq z$ and all $\lambda \in]0,1[$, the point $\lambda x + (1-\lambda)z$ is an interior point of $G(y)$ relative to $\mathbb{R}^n_+$. An extended real-valued function g on $\mathbb{R}_+$ is *strictly increasing* if $g(x) > g(y)$ for all x, y such that $x \geq y$.

Recall that for all $P \in \mathcal{P}$, $\Delta^P \equiv \{\pi \in \mathbb{R}^P_+ \mid \sum_P \pi_i = 1\}$ is the *unit simplex* in $\mathbb{R}^P_+$. Because $\bar{F}$ is homogeneous of degree 0 in π, Δ^P may be used to normalize the domain of definition for $\bar{F}$ with respect to prices π.

The axioms *P.O, CONT, B.STAB,* and *M.STAB* are now restated for the restricted solution $\bar{F}$ as follows:

Pareto-Optimality (P.O): For all $P \in \mathcal{P}$, $\pi\bar{F}(\pi, \omega) = \pi\omega$ for all $(\pi, \omega) \in \mathbb{R}^P_{++} \times \mathbb{R}^P_+$.

Continuity (CONT): For all $P \in \mathcal{P}$, if $\{(\pi^\nu, \omega^\nu)\}$ is a sequence from $\mathbb{R}^P_{++} \times \mathbb{R}^P_+$ converging to $(\pi, \omega) \in \mathbb{R}^P_{++} \times \mathbb{R}^P_+$, then $\lim_{\nu \to \infty} \bar{F}(\pi^\nu, \omega^\nu) = \bar{F}(\pi, \omega)$.

Multilateral Stability (M.STAB): For all $P, Q \in \mathcal{P}$ with $P \subset Q$, all $(\pi, \omega) \in \mathbb{R}^Q_{++} \times \mathbb{R}^Q_+$, and all $\omega' \in \mathbb{R}^P_+$, if $\bar{F}(\pi, \omega) = x$ and $\pi_P\omega' = \pi\omega - \pi_{Q\backslash P}x_{Q\backslash P}$, then $\bar{F}(\pi_P, \omega') = x_P$.

Recall that in the statement of *M.STAB* for F in Chapter 7, a provision was required in order to deal with the possibility that some subproblem $t^x_P(T)$ might not be well defined. What could go wrong is that $t^x_P(T)$ might not contain a strictly positive vector. Such a provision is not needed in the preceding statement of *M.STAB* for $\bar{F}$ because the only way that some subproblem $b(\pi_P, \omega')$ can fail to contain a strictly positive vector is by having $\omega' = 0$, in which case $b(\pi_P, \omega') = \{0\}$. This case has already been dealt with by explicitly including all such trivial problems in the domain of $\bar{F}$.

Bilateral Stability (B.STAB): This is the same as *M.STAB* except the provision that $|P| = 2$ is added.

Pursuing the interpretation of $\bar{F}$ as a demand function, *P.O* states that the whole budget is spent. *CONT* needs no comment. *M.STAB* says that if it is optimal to allocate $\pi_P\omega'$ of the total budget $\pi\omega$ to the commodities in a subset P of the set Q of all commodities, then the income $\pi_P\omega'$ can be spent optimally on the commodities in P without having to worry about how to spend the remaining income on the commodities in the set $Q\backslash P$. Thus, a consumer whose demand function satisfies *M.STAB* is one for whom two-stage budgeting is optimal for any partition of the set of commodities.

Observe that if $\bar{F}$ satisfies *P.O,* then $\bar{F}(\pi, \omega) = x$ implies $\bar{F}(\pi, x) = x$. Moreover, *M.STAB* simplifies to saying that if $\bar{F}(\pi, \omega) = x$ for some $(\pi, \omega) \in \mathbb{R}^Q_{++} \times \mathbb{R}^Q_+$, then $\bar{F}(\pi_P, x_P) = x_P$ for all $P \subset Q$.

Two additional properties that will be used in connection with the restricted solution $\bar{F}$ are introduced next. The first one is the Weak Axiom of Revealed Preference: Let $\bar{F}$ be a restricted solution and let $P \in \mathcal{P}$ be given. Given $x, y \in \mathbb{R}^P_+$ with $x \neq y$, say that *x is revealed preferred to y (by $\bar{F}$)*, written $xR_{\bar{F}}y$, if $x = \bar{F}(\pi, \omega)$ and $\pi y \leqq \pi\omega$ for some $(\pi, \omega) \in \mathbb{R}^P_{++} \times \mathbb{R}^P_+$.

Weak Axiom of Revealed Preference (W.A.R.P): For all $P \in \mathcal{P}$ and for all $x, y \in \mathbb{R}^P_+$, if $xR_{\bar{F}}y$ then not $yR_{\bar{F}}x$.

The final property is the following boundary condition, which states that if some price approaches zero in a sequence of problems, then the corresponding sequence of demand vectors must be unbounded (with respect to the Euclidean norm). Such conditions are often imposed on market excess demand functions in general equilibrium theory in order to guarantee the existence of a strictly positive equilibrium price vector. [See, e.g., Varian (1981) for an exposition.]

Boundary condition (BOUND): For all $P \in \mathcal{P}$, and for all sequences $\{\pi^\nu, \omega^\nu\}$ from $\Delta^P \times \mathbb{R}^P_+$, if $\omega^\nu \to \omega \in \mathbb{R}^P_{++}$ and $\pi^\nu_i \to 0$ for some $i \in P$, then $\lim_{\nu \to \infty} \|\bar{F}(\pi^\nu, \omega^\nu)\| = \infty$.

11.3 The main result

In this section, it is shown that *P.O, CONT,* and *M.STAB* characterize the family of CRS solutions. First it is demonstrated that a CRS solution is well defined and satisfies the three axioms.

> ***Proposition 11.1.*** *For all $\{f_i\}_{i \in I} \in \mathfrak{F}$, there exists a CRS solution F for which $\{f_i\}$ is an additively separable numerical representation such that F satisfies P.O, CONT, and M.STAB.*

Proof. The following intermediate result will be used: (i) Let $\{f_i\}_{i \in I}$ be a sequence of strictly increasing functions $f_i: \mathbb{R}^{\{i\}}_+ \to \mathbb{R}^{\{i\}} \cup \{-\infty\}$. For all $Q \in \mathcal{P}$ and all $T \in \Sigma^Q$, if $z \in \operatorname{argmax}\{\Sigma_Q f_i(x_i) \mid x \in T\}$, then for all $P \subset Q$, $z_P \in \operatorname{argmax}\{\Sigma_P f_i(x_i) \mid x \in t^z_P(T)\}$.

To prove (i), let $\{f_i\}_{i \in I}$, Q, T, and z satisfy its hypothesis. Let $P \subset Q$ be given and define $S \equiv t^z_P(T)$. By assumption,

$$\sum_Q f_i(z_i) \geqq \sum_Q f_i(x_i) \quad \text{for all } x \text{ in any subset of } T, \tag{1}$$

and in particular for all $x \in S + \{z_{Q \setminus P}\}$. Because each f_i is strictly increasing and T contains a strictly positive vector, it follows by (1) that $\Sigma_Q f_i(z_i) > -\infty$. Since T is bounded, then $\Sigma_Q f_i(z_i) < \infty$. These two inequalities imply that $-\infty < f_i(z_i) < \infty$ for all $i \in Q$. Since $x_{Q\setminus P} = z_{Q\setminus P}$ for all $x \in S + \{z_{Q\setminus P}\}$, the finite quantity $\Sigma_{Q\setminus P} f_i(z_i)$ may be subtracted from both sides of (1) to obtain that $\Sigma_P f_i(z_i) \geqq \Sigma_P f_i(x_i)$ for all $x \in S$. This completes the proof of (i).

Next, we show that CRS solutions are well defined, that is, that they associate one and only one solution outcome to every problem. To see this, let $\{f_i\}_{i\in I} \in \mathfrak{F}$ be given and let F be the CRS solution associated with $\{f_i\}_{i\in I}$. Thus, for all $P \in \mathcal{P}$ and all $S \in \Sigma^P$, $F(S) \equiv \text{argmax}\{\Sigma_P f_i(x_i) \mid x \in S\}$. Let $Q \in \mathcal{P}$ and $T \in \Sigma^Q$ be given. Since T is compact and $\Sigma_Q f_i$ is continuous, it follows that $F(T) \neq \emptyset$, and since T is convex and $\Sigma_Q f_i$ is strictly quasi-concave, then $F(T)$ is a singleton. This completes the proof that a CRS solution is well defined.

Finally, we show that all CRS solutions satisfy *P.O, CONT,* and *M.STAB*. Let F be a CRS solution. Then there exists a sequence from $\mathfrak{F}$ of functions $\{f_i\}_{i\in I}$ that represents F. The solution F satisfies *P.O* since each f_i is strictly increasing; moreover, F satisfies *CONT* since $\Sigma_P f_i$ is continuous and strictly quasi-concave on $\mathbb{R}^P_+$ for all $P \in \mathcal{P}$. It remains to show that F satisfies *M.STAB*.

Let $P, Q \in \mathcal{P}$ with $P \subset Q$ and $T \in \Sigma^Q$ be given. Let $z \equiv F(T)$ and $S \equiv t^z_P(T)$. Assume, without loss of generality, that S is a well-defined member of Σ^P (if not, then *M.STAB* holds trivially) and let $y \equiv F(S)$. Since $\{f_i\}_{i\in I}$ represents F, then

$$z = \text{argmax}\{\Sigma_Q f_i(x_i) \mid x \in T\} \quad \text{and} \quad y = \text{argmax}\{\Sigma_P f_i(x_i) \mid x \in S\},$$

which by (i) implies that $y = z_P$, the desired conclusion. Q.E.D.

The proof of the converse of Proposition 11.1 is in several steps. The first one consists of Lemmas 11.1–11.3, where it is shown that if a solution F satisfies *P.O, CONT,* and *M.STAB,* then its restriction $\bar{F}$ also satisfies *W.A.R.P* and *BOUND.*

Lemma 11.1. *If a solution satisfies P.O, CONT, and M.STAB, then it satisfies I.I.A.*

Proof. The proof, which is illustrated in Figure 11.4, is a simple adaptation of the proof of Lemma 7.3, the main step in the characterization of the Nash solution that uses Continuity. Let F be a solution satisfying *P.O, CONT,* and *M.STAB,* and let $P \in \mathcal{P}$ be given. Let S and S' be two members of Σ^P such that $S' \subset S$ and $y \equiv F(S) \in S'$. In the figure, $P = \{i, j\}$. It must be shown that $y = F(S')$ also. To do this, assume first that (i) $S' \cap U = S \cap U$ for some neighborhood U of y.

Let k be an agent who is not a member of P and let $Q \equiv P \cup \{k\}$. Define $S^1 \equiv S' + \{e_k\}$ and for all $\epsilon > 0$, let C^ϵ be the cone with vertex $(1+\epsilon)e_k$

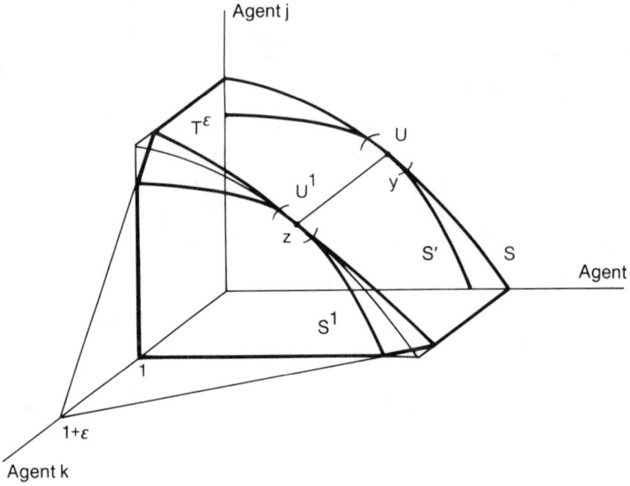

Figure 11.4. Lemma 11.1.

spanned by S^1. Define $T^\epsilon \equiv C^\epsilon \cap \text{cch}\{S+\{e_k\}\}$, $T^0 \equiv \lim_{\epsilon\to 0} T^\epsilon = \text{cch}\{S+\{e_k\}\}$ and $U^1 \equiv U+\{e_k\}$, and note that for all $\epsilon \geqq 0$, $U^1 \cap S^1 \subset T^\epsilon \in \Sigma^Q$.

Let $z \equiv F(T^0)$. We will show that $z = w \equiv (y, 1)$. To see this, note that whatever z is, it follows by construction of T^0 that $t_P^z(T^0) = S$, which by *M.STAB* implies that $z_P = y$. Since w is the only Pareto-optimal point of T^0 with the property that $w_P = y$, it follows by *P.O* that $z = w$.

Consider now $z^\epsilon \equiv F(T^\epsilon)$ as $\epsilon \to 0$. Since $z^0 = z$ and $T^\epsilon \to T^0$ as $\epsilon \to 0$, it follows by *CONT* that $z^\epsilon \to z$. Therefore, by *P.O*, there exists $\bar{\epsilon} > 0$ such that $z^\epsilon \in U^1$ for all $\epsilon \in [0, \bar{\epsilon}]$, which by *M.STAB* implies that z_P^ϵ is constant and equal to $F(S')$ for all $\epsilon \in]0, \bar{\epsilon}]$. But then $z^\epsilon = z$ for all $\epsilon \in]0, \bar{\epsilon}[$ by the fact that $z^\epsilon \to z$ in U^1 as $\epsilon \to 0$, which implies that $F(S') = z_P = y$, the desired conclusion.

To complete the proof, it suffices to observe that if S' does not satisfy condition (i), then it can be approximated by a sequence of elements from Σ^P that does. *CONT* may then be applied once more to conclude that $F(S') = F(S)$ in this case also. Q.E.D.

Lemma 11.2. *If F satisfies I.I.A, then $\bar{F}$ satisfies W.A.R.P.*

Proof. Let F be a solution that satisfies *I.I.A* and suppose, by way of contradiction, that $\bar{F}$ does not satisfy *W.A.R.P.* Since F agrees with $\bar{F}$ on the family of budget problems, there exists $P \in \mathcal{P}$ and $S, S' \in \Sigma_\Delta^P$ such that

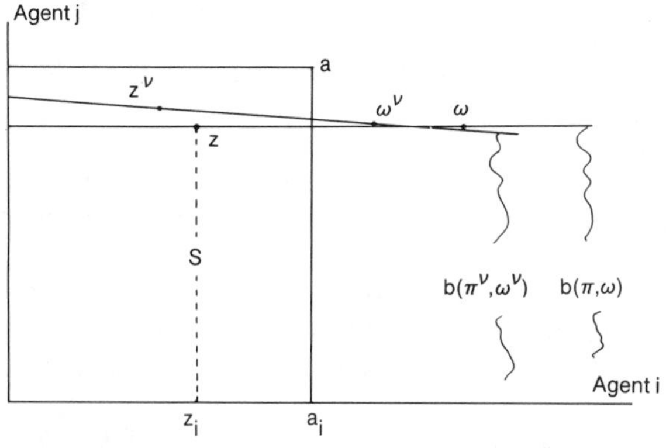

Figure 11.5. Lemma 11.3.

$F(S) \in S'$, $F(S') \in S$, and $F(S) \neq F(S')$. Let $S'' \equiv S \cap S'$ and note that $S'' \in \Sigma^P$. By *I.I.A* applied twice, $F(S'') = F(S)$ and $F(S'') = F(S')$, a contradiction, since $F(S') \neq F(S)$. Q.E.D.

The relationship between *I.I.A* and *W.A.R.P* is closer than indicated by the one-sided implication of Lemma 11.2. In fact, it is straightforward to show that *I.I.A* is *equivalent* to *W.A.R.P* if the latter axiom is restated for F instead of $\bar{F}$. No use will be made of this more general result here, however.

Lemma 11.3. *If F satisfies P.O, CONT, and I.I.A, then $\bar{F}$ satisfies BOUND.*

Proof. (See Figure 11.5 for an illustration.) Let $P \in \mathcal{P}$ be given and let $\{\pi^\nu, \omega^\nu\}$ be a sequence from $\Delta^P \times \mathbb{R}^P_+$ such that $\omega^\nu \to \omega \in \mathbb{R}^P_{++}$ and such that $\pi_i^\nu \to 0$ for some $i \in P$. For each ν, let $z^\nu \equiv \bar{F}(\pi^\nu, \omega^\nu)$ and suppose, by way of contradiction, that $\|z^\nu\|$ does not converge to infinity. Then there exists a subsequence of $\{z^\nu\}$ that converges to a point $z \in \mathbb{R}^P_+$ and a point $a \in \mathbb{R}^P_{++}$ such that $z < a$ and $z^\nu < a$ for all z^ν in that subsequence. Assume, without loss of generality, that the sequence $\{z^\nu\}$ itself has that property.

Because $\{\pi^\nu\}$ is a subset of the compact set Δ^P, it has a subsequence that converges to some $\pi \in \Delta^P$. Assume without loss of generality that $\{\pi^\nu\}$ itself has that property. For each ν, let $S^\nu \equiv b(\pi^\nu, \omega^\nu) \cap \text{cch}\{a\}$. Then $S^\nu \subset b(\pi^\nu, \omega^\nu)$, and since $z^\nu < a$, then $z^\nu \in S^\nu$. Therefore, by *I.I.A*, $z^\nu = F(S^\nu)$

for all ν. Since $(\pi^\nu, \omega^\nu) \to (\pi, \omega)$, the sequence $\{S^\nu\}$ converges to $S \equiv b(\pi, \omega) \cap \text{cch}\{a\}$, and since $z^\nu \to z$, it follows by *CONT* that $F(S) = z$. On the other hand, *P.O* requires that $F_i(S) = a_i$ because $\pi_i = 0$. Since $a_i > z_i$, this is the announced contradiction. Q.E.D.

So far we have demonstrated that if a solution F satisfies *P.O, CONT,* and *M.STAB,* then its restriction $\bar{F}$ satisfies the two additional properties of *W.A.R.P* and *BOUND*. The remainder of the proof of the main theorem consists in showing that $\bar{F}$ has an additively separable representation (Lemmas 11.4–11.14 and Proposition 11.2); the extension of that result to F (Proposition 11.3) will then follow easily from the fact that F satisfies *I.I.A*.

In the statements of Lemmas 11.4–11.14, *it is assumed that the restricted solution $\bar{F}$ satisfies P.O, CONT, M.STAB, W.A.R.P, and BOUND.*

In what follows, extensive use will be made of the *inverse choice correspondence* $\Phi: \bigcup_{P \in \mathcal{P}} \mathbb{R}^P_+ \to \bigcup_{P \in \mathcal{P}} \mathbb{R}^P_{++}$ associated with the restricted solution $\bar{F}$. Given $P \in \mathcal{P}$ and $x \in \mathbb{R}^P_+$, $\Phi(x)$ is defined by $\Phi(x) \equiv \{\pi \in \mathbb{R}^P_{++} \mid \bar{F}(\pi, \omega) = x$ for some $\omega \in \mathbb{R}^P_+\}$. Thus, Φ is the inverse of $\bar{F}$ projected on the price space. Note that for all x, either $\Phi(x)$ is empty or it is a cone with the vertex 0 removed, because $\bar{F}$ is homogeneous of degree 0 in π. Also note that for all $P, Q \in \mathcal{P}$ with $P \subset Q$, if $x \in \mathbb{R}^Q_+$ then $\Phi_P(x) \subset \Phi(x_P)$ by *M.STAB*. As already mentioned, this inclusion property is exactly what *M.STAB* says about the restricted solution $\bar{F}$. In Lemma 11.5, it will be shown that the reverse inclusion also holds if *P.O, CONT,* and *BOUND* are imposed as well. First, it is shown in Lemma 11.4 that Φ is convex-valued. This is a consequence of *W.A.R.P* alone.

Lemma 11.4. *The correspondence Φ is convex-valued.*

Proof. Let $P \in \mathcal{P}$ and $x \in \mathbb{R}^P_+$ be given. Let π^1 and π^2 be two members of $\Phi(x)$ and let $\pi^3 \equiv \alpha\pi^1 + (1-\alpha)\pi^2$ for some $\alpha \in]0, 1[$. We have to show that $\pi^3 \in \Phi(x)$. The proof is by contradiction. If $\pi^3 \notin \Phi(x)$, then, in particular, $x \neq y \equiv \bar{F}(\pi^3, x)$. Then $y R_{\bar{F}} x$, which by *W.A.R.P* implies that $\pi^1 y > \pi^1 x$ and $\pi^2 y > \pi^2 x$. Since π^3 is a convex combination of π^1 and π^2, it follows that $\pi^3 y > \pi^3 x$, which is impossible in view of the budget constraint $\pi^3 y \leqq \pi^3 x$. Q.E.D.

Lemma 11.5. *For all $P, Q \in \mathcal{P}$ with $P \subset Q$ and for all $x \in \mathbb{R}^Q_{++}$, $\Phi_P(x) = \Phi(x_P)$, that is, $\pi^0 \in \Phi(x_P)$ if and only if there exists $\pi \in \Phi(x)$ such that $\pi_P = \pi^0$.*

Proof. (See Figure 11.6.) Let P, Q, and x satisfy the hypothesis of the lemma. If $P = Q$, then $\Phi_P(x) = \Phi(x_P)$ identically. If $P \subset Q$, it follows by

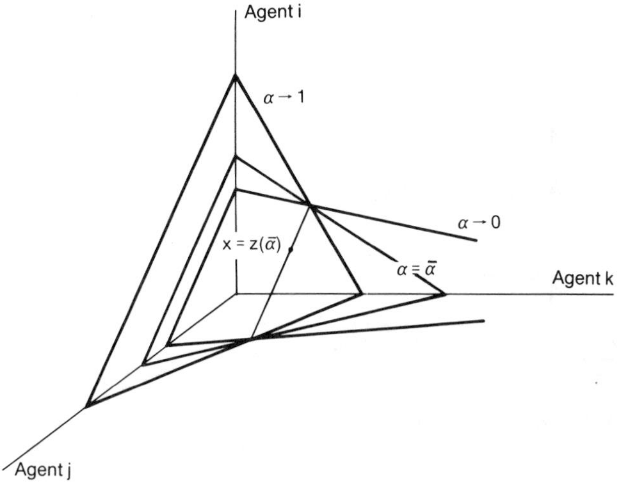

Figure 11.6. Lemma 11.5. $P=\{i,j\}$.

M.STAB that $\Phi_P(x)\subset\Phi(x_P)$. In order to establish the reverse inclusion, consider first the case where $|P|=|Q|-1$.

Let π^0 be a member of $\Phi(x_P)$. We must show that there exists $\pi\in\Phi(x)$ with $\pi_P=\pi^0$. Let $\{k\}\equiv Q\backslash P$, and let the function $\pi:]0,1[\to\Delta^Q$ be defined by $\pi_k(\alpha)\equiv\alpha$ and $\pi_P(\alpha)\equiv[(1-\alpha)/\sum_P\pi_i^0]\pi^0$. Note that $\pi_P(\alpha)\in\Phi(x_P)$ for all $\alpha\in]0,1[$ since $\pi_P(\alpha)$ is proportional to π^0 and $\Phi(x_P)$ is a cone. Therefore, since $\Phi(x)$ is also a cone, it is sufficient to show that $\pi(\alpha)\in\Phi(x)$ for some $\alpha\in]0,1[$.

To see this, let $z(\alpha)\equiv\bar{F}(\pi(\alpha),x)$ for $\alpha\in]0,1[$. As $\alpha\to1$, $\pi_P(\alpha)\to0$, and then *BOUND* implies that $\|z(\alpha)\|\to\infty$. Because $\pi_k(\alpha)=\alpha$ and $\pi(\alpha)z(\alpha)\leqq\pi(\alpha)x$, this implies that $z_k(\alpha)<x_k$ for α sufficiently close to 1. By a similar argument, $z_k(\alpha)>x_k$ for α sufficiently close to 0. Then, by the intermediate-value theorem, there exists $\bar{\alpha}\in]0,1[$ such that $z_k(\bar{\alpha})=x_k$, and it follows that

$$z_P(\bar{\alpha})=\begin{cases}\bar{F}(\pi_P(\bar{\alpha}),z_P(\bar{\alpha})) & \text{(by } P.O \text{ and } M.STAB),\\ \bar{F}(\pi_P(\bar{\alpha}),x_P)) & [\text{since } z_k(\bar{\alpha})=x_k\Rightarrow\pi_P(\bar{\alpha})z_P(\bar{\alpha})=\pi_P(\bar{\alpha})x_P],\\ x_P & [\text{since } \pi_P(\bar{\alpha})\in\Phi(x_P)].\end{cases}$$

Thus, $\bar{F}(\pi(\bar{\alpha}),x)=x$, which proves that $\pi(\bar{\alpha})\in\Phi(x)$. Hence, $\phi(x_P)\subset\Phi_P(x)$ if $|P|=|Q|-1$.

In order to show that $\Phi(x_P)\subset\Phi_P(x)$ for all $P\subset Q$, pick $\pi^0\in\Phi(x_P)$, set $P^1\equiv P\cup\{i_1\}$, where $i_1\in Q\backslash P$, and conclude by the first part of the proof that $\pi_P^1=\pi^0$ for some $\pi^1\in\Phi(x_{P^1})$. Repeating this argument by adding $i_2\in Q\backslash P^1$ to P^1, conclude that $\pi_P=\pi^0$ for some $\pi\in\Phi_P(x)$. Q.E.D.

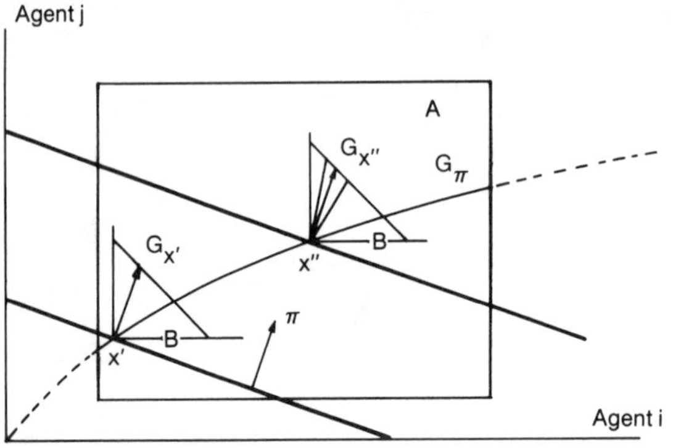

Figure 11.7. Lemma 11.7.

Lemma 11.6. *For all $P \in \mathcal{P}$, $\mathbb{R}^P_{++} \subset \bar{F}(\mathbb{R}^P_{++}, \mathbb{R}^P_+)$; that is, every positive vector is the solution outcome to some budget problem.*

Proof. Let $P \in \mathcal{P}$, $x \in \mathbb{R}^P_{++}$, and $i \in P$ be given. Because *P.O* implies that $\bar{F}(\pi_i, x_i) = x_i$ for $\pi_i > 0$, then $\Phi(x_i) \neq \emptyset$, which by Lemma 11.5 implies that $\Phi(x) \neq \emptyset$, meaning that $\Phi(x)$ contains π such that $\bar{F}(\pi, \omega) = x$ for some $\omega \in \mathbb{R}^P_{++}$. Q.E.D.

For all $P \in \mathcal{P}$, let $\mathfrak{D}^P$ be the set of points $x \in \mathbb{R}^P_{++}$ such that $\Phi(x)$ is a ray, and let $\bar{\mathfrak{D}}^P \equiv \mathbb{R}^P_+ \setminus \mathfrak{D}^P$. Define $\mathfrak{D} \equiv \bigcup_{P \in \mathcal{P}} \mathfrak{D}^P$ and $\bar{\mathfrak{D}} \equiv \bigcup_{P \in \mathcal{P}} \bar{\mathfrak{D}}^P$. The set $\mathfrak{D}$ is of particular interest because if $\bar{F}$ has a numerical representation f, then $\Phi(x)$ is the set of tangent normals to the level curve of f at x. Thus, if $x \in \mathfrak{D}^P$, then the level curve through x has a unique tangent at x, and therefore f is differentiable at x if f is additively separable.

In Lemmas 11.7–11.9, it is shown that the set $\bar{\mathfrak{D}}^P$ is negligible in the measure-theoretic sense and that it has the following simple structure: Letting μ_n denote the n-dimensional Lebesgue measure, there exists a sequence $\{\bar{D}_i\}_{i \in I}$ of subsets of $\mathbb{R}_+$ such that $\mu_1(\bar{D}_i) = 0$ for all $i \in I$ and such that $\bar{\mathfrak{D}}^P \subset \bigcup_P (\bar{D}_i \times \mathbb{R}^{P \setminus i}_+)$ for all $P \in \mathcal{P}$. Observe that if $\bar{F}$ has an additively separable numerical representation, then $\bar{\mathfrak{D}}^P$ must necessarily be of this form.

Lemma 11.7. *For all $P \in \mathcal{P}$ with $|P| = 2$, $\mu_2(\bar{\mathfrak{D}}^P) = 0$.*

Proof. An illustration is given in Figure 11.7. Let $P \in \mathcal{P}$ with $|P| = 2$ be given. Since $\mathbb{R}^P_{++}$ can be covered by a countable collection of rectangles, it is sufficient to show that $\mu_2(\bar{\mathfrak{D}}^P \cap A) = 0$ for all rectangles $A \subset \mathbb{R}^P_{++}$. Let such an A be given, let $B \equiv \{\pi \in \mathbb{R}^P_{++} \mid \sum_P \pi_i \leqq 1\}$, and let

$$G \equiv \{(x, \pi) \in A \times B \mid x = \bar{F}(\pi, \omega) \text{ for some } \omega \in \mathbb{R}^P_+\}. \tag{2}$$

For all $x \in A$ and all $\pi \in B$, let $G_x \equiv \{\pi' \mid (x, \pi') \in G\}$ and $G_\pi \equiv \{x' \mid (x', \pi) \in G\}$. Since $A \times B$ is bounded, $\mu_4(G) < \infty$, and therefore

$$\int_A \mu_2(G_x)\, d\mu_2 = \mu_4(G) = \int_B \mu_2(G_\pi)\, d\mu_2. \tag{3}$$

The sets G_x and G_π are illustrated in Figure 11.7, where $G_{x'}$ is a truncated ray of points proportional to π, that is, a set of μ_2 measure zero, and where $G_{x''}$ is a truncated convex cone with a nonempty interior, that is, a set of positive measure. We show next that the first case is the generic one.

The set G_π is an income consumption path of the continuous demand function $\bar{F}$ restricted to A. Therefore, $\mu_2(G_\pi) = 0$ for all $\pi \in B$, which by the second equality in (3) implies that $\mu_4(G) = 0$. It then follows by the first equality in (3) that $\mu_2(G_x) = 0$ for μ_2 almost all $x \in A$.

Now, $G_x = \Phi(x) \cap B$ for all $x \in A$. Since $A \subset \mathbb{R}^P_{++}$, then $\Phi(x) \neq \emptyset$ for all $x \in A$ by Lemma 11.6. Therefore, because Φ is convex-valued by Lemma 11.4, $\mu_2(\Phi(x) \cap B) > 0$ whenever $\Phi(x)$ is not a ray. Since $\mu_2(G_x) = 0$ for μ_2 almost all $x \in A$, it follows that $\mu_2(\bar{\mathfrak{D}}^P \cap A) = 0$. Q.E.D.

Given $Q \in \mathcal{P}$ and a collection $\{P^1, \ldots, P^n\}$ of subsets of Q, say that $\{P^1, \ldots, P^n\}$ is a *chain* if $P^\nu \cap P^{\nu+1} \neq \emptyset$ for $\nu = 1, \ldots, n-1$. If, in addition, $\{P^1, \ldots, P^n\}$ covers Q (i.e., if $\bigcup_{\nu=1}^n P^\nu = Q$), say that $\{P^1, \ldots, P^n\}$ is a *Q chain*. For example, if $Q = \{1, 2, 3\}$, $P^1 = \{1, 2\}$, and $P^2 = \{2, 3\}$, then $\{P^1, P^2\}$ is a Q chain.

Lemma 11.8. *For all $Q \in \mathcal{P}$, for all $x \in \mathbb{R}^Q_{++}$, and for all Q chains $\{P^1, \ldots, P^n\}$, if $x_{P^\nu} \in \mathfrak{D}$ for all P^ν in the chain, then $x_P \in \mathfrak{D}$ for all $P \subset Q$.*

Proof. Let Q, x, and $\{P^1, \ldots, P^n\}$ satisfy the hypothesis of the lemma. It is sufficient to show that $x \in \mathfrak{D}$, for then $x_P \in \mathfrak{D}$ for all $P \subset Q$ by Lemma 11.5. To this end, define for each $\nu = 1, \ldots, n$ the set $Q^\nu \equiv \bigcup_{\nu'=1}^{\nu} P^{\nu'}$. We will show by induction on ν that $x_{Q^\nu} \in \mathfrak{D}$ for $\nu = 1, \ldots, n$.

For $\nu = 1$, $Q^1 = P^1$, and $x_{Q^1} \in \mathfrak{D}$ by hypothesis. Suppose now that $x_{Q^\nu} \in \mathfrak{D}$ for $\nu < n$. We must show that $x_{Q^{\nu+1}} \in \mathfrak{D}$ also. Because $x_{Q^\nu} \in \mathfrak{D}$ and $x_{P^{\nu+1}} \in \mathfrak{D}$, then $\Phi(x_{Q^\nu})$ and $\Phi(x_{P^{\nu+1}})$ are both rays, which by Lemma 11.5 implies that $\Phi_{Q^\nu}(x_{Q^{\nu+1}})$ and $\Phi_{P^{\nu+1}}(x_{Q^{\nu+1}})$ are rays. Consequently, for all $\pi^1, \pi^2 \in \Phi(x_{Q^{\nu+1}})$, there exist positive real numbers α and β such that $\pi^1_{Q^\nu} = \alpha \pi^2_{Q^\nu}$ and $\pi^1_{P^{\nu+1}} = \beta \pi^2_{P^{\nu+1}}$. Since $P^\nu \subset Q^\nu$ and $P^\nu \cap P^{\nu+1} \neq \emptyset$,

$Q^\nu \cap P^{\nu+1} \neq \emptyset$, which implies that $\alpha = \beta$. Therefore, since $Q^\nu \cup P^{\nu+1} = Q^{\nu+1}$, it follows that $\pi^1 = \alpha\pi^2$, which proves that $\Phi(x_{Q^{\nu+1}})$ is a ray and hence that $x_{Q^{\nu+1}} \in \mathfrak{D}$. Thus, $x_{Q^\nu} \in \mathfrak{D}$ for all $\nu = 1, \ldots, n$, and since $Q^n = Q$, $x_Q = x \in \mathfrak{D}$. Q.E.D.

Lemma 11.9. *For all $i \in I$, there exists a set $D_i \subset \mathbb{R}_+^{\{i\}}$ such that* (i) *for all $Q \in \mathcal{P}$, $\times_Q D_j \subset \mathfrak{D}^Q$, and* (ii) *$\mu_1(\bar{D}_i) = 0$, where $\bar{D}_i \equiv \mathbb{R}_+^{\{i\}} \setminus D_i$.*

Proof. For all distinct $i, k \in I$, let $\bar{Z}_{ik} \equiv \{x_i \geqq 0 \mid \mu_1(\bar{\mathfrak{D}}_{x_i}^{\{i,k\}}) > 0\}$, where $\bar{\mathfrak{D}}_{x_i}^{\{i,k\}} \equiv \{x_k \geqq 0 \mid (x_i, x_k) \in \mathfrak{D}^{\{i,k\}}\}$. Define

$$\bar{Z} \equiv \bigcup_{\substack{i,k \in I \\ i \neq k}} \bar{Z}_{ik} \quad \text{and} \quad Z \equiv \mathbb{R}_{++} \setminus \bar{Z},$$

and let $D_i \equiv Z$ for all $i \in I$.

First, we prove (ii). To this end, let distinct $i, j \in I$ be given. Because $\mu_2(\bar{\mathfrak{D}}^{\{i,j\}}) = 0$ by Lemma 11.7, it follows that $\mu_1(\bar{\mathfrak{D}}_{x_i}^{\{i,j\}}) = 0$ for μ_1 almost all $x_i \geqq 0$, which implies that $\mu_1(\bar{Z}_{ij}) = 0$. Therefore, since I is countable, it follows that $\mu_1(\bar{Z}) = 0$, which proves (ii).

Next, to prove (i), let $Q \in \mathcal{P}$ and $z \in \times_Q D_i$ be given. If $|Q| = 1$, then (i) holds trivially, so assume that $|Q| \geqq 2$. Suppose, by way of contradiction, that $z \in \bar{\mathfrak{D}}^Q$. Since $|Q| \geqq 2$, by Lemma 11.8 applied twice there exists $P \equiv \{i, j\} \subset Q$ such that $(z_i, z_j) \in \bar{\mathfrak{D}}^P$ and $k \in I \setminus P$ such that for all $x_k > 0$, either $(z_i, x_k) \in \bar{\mathfrak{D}}^{\{i,k\}}$ or $(z_j, x_k) \in \bar{\mathfrak{D}}^{\{j,k\}}$. But then either $\mu_1(\bar{\mathfrak{D}}_{z_i}^{\{i,k\}}) > 0$ or $\mu_1(\bar{\mathfrak{D}}_{z_j}^{\{j,k\}}) > 0$, which is impossible since z_i and z_j both belong to Z.

Q.E.D.

For all $i \in I$, let D_i and $\bar{D}_i$ be defined as in the statement of Lemma 11.9. Also, for all $P \in \mathcal{P}$, let $D_P \equiv \times_P D_i$ and $\bar{D}_P \equiv \mathbb{R}_{++}^P \setminus D_P$. Next, let φ be a single-valued selection from Φ such that $\varphi(x) \in \Phi(x) \cap \Delta^P$ for all $P \in \mathcal{P}$ and all $x \in \mathbb{R}_{++}^P$, where Δ^P is the unit simplex in $\mathbb{R}^P$. Note that by Lemma 11.9 all such single-valued selections coincide on the sets D_P.

For all $P \equiv \{i, j\} \in \mathcal{P}$ and all $(x_i, x_j) \in D_i \times D_j$, let $M(x_i, x_j) \equiv \varphi_i(x_i, x_j)/\varphi_j(x_i, x_j)$, and similarly, $M(x_j, x_i) \equiv 1/M(x_i, x_j) = \varphi_j(x_i, x_j)/\varphi_i(x_i, x_j)$. Observe that if the P component of $\bar{F}$ has a real-valued representation f that is differentiable at (x_i, x_j), then $M(x_i, x_j)$ is equal to $f_i'(x_i, x_j)/f_j'(x_i, x_j)$, the marginal rate of substitution (MRS) at (x_i, x_j) with respect to f.

In Lemmas 11.10–11.12, we show that the MRS functions defined in this way can be integrated to obtain a sequence from $\mathfrak{F}$ of functions $\{f_i\}_{i \in I}$ such that each f_i is differentiable on D_i and such that, for all $P \in \mathcal{P}$ and $x \in D_P$, the budget plane of the unique budget problem solved at x is tangent to a level curve of the function $\sum_P f_i$ at x. The first step is Lemma

11.10, where it is shown that the function φ is sufficiently well behaved for the MRS function to be integrable.

Lemma 11.10. *For all $P \in \mathcal{P}$, the P component of the function φ is continuous on D_P, and for all $i \in P$, φ_i is bounded away from zero on compact subsets of $\mathbb{R}^P_{++}$.*

Proof. Let $P \in \mathcal{P}$ be given. To show that φ is continuous on D_P, let $\{x^\nu\}$ be a sequence from $\mathbb{R}^P_{++}$ converging to $x \in D_P$ and suppose, by way of contradiction, that $\varphi(x^\nu)$ does not converge to $\varphi(x)$. Then, because φ takes its values in Δ^P, which is a compact set, $\{x^\nu\}$ has a subsequence, which without loss of generality can be assumed to be $\{x^\nu\}$ itself, such that $\varphi(x^\nu) \to \pi \neq \varphi(x)$.

Because $\bar{F}(\varphi(x^\nu), x^\nu) = x^\nu$ for all ν by *P.O* and construction of φ, it follows by *CONT* that $\bar{F}(\pi, x) = x$ unless $\pi_i = 0$ for some $i \in P$. However, the latter possibility is ruled out by *BOUND* because $\|x^\nu\| \to \|x\| < \infty$. Since $\pi \in \Delta^P$ and $x \in D_P$ and since $\bar{F}(\pi, x) = x$ implies that $\pi \in \Phi(x)$, it follows that $\pi = \varphi(x)$. This contradiction completes the proof that φ is continuous on D_P.

To prove the second part of the lemma, let A be a compact subset of $\mathbb{R}^P_{++}$ and suppose, by way of contradiction, that φ_i is not bounded away from zero on A for some $i \in P$. Then there exists a sequence $\{x^\nu\}$ from A such that $\varphi_i(x^\nu) \to 0$. Because $\bar{F}(\varphi(x^\nu), x^\nu) = x^\nu$ for all ν, it follows by *BOUND* that $\|x^\nu\| \to \infty$, a contradiction, since $\{x^\nu\} \subset A$, which is a compact subset of $\mathbb{R}^P_{++}$. Q.E.D.

Lemma 11.11. *For all $Q \in \mathcal{P}$ with $|Q| \geqq 3$, for all $x \in D_Q$, and for all $\{i, j, k\} \subset Q$, $M(x_i, x_j) = M(x_i, x_k) \cdot M(x_k, x_j) = \varphi_i(x)/\varphi_j(x)$.*

Proof. Let Q and x satisfy the hypothesis of the lemma. Since $x \in D_Q$, by Lemma 11.9 $x \in \mathfrak{D}^Q$ and thus $\Phi(x)$ is a ray. By Lemma 11.5, $\Phi(x_P) = \Phi_P(x)$ for all $P \subset Q$, and thus $\Phi(x_P)$ is a ray for all $P \subset Q$. Therefore, by definition of the function φ, $\varphi(x_P)$ is proportional to $\varphi_P(x)$ for all $P \subset Q$, and since $M(x_i, x_j) \equiv \varphi_i(x_i, x_j)/\varphi_j(x_i, x_j)$ for all $P = \{i, j\}$, it follows that $M(x_i, x_j) = \varphi_i(x)/\varphi_j(x)$ for all such P. As $\varphi_i(x)/\varphi_j(x) = [\varphi_i(x)/\varphi_k(x)] \cdot [\varphi_k(x)/\varphi_j(x)]$, the conclusion follows. Q.E.D.

Lemma 11.12. *There exists a sequence $\{f_i\}_{i \in I}$ of functions f_i: $\mathbb{R}^{\{i\}}_{+} \to \mathbb{R}^{\{i\}} \cup \{-\infty\}$, where each f_i is continuous and strictly increasing on $\mathbb{R}^{\{i\}}_{+}$ and absolutely continuous on compact intervals in $\mathbb{R}^{\{i\}}_{++}$, such that for all $P \in \mathcal{P}$, all $x \in D_P$, and all $\{i, j\} \subset P$, $f_i'(x_i)/f_j'(x_j) = \varphi_i(x)/\varphi_j(x)$ (where f_k' denotes the derivative of f_k).*

Proof. The proof begins by constructing for each $i \in I$ a function g_i: $\mathbb{R}^{\{i\}}_{++} \to \mathbb{R}^{\{i\}}_{++}$, whose indefinite integral will be f_i. For each $i \in I$, let x_i^0 be a member of D_i. Define

$$g_1(x_1) \equiv M(x_1, x_2^0) \cdot M(x_2^0, x_1^0), \tag{4}$$

$$g_i(x_i) \equiv M(x_i, x_1^0) \quad \text{for } i \in I \backslash 1. \tag{5}$$

For all $i \in I$, let the function f_i: $\mathbb{R}^{\{i\}}_{+} \to \mathbb{R}^{\{i\}} \cup \{-\infty\}$ be defined by

$$f_i(x_i) \equiv \int_{x_i^0}^{x_i} g_i(\alpha)\, d\alpha \quad \text{for all } x_i > 0 \quad \text{and} \quad f_i(0) \equiv \lim_{x_i \to 0} f_i(x_i).$$

To see that the functions f_i are well defined, observe first that g_i is continuous on D_i and bounded on any compact interval of $\mathbb{R}^{\{i\}}_{++}$. This follows by (4), (5), and Lemma 11.10 since $M(x_i, x_j^0) \equiv \varphi_i(x_i, x_j^0)/\varphi_j(x_i, x_j^0)$ for all distinct $i, j \in I$ and since $x_i^0 \in D_i \subset \mathbb{R}^{\{i\}}_{++}$ for all $i \in I$. Therefore, g_i is integrable and f_i is absolutely continuous. Because $\varphi(x) > 0$ whenever $x > 0$, it follows that f_i is strictly increasing, which implies that $\lim_{x_i \to 0} f_i(x_i)$ exists as a real number or $-\infty$.

To complete the proof, we must show that $f_i'(x_i)/f_j'(x_j) = \varphi_i(x)/\varphi_j(x)$ for all $P \in \mathcal{P}$, all $x \in D_P$, and all $\{i, j\} \subset P$. Observe first that the derivative $f_i'(x_i)$ exists and is equal to $g_i(x_i)$ for all $x_i \in D_i$ because g_i is continuous at such points. Thus, because $\varphi_i(x)/\varphi_j(x) = M(x_i, x_j)$ whenever $x \in D_P$ by Lemma 11.11, it is sufficient to show that $g_i(x_i)/g_j(x_j) = M(x_i, x_j)$ for all distinct $i, j \in I$ and all $(x_i, x_j) \in D_i \times D_j$.

Let distinct $i, j \in I$ and $(x_i, x_j) \in D_i \times D_j$ be given. Recall that $x_k^0 \in D_k$ for all $k \in I$. Suppose first that $i \neq 1 \neq j$. Then

$$M(x_i, x_j) = M(x_i, x_1^0) \cdot M(x_1^0, x_j) \quad \text{(by Lemma 11.11)} \tag{6a}$$

$$\equiv M(x_i, x_1^0)/M(x_j, x_1^0) \tag{6b}$$

$$= g_i(x_i)/g_j(x_j) \quad \text{[by (5)].} \tag{6c}$$

Next, suppose that $i = 1$ and $j \neq 2$. Then

$$M(x_1, x_j) = M(x_1, x_2^0) \cdot M(x_2^0, x_j) \quad \text{(by Lemma 11.11)} \tag{7a}$$

$$= M(x_1, x_2^0) \cdot M(x_2^0, x_1^0) \cdot M(x_1^0, x_j) \quad \text{(by Lemma 11.11)} \tag{7b}$$

$$= g_1(x_1) \cdot M(x_1^0, x_j) \quad \text{[by (4)]} \tag{7c}$$

$$= g_1(x_1)/M(x_j, x_1^0) \tag{7d}$$

$$= g_1(x_1)/g_j(x_j) \quad \text{[by (5)].} \tag{7e}$$

Finally, if $i = 1$ and $j = 2$, let k be a member of $I \backslash \{1, 2\}$. Then

$$M(x_1, x_2) = M(x_1, x_k^0) \cdot M(x_k^0, x_2) \quad \text{(by Lemma 11.11)} \tag{8a}$$

$$= [g_1(x_1)/g_k(x_k^0)] \cdot [g_k(x_k^0)/g_2(x_2)] \quad \text{[by (7e) and (6c)]} \tag{8b}$$

$$= g_1(x_1)/g_2(x_2). \tag{8c}$$

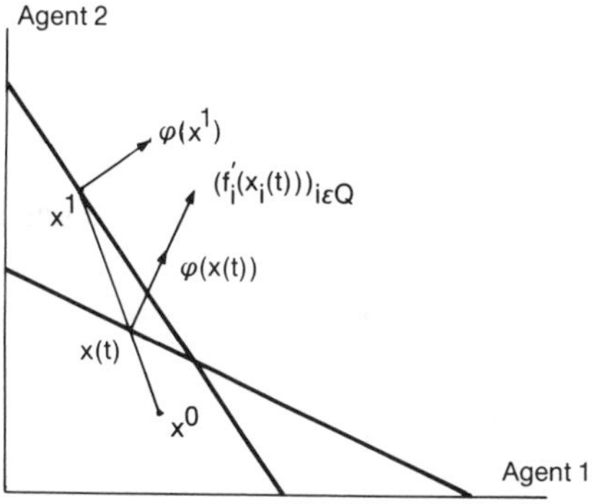

Figure 11.8. Lemma 11.13. $Q=\{1,2\}$.

Thus, $g_i(x_i)/g_j(x_j)=M(x_i,x_j)$ for all distinct $i,j\in I$ and all $(x_i,x_j)\in D_i\times D_j$. Q.E.D.

Having established that the single-valued selection φ from the inverse choice correspondence Φ can be integrated to yield the family of functions $\{f_i\}_{i\in I}$, the next step is to show that the function $\Sigma_P f_i$ has the right curvature (i.e., strict quasi-concavity) for all $P\in\mathcal{P}$. To this end, we first demonstrate in Lemma 11.13 that the ordering of $\mathbb{R}^P_+$ induced by the function $\Sigma_P f_i$ agrees with the revealed preference relation $R_{\bar{F}}$ on $\mathbb{R}^P_{++}$ induced by $\bar{F}$ in the sense that $\Sigma_P f_i(x_i^1)\geqq\Sigma_P f_i(x_i^0)$ whenever $x^1R_{\bar{F}}x^0$, with strict inequality if $\Sigma_P f_i(x_i^0)$ is finite. The quasi-concavity of the function $\Sigma_P f_i$ is then established in Lemma 11.14.

Lemma 11.13. *For all $Q\in\mathcal{P}$ and for all $x^0,x^1\in\mathbb{R}^Q_+$, if $x^1R_{\bar{F}}x^0$ and $\Sigma_Q f_i(x_i^0)>-\infty$, then $\Sigma_Q f_i(x_i^1)>\Sigma_Q f_i(x_i^0)$.*

Proof. Let Q, x^0, and x^1 satisfy the hypothesis of the lemma. Two cases are distinguished, according to whether or not $x_i^0\neq x_i^1$ for all $i\in Q$. See Figure 11.8 for an illustration.

(i) $x_i^0\neq x_i^1$ for all $i\in Q$: For all $t\in\,]0,1[$, let $x(t)\equiv tx^1+(1-t)x^0$. Since $x_i^0\neq x_i^1$ for all $i\in Q$, then $x(t)>0$ for all such t, which by Lemma 11.6 implies that $\varphi(x(t))$ exists. Because $\bar{F}(\varphi(x(t)),x(t))=x(t)$ by *P.O*, *W.A.R.P* implies that $\varphi(x(t))\cdot(x^1-x(t))>0$, and because $x^1-x(t)=(1-t)(x^1-x^0)$, it follows that

$$\varphi(x(t))\cdot(x^1-x^0)>0\quad\text{for all } t\in\,]0,1[. \tag{9}$$

Since $x_i^0\neq x_i^1$ for all $i\in Q$, each function $x_i(\cdot)$ is linear and not constant. Lemma 11.9 then implies that $x(t)\in D_Q$ for almost all $t\in\,]0,1[$.

By Lemma 11.12, the vector $(f_i'(x_i))_{i\in Q}$ is well defined and proportional to $\varphi(x)$ whenever $x\in D_Q$; thus by (9),

$$\sum_Q f_i'(x_i(t))\cdot(x_i^1-x_i^0)>0 \quad \text{for almost all } t\in\,]0,1[. \tag{10}$$

By Lemma 11.12, each f_i is absolutely continuous on compact intervals of $\mathbb{R}^{\{i\}}_{++}$. Therefore, since each $x_i(\cdot)$ is linear and strictly positive on $]0,1[$, the left side of (10) is integrable on $[\epsilon,1-\epsilon]$ for small $\epsilon>0$. Thus, by (10), for all such ϵ it follows that

$$0<\int_\epsilon^{1-\epsilon}\sum_Q f_i'(x_i(t))(x_i^1-x_i^0)\,dt \tag{11a}$$

$$=\sum_Q\int_\epsilon^{1-\epsilon} f_i'(x_i(t))\cdot(x_i^1-x_i^0)\,dt \tag{11b}$$

$$=\sum_Q f_i(x_i(1-\epsilon))-\sum_Q f_i(x_i(\epsilon)). \tag{11c}$$

As $\epsilon\to 0$, $x_i(1-\epsilon)\to x_i^1$ and $x_i(\epsilon)\to x_i^0$. Since each f_i is continuous on $\mathbb{R}^{\{i\}}_+$ by Lemma 11.12 and since the right side of (11c) is a strictly decreasing function of ϵ by (10), it follows by (11) that $\Sigma_Q f_i(x_i^1)-\Sigma_Q f_i(x_i^0)>0$. This completes the proof for case (i).

(ii) $x_i^0=x_i^1$ for some $i\in Q$: Let P be the subset of Q such that $x_i^0\neq x_i^1$ for all $i\in P$ and $x_i^0=x_i^1$ for all $i\in Q\backslash P$. Since $x^1R_{\bar F}x^0$, $P\neq\emptyset$; moreover, since $x^1_{Q\backslash P}=x^0_{Q\backslash P}$, *M.STAB* implies that $x_P^1R_{\bar F}x_P^0$. Since each f_i is strictly increasing, $f_i(x_i^0)<\infty$ for all $i\in Q$, and since $\Sigma_Q f_i(x_i^0)>-\infty$ by hypothesis, $f_i(x_i^0)$ is finite for all $i\in Q$. Since $x^1_{Q\backslash P}=x^0_{Q\backslash P}$, it follows that

$$\sum_P f_i(x_i^1)-\sum_P f_i(x_i^0)=\sum_Q f_i(x_i^1)-\sum_Q f_i(x_i^0). \tag{12}$$

Since $\Sigma_P f_i(x_i^0)>-\infty$ and $x_P^1R_{\bar F}x_P^0$, it follows by (12) and the proof of case (i) that $\Sigma_Q f_i(x_i^1)>\Sigma_Q f_i(x_i^0)$. Q.E.D.

Lemma 11.14. *For all $Q\in\mathcal{P}$, the function $\Sigma_Q f_i$ is strictly quasi-concave.*

Proof. Let $Q\in\mathcal{P}$ and $y\in\mathbb{R}^Q_+$ be given, and let $c\equiv\Sigma_Q f_i(y_i)$. We must show that the set $G(y)\equiv\{x\in\mathbb{R}^Q_+\mid\Sigma_Q f_i(x_i)\geqq c\}$ is strictly convex in $\mathbb{R}^Q_+$. This is clearly the case if $c=-\infty$, for then $G(y)=\mathbb{R}^Q_+$. Suppose $c>-\infty$; let x^0 and x^2 be two distinct points in $G(y)$, and let $x^1\equiv\alpha x^0+(1-\alpha)x^2$ for some $\alpha\in\,]0,1[$. To show that $\Sigma_Q f_i(x_i^1)>c$, two cases are distinguished according to whether or not $x_i^0\neq x_i^2$ for all $i\in Q$.

(i) If $x_i^0 \neq x_i^2$ for all $i \in Q$, then $x^1 > 0$, which by $P.O$ and Lemma 11.6 implies that $\bar{F}(\pi, x^1) = x^1$ for some $\pi > 0$. Because x^1 is a convex combination of x^0 and x^2, either $\pi x^1 \geqq \pi x^0$ or $\pi x^1 \geqq \pi x^2$. Assume, without loss of generality, that $\pi x^1 \geqq \pi x^0$. Then $x^1 R_{\bar{F}} x^0$, and since $\sum_Q f_i(x_i^0) \geqq c > -\infty$ because $x^0 \in G(y)$, it follows by Lemma 11.13 that $\sum_Q f_i(x_i^1) > \sum_Q f_i(x_i^0) \geqq c$.

(ii) If $x_i^0 = x_i^2$ for some $i \in Q$, one may use the fact that $c > -\infty$ in an argument similar to the one used to prove (ii) of Lemma 11.13 to obtain the same conclusion as in (i). Q.E.D.

The main result concerning the restricted solution $\bar{F}$ can now be established.

> ***Proposition 11.2.*** *If $\bar{F}$ satisfies P.O, CONT, M.STAB, W.A.R.P, and BOUND, then it has an additively separable numerical representation.*

Proof. Let $\{f_i\}_{i \in I}$ be the sequence of functions introduced in Lemma 11.12. By Lemma 11.12, each f_i is continuous and strictly increasing, and by Lemma 11.14, $\sum_P f_i$ is strictly quasi-concave for all $P \in \mathcal{P}$. It remains to show that $\sum_P f_i$ represents the P component of $\bar{F}$ for all $P \in \mathcal{P}$.

To see this, let $P \in \mathcal{P}$ and $(\pi, \omega) \in \mathbb{R}^P_{++} \times \mathbb{R}^P_{+}$ be given, and let $S \equiv b(\pi, \omega)$. We must show that $z \equiv \operatorname{argmax}\{\sum_P f_i(x_i) \mid x \in S\} = \bar{F}(\pi, \omega)$. If $\omega = 0$, the proof is trivial, so assume that $\omega \geq 0$. Then S contains a strictly positive vector y because $\pi > 0$. Therefore, since S is compact and convex, it follows by the existence part of the proof of Proposition 11.1 that z exists and is unique. Moreover, $\sum_P f_i(z_i) \geqq \sum_P f_i(y_i) > -\infty$ because each f_i is strictly increasing and $y > 0$. It then follows that $\bar{F}(\pi, \omega) = z$, for otherwise $\bar{F}(\pi, \omega) R_{\bar{F}} z$ and $\sum_P f_i(z_i) > -\infty$, which is impossible in view of Lemma 11.13 since z maximizes $\sum_P f_i$ on S. Q.E.D.

Proposition 11.2 is an interesting by-product of the analysis, as it gives sufficient conditions for a demand function to be consistent with the maximization of an additively separable utility function. It may well be that Proposition 11.2 is not the strongest result that can be proved in that respect. A question that is left open for further investigation is whether *W.A.R.P* is implied by the other four axioms in Proposition 11.2. Note, however, that *P.O, CONT,* and *M.STAB* alone are not sufficient conditions for utility maximization, as these conditions are also consistent with the minimization of a strictly increasing, strictly quasi-convex, continuous, and additively separable function on the budget plane.

Our next task is to extend the result obtained in Proposition 11.2 from budget problems to general problems.

Proposition 11.3. *If a solution satisfies P.O, CONT, and M.STAB, then it has an additively separable numerical representation.*

Proof. Let F be a solution satisfying *P.O, CONT,* and *M.STAB*. By Lemma 11.1, F satisfies *I.I.A,* and by Lemmas 11.2 and 11.3, the restricted solution $\bar{F}$ satisfies the additional properties of *W.A.R.P* and *BOUND*. By Proposition 11.2, $\bar{F}$ has an additively separable numerical representation $\{f_i\}_{i \in I}$. We must show that $\{f_i\}_{i \in I}$ represents F also.

Let $P \in \mathcal{P}$ and $S \in \Sigma^P$ be given, and let $z \equiv \text{argmax}\{\Sigma_P f_i(x_i) \mid x \in S\}$. Proposition 11.1 implies that z exists and is unique. By convexity of S and quasiconcavity of $\Sigma_P f_i$, there exists a hyperplane H in $\mathbb{R}^P$ with normal π separating S and $\{x \in \mathbb{R}^P_+ \mid \Sigma_P f_i(x_i) > \Sigma_P f_i(z_i)\}$. Here, π is strictly positive since $\Sigma_P f_i$ is strictly increasing. This implies that $S' \equiv \text{cch}\{H \cap \mathbb{R}^P_+\}$ is a member of Σ^P_Δ. By Proposition 11.2, $F(S') \equiv \bar{F}(\pi, z) = z$, and since $z \in S \subset S'$, it follows by *I.I.A* that $F(S) = z$. Q.E.D.

The announced characterization of the family of CRS solutions is now obtained by combining Propositions 11.1 and 11.3:

Theorem 11.1. *A solution satisfies P.O, CONT, and M.STAB if and only if it is a CRS solution.*

11.4 Variants

In this section, we first show that the three axioms *P.O, CONT,* and *M.STAB* are independent in the sense that removing any one of them will yield solutions that are not collectively rational. Then the consequences of adding more axioms to this list are investigated. Finally, we show that when the requirement that the number of agents be infinite is removed and *M.STAB* is weakened to *B.STAB,* the conclusion of Proposition 11.3 still holds.

11.4.1 Removal of the axiom of Pareto-optimality

The following solution satisfies *CONT* and *M.STAB* but is not collectively rational: Let $k \in I$ and $\lambda \in]0,1[$ be given. For all $P \in \mathcal{P}$ and all $S \in \Sigma^P$, set $F_i(S) \equiv 0$ if $i \neq k$ and $F_i(S) \equiv \lambda \max\{x_i \mid x \in S\}$ if $i = k$. Clearly, F satisfies *CONT* and *M.STAB* but not *I.I.A,* and therefore F is not collectively rational.

11.4.2 Removal of the axiom of Continuity

For all $P \in \mathcal{P}$, let $\succsim^2_P$ be the lexicographic ordering of $\mathbb{R}^P_+$ such that for all $i, j \in P$, i has priority over j if and only if $i > j$, and let $\succsim^2 \equiv \{\succsim^2_P \mid P \in \mathcal{P}\}$.

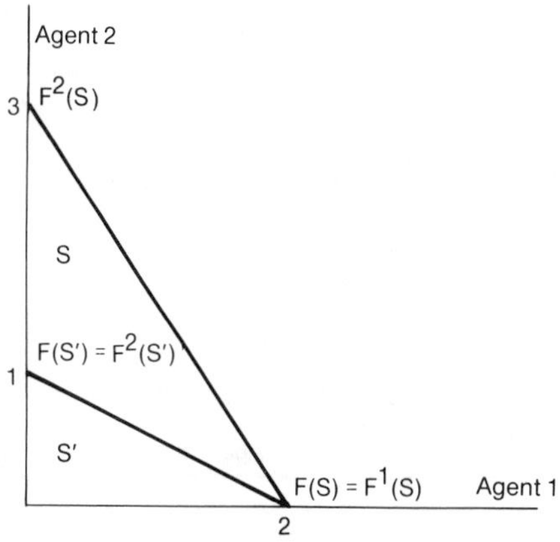

Figure 11.9. A solution satisfying *P.O* and *M.STAB* but not *I.I.A*.

Also, let the family $\succsim^1$ of lexicographic orderings be obtained from $\succsim^2$ by interchanging the roles of agents 1 and 2. Thus, $\succsim^1$ differs from $\succsim^2$ only in that the members of $\succsim^1$ give priority to 1 over 2, whereas the members of $\succsim^2$ give priority to 2 over 1. Note that for all $P \in \mathcal{P}$, $\succsim_P^1 = \succsim_P^2$ unless both 1 and 2 belong to P.

For $i = 1, 2$, there exists a collectively rational solution F^i for which $\succsim^i$ is a representation. Clearly, F^i satisfies *P.O;* moreover, it satisfies *M.STAB* since each $\succsim^i$ is a family of separable orderings. Let the solution F be defined as follows: For all $P \in \mathcal{P}$ and all $S \in \Sigma^P$,

$$F(S) \equiv \begin{cases} F^1(S) & \text{if } \{1,2\} \subset P \text{ and } F_1^1(S) \leqq F_2^2(S), \\ F^2(S) & \text{otherwise.} \end{cases}$$

It is easy to verify that F is a well-defined solution that inherits the properties of *P.O* and *M.STAB* from the solutions F^i. However, F does not satisfy *I.I.A*, as shown in Figure 11.9, and therefore it is not collectively rational.

These two examples show that *P.O, CONT,* and *M.STAB* constitute a minimal set of conditions for a solution to be a member of the CRS family. (Removing *M.STAB* would admit a large set of solutions that are not collectively rational.) With the aid of Theorem 11.1, it is easy to analyze the implications of adding more conditions to this list. This is done in the next section.

11.4.3 Adding Homogeneity and Symmetry to the list of axioms

The examples given in the preceding of solutions violating either *P.O* or *CONT* indicate that the main role of these two axioms is to rule out some

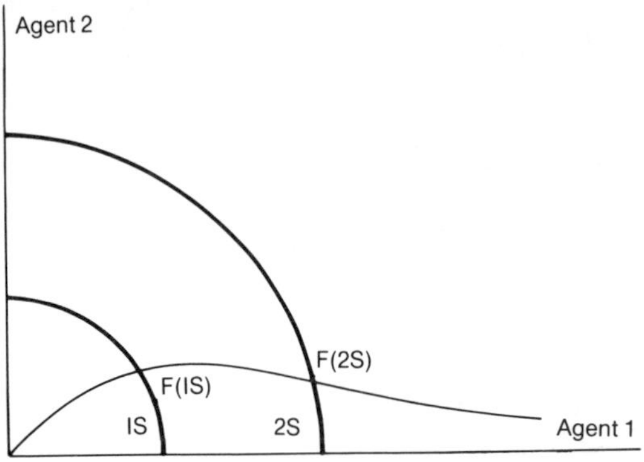

Figure 11.10. Agent 1 is an eventual dictator.

peculiarities that *M.STAB* permits. However, a certain peculiarity turns out to survive all three axioms, as shown next.

For all $P \in \mathcal{P}$, all $S \in \Sigma^P$, and all real numbers $\alpha > 0$, let αS denote the problem $\{x \in \mathbb{R}^P_+ \mid x/\alpha \in S\}$. Given $S \in \Sigma^P$ and $\alpha > 1$, the symmetric expansion of the set of feasible alternatives from S to αS could come about as the result of what may be called a *welfare-neutral growth* in the underlying set of physical alternatives. It turns out that the response of a solution to welfare-neutral growth may be quite pathological. Given a solution F and an agent k, say that *k is an eventual dictator for F* if for all $P \in \mathcal{P}$ with $k \in P$ and all $S \in \Sigma^P$, $F_k(\alpha S)/\max\{x_k \mid x \in \alpha S\} \to 1$ as $\alpha \to \infty$. In other words, agent k is an eventual dictator for F if persistent welfare-neutral growth always causes the income distribution to approach his preferred alternative.

As an example of a CRS solution that creates an eventual dictator, let $f_1 \equiv e^{x_1}$ and $f_j \equiv (\frac{1}{2})^{j-1}\log(x_j)$ for all $j \neq 1$. Then each f_i is continuous and strictly increasing; moreover, $\Sigma_P f_i$ is strictly quasi-concave for all $P \in \mathcal{P}$ by Theorem 11 in Debreu and Koopmans (1982) even though f_1 is strictly convex. Thus, there exists a CRS solution F that is represented by the sequence of functions $\{f_i\}_{i \in I}$. The eventual dictator is agent 1, and it is the strict convexity of the function f_1 that is responsible for that fact. The response of the solution F to welfare-neutral growth is illustrated in Figure 11.10, where the thin curve shows the income expansion path for $P = \{1, 2\}$ and $\alpha S = \{x \in \mathbb{R}^P_+ \mid (x_1/\alpha)^2 + (x_2/\alpha)^2 \leq 1\}$. For low levels of aggregate income, measured by the parameter α, both agents gain from an increase in income. However, at some point, agent 1's dictatorial tendencies start to dominate, and in the limit he will end up with his preferred alternative, leaving nothing to agent 2. In order to eliminate this type of phenomenon, one might want to impose additional restrictions on the solution.

Two conditions that are satisfied by the solutions associated with the four Bergson–Samuelson SWFs mentioned in the introduction of this chapter (the Utilitarian, Rawlsian, Leximin, and Nash SWFs) are Homogeneity (*HOM*) and Symmetry (*SY*). *HOM* says that if two problems S and S' have the property that $S' = \alpha S$ for some $\alpha > 0$, then $F(S') = \alpha F(S)$. Any of these two axioms will, in conjunction with the standard ones, prevent a solution from creating an eventual dictator.

Adding *HOM* to the list of axioms in Theorem 11.1 implies that the functions $\Sigma_P f_i$ must be homothetic for all $P \in \mathcal{P}$. This means (Eichhorn, 1978, Theorem 2.2.1) that (except for arbitrary constant terms) there exists $\rho > -1$ and a sequence $\{\alpha_i\}_{i \in I}$ of positive real numbers such that $f_i(x_i) = -(\alpha_i/\rho)x_i^{-\rho}$ for all $i \in I$ if $\rho \neq 0$, and $f_i(x_i) = \alpha_i \log(x_i)$ for all $i \in I$ if $\rho = 0$. Thus, $\Sigma_P f_i$ is a constant elasticity of substitution (CES) function for all $P \in \mathcal{P}$. If *SY* is also imposed, then f_i, and hence α_i, must be the same for all i. The Nash SWF is obtained when $\rho \to 0$, the Utilitarian SWF when $\rho \to -1$, and the Rawlsian SWF when $\rho \to \infty$. [See Roberts (1980) for related results in the Arrow tradition of social choice theory.]

It should be noted that the Utilitarian and Rawlsian SWFs do not themselves yield well-defined solutions, since their maximizers are not always unique on the domain considered here. One may then consider single-valued selections, but this will be at the necessary cost of relaxing either *P.O* or *CONT*. For example, keeping *P.O* and dropping *CONT* will admit the lexicographic extension of the Rawlsian SWF, as shown in Chapter 9.

11.4.4 Removing the requirement that the number of potential agents be infinite

In the proof of Theorem 11.1, the requirement that the set I of potential agents be infinite was only used in the proof of Lemma 11.1, which says that *P.O, CONT,* and *M.STAB* imply *I.I.A*. If I were finite, the rest of the proof would still go through as long as $|I| \geqq 3$.

In this section, we only assume that the number of potential agents is at least 3. We show in Lemma 11.19, which differs from 11.1 by using *B.STAB* instead of *M.STAB,* that the conclusion of Lemma 11.1 still holds. On the way to its proof, we show that *P.O, CONT,* and *B.STAB* imply that the restricted solution $\bar{F}$ must satisfy *M.STAB* as well. Because the proof of Proposition 11.3 makes no use of *M.STAB,* this result strengthens the "only if" part of Theorem 11.1 in two ways: by reducing the minimum number of potential agents from infinite to finite, and by weakening *M.STAB* to *B.STAB*.

Some additional notation and a new axiom that will be useful in the proof of Lemma 11.19 are first introduced. The new axiom is a *localness condition,* which is closely related to *I.I.A*.

Given a solution F and given $Q \in \mathcal{P}$ and $T \in \Sigma^Q$, recall from Chapter 7 that $B_F(T)$ denotes the set of F bilaterally stable points of T. The set $B_F(T)$ is the set of points $x \in T$ such that for all $P \in \mathcal{P}$ with $P \subset Q$ and $|P| = 2$, and for all $S \in \Sigma^P$, if $S = t_P^x(T)$ then $F(S) = x_P$. Given $P \in \mathcal{P}$ and a subset A of $\mathbb{R}^P$, $\text{cl}\{A\}$ denotes the closure of A. Finally, given $P \in \mathcal{P}$ and $S, S' \in \Sigma^P$, say that *S and S′ coincide in a neighborhood U* if $S \cap U = S' \cap U$.

Localness condition (LOC): For all $P \in \mathcal{P}$ and for all $S, S' \in \Sigma^P$, if S and S' coincide in a neighborhood U of $F(S)$ then $F(S') = F(S)$.

> ***Lemma 11.15.*** *A continuous solution satisfies I.I.A if and only if it satisfies LOC.*

Proof. First we show that if a solution F satisfies *LOC* and *CONT,* then it satisfies *I.I.A*. Let $P \in \mathcal{P}$ and $S, S' \in \Sigma^P$ be given such that $S' \subset S$ and $z \equiv F(S) \in S'$. For all $\nu \geqq 1$, let U^ν be an open ball with center z and radius $1/\nu$, let $V^\nu \equiv S \cap \text{cl}\{U^\nu\}$, $S^\nu \equiv \text{cch}(S' \cup V^\nu)$, and note that $S^\nu \cap U^\nu = S \cap U^\nu$ and $S' \subset S^\nu \subset S$.

We claim that $F(S^\nu) = z$ for all ν. To see this let ν be given, and for all $\alpha \in [0,1]$ let $S(\alpha) \equiv \alpha S^\nu + (1-\alpha)S$ and $z(\alpha) \equiv F(S(\alpha))$. Since $S^\nu \subset S$ and $S^\nu \cap U^\nu = S \cap U^\nu$, then $S(\alpha) \subset S$ and $S(\alpha) \cap U^\nu = S \cap U^\nu$ for all $\alpha \in [0,1]$. The proof that $z(1) = z$ is by contradiction. If $z(1) \neq z$ then $z(\alpha) \in U^\nu \backslash \{z\}$ for some $\alpha \in]0,1[$, since $z(0) = z \in U^\nu$ and since the function $z(\cdot)$ is continuous by continuity of F. Because $z(\alpha) \in U^\nu$ and $S(\alpha) \cap U^\nu = S \cap U^\nu$, it follows by *LOC* that $F(S) = z(\alpha)$, a contradiction since $z(\alpha) \neq z = F(S)$. Hence, $F(S^\nu) = z$.

Since $F(S^\nu) = z$ for all ν and since $S^\nu \to S'$ as $\nu \to \infty$, it follows by *CONT* that $F(S') = z = F(S)$. Thus, F satisfies *I.I.A* if it satisfies *LOC* and *CONT.*

Next, we show that if F satisfies *CONT* and *I.I.A,* then it satisfies *LOC.* Let $P \in \mathcal{P}$ and $S, S' \in \Sigma^P$ be given such that S and S' coincide in a neighborhood U of $z \equiv F(S)$. Define $S'' \equiv S \cap S'$ and note that $F(S'') = z$ by *I.I.A*.

For all $\alpha \in [0,1]$, let $S(\alpha) \equiv \alpha S' + (1-\alpha)S''$ and $z(\alpha) \equiv F(S(\alpha))$. Then $S'' \subset S(\alpha)$ for all $\alpha \in [0,1]$. Moreover, since S and S' coincide in U, so do S' and S'' and hence $S(\alpha)$ and S'' for all $\alpha \in [0,1]$. We must show that $z(1) = z$, and the proof is by contradiction. If $z(1) \neq z$ then $z(\alpha) \in U \backslash \{z\}$ for some $\alpha \in]0,1[$, since $z(0) = z \in U$ and since the function $z(\cdot)$ is continuous. Since $S(\alpha)$ and S'' coincide in U, this implies that $z(\alpha)\in S''\subset S(\alpha)$, which by *I.I.A* implies that $F(S'')=z(\alpha)$, a contradiction since $z(\alpha)\neq z=F(S'')$. Hence $z(1)=z$; that is, $F(S')=F(S)$. Q.E.D.

Lemma 11.16. *If F satisfies P.O, CONT, and B.STAB, then*

(1) *for all $P\in\mathcal{P}$, F satisfies M.STAB on Σ_Δ^P; and*
(2) *for all $P\in\mathcal{P}$ with $|P|\geqq 2$ and for all $S\in\Sigma_\Delta^P$, $B_F(S)$ is a singleton.*

Proof. For the purpose of the proof, the convention is adopted that $\{0\}\in\Sigma_\Delta^P$ and $F(\{0\})=0$ for all $P\in\mathcal{P}$. If the lemma holds for this extension of F, then by definition of *M.STAB* and $B_F(\cdot)$ it holds for F as well.

It is to be shown that (1) and (2) hold for each P component of F. The proof is by induction on the number of elements in P. Clearly, the desired conclusion holds for $|P|\leqq 2$. Suppose it holds for $|P|=n\geqq 2$ and let $Q\in\mathcal{P}$ with $|Q|=n+1$ be given. We claim that: (i) for all $T\in\Sigma_\Delta^Q$, for all $x\in B_F(T)$, and for all $P\subset Q$ with $|P|<|Q|$, $F(t_P^x(T))=x_P$.

To see this, let T, x, and P satisfy the hypothesis of (i). If $|P|=1$, then $F(t_P^x(T))=x_P$ by *P.O*, so assume that $|P|\geqq 2$. Since $x\in B_F(T)$, $x_P\in B_F(t_P^x(T))$, which is a singleton by induction hypothesis (2). *B.STAB* then implies that $F(t_P^x(T))=x_P$, and thus (i) holds. This proves (1) as well, for if $F(T)=x$ then $x\in B_F(T)$ by *B.STAB*.

Next, we show that (2) holds for this Q. The proof, which is by contradiction, is illustrated in Figure 11.11. Let $T\in\Sigma_\Delta^Q$ be given, let $z\equiv F(T)$, and suppose that $B_F(T)$ contains a point $y\neq z$. Then $y_{Q^i}\in B_F(t_{Q^i}^y(T))$ for all $i\in Q$, where $Q^i\equiv Q\backslash i$. Moreover, since $B_F(T)\subset\mathrm{PO}(T)$ by *P.O*, then $z,y\in\mathrm{PO}(T)$. Let π be the normal to $\mathrm{PO}(T)$. For all $\alpha>0$, let $z(\alpha)\equiv F(\alpha T)$, and for all $i\in Q$, let $\underline{K}^i(\alpha)\equiv\{x\in\mathrm{PO}(\alpha T)\mid \pi_{Q^i}x_{Q^i}\geqq\pi_{Q^i}y_{Q^i}\}$ and $\bar{K}^i(\alpha)\equiv\{x\in\mathrm{PO}(\alpha T)\mid\pi_{Q^i}x_{Q^i}\leqq\pi_{Q^i}y_{Q^i}\}$. Note that $z(1)=z$ and that $\alpha T=\{x\in\mathbb{R}_+^Q\mid\pi x\leqq\alpha\pi y\}$ for all $\alpha>0$ since $y\in\mathrm{PO}(T)$. If $z(\alpha)\in\underline{K}^i(\alpha)\cap\bar{K}^i(\alpha)$, then $t_{Q^i}^{z(\alpha)}(\alpha T)=t_{Q^i}^y(T)$. Therefore, since $y_{Q^i}\in B(t_{Q^i}^y(T))$, it follows by (2) that $F(t_{Q^i}^{z(\alpha)}(\alpha T))=y_{Q^i}$. Thus, by *M.STAB*, it follows that: (ii) for all $\alpha>0$ and for all $i\in Q$, if $z(\alpha)\in\underline{K}^i(\alpha)\cap\bar{K}^i(\alpha)$ then $z_{Q^i}(\alpha)=y_{Q^i}$.

Because $|Q|\geqq 3$, there exists $P\subset Q$ with $|P|=2$ such that $z_P\geqq y_P$ or $z_P\leqq y_P$. Suppose first that $z_P\geqq y_P$. We prove by contradiction that $z(\alpha)\in\bigcap_P\bar{K}^i(\alpha)$ for all $\alpha\geqq 1$. Consider the path $\sigma\equiv z([1,\infty[)$ traced out by $z(\cdot)$ as α increases from 1. *P.O* implies that $z(\alpha)\in\mathrm{PO}(\alpha T)$ for all α and *CONT* implies that σ is a continuous curve. Here, $z(\alpha)$ starts in $\bigcap_P\bar{K}^i(1)$ for $\alpha=1$ since $z_P\geqq y_P$, and if it does not stay in $\bigcap_P\bar{K}^i(\alpha)$ for all $\alpha\geqq 1$ then there exists $\bar{\alpha}\geqq 1$ and $j\in P$ such that $z(\bar{\alpha})\in[\bigcap_P\bar{K}^i(\bar{\alpha})]\cap\underline{K}^j(\bar{\alpha})$. This is the situation represented in Figure 11.11. Let i be the other member of P.

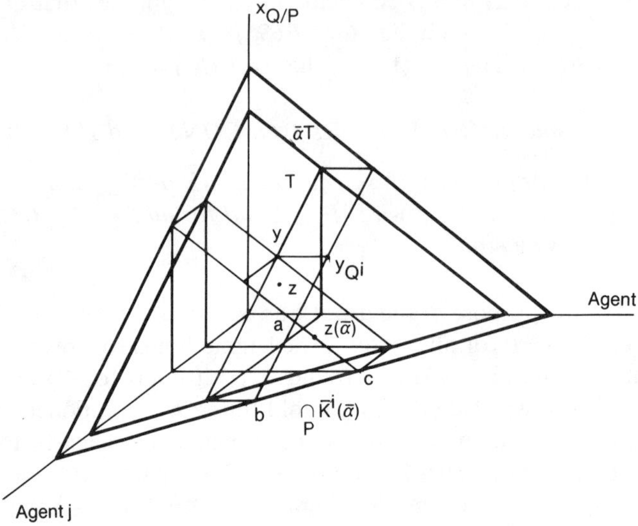

Figure 11.11. Lemma 11.16. $P=\{i,j\}$; $\bigcap_P \bar{K}^i(\bar{\alpha})=\text{cch}\{a,b,c\}$.

It follows by (ii) that $z_{Q^j}(\bar{\alpha})=y_{Q^j}$. Because $z(1)$ and y belong to PO(T), this implies that $\bar{\alpha}>1$; otherwise, $z(1)=y$, contrary to assumption. Since $z_{Q^j}(\bar{\alpha})=y_{Q^j}$ and $\bar{\alpha}>1$, it follows that $z_j(\bar{\alpha})>y_j$. But then $\pi_{Q^i}z_{Q^i}(\bar{\alpha})>\pi_{Q^i}y_{Q^i}$ since $z(\bar{\alpha})\in \text{PO}(\bar{\alpha}T)$, and therefore $z(\bar{\alpha})\notin \bar{K}^i(\bar{\alpha})$, a contradiction. Thus, $z(\alpha)\in \bigcap_P \bar{K}^i(\alpha)$ for all $\alpha \geqq 1$, as claimed.

This completes the proof for the case where $z_P \geqq y_P$ because $\bigcap_P \bar{K}^i(\alpha)$ is empty for sufficiently large α. If $z_P \leqq y_P$, then the argument in the previous paragraph is used to show that $z(\alpha)\in \bigcap_P \underline{K}^i(\alpha)$ for all $\alpha \in]0,1]$, and a similar contradiction follows by the fact that $\bigcap_P \underline{K}^i(\alpha)$ is empty for α sufficiently close to zero. Q.E.D.

Lemma 11.17. *If F satisfies P.O, CONT, and B.STAB, then for all $Q\in \mathcal{P}$ and all $T^1, T^2 \in \Sigma^Q$, if there exists $T\in \Sigma^Q_\Delta$ such that T, T^1, and T^2 coincide in a neighborhood U of $F(T^1)$, then $F(T)=F(T^2)=F(T^1)$.*

Proof. Let Q, T, T^1, T^2, and U satisfy the hypothesis of the lemma, and let $z\equiv F(T^1)$. First we show that $F(T)=z$ also.

To see this, observe first that since F satisfies *P.O, CONT,* and *B.STAB,* it follows by the same argument used to prove Lemma 11.1 that each two-person component of F must satisfy *I.I.A;* hence, by Lemma 11.15 each two-person component of F satisfies *LOC*. Since $z\in B_F(T^1)$ by *B.STAB,*

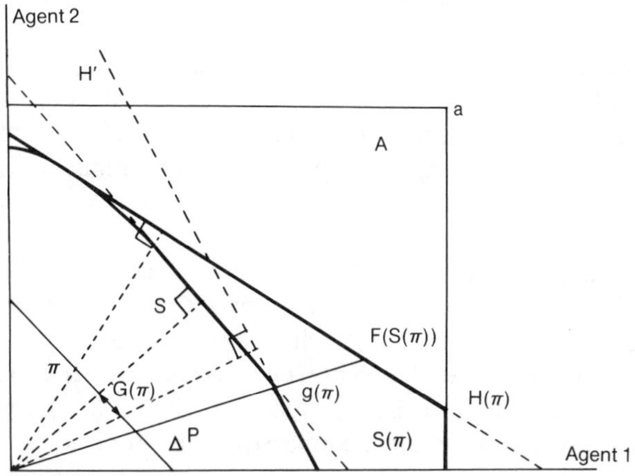

Figure 11.12. Lemma 11.18.

this implies that $z \in B_F(T)$ also. Since T is a budget problem, it follows by Lemma 11.16 that $B_F(T)$ is a singleton; hence by *B.STAB*, $F(T)=z=F(T^1)$.

Next we show that $F(T^2)=z$. To this end, define for each $\alpha \in [0,1]$ the problem $T(\alpha) \equiv \alpha T^2+(1-\alpha)T$ and set $z(\alpha) \equiv F(T(\alpha))$. We show by contradiction that $z(1)=z$. If $z(1) \neq z$, then $z(\alpha) \in U \setminus \{z\}$ for some $\alpha \in]0,1[$ since $z(0)=z \in U$ and the function $z(\cdot)$ is continuous. Because T and T^2 coincide in U, so do T and $T(\alpha)$, and therefore $F(T)=F(T(\alpha))=z(\alpha)$ by the same argument used to prove that $F(T)=F(T^1)$. Since $z(\alpha) \neq z = F(T)$, this is the announced contradiction. Hence, $z(1)=z$; that is, $z(1)=F(T^2)=F(T^1)$. Q.E.D.

Lemma 11.18. *If F satisfies P.O, CONT, and B.STAB, then for all $P \in \mathcal{P}$ and all $S \in \Sigma^P$, there exists $S' \in \Sigma^P_\Delta$ such that $S \subset S'$ and $F(S') \in S$.*

Proof. The proof is done using a fixed-point argument, and the mapping is illustrated in Figure 11.12. Let $P \in \mathcal{P}$ and $S \in \Sigma^P$ be given (in Figure 11.12, $P=\{1,2\}$). Let a be a point in $\mathbb{R}^P_{++}$ such that $x<a$ for all $x \in S$ and let $A \equiv \text{cch}\{a\}$. A correspondence G from the unit simplex Δ^P to itself is constructed as follows: For all $\pi \in \Delta^P$, let $H(\pi)$ be the unique hyperplane with normal π supporting S at some point in WPO(S), and let $S(\pi) \equiv \text{cch}\{H(\pi) \cap A\}$. Next, let $g(\pi)$ be the point of intersection between the line segment $[0, F(S(\pi))]$ and WPO(S), and define $G(\pi)$ to be the set

of points $\pi' \in \Delta^P$ such that π' is normal to a hyperplane H' supporting S at $g(\pi)$.

Clearly, the function $S(\cdot)$ is continuous. Because $S \subset S(\pi)$ for all $\pi \in \Delta^P$, it follows by *P.O* and comprehensiveness of S that $g(\pi)$ exists and is unique. Moreover, g is continuous since $S(\cdot)$ and F are continuous. Therefore, since S is convex, G is upper hemi-continuous and convex-valued. By Kakutani's fixed-point theorem, there exists $\bar{\pi} \in \Delta^P$ such that $\bar{\pi} \in G(\bar{\pi})$.

Since $\bar{\pi} \in G(\bar{\pi})$, the hyperplane $H(\bar{\pi})$ supports S at $g(\bar{\pi})$. This in turn implies that $F(S(\bar{\pi})) = z \equiv g(\bar{\pi})$. It follows by *P.O* that $\bar{\pi} > 0$; otherwise, z would belong to the boundary of A, which is impossible since $A = \text{cch}\{a\}$ and $a > x$ for all $x \in S$. Let $S' \equiv \text{cch}\{H(\bar{\pi}) \cap \mathbb{R}^P_+\}$. The set S' is a well-defined budget problem since $\bar{\pi} > 0$; moreover, S' and $S(\bar{\pi})$ coincide in a neighborhood of z since $z < a$. Lemma 11.17 then implies that $F(S') = z \in S$. Q.E.D.

Lemma 11.19. *If a solution satisfies P.O, CONT, and B.STAB, then it satisfies I.I.A.*

Proof. Let F be a solution satisfying *P.O, CONT,* and *B.STAB*. Let $P \in \mathcal{P}$ and $S', S \in \Sigma^P$ be given such that $S' \subset S$ and $F(S) \in S'$. We have to show that $F(S') = F(S)$.

By Lemma 11.18, there exists $S'' \in \Sigma^Q_\Delta$ with $S \subset S''$ and $z \equiv F(S'') \in S$. We claim that $F(S) = z$ also.

For all $\nu \geqq 1$, let U^ν be the closed ball in $\mathbb{R}^P$ with center z and radius $1/\nu$. Let $V^\nu \equiv S'' \cap U^\nu$ and $S^\nu \equiv \text{cch}\{S \cup V^\nu\}$. Because S^ν and S'' coincide in U^ν for all ν, it follows by Lemma 11.17 that $F(S^\nu) = z$ for all ν and by *CONT* that $F(S) = z$ since $S^\nu \to S$ as $\nu \to \infty$. This proves the claim.

Since $S' \subset S \subset S''$ and $F(S'') = F(S) \in S'$, the argument in the previous paragraph may be applied to S' as well, and therefore $F(S') = z = F(S)$. Q.E.D.

The main result of this section can now be stated.

Theorem 11.2. *Suppose the number of potential agents is at least 3. A solution satisfies P.O, CONT, and B.STAB if and only if it is a CRS solution.*

Proof. Because *M.STAB* implies *B.STAB,* it follows by Proposition 11.1 that a CRS solution satisfies *PO, CONT,* and *B.STAB*.

To prove the converse, let F satisfy *P.O, CONT,* and *B.STAB*. Then F satisfies *I.I.A* by Lemma 11.19. Moreover, the restricted solution $\bar{F}$ satisfies *M.STAB* by Lemma 11.16, *W.A.R.P* by Lemma 11.2, and *BOUND* by Lemma 11.3. By Proposition 11.2, $\bar{F}$ has an additively separable numerical representation that, by the second paragraph in the proof of Proposition 11.3, represents F as well. Q.E.D.

11.5 Concluding remarks

Although at first sight, the idea of Bilateral Stability appears to be quite different from that of collective rationality, it turned out to have quite strong implications in that respect. What then does a bilaterally stable solution have in common with a collectively rational one that can explain this fact?

Intuitively, both types of solutions are based on some version of what may be called the *principle of pairwise comparisons.* Consider first a collectively rational solution. The social ordering corresponding to such a solution provides a way of determining the solution outcome to all problems involving *any pair of alternatives,* and a utility vector z is the solution outcome to a particular problem S only if z agrees with the solution outcome to any subproblem of S involving a pair of alternatives $\{z,x\}$. This is a requirement similar to the one expressed by *B.STAB:* The generalized solution concept used here provides a way of solving all problems involving *any pair of agents,* and *B.STAB* says that a utility allocation z is the solution outcome to a particular problem S only if z agrees with the solution outcome to any subproblem of S involving any pair of agents.

Our characterization result (in particular, Theorem 11.2) shows that the second version of this principle is closely related to the first one, although – as shown in Sections 11.4.1 and 11.4.2 – there is no direct implication.

CHAPTER 12

Invariance under Replication and Juxtaposition

12.1 Introduction

In all of the previous chapters, we considered variations in the number of agents without imposing any restriction on the preferences of the new agents in relation to the preferences of the agents originally present. In contrast, we formulate here various notions of "similarity" between old agents and new agents, and we examine the behavior of solutions in these special cases.

The chapter starts with notions of "replication," and we ask whether and in what sense solutions can be said to be invariant under such replications. Then, we consider related notions of "juxtaposition" and ask similar questions.

This chapter is partly inspired by the literature on replica economies initiated by Edgeworth (1881) and taken up by Debreu and Scarf (1963) and many subsequent writers. The replication of economies turned out to be a powerful tool in the study of large economies, opening up a line of investigation that provided valuable insights into the classical concept of perfect competition.

The cores of replicated games in coalitional form were recently analyzed by Wooders (1981) and various coauthors, but to our knowledge, the only author who concerned himself with the replication of unanimity games of the kind examined in this book is Kalai (1977a).

Kalai showed that each two-person asymmetric Nash solution is equivalent to the Nash solution under appropriate replications (or limits of such replications). He also noted the invariance of the Kalai–Smorodinsky solution under replications. We will start by reproducing Kalai's result and generalize it to the replication of n-person (instead of two-person) problems. We will also establish that the Utilitarian solution behaves like the Nash solution and that the Egalitarian solution behaves like the Kalai–Smorodinsky solution.

Then, we will show that these results crucially depend on the manner in which the replications are performed. Under another replication method that is just as natural, the asymmetric generalizations of all four major solutions become equivalent to their symmetric counterparts under appropriate replications (or limits of such replications).

The two replication methods are polar opposites. Kalai's method models maximal compatibility of interests between the original agents and the newcomers whereas the second method models minimal compatibility.

Both methods have natural interpretations and applications in economic contexts. Kalai's method is particularly appropriate in public good economies, and the second method is appropriate in private good economies. Replication of economies with both private goods and public goods or with local public goods would have to be modeled in an intermediate manner.

A notion related to the notion of replication is that of "juxtaposition." There, the new agents are not required to be "clones" of the original agents, but the interaction between original and new agents still takes a very simple form. Again, we will examine two extreme cases, the case of maximal compatibility of interests and that of minimal compatibility of interests between the groups of agents that are being juxtaposed, and we will formulate two corresponding notions of invariance of solutions. The main solutions satisfy the second notion, but only the Nash and Utilitarian solutions satisfy the first notion. However, the Kalai–Smorodinsky and Egalitarian solutions satisfy a slightly weaker version of this first notion.

An example of an economic situation to which the notions of juxtaposition apply is when the tastes of the new agents are identical to those of the old agents but for different sets of goods.

The results reported here tell us when groups of similar agents benefit from being represented by a single agent and, conversely, when an agent gains from recruiting supporters similar to himself.

Sections 12.2 and 12.3 are devoted to replication and juxtaposition (respectively), and Section 12.4 concludes. This chapter is based on Thomson (1986).

12.2 Replication

We start with some definitions. Given $P \in \mathcal{P}$, $S \in \Sigma^P$, and $n \in \mathbb{N}^P$, the *n-replica of S* is obtained by first composing an enlarged group Q containing $\sum_P n_i$ agents, each agent $i \in P$ being replicated n_i times. Then we require that each subgroup of Q with a composition identical to that of P face a problem that is a copy of S and that the problem faced by Q be the intersection of the cylinders in $\mathbb{R}^Q_+$ spanned by these subproblems.

Formally, let $Q \in \mathcal{P}$ be such that $|Q| = \sum_P n_i$. Let $\{Q^i \mid i \in P\}$ be a partition of Q with $|Q^i| = n_i$ for all $i \in P$. The members of Q^i are called the *agents of type i.* Given any $P' \subset Q$ containing exactly one agent of each type, let $S^{P'} \subset \mathbb{R}^{P'}$ be defined by

$$S^{P'} \equiv \{x' \in \mathbb{R}^{P'}_{+} \mid \exists x \in S \text{ with } x'_j = x_{t(j)}\ \forall j \in P'\},$$

where $t(j)$ designates the agent in P of whose type agent j is. Finally, let $S^{\max}(n) \subset \mathbb{R}^{Q}_{+}$ be defined by

$$S^{\max}(n) \equiv \{y \in \mathbb{R}^{Q}_{+} \mid \forall P' \subset Q \text{ with } \operatorname{comp} P' = \operatorname{comp} P,\ y_{P'} \in S^{P'}\},$$

where comp P should be read as "composition of P." The problem $S^{\max}(n)$ is the intersection, for all $P' \subset Q$ of composition identical to that of P, of the cylinders spanned by $S^{P'}$ with generators parallel to $\mathbb{R}^{Q \setminus P'}$.

Since in the introduction we alluded to the literature on replica economies, it is worth emphasizing that here we allow the orders of replication of different types of agents to differ, in contrast with that literature where the order of replication is always chosen to be uniform across types.

Finally, in this chapter we will make use of the notation O_P to designate the origin of $\mathbb{R}^P$.

We can now state our first invariance axiom. It says that all of the agents of a given type receive in the replicated problem the amount received in the original problem by the agent they are replicating.

Nonconflictual Replication (N.C.R): For all $P \in \mathcal{P}$, for all $S \in \Sigma^P$, for all $n \in \mathbb{N}^P$, and for all $i \in P$ and $j \in Q^i$, $F_j(S^{\max}(n)) = F_i(S)$ [where Q^i is as in the definition of $S^{\max}(n)$].

Theorems 12.1 and 12.2 follow directly from Kalai (1977a). (Kalai limited his attention to the replication of two-person problems and did not examine the Egalitarian or the Utilitarian solutions.)

Theorem 12.1. *The Kalai–Smorodinsky and Egalitarian solutions satisfy Nonconflictual Replication.*

Proof. (See Figure 12.1.) Let $P \in \mathcal{P}$, $S \in \Sigma^P$, and $n \in \mathbb{N}^P$ be given as in the statement of *N.C.R,* and let Q be as in the definition of $S^{\max}(n)$. (In Figure 12.1, $P = \{1,2\}$ and $n = (2,1)$ with agent 3 replicating agent 1.) Also, let $x \equiv K(S)$ and $y \in \mathbb{R}^Q$ be such that for all $i \in P$ and $j \in Q^i$, $y_j = x_i$. We will show that $y = K(S^{\max}(n))$. Since for each $P' \subset Q$ with comp $P' =$ comp P, $y_{P'} = K(S^{P'}) \in S^{P'}$ [where $S^{P'}$ is as in the definition of $S^{\max}(n)$], it follows that $y \in S^{\max}(n)$. (In the figure, the only $P' \neq P$ is $\{2,3\}$.) To show that $y \in \mathrm{WPO}(S^{\max}(n))$, suppose, by way of contradiction, that for some $y' \in S^{\max}(n)$, $y' > y$. Then $y'_P > y_P$ and, since $y_P = x \in \mathrm{WPO}(S)$, $y'_P \notin S$ and a contradiction follows with the definition of $S^{\max}(n)$. Finally, since $x = K(S)$, $x = \lambda a(S)$ for some $\lambda > 0$. Also, $a_j(S^{\max}(n)) = a_i(S)$ for all $i \in P$

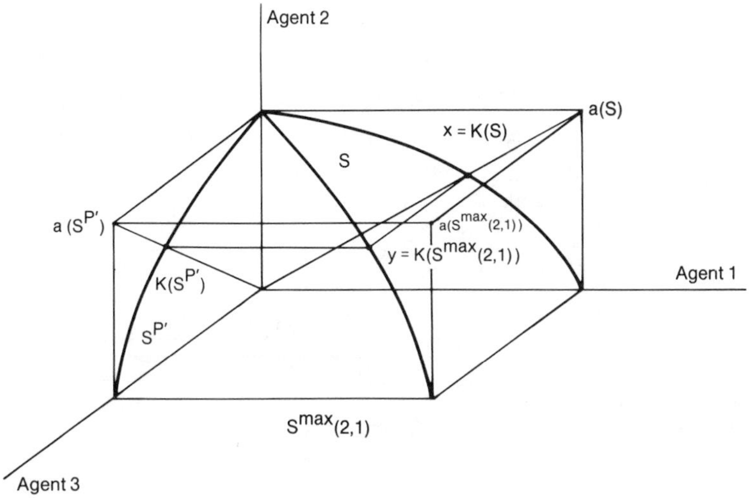

Figure 12.1. Theorem 12.1. The Kalai–Smorodinsky solution satisfies Nonconflictual Replication.

and $j \in Q^i$; thus $y = \lambda a(S^{\max}(n))$. This, together with our previous conclusion that $y \in \text{WPO}(S^{\max}(n))$, implies that $y = K(S^{\max}(n))$, as desired.

The proof that E satisfies $N.C.R$ is obtained from the previous one by replacing everywhere K by E and changing the last three sentences to: Finally, since $x \in E(S)$, $x = \lambda e_P$ for some λ; thus $y = \lambda e_Q$. This, together with our previous conclusion that $y \in \text{WPO}(S^{\max}(n))$, implies that $y = E(S^{\max}(n))$, as desired. Q.E.D.

The Nash solution does not satisfy $N.C.R$, but we show next that the Nash solution outcome of $S^{\max}(n)$ is closely related to the asymmetric Nash solution outcome of S if the coefficients of asymmetry are proportional to the orders of replication of the different types. Asymmetric generalizations of the Utilitarian solutions can also be defined, and a similar result can be formulated.

First recall the definition of the asymmetric Nash solutions encountered in Chapter 7. Given a list of positive weights $\alpha = \{\alpha_i \mid i \in I\}$, the *asymmetric Nash solution relative to* α, N^α, is defined by setting, for each $P \in \mathcal{P}$ and for each $S \in \Sigma^P$, $N^\alpha(S)$ equal to the maximizer of $\prod_P x_i^{\alpha_i}$ for $x \in S$. Similarly, given a list of positive weights $\alpha = \{\alpha_i \mid i \in I\}$, an *asymmetric Utilitarian solution relative to* α, U^α, is defined by choosing, for each $P \in \mathcal{P}$ and for each $S \in \Sigma^P$, $U^\alpha(S)$ among the maximizers of $\sum_P \alpha_i x_i$ for $x \in S$. In the statement of the next theorem, it is assumed that appropriate selections, if there are multiple maximizers, are made.

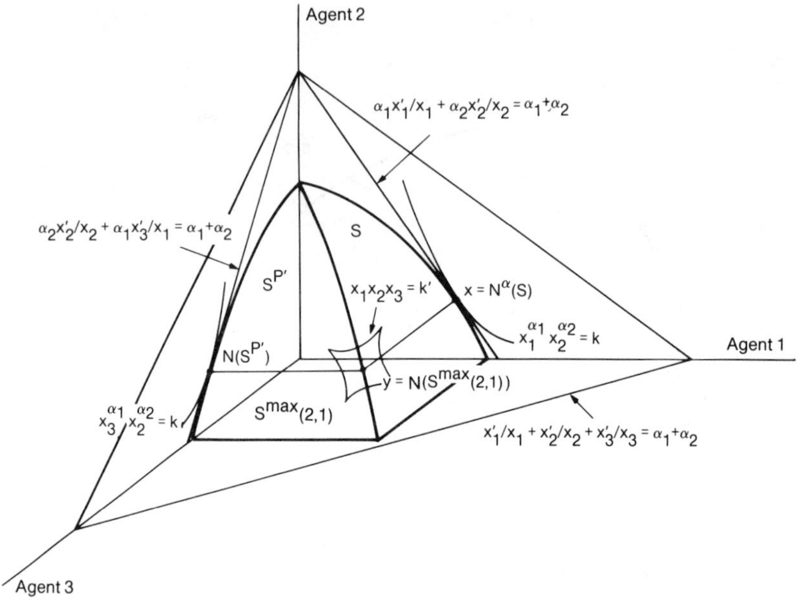

Figure 12.2. Theorem 12.2. The Nash solution coincides with its asymmetric generalizations under nonconflictual replication.

Theorem 12.2. *For all $P \in \mathcal{P}$, all $S \in \Sigma^P$, all $n \in \mathbb{N}^P$, and all $i \in P$ and $j \in Q^i$, $N_j(S^{\max}(n)) = N_i^\alpha(S)$ where α is such that for each $i \in P$, $\alpha_i = n_i$ [and Q^i is as in the definition of $S^{\max}(n)$]. Also, $U_j(S^{\max}(n)) = U_i^\alpha(S)$.*

Note that since in the statement of the theorem we have specified only finitely many of the coordinates of α, N^α is not entirely determined. However, the remaining indeterminacy is irrelevant to our computations. The same comment applies to the Utilitarian solutions and to the statements of several other results presented in what follows.

Proof. (See Figure 12.2.) Let $P \in \mathcal{P}$, $S \in \Sigma^P$, and $n \in \mathbb{N}^P$ be given, and let Q be as in the definition of $S^{\max}(n)$; also, let α be such that $\alpha_i = n_i$ for all $i \in P$. Let $x \equiv N^\alpha(S)$ and $y \in \mathbb{R}^Q_+$ be such that for all $i \in P$ and $j \in Q^i$, $y_j = x_i$. [In Figure 12.2, $P = \{1, 2\}$ and $n = (2, 1)$, with agent 3 replicating agent 1.] We will show that $y = N(S^{\max}(n))$. Since for each $P' \subset Q$ with $\operatorname{comp} P' = \operatorname{comp} P$, $y_{P'} = N(S^{P'})$, it follows from the definition of $S^{\max}(n)$ that $y \in S^{\max}(n)$. (In Figure 12.2, the only $P' \neq P$ is $\{2, 3\}$.) It remains to show that $S^{\max}(n)$ is supported at y by the hyperplane H in $\mathbb{R}^Q_+$ of equation $\Sigma_Q y'_j/y_j = |Q| = \Sigma_P \alpha_i$, which also supports the set $\{y' \in \mathbb{R}^Q_+ \mid \Pi_Q y'_j = \Pi_Q y_j\}$. To see this, note first that since $x = N^\alpha(S)$, the hyperplane in $\mathbb{R}^P$ of equation $\Sigma_P \alpha_i x'_i/x_i = \Sigma_P \alpha_i$ supports S at x and that consequently (i) for all $P' \subset Q$ with comp P' = comp P, the hyperplane in $\mathbb{R}^{P'}$ of equation $\Sigma_{P'} \alpha_{t(j)} x'_j/x_{t(j)} = \Sigma_P \alpha_i$ supports $S^{P'}$ at $y_{P'}$ [where $S^{P'}$ is as in the definition of $S^{\max}(n)$]. Assume, by way of contradiction, that there exists some $y' \in S^{\max}(n)$ that lies above H, that is, such that (ii) $\Sigma_Q y'_j/y_j > \Sigma_P \alpha_i$. For each $i \in P$, let $c(i) \in Q^i$ be such that $y'_{c(i)} \geqq y'_j$ for all $j \in Q^i$. Let $P' \equiv c(P)$. Then it follows from (ii) that $\Sigma_P \alpha_i y'_{c(i)}/y_i = \Sigma_P \alpha_{t(j)} y'_j/x_i > \Sigma_P \alpha_i$; also, the definition of $S^{\max}(n)$ and the fact that $y' \in S^{\max}(n)$ imply that $y'_{P'} \in S^{P'}$. But these two conclusions are in contradiction to (i).

The proof for U is very similar except for the difficulties that arise due to the possible existence of multiple maximizers of the sum of utilities.
Q.E.D.

Kalai established a converse of Theorem 12.2. Given $P \in \mathcal{P}$, $S \in \Sigma^P$, and an asymmetric Nash solution N^α, the solution outcome of S resulting from applying N^α can be obtained by applying the (symmetric) Nash solution to S after appropriate replications or by limits of such replications. If for some $k \in \mathbb{R}_+$ and $n \in \mathbb{N}^P$, $\alpha_i = kn_i$ for all $i \in P$, then $S^{\max}(n)$ is a desired replica of S [$S^{\max}(tn)$ for any $t \in \mathbb{N}$ would also work]. Otherwise, sequences $\{k^\nu\}$ in $\mathbb{R}_+$ and $\{n^\nu\}$ in $\mathbb{N}^P$ should be found with $k^\nu n_i^\nu \to \alpha_i$ as $\nu \to \infty$ for all $i \in P$, and the sequence of problems $S^{\max}(n^\nu)$ will have the desired property. Again, a similar statement can be made about the asymmetric Utilitarian solutions.

Kalai's replication method is best motivated by reproducing the economic example that appears in his paper (1977a, p. 131): There is one unit of one good available for distribution between two agents, numbered 1 and 2. For each i, agent i's utility $u_i: \mathbb{R}_+ \to \mathbb{R}_+$ is defined by $u_i(z_i) = z_i$ for all $z_i \in \mathbb{R}_+$. Therefore, the problem $S \subset \mathbb{R}^2_+$ they face is $S \equiv \{x \in \mathbb{R}^2_+ \mid x_1 + x_2 \leqq 1\}$. Equal payoffs (i.e., equal division) is recommended for that problem by all solutions satisfying *W.P.O* and *AN*. Now a third agent comes in, numbered 3, identical to agent 2 in that he derives exactly the same utility as agent 2 *from what agent 2 consumes:* Given a distribution $z = (z_1, z_2, z_3)$ of the good, $u_3: \mathbb{R}^3_+ \to \mathbb{R}_+$ is such that $u_3(z) = z_2$. (Note that it is the first time that we use an economic example exhibiting external effects.) The implication of this form of agent 2's utility on the problem faced by the three-agent group is that it is the *largest* convex and comprehensive set with projections S on $\mathbb{R}^{\{1,2\}}$ and the replica S' of S on $\mathbb{R}^{\{1,3\}}$ (obtained from S by having agent 3 play the role of agent 2). This problem is precisely $S^{\max}(1,2)$. The construction amounts to assuming maximal compatibility of interests among agents 2 and 3. Agent 2's consumption is similar to a public good for the two of them.

The opposite extreme, in replicating agent 2, is that of minimal compatibility of interests: This is achieved by supposing that agent 3's utility $u_3: \mathbb{R}_+ \to \mathbb{R}_+$ satisfies $u_3(z_3) = z_3$. Then allocating a given amount of the good to agents 2 and 3 together yields an aggregate utility that is independent of how much each receives. The resulting problem faced by the three-agent group is $\text{cch}\{S, S'\}$. This is the *smallest* convex and comprehensive set with projections S on $\mathbb{R}^{\{1,2\}}$ and S' on $\mathbb{R}^{\{1,3\}}$.

This sort of replication is formalized in the following definition.

Given $P \in \mathcal{P}$, $S \in \Sigma^P$, and $n \in \mathbb{N}^P$, let Q and the $S^{P'}$ be as in the definition of $S^{\max}(n)$, and let $S^{\min}(n) \subset \mathbb{R}^Q_+$ be defined by

$$S^{\min}(n) \equiv \text{cch}\{S^{P'} \mid P' \subset Q, \text{ comp } P' = \text{comp } P\}.$$

The natural notion of invariance for this situation may appear to be that the sum of what the agents of a given type get in the replicated problem is equal to what the agent they are representing gets in the original problem. However, this is not the appropriate notion since it cannot be met by any solution satisfying *W.P.O* and *AN*. Indeed, let $P \equiv \{1, 2\}$, $S \equiv \text{cch}\{e_1, e_2\}$, $n = (2, 1)$, and $Q \equiv \{1, 2, 3\}$, with agent 3 replicating agent 1. Then $S^{\min}(n) \equiv \text{cch}\{e_1, e_2, e_3\}$. If F satisfies *W.P.O* and *AN*, then $F(S) = \frac{1}{2}e_P$ and $F(S^{\min}(n)) = \frac{1}{3}e_Q$. Therefore, $\frac{2}{3} = F_1(S^{\min}(n)) + F_3(S^{\min}(n)) \neq F_1(S) = \frac{1}{2}$.

Just as when Kalai's notion of replication is considered, it turns out however, that the sum of what the agents of a given type get in the replicated problem may often be simply related to what the agent of the original group they are representing gets in the original problem under the application of the asymmetric generalization of the solution that has weights proportional to the orders of replication.

To state this result formally, we need to define asymmetric generalizations of the Kalai–Smorodinsky and Egalitarian solutions. Given a list of positive weights $\alpha = \{\alpha_i \mid i \in I\}$, the *asymmetric Kalai–Smorodinsky solution relative to* α, K^α, is given by setting, for each $P \in \mathcal{P}$ and for each $S \in \Sigma^P$, $K^\alpha(S)$ equal to the maximal point of S on the segment connecting the origin to the *α-ideal point of S*, $a^\alpha(S)$, defined by $a_i^\alpha(S) = \alpha_i a_i(S)$ for all $i \in P$. Similarly, the *asymmetric Egalitarian solution relative to* α, E^α, is defined by setting $E^\alpha(S)$ equal to the maximal point of S of coordinates proportional to α. The next axiom is stated for solutions F assumed to have asymmetric generalizations F^α relative to all positive $\alpha = \{\alpha_i \mid i \in I\}$. It says that the agents of a given type receive in the replicated problem the amount the agent they are replicating would receive in the original problem under an application of the asymmetric generalization of the solution under consideration having weights proportional to the orders of replication of the different types.

Conflictual replication (C.R): For all $P \in \mathcal{P}$, all $S \in \Sigma^P$, all $n \in \mathbb{N}^P$, and all $i \in P$, $\sum_{Q^i} F_j(S^{\min}(n)) = F_i^{\alpha}(S)$, where $\alpha_i = n_i$ for all $i \in P$ [and Q^i is as in the definition of $S^{\max}(n)$].

Theorem 12.3. *The Nash, Kalai–Smorodinsky, Egalitarian, and Utilitarian solutions satisfy Conflictual Replication.*

Proof. Let $P \in \mathcal{P}$, $S \in \Sigma^P$, and $n \in \mathbb{N}^P$ be given, and let Q be as in the definition of $S^{\min}(n)$. Also, let α be such that $\alpha_i \equiv n_i$ for all $i \in P$.

(i) First, we consider N. Let $x \equiv N^{\alpha}(S)$ and $y \in \mathbb{R}^Q$ be such that for all i and $j \in Q^i$, $y_j = x_i/\alpha_i$ [where Q^i is as in the definition of $S^{\max}(n)$]. We will show that $y = N(S^{\min}(n))$. First, note that the number of subsets P' of Q with $\operatorname{comp} P' = \operatorname{comp} P$ is equal to $\prod_P n_i$. Given any such P', let $x^{P'} \in \mathbb{R}^{P'}$ be defined by $x_j^{P'} = x_{t(j)}$ for all $j \in P'$ [where $t(j)$ is as in the definition of $S^{\max}(n)$]. Clearly, $x^{P'} \in S^{P'}$ [where $S^{P'}$ is as in the definition of $S^{\max}(n)$]. Then, we observe that

$$y = \sum \{(x^{P'}, O_{Q \setminus P'}) \mid P' \subset Q,\ \operatorname{comp} P' = \operatorname{comp} P\} / \prod_P n_i,$$

so that $y \in S^{\min}(n)$. Next, we show that $S^{\min}(n)$ is supported at y by the hyperplane H of equation $\sum_Q y_j'/y_j = |Q| = \sum_P \alpha_i$. Indeed, the intersection of H with $\mathbb{R}^P$ is the hyperplane H^P in $\mathbb{R}^P$ of equation $\sum_P y_i'/y_i = \sum_P \alpha_i$, which can also be written as $\sum_P \alpha_i y_i'/x_i = \sum_P \alpha_i$. The hyperplane H^P contains x and separates S at x from the set $\{x' \in \mathbb{R}_+^P \mid \prod_P \alpha_i x_i' = \prod_P \alpha_i x_i\}$. By a similar computation, for all $P' \subset Q$ with $\operatorname{comp} P' = \operatorname{comp} P$, the intersection of H with $\mathbb{R}^{P'}$ is a hyperplane in $\mathbb{R}^{P'}$ that contains $x^{P'}$ and separates $S^{P'}$ at $x^{P'}$ from the set $\{x' \in \mathbb{R}_+^{P'} \mid \prod_{P'} \alpha_{t(j)} x_j' = \prod_P \alpha_i x_i\}$. It now follows from the definition of $S^{\min}(n)$ that H supports it at y. Since H also supports at y the set $\{y' \in \mathbb{R}_+^Q \mid \prod_Q y_j' = \prod_Q y_j\}$, it follows that $y = N(S^{\min}(n))$, which proves the claim for N.

(ii) The proof of the claim for K is similar. Let $x \equiv K^{\alpha}(S)$ and $y \in \mathbb{R}^Q$ be such that for all $i \in P$ and $j \in Q^i$, $y_j = x_i/\alpha_i$. To show that $y = K(S^{\min}(n))$, we first establish as in (i) that $y \in S^{\min}(n)$. Since $x \in \mathrm{WPO}(S)$, there is a hyperplane in $\mathbb{R}^P$ of equation $\sum_P \beta_i x_i' = \sum_P \beta_i x_i$, supporting S at x. For each $P' \in \mathcal{P}$ with $\operatorname{comp} P' = \operatorname{comp} P$, let $x^{P'}$ be as in (i). By construction of $S^{\min}(n)$, for each $P' \subset Q$ with $\operatorname{comp} P' = \operatorname{comp} P$, the hyperplane in $\mathbb{R}^{P'}$ of equation $\sum_{P'} \beta_{t(j)} x_j' = \sum_{P'} \beta_{t(j)} x_{t(j)}$ supports $S^{P'}$ at $x^{P'}$. It then follows that the hyperplane of equation $\sum_Q \beta_{t(j)} y_j' = \sum_Q \beta_{t(j)} x_{t(j)}/\alpha_{t(j)} = \sum_P \beta_i x_i$, which contains y, supports $S^{\min}(n)$ at y. This implies that $x \in \mathrm{WPO}(S^{\min}(n))$. Finally, for all $i \in P$ and $j \in Q^i$, $a_j(S^{\min}(n)) = a_i(S)$. Thus $y = K(S^{\min}(n))$, the desired conclusion.

(ii) The proofs for E and U are omitted. Q.E.D.

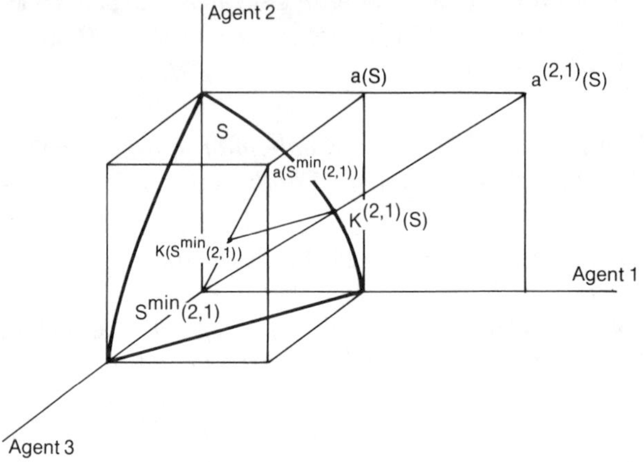

Figure 12.3. Theorem 12.3. The Kalai–Smorodinsky solution coincides with its asymmetric generalizations under conflictual replication.

Theorem 12.3 is illustrated in Figure 12.3, where $S^{\min}(n)$ is represented for $P=\{1,2\}$ and $n=(2,1)$, and with agent 3 replicating agent 1. Note that both $K(S^{\min}(2,1))$ and $K^{(2,1)}(S)$ belong to the same generator of the ruled surface defining $\text{WPO}(S^{\min}(2,1))$. Similarly, for $F=N,E,U$, $F(S^{\min}(2,1))$ and $F^{(2,1)}(S)$ (not represented) belong to the same generator of $\text{WPO}(S^{\min}(2,1))$.

12.3 Juxtaposition

In this section we model situations in which the old and new agents are simply "juxtaposed." We propose two notions of juxtaposition paralleling the two notions of replication of the previous section.

The first juxtaposition axiom models maximal compatibility of interests among the members of P and P': Starting from the problems S and S' faced by P and P', the problem T faced by $P\cup P'$ is taken to be the set of all points of $\mathbb{R}^{P\cup P'}$ obtained by juxtaposing a point of S to a point of S'. Then a natural requirement on F is that $F(T)$ be obtained by simply juxtaposing the solution outcomes of the constituent problems.

An economic situation giving rise to this configuration is as follows: The two groups P and P' care about two different sets of goods available in the amounts Ω and Ω'. If the aggregate vector of goods (Ω,Ω') is entirely allocated to P (P'), the resulting feasible set is $S\in\Sigma^P$ ($S'\in\Sigma^{P'}$). If the goods are allocated to $P\cup P'$, the resulting feasible set is $T=\{x\in\mathbb{R}^{P\cup P'} \mid x_P\in S, x_{P'}\in S'\}\in\Sigma^{P\cup P'}$.

Our first axiom of juxtaposition is as follows.

Nonconflictual Juxtaposition (N.C.J): For all $P, P' \in \mathcal{P}$ with $P \cap P' = \emptyset$, for all $S \in \Sigma^P$, $S' \in \Sigma^{P'}$, and $T \in \mathbb{R}^{P \cup P'}$, if $T = \{x \in \mathbb{R}^{P \cup P'} \mid x_P \in S, x_{P'} \in S'\}$, then $F(T) = (F(S), F(S'))$.

Only two of the main solutions satisfy this axiom.

Theorem 12.4. *The Nash and Utilitarian solutions satisfy Nonconflictual Juxtaposition.*

Proof. Let P, P', S, S', and T be as in the statement of the axiom.

(i) First, we consider the Nash solution. Let $x \equiv N(S)$ and $x' \equiv N(S')$. By definition of N, $\prod_P x_i \geqq \prod_P y_i$ for all $y \in S$ and $\prod_{P'} x_i' \geqq \prod_{P'} y_i'$ for all $y' \in S'$. Since these products are positive, $\prod_P x_i \prod_{P'} x_i' \geqq \prod_P y_i \prod_{P'} y_i'$ for all $y \in S$ and $y' \in S'$, that is, $\prod_P x_i \prod_{P'} x_i' \geqq \prod_Q y_i$ for all $y \in T$. This says that $N(T) = (x, x') = (N(S), N(S'))$ and proves the claim for N.

(ii) The proof for U is omitted. Q.E.D.

Although neither the Kalai–Smorodinsky nor the Egalitarian solutions satisfy *N.C.J,* they satisfy a closely related property that is also of interest. It is obtained from *N.C.J* by simply weakening its conclusion to

$$F(T) = \begin{cases} (F(S), \lambda F(S')) & \text{for some } \lambda \in [0,1] \\ \text{or} & \\ (\lambda F(S), F(S')) & \text{for some } \lambda \in [0,1]. \end{cases}$$

This axiom will be referred to as *Weak Nonconflictual Juxtaposition (W.N.C.J).* Of course, *N.C.J* implies *W.N.C.J.*

Theorem 12.5. *The Kalai–Smorodinsky and Egalitarian solutions satisfy Weak Nonconflictual Juxtaposition.*

Proof. Let P, P', S, S', and T be as in the statement of the axiom.

(i) First, we consider the Kalai–Smorodinsky solution. By definition of K, $K(S) = \mu a(S)$ for some $\mu > 0$ and $K(S') = \mu' a(S')$ for some $\mu' > 0$. By construction of T, $a(T) = (a(S), a(S'))$. Let

$$A \equiv [(K(S), O_{P'}), (K(S), K(S'))] \cup [(O_P, K(S')), (K(S), K(S'))].$$

Because $A \subset \text{WPO}(T)$ and A contains a point proportional to $a(T)$, this point is $K(T)$. If $\mu \leqq \mu'$ then $K(T) = (K(S), (\mu/\mu')K(S'))$. If $\mu > \mu'$ then $K(T) = ((\mu'/\mu)K(S), K(S'))$. This proves the claim for K.

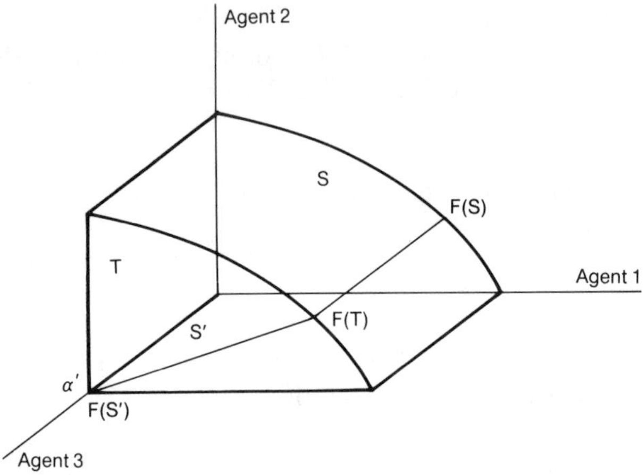

Figure 12.4. Axiom of Nonconflictual Juxtaposition for $P=\{1,2\}$ and $P'=\{3\}$.

(ii) Next, we consider E. We define similarly

$$B \equiv [(E(S), O_{P'}), (E(S), E(S'))] \cup [(O_P, E(S')), (E(S), E(S'))].$$

Note that $B \subset \mathrm{WPO}(T)$ and that B contains a point of coordinates all equal to $\min\{E_i(S), E_j(S)\}$ where $i \in P$ and $j \in P'$. This point is $E(T)$.

Q.E.D.

An interesting version of *N.C.J* obtains when $|P'|=1$. Then S' is simply a segment $[0, \alpha'] \subset \mathbb{R}^{P'}$ and T is the cylinder spanned by S with generators parallel to $e_{P'}$ truncated by the hyperplane in $\mathbb{R}^Q$ of equation $x_{P'} = \alpha'$. (See Figure 12.4.) The arrival of the individual in P' does not disturb at all the trade-offs available to the members of P. It is therefore natural to require that their payoffs be unaffected, as required by *N.C.J.* Axiom *W.N.C.J* simply says that their *relative* payoffs be unaffected. Note the resemblance of this version of *N.C.J* to the axiom known in social choice theory as Elimination of Indifferent Individuals, which says that if an agent is indifferent between all alternatives, the social choice should be made as if that agent were not present. Because of our condition on domains (the feasible set should contain a point giving positive utility to all agents and be comprehensive), no agent can ever be indifferent between all alternatives, but the closest situation is when there is an agent such that the set of utility vectors attainable by the others is independent of the (feasible) utility level assigned to him.

In order to motivate the second notion of juxtaposition, we first describe an economic problem. There are two groups P and P' of consumers who care about two different sets of goods. These goods are producible from primary factors, available in some given amounts, according to the following technology: If all factors are allocated to the production of the goods that the members of P (P') care about, the vector Ω (Ω') can be obtained, resulting in the set $S \in \Sigma^P$ ($S' \in \Sigma^{P'}$) of utility vectors achievable by P (P'). By allocating the factors of production between the productions of both sets of goods proportionately to q and $1-q$ where $q \in [0,1]$, the outputs of the two sets of goods are $q\Omega$ and $(1-q)\Omega'$. Finally, agents have homogeneous utility functions. Then, the set of feasible utility vectors achievable by $P \cup P'$ is $T \equiv \text{cch}\{S, S'\}$. This specification of T implies that the interests of P and P' are exactly opposed. Indeed, the smallest admissible problem in $\Sigma^{P \cup P'}$ containing S and S' is $\text{cch}\{S, S'\}$; by taking T to be equal to $\text{cch}\{S, S'\}$, we formalize a situation in which there is no positive interaction between the two groups. Given that T is a "linear combination" of S and S', it is then natural to require that $F(T)$ be a linear combination of $F(S)$ and $F(S')$ also. This gives the following juxtaposition axiom.

Conflictual Juxtaposition (C.J): For all $P, P' \in \mathcal{P}$ with $P \cap P' = \emptyset$, for all $S \in \Sigma^P$, $S' \in \Sigma^{P'}$, and $T \in \Sigma^{P \cup P'}$, if $T = \text{cch}\{S, S'\}$ then

$$F(T) = (\lambda F(S), (1-\lambda)F(S')) \quad \text{for some } \lambda \in [0,1].$$

All the main solutions satisfy this condition, as now established.

Theorem 12.6. *The Nash, Kalai–Smorodinsky, Egalitarian, and Utilitarian solutions satisfy Conflictual Juxtaposition.*

Proof. Let P, P', S, S', and T be as in the statement of the axiom.

(i) First, we consider the Nash solution. Let $x \equiv N(S)$, $x' \equiv N(S')$, $m = |P|$, and $m' = |P'|$. We identify the two hyperplanes of equation $\sum_P y_i/x_i = m$ and $\sum_{P'} y_i/x_i' = m'$ separating S at x from the set $\{y \in \mathbb{R}^P_+ \mid \prod_P y_i = \prod_P x_i\}$ and S' at x' from the set $\{y \in \mathbb{R}^P_+ \mid \prod_{P'} y_i = \prod_{P'} x_i'\}$, respectively. It follows that the hyperplane H in $\mathbb{R}^{P \cup P'}$ of equation

$$\frac{1}{m} \sum_P \frac{y_i}{x_i} + \frac{1}{m'} \sum_{P'} \frac{y_i}{x_i'} = 1$$

supports S at x and S' at x'. Also, since $x \in S$, $x' \in S'$, and $T = \text{cch}\{S, S'\}$, then $(\lambda x, (1-\lambda)x') \in T$ for all $\lambda \in [0,1]$. Finally, we claim that for some λ, H separates T at $(\lambda x, (1-\lambda)x')$ from the set

$$A \equiv \{y \in \mathbb{R}^{P \cup P'} \mid \prod_{P \cup P'} y_i = \lambda^m (1-\lambda)^{m'} \prod_P x_i \prod_{P'} x_i'\}.$$

This will establish that $N(T) = (\lambda x, (1-\lambda)x') = (\lambda N(S), (1-\lambda)N(S'))$, as desired. To prove the claim, note that A is supported at $(\lambda x, (1-\lambda)x')$ by the hyperplane of equation

$$\sum_P \frac{y_i}{\lambda x_i} + \sum_{P'} \frac{y_i}{(1-\lambda)x_i'} = m + m',$$

which coincides with H if

$$mx_i = \lambda x_i (m+m') \quad \text{for all } i \in P,$$
$$m'x_i' = (1-\lambda)x_i'(m+m') \quad \text{for all } i \in P.$$

All of these equalities are satisfied for $\lambda = m/(m+m')$.

(ii) Next, we consider K. By definition of K, $K(S) = \mu a(S)$ for some $\mu > 0$ and $K(S') = \mu' a(S')$ for some $\mu' > 0$. Also, $a(T) = (a(S), a(S'))$. Because $K(S) \in \text{WPO}(S)$, $K(S') \in \text{WPO}(S')$, and $T = \text{cch}\{S, S'\}$, it follows that $(\lambda K(S), (1-\lambda)K(S')) \in \text{WPO}(T)$ for all $\lambda \in [0,1]$ and for some λ, namely, $\lambda = \mu'/(\mu+\mu')$; this point is proportional to $a(T)$. This shows that $K(T) = (\lambda K(S), (1-\lambda)K(S'))$ as desired.

(iii) Next, we consider E. By definition of E, $E(S) = \mu e_P$ for some $\mu > 0$ and $E(S') = \mu' e_{P'}$ for some $\mu' > 0$. Because $E(S) \in \text{WPO}(S)$, $E(S') \in \text{WPO}(S')$, and $T = \text{cch}\{S, S'\}$, $(\lambda E(S), (1-\lambda)E(S')) \in \text{WPO}(T)$ for all $\lambda \in [0,1]$ and for some λ, namely, $\lambda = \mu'/(\mu+\mu')$; this point has equal coordinates. This shows that $E(T) = (\lambda E(S), (1-\lambda)E(S'))$, as desired.

(iv) Finally, we consider U. As in the previous results involving U, a slight difficulty occurs here because of the possible multiplicities of maximizers, so we will be a little more explicit in this case. Multiplicities may indeed be resolved in a way that leads to a violation of the axiom. However, they can also be resolved in such a way that the axiom is satisfied. Indeed, let x be a maximizer of $\sum_P y_i$ over S and let x' be a maximizer of $\sum_P y_i$ over S'. If $\sum_P x_i > \sum_{P'} x_i'$, then $\sum_{P \cup P'} y_i$ is maximized over T at $(x, O_{P'})$; if $\sum_P x_i < \sum_{P'} x_i'$, $\sum_{P \cup P'} y_i$ is maximized over T at (O_P, x'); if $\sum_P x_i = \sum_{P'} x_i'$, then $\sum_{P \cup P'} y_i$ is maximized over T at any point of the form $(\lambda x, (1-\lambda)x')$ for $\lambda \in [0,1]$. This proves the claim. Q.E.D.

Note that the weights λ and $1-\lambda$ placed on $F(S)$ and $F(S')$ to obtain $F(T)$ have different values for the different solutions F we considered. For the Nash solution, they are proportional to the cardinalities of P and P' and therefore do not depend on S and S' at all. For the Kalai–Smorodinsky solution, they are proportional to how close to the ideal points the Kalai–Smorodinsky solution outcomes of the two constituent problems are. For the Egalitarian solution, they are proportional to the values of

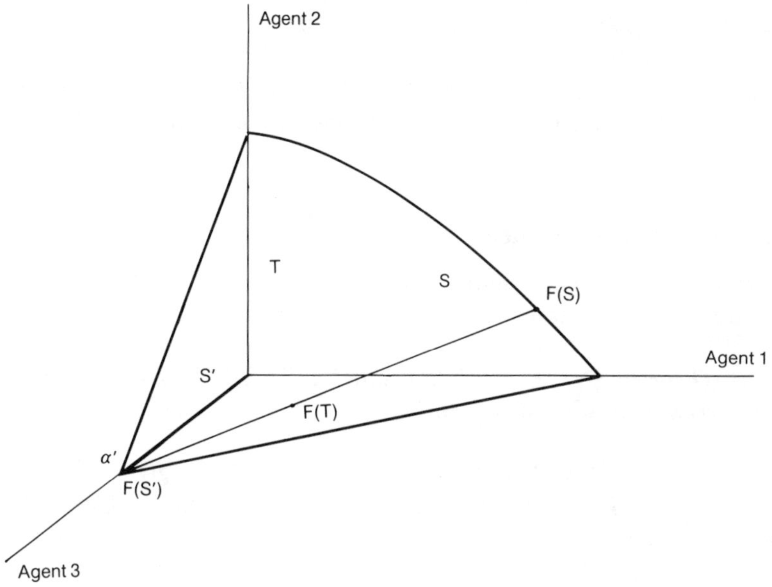

Figure 12.5. Axiom of Conflictual Juxtaposition for $P=\{1,2\}$ and $P'=\{3\}$.

the coordinates of the Egalitarian outcomes of the two constituent problems. For the Utilitarian solution, they are (usually) equal to 0 or 1, or they do not matter.

A particularly interesting version of axiom $C.J$ is obtained when $|P'|=1$. (See Figure 12.5). Then S' is simply a segment $[0,\alpha'] \subset \mathbb{R}^{P'}$, and $T \equiv \text{cch}\{S, S'\}$ is the cone spanned by S with the vertex $\alpha' e_{P'}$; T is obtained from S by adding one alternative that gives nothing to all of the agents in P and by convexifying. The axiom requires that the solution outcome of T be a linear combination of the solution outcome of S and of that of S'. [The latter, of course, is $\alpha' e_{P'}$ as soon as F satisfies $W.P.O$. This means that $F(S')$ is the vertex of the cone and that $F(S)$ and $F(T)$ lie on the same generator.]

An application worth noting of our two juxtaposition axioms is to the case $S=S'$. Then the problems can be thought of as being "replicated," but the resulting notions of replication are different from the notions considered earlier since it is not required here that groups of identical compositions face the same problem.

If only such replications are considered, $C.J$ can be rewritten as: For all $P, P' \in \mathcal{P}$ with $P \cap P' = \emptyset$ and $|P|=|P'|$, for all $S \in \Sigma^P$, $S' \in \Sigma^{P'}$, and

$T \in \Sigma^{P \cup P'}$, if there exists a one-to-one function $\gamma: P \to P'$ such that $S' = \{x' \in \mathbb{R}^{P'} \mid \exists x \in S \text{ s.t. } x'_{\gamma(i)} = x_i, \forall i \in P\}$, and if $T = \text{cch}\{S, S'\}$, then $F(T) = (F(S)/2, F(S')/2)$.

Analogous reformulations of *N.C.J* and *W.N.C.J* could also be written out. It is easily verified that all the solutions we considered satisfy these weaker axioms.

12.4 Concluding comment

To conclude, we present a simple result relating one of the notions of juxtaposition to other axioms encountered in previous chapters.

> ***Theorem 12.7.*** *If a solution satisfies ST.I.R, N.C.J, and I.I.A, then it satisfies M.STAB.*

Proof. Let $P, Q \in \mathcal{P}$ with $P \subset Q$, $S \in \Sigma^P$, and $T \in \Sigma^Q$ be given with $S = t_P^x(T)$ where $x = F(T)$. We show that $F(S) = x_P$. Indeed, let $T' \in \Sigma^Q$ be defined by $T' \equiv \{x' \in T \mid x'_i \leqq x_i \text{ for all } i \in Q \backslash P, x_P \in S\}$. By *ST.I.R*, $x > 0$, so that $T' \in \Sigma^Q$, and by *I.I.A*, $F(T') = F(T) = x$. But T' is the cylinder spanned by S with generators parallel to $\mathbb{R}^{Q \backslash P}$. By *N.C.J*, $F_P(T) = F(S)$.
Q.E.D.

Bibliography

Arrow, K. J. (1951), *Social Choice and Individual Values,* New York, Wiley.

Aumann, R. J. (1977), "The St. Petersburg Paradox: A Discussion of Some Recent Comments," *Journal of Economic Theory* 17, 443–5.

Aumann, R. J. and M. Maschler (1985), "Game Theoretic Analysis of a Bankruptcy Problem from the Talmud," *Journal of Economic Theory* 36, 195–213.

d'Aspremont, C. and L. Gevers (1977), "Equity and the Informational Basis of Collective Choice," *Review of Economic Studies* 44, 199–203.

Balinski, M. and H. P. Young (1982), *Fair Representation: Meeting the Ideal of One Man One Vote,* New Haven, Yale University Press.

Bergson, A. (1938), "A Reformulation of Certain Aspects of Welfare Economics," *Quarterly Journal of Economics* 52, 310–34.

Billera, L. F. and R. E. Bixby (1973), "A Characterization of Pareto Surfaces," *Proceedings of the American Mathematical Society* 41, 261–7.

Blackorby, C. and D. Donaldson (1982), "Social Criteria for Evaluating Population Change," University of British Columbia Discussion Paper No. 82-04.

Chichilnisky, G. and W. Thomson (1987), "The Walrasian Mechanism from Equal Division Is Not Monotonic with Respect to Variations in the Number of Agents," *Journal of Public Economics* 32, 119–24.

Chipman, J. S., L. Hurwicz, M. K. Richter, and H. F. Sonnenschein (1971), *Preferences, Utility and Demand,* New York, Harcourt Brace Jovanovich.

Chun, Y. and W. Thomson (1988), "Bargaining Solutions and Stability of Groups," *Mathematical Social Sciences,* forthcoming.

Debreu, G. (1954), "Representation of a Preference Ordering by a Numerical Function," in *Decision Processes* (R. M. Thrall et al., eds.), Wiley, New York, pp. 159–65.

(1960), "Topological Methods in Cardinal Utility Theory," in *Mathematical Methods in the Social Sciences* (K. J. Arrow, S. Karlin, and P. Suppes, eds.), Stanford, Stanford University Press.

Debreu, G. and T. C. Koopmans (1982), "Additively Decomposed Quasi-Convex Functions," *Mathematical Programming* 24, 1–38.

Debreu, G. and H. Scarf (1963), "A Limit Theorem on the Core of an Economy," *International Economic Review* 4, 235–46.

Deschamps, R. and L. Gevers (1978), "Leximin and Utilitarian Rules: A Joint Characterization," *Journal of Economic Theory* 17, 143–63.

Edgeworth, F. Y. (1881), *Mathematical Psychics,* London, Kegan Paul.

Eichhorn, W. (1978), *Functional Equations in Economics,* Reading, MA, Addison-Wesley.

Foley, D. (1967), "Resource Allocation and the Public Sector," *Yale Economic Essays* 7, 45–98.

Fleming, M. (1952), "A Cardinal Concept of Welfare," *Quarterly Journal of Economics* 66, 366–84.

Gale, D. (1960), "A Note on Revealed Preference," *Economica* 27, 348–54.

Harsanyi, J. C. (1959), "A Bargaining Model for the Cooperative *N*-Person Game," in *Contributions to the Theory of Games IV* (A. W. Tucker and R. D. Luce, eds.), Annals of Mathematics Studies, No. 40, Princeton, Princeton University Press.

(1977), *Rational Behavior and Bargaining Equilibrium in Games and Social Situations,* Cambridge, Cambridge University Press.

Harsanyi, J. C. and R. Selten (1972), "A Generalized Nash Solution for Two-Person Bargaining Games with Incomplete Information," *Management Science* 18, 80–106.

Hart, S. and A. Mas-Colell (forthcoming), "Potential, Value and Consistency," *Econometrica.*

Houthakker, H. S. (1950), "Revealed Preference and the Utility Function," *Economica* 7, 159–74.

Hurwicz, L. (1971), "On the Problem of Integrability of Demand Functions," in *Preferences, Utility and Demand* (J. Chipman, L. Hurwicz, M. K. Richter, and H. F. Sonnenschein, eds.), New York, Harcourt Brace Jovanovich, pp. 174–214.

Hurwicz, L. and M. K. Richter (1971), "Revealed Preference without Demand Continuity Assumptions," in *Preferences, Utility and Demand* (J. Chipman, L. Hurwicz, M. K. Richter, and H. F. Sonnenschein, eds.), New York, Harcourt Brace Jovanovich, pp. 59–76.

(1979), "Ville Axioms and Consumer Theory," *Econometrica* 47, 603–19.

Imai, H. (1983), "Individual Monotonicity and Lexicographic Maximin Solutions," *Econometrica* 51, 389–401.

Jones, R. (1987), "The Population Monotonicity Paradox and the Transfer Paradox," *Journal of Public Economics* 32, 125–32.

Kalai, E. (1977a), "Nonsymmetric Nash Solutions and Replications of Two-Person Bargaining," *International Journal of Game Theory* 6, 129–33.

(1977b), "Proportional Solutions to Bargaining Situations: Interpersonal Utility Comparisons," *Econometrica* 45, 1623–30.

Kalai, E. and M. Smorodinsky (1975), "Other Solutions to Nash's Bargaining Problem," *Econometrica* 43, 513–18.

Kihlstrom, R., A. Mas-Colell, and H. F. Sonnenschein (1976), "The Demand Theory of the Weak Axiom of Revealed Preference," *Econometrica* 44, 971–8.

Lensberg, T. (1985a), "Stability, Collective Choice and Separable Welfare," Ph.D. Dissertation, Norwegian School of Economics and Business Administration.

(1985b), "Bargaining and Fair Allocation," in *Cost Allocation: Methods, Principles, Applications* (H. P. Young, ed.), Amsterdam, North-Holland, pp. 101–16.

(1987), "Stability and Collective Rationality," *Econometrica* 55, 935–61.

(1988), "Stability and the Nash Solution," *Journal of Economic Theory* 45, 330–41.

Lensberg, T. and W. Thomson (1988), "Characterizing the Nash Bargaining Solution without Pareto-Optimality," *Social Choice and Welfare* 5, 247–59.

Luce, R. D. and H. Raiffa (1957), *Games and Decisions: Introduction and Critical Survey,* New York, Wiley.

Maschler, M. and M. A. Perles (1981), "The Present Status of the Super Additive Solution," in *Essays in Game Theory and Mathematical Economics in Honor of Oskar Morgenstern* (R. Aumann et al., eds.), pp. 103–10.

Moulin, H. (1985a), "Egalitarianism and Utilitarianism in Quasi-Linear Bargaining," *Econometrica* 53, 49–67.

(1985b), "The Separability Axiom and Equal-Sharing Methods," *Journal of Economic Theory* 36, 120–48.

(1987), "Equal or Proportional Division of a Surplus, and Other Methods," *International Journal of Game Theory* 16, 161–86.

Myerson, R. B. (1977), "Two-Person Bargaining Problems and Comparable Utility," *Econometrica* 45, 1631–7.

(1981), "Utilitarianism, Egalitarianism and the Timing Effect in Social Choice Problems," *Econometrica* 49, 883–97.

Nash, J. F. (1950), "The Bargaining Problem," *Econometrica* 18, 155–62.

(1953), "Two-Person Cooperative Games," *Econometrica* 21, 129–40.

O'Neill, B. (1981), "Comparison of Bargaining Solutions, Utilitarianism and the Minmax Rule by Their Effectiveness," Northwestern University Discussion Paper.

Peleg, B. (1985), "An Axiomatization of the Core of Cooperative Games without Side Payments," *Journal of Mathematical Economics* 14, 203–14.

(1986), "On the Reduced Game Property and Its Converse," *International Journal of Game Theory* 15, 187–200.

Perles, M. A. and M. Maschler (1981), "A Superadditive Solution to Nash Bargaining Games," *International Journal of Game Theory* 10, 163–93.

Peters, H. (1983), "Independence of Irrelevant Alternatives for *n*-Person Bargaining Solutions," Nijmegen University Discussion Paper 8318.

(1986), "Simultaneity of Issues and Additivity in Bargaining," *Econometrica* 54, 153–69.

Peters, H. and S. Tijs (1984), "Individually Monotonic Bargaining Solutions for *n*-Person Bargaining Games," *Methods of Operations Research* 51, 377–84.

(1985). "Characterization of All Individually Monotonic Bargaining Solutions," *International Journal of Game Theory* 14, 219–28.

Peters, H., S. Tijs, and R. de Koster (1983), "Solutions and Multisolutions for Bargaining Games," *Methods of Operations Research* 46, 465–76.

Raiffa, H. (1953), "Arbitration Schemes for Generalized Two-Person Games," in *Contributions to the Theory of Games II* (H. W. Kuhn and A. W. Tucker, eds.), Annals of Mathematics Studies, No. 28, Princeton, Princeton University Press, pp. 361–87.

Rawls, J. (1971), *A Theory of Justice,* Cambridge, MA, Harvard University Press.

Richter, M. K. (1966), "Revealed Preference Theory," *Econometrica* 34, 634–45.

(1971), "Rational Choice," in *Preferences, Utility and Demand* (J. S. Chipman, L. Hurwicz, M. K. Richter, and H. F. Sonnenschein, eds.), New York, Harcourt Brace Jovanovich, pp. 29–58.

Roberts, K. W. S. (1980), "Interpersonal Comparability and Social Choice Theory," *Review of Economic Studies* 47, 421–39.

Roemer, J. (1986), "The Mismarriage of Bargaining Theory and Distributive Justice," *Ethics* 97, 88–110.

Roth, A. E. (1977a), "Individual Rationality and Nash's Solution to the Bargaining Problem," *Mathematics of Operations Research* 2, 64–5.

(1977b), "Independence of Irrelevant Alternatives and Solutions to Nash's Bargaining Problem," *Journal of Economic Theory* 16, 247–51.

(1979a), "Proportional Solutions to the Bargaining Problem," *Econometrica* 47, 775–80.

(1979b), "Interpersonal Comparisons and Equal Gains in Bargaining," mimeo.

(1979c), *Axiomatic Models of Bargaining,* Berlin and New York, Springer-Verlag.

(1979d), "An Impossibility Result Concerning *n*-Person Bargaining Games," *International Journal of Game Theory* 8, 129–32.

Salonen, H. (1985), "A Solution for Two-Person Bargaining Problems," *Social Choice and Welfare* 2, 139–46.

Samuelson, P. A. (1938), "A Note on the Pure Theory of Consumer's Behaviour," *Economica* 5, 61–71.

(1947), *Foundations of Economic Analysis,* Cambridge, MA, Harvard University Press.

Segal, U. (1980), "The Monotonic Solution for the Bargaining Problem: A Note," Hebrew University of Jerusalem mimeo.

Sen, A. K. (1970), *Collective Choice and Social Welfare,* San Francisco, Holden Day.

(1979), "Utilitarianism and Welfarism," *Journal of Philosophy* 76, 463–89.

Shapley, L. S. (1969), "Utility Comparison and the Theory of Games," in *La Decision* (G. Th. Guilbaud, ed.), Editions du CNRS, Paris, pp. 251–63.

Sobolev, A. I. (1975), "The Characterization of Optimality Principles in Cooperative Games by Functional Equations," in *Matematicheskie Metody v Socialnix Naukax* (N. Vorobiev, ed.), pp. 94–151 (in Russian).

Thomson, W. (1980), "Two Characterizations of the Raiffa Solution," *Economics Letters* 6, 225–31.

(1981a), "A Class of Solutions to Bargaining Problems," *Journal of Economic Theory* 25, 431–41.

(1981b), "Independence of Irrelevant Expansions," *International Journal of Game Theory* 10, 107–14.

(1981c), "Nash's Bargaining Solution and Utilitarian Choice Rules," *Econometrica* 49, 535–8.

(1983a), "Truncated Egalitarian and Monotone Path Solutions," University of Minnesota Discussion Paper (January).

(1983b), "Collective Guarantee Structures," *Economics Letters* 11, 63–8.

(1983c), "The Fair Division of a Fixed Supply Among a Growing Population," *Mathematics of Operations Research* 8, 319–26.

(1983d), "Problems of Fair Division and the Egalitarian Solution," *Journal of Economic Theory* 31, 211–26.

(1984a), "Truncated Egalitarian Solutions," *Social Choice and Welfare* 1, 25–32.

(1984b), "Two Aspects of the Axiomatic Theory of Bargaining," University of Rochester Discussion Paper No. 6.

(1984c), "Monotonicity, Stability, and Egalitarianism," *Mathematical Social Sciences* 8, 15–28.

(1985a), "Axiomatic Theory of Bargaining with a Variable Population: A Survey of Recent Results," in *Game Theoretic Models of Bargaining* (A. E. Roth, ed.), Cambridge, Cambridge University Press, pp. 233–58.

(1985b), "On the Nash Bargaining Solution," University of Rochester mimeo.

(1986), "Replication Invariance of Bargaining Solutions," *International Journal of Game Theory* 15, 59–63.

(1987a), "Individual and Collective Opportunities," *International Journal of Game Theory* 16, 245–52.

(1987b), "Bargaining Theory; The Axiomatic Approach," University of Rochester, Lecture notes.

(forthcoming), "A Study of Choice Correspondences in Economies with a Variable Number of Agents," *Journal of Economic Theory*.

Thomson, W. and T. Lensberg (1983), "Guarantee Structures for Problems of Fair Division," *Mathematical Social Sciences* 4, 205–18.

Thomson, W. and R. B. Myerson (1980), "Monotonicity and Independence Axioms," *International Journal of Game Theory* 9, 37–49.

Uzawa, H. (1971), "Preference and Rational Choice in the Theory of Consumption," in *Preferences, Utility and Demand* (J. Chipman, L. Hurwicz, M. K. Richter, and H. F. Sonnenschein, eds.), New York, Harcourt Brace Jovanovich, pp. 7–28.

Varian, H. (1981), "Dynamical Systems with Applications to Economics," in *Handbook of Mathematical Economics* (K. J. Arrow and M. D. Intrilligator, eds.), Vol. 1, Amsterdam, North-Holland, pp. 93–109.

Ville, J. (1951), "The Existence of a Total Utility Function," *Review of Economic Studies* 19, 123–8.

von Neumann, J. and O. Morgenstern (1944), *Theory of Games and Economic Behavior,* Princeton, Princeton University Press.

Wooders, M. (1981), "The Epsilon Core of a Large Game," Yale University Discussion Paper (December).

Young, H. P. (1984), "Consistency and Optimality in Taxation," mimeo, University of Maryland.

(1987), "On Dividing an Amount According to Individual Claims or Liabilities," *Mathematics of Operations Research* 12, 398–414.
(1988), "Distributive Justice in Taxation," *Journal of Economic Theory* 44, 321–35.

Index